SLAVERY
and
POLITICS
in the
EARLY
AMERICAN
REPUBLIC

SLAVERY
and
POLITICS
in the
EARLY
AMERICAN
REPUBLIC

Matthew Mason

The University of North Carolina Press

CHAPEL HILL

Set in MT Baskerville
by Keystone Typesetting, Inc.

This book was published with the assistance of the Fred W. Morrison
Fund for Southern Studies of the University of North Carolina Press.

Parts of this book have been reprinted in revised form from the following works:
"Slavery Overshadowed: Congress Debates Prohibiting the Atlantic Slave
Trade to the United States, 1806–1807," *Journal of the Early Republic* 20 (Spring
2000): 59–81; " 'Nothing Is Better Calculated to Excite Divisions': Federalist
Agitation against Slave Representation during the War of 1812," *New England
Quarterly* 75 (December 2002): 531–61; and "The Battle of the Slaveholding Lib-
erators: Great Britain, the United States, and Slavery in the Early Nineteenth
Century," *William and Mary Quarterly*, 3d ser., 59 (July 2002): 665–96.

ISBN-13: 978-0-8078-3049-9
ISBN-10: 0-8078-3049-6

Book Club Edition

For Stacie

Contents

Illustrations and Maps

Acknowledgments

This book is much better than it would have been without the aid of several people over the course of several years. I assume no one in their right mind would charge them with any of the errors or infelicities that may remain in it, so I will offer no long disclaimer to that effect.

In addition to receiving invaluable financial support, I have benefited from the encouragement and criticisms of generous colleagues and mentors in three different home institutions. At the University of Maryland, I had a wealth of faculty strength on which to draw, and I drew liberally. Thanks to the critiques of these faculty members of the dissertation I wrote there, this book is substantially different—and, I'm confident, in a good way—from what they read then. Two members of my dissertation committee were of particular help: Leslie Rowland's conscientious reading and stylistic suggestions made later revisions easier. And James Henretta offered helpful comments, especially on the new and improved chapter 1 here. At Eastern Michigan University, Richard Nation in particular was a wonderful colleague, and he offered comments and source material that aided greatly in the development of chapter 6. At Brigham Young University, I am surrounded by talented peers, many of whom share my interests and have been a great help to me. Jenny Hale Pulsipher helped make chapter 1 better, as did Susan Sessions Rugh with chapter 6. Neil York offered insightful critiques on various portions of the manuscript, with such quick turnaround time as to shame us all.

Nor have colleagues in my home institutions been alone in their helpfulness. I am grateful to the University of North Carolina Press for arranging for two such generous and perceptive readers as James Brewer Stewart and Richard Newman. Their wise suggestions and the collegial spirit of our give-and-take concerning the manuscript rendered the final stages of revisions a relative pleasure as well as a useful process. Donald R. Hickey graciously read and offered valuable comments on the first few chapters. And I have benefited from presenting earlier drafts of material here to various conferences and seminars.

Sponsors of and participants in the International Seminar on the History of the Atlantic World at Harvard University, the New England Slavery and the Slave Trade Conference of the Colonial Society of Massachusetts, and especially the Newberry Library Early American History Seminar provided valuable insights and critiques of my work. I thank them for their attention to it.

Ira Berlin deserves special thanks. As my final graduate advisor at the University of Maryland, he provided not only invaluable aid, especially in improving my writing, but also a model of the engaged and influential scholar and teacher. In the years since, he has stayed involved in my work, offering commentaries on various chapters here. He has also given treasured professional advice and in general been a valued friend.

Then there is my family. Thanks for things too numerous to list here go to our parents. I started this project at the time our oldest daughter, Emily, was born, and it is gratifying to see it hit a few library bookshelves before she is old enough to offer her own critiques of it. Both she and her sisters, Hannah and Rachel, are our pride and joy and help provide incentive for me to do my best in whatever I do. I dedicate this effort to my wife, Stacie, who has read less of it than she has wished—a trio of high-energy girls running around the house will do that. But as a smart nonspecialist she has long been the kind of reader I aim for when I write. And more importantly, she has made the last fifteen-plus years of our life together a great joy.

Introduction

ON II JANUARY 1820, as a debate raged in Congress and throughout the nation over whether to restrict slavery in the prospective state of Missouri, a massive fire broke out in Savannah, Georgia. So many people suffered and lost homes in this conflagration that donors throughout the country contributed almost $100,000 to their relief.[1] Many observers welcomed this outpouring of benevolence, especially from the North, as a sign of goodwill in a time of sectional controversy. A member of Pennsylvania's senate urged his colleagues to embrace this "opportunity to cultivate the feelings of friendship and of mutual good will, between the inhabitants of different states," for this "was one of the surest and most effectual modes to perpetuate the existence of the union." Such a course was especially pressing given that the Missouri debates "had occasioned some warmth and temper between the citizens of the slave-holding, and non-slaveholding states." As Pennsylvanians had led the way in fighting against slavery's extension to Missouri, so they should now be foremost in extending a helping hand to the South. This would prove that "charity and benevolence are the principles which actuate the policy of our state." The legislature unanimously passed a bill providing $10,000 worth of relief.[2] Georgians gladly accepted such charity and agreed that "it links closer and closer the chain of Union."[3]

But the Savannah fire incident, far from the hoped-for balm for the Union's wounds, became yet another sectional irritant. For other Northerners were not prepared to set aside their antagonism toward the South. A private committee gathering funds in Philadelphia encountered a group of donors who gave money "for the use exclusively of persons in Savannah not Slave-holders." This restriction faded from public view when the committee returned these donors' funds.[4] The mayor and general relief committee of New York City caused a greater stir by sending money to Savannah but stipulating that it "be applied exclusively to the relief of all indigent persons, *without distinction of color.*" Savannah's mayor and council, insulted by this condition, returned the donation with a sharp retort. "The language of the resolution," Savannah's mayor, Thomas Charlton, lectured, was not only an affront to "the humanity of our citizens" but also "dangerous to the tranquility of this section of the United States." "It is," he pursued, "in short, throwing among us the fire-brand of discord, and, if persevered in, will . . . place in jeopardy the federal unity of our now glorious republic."[5]

True to Charlton's prognostication, the Savannah fire episode became yet another "fire-brand of discord" in the already divided States. Other white Southerners joined the mayor in expressing their outrage, vowing to remember the Yankees' ungenerous sentiments.[6] Northerners responded in kind. Upon reading Charlton's rejoinder, the people of other Northern towns withheld the money they had collected for Savannah.[7] The Philadelphia-based American Fire Insurance Company replied to a Savannah resident's inquiry about insuring his home and furniture by decreeing "that this company, for the present, decline making insurances in any of the slave states." Although this was probably just good business, given the frequency of slave arson, Southern newspapers reprinted it as proof of the "temper and tone of the northern section of the country towards the people of the south."[8] Less business-minded Northerners thought nothing would ensure Southerners' safety, given that they were tempting the wrath of God. One declared that his "heart sickens to think" that Northern generosity had been "perverted to the reinstating [of] a *slave* city in all her former prosperity." Yankees "might evince a higher humanity by withholding than bestowing our contributions" and by warning Georgians that if they did not expunge their horrid slave codes, "you can have no encouragement to ask of Heaven, that it would arrest the progress of the destroying angel through your dwellings, nor of us, that we would assist in repairing its devastations."[9] Abolitionist Elihu Embree reasoned that Charlton's haughty reply illustrated "the effects of slavery on the minds of slaveholders." Given their wickedness, Embree marveled "at the mercy of the supreme being, that instead of burning the town of Savannah, he has not destroyed its proud inhabitants with fire unquenchable!!!"[10]

Keen observers saw the influence of the Missouri Crisis in the Savannah imbroglio. Baltimore editor Hezekiah Niles opined that Charlton's screed proved that "public feeling must have been exceedingly stirred up at Savannah, by the *Missouri* question, to have caused such a warmth of proceeding."[11] And this was just one supposedly unrelated affair that the Missouri debate had touched. In its wake, sectional conflict infected the contest for Speaker of the House of Representatives in late 1820, whether to count Missouri's three electoral votes in that year's presidential election, and even the naming of U.S. Navy battleships![12] Secretary of State John Quincy Adams offered an apt sum in his journal: "The Missouri question is indeed a flaming sword that waves round on all sides and cuts in every direction."[13]

The bitterness of the Missouri debates was many years in the making. The passions it brought forth and the particular shape it took were the product of what preceded it. Yet this is not the conventional wisdom. Many historians either ignore or downplay the political significance of slavery in the early national period—that is, until Missouri bursts upon their view as if out of nowhere. This is not a new perspective. In 1835, for example, antislavery journalist Gamaliel Bradford wrote that upon the close of the international slave trade in 1808 "the attention of the community was diverted by the convulsions of Europe, the din of party, the increase of wealth, commerce, and manufactures, and other Delilahs of the time, till, in 1820, on the fatal Missouri question, the Samson of Abolition found his struggles unavailing."[14] Bradford's portrayal of this period echoed in the works of twentieth-century historians. By their accounts, slavery dropped from the national radar screen with the abolition of the Atlantic slave trade in 1808, only to reappear suddenly in 1819 once the distractions relative to war with England had disappeared.[15] Others realized the unlikelihood of such a crisis as Missouri being created out of whole cloth, but their attempts to account for its origins were vague or otherwise inadequate.[16] The out-of-nowhere interpretation remains alive and well in the twenty-first century and in some of the best works of history. "For the most part," Don E. Fehrenbacher has suggested, "national discord over slavery was muted during the years of maritime contention and then outright warfare with England. Even after peace returned, the subject did not for a time cause much disturbance in the deliberations of Congress."[17] Even as limited to Congress, this observation does not withstand scrutiny. Early in the Missouri controversy, New York's elder statesman, John Jay, rightly remarked that "little can be added to what has been said and written on the subject of slavery."[18]

There had indeed been a great deal said on the matter before the Missouri contest erupted, beginning with the American Revolution, which put slavery on the political and moral agenda of the new nation and of its British antagonists. But the Revolutionary generation, whose engagement with slavery culminated with the slave trade ban of 1808, left much undecided. The Revolution had set the split between slave states and free states in motion, but that division took clearer shape and assumed greater importance in the early nineteenth century. Especially in its second decade, slavery's unexpected expansion, and tangential debates in which slavery became a weapon, kept slavery on the table and defined the identity of both the free and the slave states.

To begin with, the partisan and geopolitical strife surrounding the War of 1812, far from suppressing divisions over slavery, intensified them. Participants in the bitter domestic disputes of the war years rarely hesitated to draw on the rhetoric of slavery to attack their opponents. The war years also witnessed the high point in New England Federalists' agitation against the representation of Southern slaves in the federal government. The nervousness of the Republicans' response to such uses of slavery bore witness to its divisive power. As slavery entered the domestic politics of the war, it exacerbated the rift between North and South.

Politicians and constituents (especially newspaper editors) in both sections took note of the broad Northern popularity of the Yankee Federalists' attacks on slaveholders and their power. Accordingly, when some Northern Republicans abandoned the mainstream of their party in the immediate postwar period, they mimicked the Federalists in stirring up sectional grievances against the Monroe administration. Seeing antislavery Northern sectionalism wed again to partisan politics, loyal Republicans in both sections again feared for their party and the Union. They thus resurrected wartime tactics, chiefly appealing to the value of the Union. Political struggles that bore no direct relation to slavery thus revealed that a sectionalist, political brand of antislavery was becoming an integral part of Northern sectional identity, an identity that menaced the Union in its more forceful manifestations.

In all of this, politicians and editors were not creating the issue of slavery so much as manipulating existing antislavery sentiment in the North. This does not mean that the sentiment itself was insincere, or that the politicos in question did not hold that sentiment themselves.[19] Indeed, some remained engaged in slavery politics after the initial cause that brought them to it had passed. But the timing and nature of especially most New England Federalists' agitation in regard to slavery suggest that partisan politics prompted them to act on that sentiment—to organize it into a sectional force in American politics. This distinction between belief and action is a critical one. The Revolution bequeathed a dislike for slavery to almost every Northerner, but after they had rid their own states of slavery and banned the Atlantic slave trade, most Northerners' antislavery remained only as inert opinion. As with most humans throughout history, they saw no need to convert opinion to organized action unless the evil they deplored somehow affected them. The Federalists demonstrated that masses of Northern voters would organize and act against slaveholders when their leaders showed them how slavery impinged on their rights and interests.

American slavery also permeated the Anglo-American disputes that historians have so often assumed submerged it as an issue. It played a vital role in Britain's military and political strategy during the War of 1812. It was also a key weapon in both sides' attacks on the other's political institutions and national identity. The involvement of the British in the debate served to harden the nascent positions of nationalists and sectionalists, as well as of opponents and defenders of slavery.

All these injections of slavery into American and Anglo-American politics illustrated important truths. One was that there was never a time between the Revolution and the Civil War in which slavery went unchallenged. Another was how central chattel bondage was in American life. Furthermore, the Federalist campaign against slave representation pioneered a sectional politics of slavery in the United States, revealing the potentialities of antislavery sectionalist appeals in Northern politics. And these and other debates of the period proved that slavery did not have to be the main issue at hand to elicit Southern defensiveness or threaten the Union. To attack slavery's auxiliaries—whether it be slave representation, the Atlantic or domestic slave trade, or kidnapping— was tantamount to attacking slavery itself, as far as its defenders were concerned. Indeed, some of the Federalists and others who campaigned against these ancillary features of American slavery set the institution itself in their sights, provoking some Southerners to respond accordingly. Similarly, although many Britons who reproved Americans for slavery meant to assault American political institutions, they produced defenses of slavery as well as of republican government. In short, partisans and patriots, not just abolitionists and advocates of slavery, should be considered important players in the politics of slavery in the United States.

So should the slaves themselves, along with free blacks. Most historians have neglected or denied African Americans' impact on the politics of the early republic.[20] William W. Freehling has made eloquent and persistent appeals to reintegrate social and political history, in part by linking slave resistance to slaveholder politics.[21] The likes of John Ashworth, James Oakes, William A. Link, and Ira Berlin and Leslie Rowland and their associates, along with Freehling himself, have practiced what Freehling preached, examining, in Link's words, "how slaves' actions affected politics" and "how politics affected slaves' actions." Yet these works, even those in which this theme is fully developed, are confined to the Civil War and the years immediately preceding it.[22] Nearly all of the scholarship depicting black people as actors on the early national stage is limited to relations between slaves and their masters. As a valuable recent study by Steven Hahn has shown, the slaves' defiance within that relationship and attempts to escape it were political in a broad sense, for they challenged "the fictions of domination and submission around which slavery was constructed, and [were] thereby imbued with a political resonance." Furthermore, as slaves passed rumors along their grapevine, they taught each other of the possibilities for freedom opening up in the larger world, such as in the North or in Haiti; for slaves, these were the "basic lessons of the new national politics."[23] Hahn, however, seemingly arbitrarily begins his exploration of the black political tradition in the late antebellum period. And this informal or broadly defined political struggle had an impact on formal Southern and national politics that Hahn does not fully explore. In the early national, as in the antebellum and Civil War eras, the consequences of slave resistance and free blacks' increasing independence reverberated far from the plantation, and individual master-slave contests took place in and helped shape the larger political context. In the hands of partisans and sectionalists, perceptions of and changes in black people's behavior became yet another wedge between North and South in the early republic.

If African Americans' growing assertiveness played a key role in the politics of slavery, so did other developments within the peculiar institution. The rapid expansion of cotton cultivation into the Southwest, particularly after the War of 1812, intensified the slave regime's hunger for labor. Its agents roamed the North in far greater numbers to buy Northern blacks still in slavery and to kidnap free blacks. In an age of relative liberality in racial thought among whites, many protested such practices on humanitarian grounds. The slave dealers and kidnappers also hampered the free states' efforts to distance themselves from slavery and thus provoked heated denunciations, especially in the Mid-Atlantic states whose territory they encroached upon. It was therefore no accident that New Yorkers started the quarrel with Savannah in 1820, just as a New Yorker in Congress had initiated the Missouri debates in the first place. Slavery also put the Northwest on the defensive by threatening to burst its traditional bounds by spreading there. Most white Northerners' brand of anti-slavery allowed them to coexist with Southern slavery so long as it stayed at a distance. But the institution's postwar expansion brought slavery home to white Northerners by violating their notions that its proper sphere lay south of the

Mason-Dixon Line and the Ohio River. The social and political histories of slavery had collided, as they so often did.

Although a type of antislavery sentiment ruled supreme in the North's public discourse, then, the reasons particular Northerners became ardently opposed to slavery varied from person to person and especially region to region. The vague but latently powerful ideological impulses of the Revolution gained concrete meaning as Northerners in various subregions defended against the particular threat slavery posed in their neighborhoods. The timing and reasons for that threat varied, especially between New England and subregions to the south and west, which helps explain who took the lead in the Missouri controversy, as opposed to earlier contests.

But if Northerners came to similar opinions by different routes, white Southerners displayed a wider range of opinion on the rightness of slavery. Ironically, it was in the early national North that orthodoxy reigned, even as some Southerners fumbled toward embracing slavery. It is therefore less useful to talk of "Southern opinion" in the aggregate, even on slavery, than of intrasectional debates in which certain groups gained the upper hand at various times. And in the realms of ideology and ethics, slaveholders and their allies found themselves on the defensive. This rendered their attempts to defend slavery hesitant and confused.[24]

Thus, the sectional politics of slavery presented striking paradoxes throughout the early nineteenth century. The North was proud to denominate itself as "the free states" in an ideological world that proscribed bondage as immoral. No one in the South seemed proud to call the region "the slave states." Yet slavery itself was on the march, throwing the North on the defensive. And if Northern sectionalism was more confident than Southern, the national political structure inhibited its expression. The national two-party system required that significant numbers of Northern politicians subordinate their antislavery convictions and sectional chauvinism to the imperatives of party and national unity. Thus only when Northern Federalists—and after the War of 1812 some Northern Republicans—abandoned the idea of an intersectional party strategy did they give full vent to their detestation of slavery and slaveholders. When outsiders attacked the increasingly peculiar institution, white Southerners could couch their defenses in patriotic terms. Therefore, not only were Southern spokesmen reactive rather than proactive on the issue, but the political advantage in posing as patriots—and the ignominy the age attached to slavery —diverted them from developing a consistent, principled defense of slavery.

One result of all these developments in the early nineteenth century was that ordinary as well as prominent Americans found themselves engaged in the politics of slavery. Some historians, notably Eric Foner, have seen early national sectional differences over slavery as disorganized and only "latent." Foner has approvingly quoted Glover Moore, "the historian of the Missouri Compromise," who wrote that "if there had been a civil war in 1819–1821 it would have been between the members of Congress, with the rest of the country looking on in amazement." It was not until "the mass . . . politics of the Jackson era" that "agitators" could use "politics as a way of heightening sectional self-consciousness and antagonism in the populace at large." Thus, in short, Foner has argued that only with the Missouri Crisis did Americans grasp the "political possibilities inherent in a sectional attack on slavery," and only in the 1830s did popular parties arise to fully explore those possibilities.[25]

But this formulation overlooks several things. For starters, it overlooks the broad popular participation in the Missouri debates; these were hardly carried on by congressmen in isolation. Failing to recognize this, Moore and Foner thus miss the broad public concern over slavery, as a result of its expansion and African American resistance to it, which created the popular engagement with the Missouri Crisis. Furthermore, it has been easy for historians such as these to assume most Americans to be untouched by agitation over slavery in the early nineteenth century because they have ignored the links between sectionalism and partisan politics. Finally, Foner glosses over partisan usages of slavery in the early republic, because he posits that the Federalists and Republicans were not popular parties that connected with the people. This assumption does not hold, in light of the evidence of high voter turnout in the early nineteenth century compiled long ago by historians such as David Hackett Fischer.[26] And more recent studies of the popular mobilization achieved by partisan celebrations and newspaper editors have further demonstrated that the usual story line of elite politics in the early national period giving way to antebellum mass politics is overdrawn.[27]

Therefore, citizens of various walks of life in both North and South entered the Missouri controversy with existing grievances as well as half-baked ideological positions. The course of the debate pushed some participants toward greater consistency, even as it displayed the legacy of the previous decades of conflict over slavery. But as much as this contest changed and clarified, only the most consistent antebellum extremists departed much from patterns set in the early republic. The Missouri Crisis thus bridged the early national and antebellum politics of slavery. But more ideas and tactics crossed that bridge than many people would suspect.

1

Slavery and Politics to 1808

THE POLITICAL HISTORY of slavery in North America began in earnest with the American Revolution. The years of struggle against Great Britain took what had been weak and disparate strands of opposition to slavery and bound them into a powerful antislavery ideology and movement. The new concern with human bondage also transformed slavery into a potent weapon with a variety of political uses, both international and domestic. Americans, both slaveholders and nonslaveholders, felt compelled to respond to these developments. The contrast between the responses of the Northern and the Southern states opened up a sectional division over slavery for the first time, with consequences that could not have been more momentous. The era of the Revolution set these developments in motion, but their impact and implications were still unclear when this epoch closed with the abolition of the Atlantic slave trade to the United States in 1808.

———

Serious, sustained scrutiny of slavery in North America—indeed, in the Western world—arose for the first time in the 1760s in tandem with the political and military strife between Great Britain and her colonies. This is not to assert that slavery had never troubled Western man before then. Indeed, as David Brion Davis has written, "slavery had long been a source of latent tension in Western culture."[1] But before the late eighteenth century, Western intellectual traditions presented "a framework of thought that would exclude any attempt to abolish slavery as an institution." There were exceptions to this rule, but they were aberrations in their respective times and places and cannot be called part of any antislavery tradition.[2] Even in the late seventeenth century and first half of the eighteenth century, only occasional rhetorical flourishes and faint glimmerings of moral opposition to slavery appeared, demonstrating "how remote abolitionism was from even the more liberal minds of" the world.[3]

What was true of the Western world generally held for Britain's North American colonies before their conflict with the imperial power. Attempts to keep particular colonies free of slavery were not actuated by principled opposition to the institution; moreover, they failed. For instance, Rhode Island's 1652 effort to limit involuntary servitude to ten-year terms floundered, and in short order the colony's ports became leading centers of the African slave trade.[4] Georgia's leading lights were more persistent but just as unsuccessful. For much of the 1730s and 1740s, the proprietors and settlers of this new colony debated whether to retain the original ban on African slavery. In the course of this debate, moral opposition to slavery surfaced only rarely, as the antislavery side emphasized practical reasons to exclude slaves. And after 1750, Georgia joined its neighbor to the north, South Carolina, as a colony fully committed to plantation slavery.[5]

Georgia joined more than South Carolina, for slavery was of vital importance in Northern as well as Southern colonies. The institution took different forms in different colonies and was more important in some than in others. But, especially in New England, the Atlantic slave trade was a key contributor to economic growth. Accordingly, holding or trading in slaves was far from an impediment to respectability—indeed, many of New England's first families participated in the African slave trade.[6] In parts of colonies such as New York, New Jersey, and Pennsylvania, slave labor was becoming more rather than less important at midcentury.[7]

Protests against the growth and importance of slavery in the colonies were few and far between, and protests against slavery per se were even scarcer. A well-known exception was Puritan divine Samuel Sewall's pamphlet *The Selling of Joseph*, published in Boston in 1700. But after this protest against the slave trade, Sewall did not pay public attention to the subject. This flicker of antislavery sentiment hardly constituted an antislavery movement.[8] Preachers, especially in New England, had no hesitance in reproving sin, but in the early and mid-eighteenth century, slavery was not yet on their list of crying offenses. Colonists of various denominations grappled with the righteousness of slavery before the American Revolution, but they rarely if ever came to any conclusion that fundamentally challenged slavery.[9] Later depictions of a transhistorically antislavery New England notwithstanding, even there opposition to the principle of slaveholding was fleeting and rare.

The Quakers formed the strongest exception to this rule of nonengagement, for they wrangled over the question of slavery's rectitude early and often. As early as 1682, George Fox, the English founder of the Society of Friends, questioned slavery's morality. In North America, the first Quaker protest against slaveholding came from a meeting of Friends in Germantown, Pennsylvania, in 1688. These Quakers appealed in large part to the Golden Rule and to the preservation of Pennsylvania's good name in Europe. For their part, the recipients of this memorial—Society of Friends meetings in Philadelphia and Burlington—hoped to avoid the issue altogether, protesting that it was "of too great a weight" for them to decide.[10] Other Quaker assaults on slavery followed in rapid succession, demonstrating the Quaker meetings' inability to quiet the question. These arguments, and their reception, would become some of the timeless themes of antislavery agitation.

Yet even among the Quakers, antislavery progressed painfully and slowly before the Revolution, in part because wealthy slaveholders predominated in many of their meetings.[11] The opponents of slavery were more vocal and published their views more often. But whole sections of Quaker antislavery tracts were devoted to refuting arguments, biblical and otherwise, that their fellow Friends had advanced in defense of slavery.[12] It appears that the Friends pioneered both antislavery *and* proslavery in British North America.

Moreover, between the 1680s and the 1760s, this debate was almost entirely carried on among the Quakers themselves. Despite their power in Pennsylvania, both the Quakers as a sect and their concerns over slavery were marginal in both England and its colonies. Leading Quaker abolitionist Benjamin Lay, for instance, gained notoriety for his striking object lessons, but his main audience was his coreligionists. He was an eccentric character—even those sympathetic to him have conceded that he may have been mentally deranged—who lived in "a cottage resembling, in its construction, a cave."[13] A colorful lunatic living in a cave embodied the place of antislavery in the colonial consciousness as late as the mid-eighteenth century.

In the midst of the Great Awakening, another liminal group arose whose members evinced at least some sympathy for the slave: evangelical Protestants. They shared a common experience of persecution with other sects who became leaders in religious antislavery, such as Quakers and Moravians. Indeed, they gloried in the fact that proud, worldly slaveholders persecuted both evangelicals and the lowest form of outcasts, slaves.[14] This prepared some evangelical minds for antislavery, but not all embraced it. Leaders of the Great Awakening such as George Whitefield and Samuel Davies rebuked planters for abusing their slaves but not for holding them. They advocated a benevolent form of Christian slaveholding, and Whitefield employed slave labor at his orphanage in Georgia.[15]

If there was no automatic link between evangelicalism and opposition to slavery, neither was there such a connection between antislavery and more secular philosophies. The precepts of the Enlightenment brought some minds to the conclusion that slavery was unnatural and immoral. Yet to other Enlightenment thinkers, especially early in the movement, the slave trade and colonial plantation slavery were key elements in a grand, even "divinely contrived system" that was beneficial to all.[16] Indeed, both sides of a Harvard forensic dispute over the justice of slavery appealed to Enlightenment notions of natural rights to support their position.[17] Neither did the more specific ideology of the American Revolution automatically produce abolitionists, even when combined with evangelical religion. Many white patriots conceived of the struggle with Britain as designed only to preserve the rights of those who "were free-born, never made slaves" by conquest or sale.[18] In the mid-1780s, hundreds of Virginia evangelicals employed both their religious beliefs and the Revolution's stress on property rights in a series of petitions against emancipation. They also branded their antislavery opponents "Enemies of our Country, Tools of the British Administration."[19]

Notwithstanding the overall ambiguity of these religious and secular philosophies on slavery, they proved unfriendly to it when they converged in the late eighteenth century, when a sense of a confrontation between freedom and tyranny was international. This gave many Western people an apocalyptic sense of urgency that turned their faith and political precepts into strong rhetoric—and often action—against human bondage. Many more people than ever before thus awoke to the issue for the first time, feeling personally implicated in or affected by slavery.[20]

The days of the Revolution were heady indeed, and this headiness included some remarkable changes for slavery in North America. In 1777, as Captain William Whipple of New Hampshire went off to fight the British, he noticed that his slave, Prince, was dejected. When Whipple asked him why, Prince responded: "Master, *you* are going to fight for your *liberty*, but I have none to fight for." Whipple, "struck by the essential truth of Prince's complaint," immediately freed him.[21] Whipple was unusual in his haste, but he was far from alone in coming to the conviction that slavery was wrong. In 1773, Philadelphia doctor and patriot Benjamin Rush observed that a small cadre of Quaker abolitionists "stood alone a few years ago in opposing Negro slavery in Philadelphia, and now three-fourths of the province as well as the city cry out against it."[22] By 1797, a New York diarist estimated that "within 20 years the opinion of the injustice of slaveholding has become almost universal."[23] By the late eighteenth and early nineteenth centuries, Americans of all ages—especially Northerners—could and did read antislavery textbooks and literature, see antislavery plays, and sing antislavery songs.[24]

White Americans came to this destination by many roads, although two were particularly well traveled. In the midst of the political contention and war with Britain, especially when the war went badly for the patriots, a multitude of clergymen—especially but not exclusively New England Congregationalists—preached that God was punishing the colonists for their iniquities. Although this message was not new, it was novel to see slavery listed as "an Achan, an accursed thing that is the troubler of our land, and for which God is at this day contending with us." In fact, some preachers even denounced "negro slavery" as "the most crying sin in our land." Moreover, many contended that slavery was a *national* sin, for which God was using the British ministry as a rod to chasten all the colonists.[25] Legions of patriots also rebuked their fellows for inconsistency in holding slaves while striving for their own liberty. One writer only formulated this in a more extreme form than others when he compared American slaveholders condemning Britain's tyranny to "an atrocious pirate, setting [*sic*] in all the solemn pomp of a judge, passing sentence of death on a petty thief."[26]

Many Revolutionary Americans' opposition to slavery was more than rhetorical, and they formed the first non-Quaker antislavery movement in American history. For all its novelty and its connection to the political ideology of the American Revolution, Quakers and evangelicals remained prominent in the antislavery cause.[27] But this new movement was far more universal than the intrasectarian disputes of the colonial period—indeed, it was transatlantic. American and European—especially British—abolitionists corresponded, published each others' works, and generally nourished each other's efforts.[28]

The new breed of abolitionists gave no quarter to slaveholders, branding them as tyrants, villains in this age when human liberty was the cause célèbre. They repeatedly argued that no man's liberty—no matter his color—could safely be entrusted to those who had been "habituated to despotism by being the sovereigns of slaves." Only their fear of white men's political power kept them from enslaving whites as well as blacks.[29] After the publication of Thomas Jefferson's *Notes on the State of Virginia* in 1785, abolitionists delighted in quoting a slaveholder's denunciation of the tyranny of the commerce between master and slave.[30] But although they drew on his antislavery passage, many abolitionists had nothing but disdain for Jefferson's conclusion that slavery was for the time being a necessary evil given the obstacles to emancipation. They attributed this defense of slavery's continuation to "interested motives," arguing that if its proponents were not so blinded by selfish greed, "the mountains that are now raised up in the imagination would become a plain."[31] Thus some of the bolder abolitionists of the Revolutionary era sought to dismantle the necessary-evil apology for slavery even as it was being erected and to discredit slaveholders' claims to share in the liberal impulses of their time.

But if their rhetoric was uncompromising, this generation of abolitionists' programs was often limited and cautious. To be sure, since many believed that slaves were at least theoretically entitled to immediate freedom, early abolitionists did not think themselves conservative.[32] And occasionally a call for immediate abolition broke out.[33] But even the evangelicals, whose characterization of slavery as a sin logically precluded compromise with the institution, shrank from demanding an immediate emancipation of all slaves. Presbyterian preacher Alexander McLeod of New York, a key contributor to his denomination's antislavery tradition, believed an immediate abolition would entail great risk and only vaguely called for "a national repenting and forsaking."[34] Similarly, Methodist divine John Wesley's language was strident, but his proposal for dealing with slavery was limited to halting the Atlantic slave trade and beginning a long preparation of blacks for freedom.[35] "In its early appearances," one historian has aptly written, "immediatism was rhetorical rather than programmatic."[36] Indeed, one of the calling cards of abolitionists of all stripes was the gradual emancipation scheme. Even slavery's strongest opponents presented their own pet project for freeing slaves gradually.[37] The emphasis on gradualism fit well with the Enlightenment's faith in orderly, incremental reform.[38]

If the call for gradual emancipation was a limit on the early abolitionist movement, it also represented a concrete and progressive program and led to significant achievements. Urging all Americans, and usually the government, to aid in eradicating slavery was itself an advance from the pre-Revolutionary Quakers' almost exclusively intradenominational abolitionism.[39] The policy of gradual emancipation was also a success in the Northern states. By 1804, every Northern state had committed itself to abolition, the result of a process that ranged from the efforts of the General Court of Massachusetts to establish gradual abolition laws in 1773 and 1774 to New Jersey's gradual emancipation statute of 1804. Most of these state actions provided only for gradual abolition so as to protect slaveholders' property rights, with the result that well into the 1840s some "free states" still had some few slaves living within their borders. Yet the Revolutionary generation set the North firmly on the path to emancipation.[40]

If any one thing characterized abolitionism in its early years, however, it was opposition to the Atlantic slave trade. For this reason it makes sense to date the end of the Revolutionary phase of antislavery at 1808. Focusing on the slave trade was politically savvy, for the horrors of the Middle Passage, once publicized, made it the most odious and least defensible aspect of the New World slave system. Strong evidence of this came when Congress voted in 1807 to abolish the trade, effective 1 January 1808. At one point in the debate on this bill, the Speaker of the House, Nathaniel Macon of North Carolina, responded testily when a Northern representative questioned Southern commitment to abolition. "Though our sincerity has been doubted with an *if*," Macon scolded, "yet I believe every member in this House is solicitous to put a complete stop to this nefarious traffic." No one was eager to appear as the slave trade's defender, as the vote of 113 to 5 in favor of the ban also suggested.[41]

Abolitionists had other practical reasons to center their attention on the foreign slave trade. If immediate abolition of slavery was unfeasible, abolitionists argued, immediate abolition of the slave trade was not.[42] And while they celebrated the growth of antislavery sentiment, abolitionists like Benjamin Rush reasoned that "nothing of consequence, however, can be done here till the ax is laid to the root of" slavery, the African slave trade.[43] Indeed, all gradual emancipation plans presupposed abolition of the foreign slave trade as their first step. It may be charged that these men and women placed too much emphasis on abolishing the slave trade, which did not end slavery in the United States because the U.S. slave population continued to grow through reproduction. But the slave population's natural increase in the United States was an exception; everywhere else in the New World, the African slave trade was the lifeblood of the plantation labor system.[44]

Misplaced or not, optimism was another hallmark of the Revolutionary and early national antislavery movement. At the Constitutional Convention in 1787, some Northern delegates affirmed that slavery would soon disappear from the United States, whether or not they interfered with it. The Constitution moved beyond noninterference to allow for the abolition of the slave trade in 1808. In the ratification debates, many Northern Federalists cited this clause as proof that the Constitution had dealt slavery such a "mortal wound" that it would soon die.[45] As gradual emancipation moved forward, Northerners' confidence in abolition's ultimate success soared. Even in New York, where gradual abolition did not pass until 1799, this optimism—and a strong concomitant dose of complacency—thrived in the 1780s and 1790s. In 1793, a Presbyterian preacher in New York City regretted slavery's continuance in Christian lands but also declared his conviction that "domestic slavery . . . flies before" Christianity, "unable to stand the test of her pure and holy tribunal." And in America, "this monster has received a fatal blow, and will soon, we hope, fall expiring to the ground."[46] If Northern abolition inspired such buoyancy, the abolition of the slave trade by Congress only increased the expectations. A Philadelphia newspaper spoke for the hopes of many when it reported the introduction of the slave trade bill in Congress under the headline, "Abolition of Slavery."[47] Nor were white Americans alone; beginning on 1 January 1808, blacks in the North began to celebrate this anniversary as an alternative Fourth of July. The preacher at black Philadelphia's first such celebration, Absalom Jones, rejoiced that no longer would "the shores . . . of the United States, any more witness the anguish of families, parted for ever by a publick sale." Meanwhile, congregants in the black churches of Philadelphia sang that Britain had set slaves free by abolishing the slave trade in 1807, and that by a similar act "Columbia tears the galling bands, / And gives the sweets of Liberty."[48]

Given the revolution in sentiment that citizens of the new republic had seen in their own lifetimes, and given the Enlightenment's faith in Progress, they felt perfectly justified in their optimism. But because of their successes, and because they were so driven to abolish the slave trade, in 1808 the movement faced the malaise that comes to all movements when their members feel their work is done. It would take new issues to maintain the momentum of antislavery in America.

————

As slavery came under scrutiny, Southern slaveholders could not hope to continue unopposed in their possession of human property. Their property in man, for centuries virtually unquestioned, was now castigated as abolitionism spread not only within their own country but also in Europe, especially in Britain and Revolutionary France. All this required a response from the United States' remaining slaveholders and what were now known as slave states.

Nor were these the only threats slaveholders in the new nation faced, for at the same time their slave population was unusually restive. Slaveholders have never lorded it over a contented slave population, and the masters of colonial North America had long feared their slaves, especially in times of disruption and foreign war.[49] But during the American Revolution, slave flight and rebellion increased dramatically, as slaves took advantage of revolutionary rhetoric and the dislocations of the war to effect their freedom. Virginia, South

Carolina, and Georgia lost thousands of slaves in the wake of the famous 1775 proclamation of Virginia's royal governor Lord Dunmore, freeing all slaves who fought for the British cause.[50] As late as the 1790s, maroon communities endured in Low Country South Carolina and Georgia.[51]

As the maroons' persistence suggests, long after the war for independence, American slaveholders held onto a slave population with an explosive mix of grievances and ideological influences. The establishment of the free black republic of Haiti in the former French colony of St. Domingue, after over a decade of slave revolt and successful defensive wars against the powers of Europe, stood as a dangerous example to American slaves as well as an illustration of the dangers of the revolutionary ideology spreading throughout the Atlantic world.[52] The dangers of that ideology came even closer to home in 1800 when Virginia authorities discovered a massive plot to revolt among the slaves in and around Richmond. The rebels' leader, Gabriel, and his fellow conspirators spoke in the language of the American and French Revolutions.[53] Planter John Randolph of Roanoke had attended some of the interrogations of Gabriel's lieutenants and was alarmed to hear them speaking in terms of their rights and of vengeance. They "exhibited a spirit," he fretted, "which, if it becomes general, must deluge the Southern country in blood." St. Domingue had appeared in the South.[54]

Free African Americans also posed a threat, both actual and theoretical. Manumissions in the South and emancipation in the North spurred the growth of a vigorous free black population in both sections. This population stood as a continual symbolic threat to slaveowners, challenging the idea that "black" and "slave" were synonymous. Moreover, Northern emancipation had been precipitated in no small measure by the aggressiveness of Northern slaves in seizing their own freedom, rendering their example doubly bad.[55]

Urban concentrations of free black people in both the North and the South posed more than a symbolic danger to the slaveholders' property in man. In the runaway slave advertisements they placed in Virginia in the early nineteenth century, masters—who had no reason to publish anything other than what they thought was accurate information that would aid in the recovery of their human property—bespoke their assumption that free people of color gave runaway slaves aid. They presumed that black seamen hid runaways on their ships, or that free black populations in cities throughout the Chesapeake and Northern states offered the possibility of anonymity to fugitives from bondage. "I believe," wrote one typical master, that a particular slave "is in Alexandria [Virginia] or its vicinity, harbored by some of those numerous shops and negro houses that infest every city." Often that safe haven was temporary, for cities in the Upper South served as way stations when fugitives followed the North Star to freedom. Furthermore, the growing presence of free black people in the Upper South helped other runaways indirectly by lending plausibility to the free papers forged by many runaways.[56] Despite Congress's Fugitive Slave Act of 1793, Northern free black communities also made their influence felt in the South. Several years after James Madison freed his slave Billey and left him in Philadelphia, Madison was convinced that a runaway from his plantation might try to seek Billey out for shelter.[57]

Slaveholders bore witness to their fear and loathing of free blacks in no uncertain terms. A white North Carolinian flatly declared that "it is impossible for us to be happy, if, after manumission, they are to stay among us."[58] Virginia's antimanumission petitioners spoke of free people of color as "a vast Multitude of unprincipled, unpropertied, revengeful, and remorseless Banditti."[59] Southern politicians heard such constituents. As Congress debated the slave trade ban, Representative Peter Early of Georgia asserted that "to have among us in any considerable quantity persons of this description" would be "an evil far greater than slavery itself." If the number increased beyond what Southern whites considered reasonable, Early explained, "we must in self-defense—gentlemen will understand me—get rid of them in some way. We must either get rid of them, or they of us; there is no alternative."[60]

Accordingly, Northern abolitionists made a contribution to antislavery when they protected fugitives. By so doing, they preserved the integrity of the free black communities in their midst, thereby perpetuating a menace to Southern slaveholders. Certainly they irritated slaveholders, including George Washington, who thought the Pennsylvania Abolition Society a bunch of bullies whose resources far exceeded those of most Virginia slaveholders seeking to recover their slippery human property.[61]

In short, Southern slaves in the early national period bore more than the usual heavy grievances against their masters and had opportunities to act on them. In addition to American-born slaves and free people of color who had drunk in the ideology of the American and French and Haitian revolutions, the South in the early nineteenth century was inhabited by almost 200,000 slaves brought from Africa since the close of the Revolutionary war.[62] Slaveholders were never absolutely sure from which quarter revolt might break out, but they seemed particularly confident that slaves from outside the United States, whether West Indians infected with the St. Domingue political fever or West Africans stewing after the horrors of the Middle Passage, were a peculiarly unruly element. Such fears were a powerful reason for Southerners to join Northerners in abolishing the foreign slave trade.[63] Furthermore, as the expansion of slavery accelerated in the early nineteenth century, the forced migration of slaves to the Southwest frayed the fragile ties between master and slave. Whether dragged to the Southwest or left behind with families torn asunder, slaves affected by this Great Migration had good reasons for their deep discontent. Slaves from the late colonial period to the Great Migration had attained a large measure of stability in their family and community life and had developed strong attachments to their home places.[64] If forcible migration shattered such ties, it also broke the delicate web of customary privileges and practices that slaves had hammered out with their masters in each particular location. Thus the forced southwesterly march, as Steven Miller has written, "strained the always unstable entente" between owner and owned.[65] It was with good reason, then, that slaveholders feared their slaves in the early republic. One white Virginian spoke for many when he wrote that "if we will keep a ferocious monster in our country, we must keep him in chains."[66]

The "if" spoke volumes, and many masters, particularly in the Upper South, decided to let the monster go. In 1782, Virginia passed a law giving slaves easier access to manumissions by reducing restrictions on their masters. In the decade following the act, Virginia masters alone manumitted roughly 10,000 slaves.[67] So liberalized did Maryland's manumission laws become that some slaves reversed the traditional assumption that African descent conferred slave status by suing (sometimes successfully) for their liberty on grounds of descent from at least one white person.[68] Southern manumission and abolition societies had their heyday in the late eighteenth century; the wrath they provoked in many planters bore testimony to their effectiveness.[69]

Yet genuine, vital antislavery commitment seems to have been a growth of short duration among white Southerners, and in some it never took root. Many—such as Jefferson—professed their opposition to slavery, but it seems that much of that was for consumption beyond the South, for those same Southern spokesmen upheld slavery by their political actions at home and abroad. Even if their antislavery professions were sincere, many backed away from them rather quickly.[70] James Monroe spoke for many when he wrote to Jefferson to express support for abolition—provided it could be effected "without expense or inconvenience to ourselves."[71]

Indeed, the majority of white Southerners answered the "if" in the affirmative, deciding in the end to keep the monster in strengthened chains. This was especially true in the Lower South, where opposition to slavery made precious few inroads even in the late eighteenth century. Even in the revolutionary year of 1776, South Carolinian John Laurens lamented that he had "scarcely ever met with a Native of" South Carolina or Georgia "who did not obstinately" support slavery by any argument at hand.[72] Nothing had changed by 1790, when a Charleston resident attested that it would "be more safe for a man to proclaim through this city that there was no God, than that slave-holding was inconsistent with his holy law."[73] By the early nineteenth century, the small traces of antislavery in the Lower South became almost undetectable. Between 1805 and 1819, over a thousand Quakers retreated from South Carolina, headed for the Northwest.[74] Such departures heralded a migration from the South that continued for decades—and which not only vitiated the remnants of Southern antislavery but also presented visual proof of the sectional logic of free and slave states working itself out in the early decades of the nineteenth century.[75]

The Upper South manifested a greater degree of uncertainty on slavery, but it was no den of abolitionists. The antimanumission petitioners to Virginia's legislature were at least as organized as any abolitionist society, echoing each other's language calling for the same policy: rejection of emancipation plans and repeal of the 1782 manumission law. Furthermore, they gathered hundreds of signatures from throughout the tobacco-planting counties of the state.[76] In 1791, Robert Carter initiated the gradual manumission of his slaves, more than five hundred in all. Despite Carter's gradualism, his neighbors complained bitterly of the bad effect his example was having on their slaves. Even his sons, whom he had sent to the North to be educated away from slavery's influence, sought to overturn or counteract the effects of this act. One even bought slaves from slave traders while he was freeing others in reluctant compliance with his father's wishes. Carter, like other manumitters, was anomalous in his neighborhood and even in his family.[77] Likewise, many white Virginians saw in George Washington's manumitted slaves not a noble example of liberty but a harbor for runaways.[78]

The Upper South's ambivalence toward the perpetuation of slavery diminished even more in the first decade of the nineteenth century. To be sure, the Upper South still hosted many vocal opponents to slavery.[79] Yet in the aftermath of Gabriel's conspiracy in 1800, they began losing the debate. Methodist ministers in the South found themselves the objects of persecution for their antislavery reputation in the days after the plot was discovered and thereafter distanced themselves from what they deemed the lost cause of Southern emancipation.[80] The proponents of perpetual slavery gained the upper hand within the bellwether state of Virginia, where whites were increasingly reconciling themselves to the institution. In 1806, Virginia passed an antimanumission law that epitomized the changing commitment of the Upper South. It required freed blacks to leave the state within a year and checked the post-Revolutionary rise in manumissions.[81] Tennessee's legislature similarly restricted slaves' access to freedom in the first years of the nineteenth century. Although North Carolina, Tennessee, and Kentucky harbored many antislavery societies, their members were a hopeless minority and faced an increasingly chilly public reception after 1800.[82]

But if the South was accommodating itself to slavery in practice, almost none of its spokesmen were prepared to announce that to the world. They continued to defend slavery as a necessary evil rather than embracing it as a positive good in theory. This was true in part because many of them still wrestled with the moral and practical dilemmas slavery posed.[83] Those who cared about the outside world also had to wrestle with the antislavery zeitgeist. They feared the political isolation that would come from defending slavery in the abstract. In 1789, for instance, a South Carolina contributor to a Philadelphia magazine, contrary to all other available evidence, protested that "the most elevated and liberal Carolinians abhor slavery; and will not debase themselves by attempting to vindicate it."[84] Most of those who rose to parry the blows aimed at slavery were in the difficult position of seeking to justify slavery's continuance in the South while denying that they were justifying it.[85] Thus, their apologies and defenses were often tortured, for few of them were as candid as Patrick Henry, who declared that although he could not defend slavery, he could not imagine living without slave labor.[86]

To be sure, some Southerners did move in the direction of a principled endorsement of chattel bondage. Most of the antimanumission petitions in Virginia spoke circumspectly of God having "permitted" slavery, but one memorial took a more advanced position. Its authors declared that slavery "was ordained by the Great and wise Disposer of all things," who "Licensed or Commanded his People" in biblical times to own slaves.[87] During South Carolina's convention to ratify the federal Constitution, Rawlins Lowndes ventured to say that the African slave trade "could be justified on the principles of religion, humanity and justice; for certainly to translate a set of human beings from a bad country to a better, was fulfilling every part of those principles."[88]

Such reasoning surfaced only in intra-Southern debates such as these, however. In the national arena, Southerners were more reticent. In May 1789, during a debate over taxing imported slaves, Georgia's James Jackson averred that although "it was the fashion of the day, to favor the liberty of slaves," experience had shown that emancipation had not improved their condition in any respect. They certainly were better off in American slavery than they had been in Africa, he declared.[89] Ironically, Jackson upheld the African slave trade but did not fully commit to the superiority of slavery over freedom in America. Yet Jackson's was the most advanced position Southerners took in national councils, where they found it much easier to abuse abolitionists than to uphold slavery outright. In 1790, Congressman William L. Smith of South Carolina professed his certainty that by any measure "the folly of emancipation was manifest." But all he would say about slavery itself was that it was of ancient date and "was not disapproved of by the apostles." "If it be a moral evil," he suggested, "it is like many others" that the civilized world accepted, and seeking to remove it would likely cause more harm than good.[90] In response to this speech, Representative Thomas Scott of Pennsylvania expressed his shock at hearing, "at this age of the world" and in the hallowed halls of Congress, "an advocate for slavery, in its fullest latitude." Such constituted "a phenomenon in politics."[91] But Scott had misread Smith. While bitterly opposed to emancipation, Smith was but a tepid supporter of slavery in the abstract.

Others joined Smith in inching only hesitantly toward a full proslavery position on the national stage. "If slavery be wrong," South Carolina's Charles Pinckney told his fellow delegates in the Constitutional Convention, "it is justified by the example of all the world."[92] In the debates over abolishing the slave trade in 1806–1807, Southern congressmen could not quite bring themselves to call slavery or the slave trade a positive good. North Carolinian James Holland echoed James Jackson when he posited that the Atlantic trade was "only a transfer from one master to another, and it is admitted that the condition of slaves in the Southern States is much superior to that of those in Africa. Who, then, will say that the trade is immoral?" Meanwhile, Georgia's Peter Early informed his colleagues that "in the Southern section of the Union," the foreign commerce in slaves was not "an offense which nature revolts at. They do not consider it as a crime." He also instructed his fellows on white Southerners' feelings about slavery itself. "All the people in the Southern States are concerned in slavery. It is not then considered as criminal. . . . Many deprecate slavery as an evil; as a political evil, but not as a crime."[93] These men could not bring themselves to say that slavery or the slave trade were *moral*, only that they were not (and were not considered by most white Southerners to be) *immoral*. These defenses, and the hesitant manner in which they were offered, illustrated the difficulties of trying to speak for slavery in the Revolutionary and early national era.

ADVERTISEMENT.

RUN away laſt Night, from on board the Sloop Grace and Sally. Chriſtopher Wilſon, Maſter, lying in this Harbour ; A Yellow negro fellow named Caeſer, about five feet ſeven or eight Inches high, 29 or 27 years old, much pitted with the ſmall Pox, has a wild ſtare in his Eyes, which is obſervable at firſt ſight; he is an artful ſpecious fellow, and may paſs himſelf, for a free Man: We cannot deſcribe his dreſs, as he carried off with him all the Sailors Cloaths he could lay his hands on.

He was formerly the property of Mr. Charles Yates on Rappahanock River, and lately ſold in Antigua, whoever ſecures him in any Goal, and informs the ſub-ſcribers ſo that they may get him again, ſhall receive forty Shillings Reward.

GILCHRIST and TAYLOR.

N. B. It is ſuppoſed he went up Rappahanock in a Craft that left this place laſt Night.

NORFOLK, June 9th, 1774

This runaway slave advertisement is a specimen of the idea that demons or other outside agitators drove otherwise happy American slaves to flee their bondage. (From *Virginia Gazette and General Advertiser*, 9 June 1774)

The arguments of slavery's early pseudochampions contained many elements that would later make up the proslavery creed, even if they were experimental and directed mainly at fellow Southerners. Some slaveholders, for instance, refused to admit publicly that their slaves would want to flee their service, preferring instead to depict their slaves as contented. Thus at least one fugitive slave advertisement in the 1770s replaced the standard icon of a runaway with a demon goading a reluctant slave to flight. During the Revolutionary War, such men spoke of the British "stealing" and "seducing" their slaves away from their masters during the American Revolution. Historian Gerald Mullin has suggested that this image only gained in frequency as ambivalence about slavery faded in the South beginning in the 1790s.[94] Virginia's anti-emancipation petitioners also prefigured future arguments by castigating their opponents as meddlers whose officiousness was prompted either by interested motives or "the chimerical Flights of a fanatic Spirit."[95] And, as early as 1801, some Southern evangelicals forged ahead of their time by seeking to persuade their countrymen to sanctify slavery by initiating reforms in the interests of strengthening the institution.[96]

To be sure, slavery's defenders were generally more innovative than were its attackers in the early national period.[97] Yet for all their creativity, slavery's spokesmen were on the defensive ideologically and politically. For instance, between 1787 and 1807, slaveholders in the Northwest territories repeatedly petitioned Congress to overturn the clause in the Northwest Ordinance that outlawed slavery there. When they failed to gain this repeal from Congress, they turned more forcefully to exercising their local power to keep their black servants in de facto slavery. This revealed the Northwestern slaveholders' re-sourcefulness. But Congress's repeated rebuffs of these petitions were also telling. Furthermore, the language of the petitioners for slavery demonstrated their defensive position. They "accepted the idea that slavery was a violation of republican principles" and couched their arguments in terms of the diffusion of slavery as a means toward its distant and gradual abolition.[98] Slaveholders in the Northwest had met nothing but frustration at the hands of the same Congress that outlawed the Atlantic slave trade. Although they were assertive and creative, theirs was a curiously defensive offensive; they sought to take slavery into enemy territory while granting the enemy's arguments.

Yet if Congress's rejection of the Northwest petitioners revealed the ideological position of slavery, the slaveholders' drive to expand slavery there illuminated the fact that slavery was on the march on the ground in the early national era. The reason Congress rejected the claims highlighted why this was so. The rejection of these petitions was based less on antislavery principles than on the idea that slavery should not expand beyond what most Americans regarded as its natural or proper limits. In this instance as in many others, Northerners proved more concerned about preserving their cherished distance from slavery than about slavery in the distant South. Such limits to the antislavery sentiment of the age restricted the threat it posed to slavery in the United States.

Northerners made only fleeting and ineffectual efforts to restrict slavery in territories where it was already entrenched. In 1787, James Wilson assured Pennsylvania's ratification convention that under the Constitution, Congress would be able to ensure that "slaves will never be introduced" into any new states.[99] Yet when Kentucky entered the Union in 1792 and Tennessee in 1796,

Congress did no such thing. Indeed, Northern resistance to the admission of these slave states was weak and largely unconnected to the issue of slavery.[100] When the Mississippi Territory and Louisiana Purchase became territories of the United States, slavery in these regions did generate disputes. Southern representatives won both of them. In 1798, Congress debated whether Article VI of the Northwest Ordinance, which prohibited slavery from the Northwest Territory, should be applied to Mississippi Territory. In the end, Congress declared that the Ordinance was applicable in all ways to Mississippi—with the explicit exception of Article VI.[101] When it came time for Congress to ratify the Louisiana Purchase in 1803, New England Federalists declared that it had fundamentally altered the whole nature of the Union, shifting the balance of power decidedly toward the South and the Republicans. New Englanders experimented with ideas of a Northern confederacy in 1804, and the whole episode focused their scrutiny even more upon the constitutional clause that granted Southerners representation for three-fifths of their slave population.[102] Yet such opposition was not only weak and isolated, but it also focused at least as much on whether to ratify the treaty as on whether to restrict slavery in the Southwest.[103]

A key reason for most Northerners' acquiescence in slavery's expansion was their belief that slavery was a necessity in the Deep South. They believed in a doctrine of separate spheres for slavery and freedom that grew from two basic assumptions: first, that it would be fruitless or even dangerous to try to outlaw slavery where it had taken firm root; and second, that African slavery was best suited—or perhaps indispensable—to agricultural labor in the Southern climate. Subscription to these maxims made it possible for most white Northerners to concede that slavery was a necessary evil, indefensible in principle but only very gradually eradicable in the South.

Unlike other widely held doctrines of the time, this idea strengthened the slaveholders' position, allowing for the spread of slavery within its accepted sphere. Northerners and Southerners alike had voted for slavery's restriction above the Ohio River but for allowing slavery to spread to the Southwest.[104] This policy of nonintervention, as opposed to one that would have formally established slavery, reinforced the sense that slavery was "natural" in southerly climes. Some Revolutionary-era abolitionists sought to explode the climatic defense of slavery in the tropics or semitropical Southern states. They pointed to many instances in which white men had labored profitably, even in the West Indies. But they were fighting an uphill battle against this old and popular stereotype.[105] This common wisdom echoed in the halls of Congress, helping to win the day for Louisiana's accession as a slave territory. When a Senator from Georgia insisted that "slaves must be admitted into that territory" because "it cannot be cultivated without them," he found many Northerners in agreement. Some charged that the climatic argument was a specious cover for the continued practice of slavery, but others echoed the Georgian's assertion, and still others pointed to the futility of restriction given the existence of slavery in the territory.[106] Most white Americans in both sections shared vague notions that slavery had a proper territorial orbit that included the Southwest.

Furthermore, most white Northerners saw slavery in the Southwest as sufficiently distant that it need not affect them. Northerners' assent to the expansion of slavery in the South and opposition to it in the Northwest were two sides of the same coin: antislavery for the vast majority of white Yankees consisted mostly of a desire to separate themselves from it. They had abolished slavery in their states, but only a few abolitionists concerned themselves beyond the state level.

Many white Northerners sought to maintain a healthy distance not only from slavery but also from what they perceived to be its legacy—African Americans. Northerners did not need to be racial egalitarians to support emancipation acts; indeed, some fantasized that these laws would somehow rid them of African Americans as well as the institution of slavery.[107] Thomas Branagan, a Philadelphia abolitionist, contended that since "slavery debases and contaminates the immortal soul," Northerners were justly alarmed when Southerners manumitted their victims without preparing them for freedom and they flooded into Northern cities. He compared slavery "to a large tree planted in the south, whose spreading branches extends to the North; the poisonous fruit of that tree when ripe falls upon these states, to the annoyance of the inhabitants, and contamination of the land which is sacred to liberty." He preferred cutting off the branches and taking them to a more distant territory.[108] In his influential geography text, Jedidiah Morse rejoiced that since the 1770s, the black population of New York state had "decreased 1000, which is a happy circumstance."[109] A New York City merchant told English traveler William Strickland that "the general opinion which prevails here with regard to the Slaves, when emancipated is, that they will dwindle away and soon disappear"—much "like the Indians."[110] Some who wished to keep African Americans at arm's length went beyond pleading and entertaining convenient fantasies. Thus laws such as Ohio's black codes of 1804, which sought to bar free African Americans from entering the state and restricted the rights of those already there, often accompanied abolition in the North.[111]

Whenever slavery or its side effects threatened to bridge that distance, the Northern populace could be expected to resist. Northern Antifederalists understood this, and they exploited it in the struggle over ratification of the Constitution. One of their scare tactics was to charge, rather implausibly, that by encouraging the slave trade for twenty years or more, the Constitution would allow Congress to authorize the importation of slaves even into Pennsylvania. Thus "SLAVERY will probably resume its empire in Pennsylvania," they warned.[112] Similarly, and more reasonably, Northern Antifederalists told their audiences that by ratifying such a compact they would be complicit in slavery and the slave trade, despite their confidence that they were far from such moral guilt.[113]

Such appeals demonstrated the Antifederalists' grasp on white Northerners' immense pride in living in the free states. White Northerners' sectional pride in having acted on the libertarian premise of the American Revolution was widely shared throughout the section and was especially strong in New England. Citizens of Massachusetts, for instance, claimed that their state was "the special home of liberty. . . . In contrast to slave society, she had nurtured the masculine virtues among a people who prospered '*with the labor of their own hands, —with the sweat of their own brows.*'" Distance from—even opposition to—slavery thus became an integral part of an exclusive New England identity that was at once partisan, sectional, state-centric, and national, for Massachusetts Federalists posed as the preservers of their state's and region's special bequests to America.[114] In Royall Tyler's novel *The Algerine Captive*, the main character visits an unspecified Southern state, where he sees a minister lashing his slave on the way to church. "A certain staple of New England which I had with me, called conscience," forces him to remonstrate with the parson, but his remarks are lost on the Southerner. Although at times in the novel slavery is treated as a national disgrace, Tyler lays its guilt directly at the feet of the Southern states.[115] By such means, Northerners could sectionalize the national embarrassment slavery caused.

Sectional pride often brought out the bright side of Northerners' desire for distance from slavery, as they resented anything that might implicate them morally in slavery. This included resentment toward the idea of returning fugitive slaves from the North to the South. In 1796, for instance, when President George Washington's agents arrived in Portsmouth, New Hampshire, seeking a fugitive slave from his estate, the community arose in such fury that they had to call their search off.[116]

But the success and prevalence as well as the limited focus of popular antislavery in the North also bred overconfidence. Many were blinded to or at least apathetic toward the expansion of slavery in the South because abolition seemed like a done deal in their own backyard. To such minds, slavery was a distant, sectional problem as a result of the American Revolution, no longer a national evil. Such complacency, together with the widespread acceptance that slave labor had a proper sphere, left slavery free to roam across the continent, even as it was under attack in the abstract. Most Northerners trusted that slavery would effortlessly disappear once they abolished the slave trade and hoped that it would keep to itself in the meantime.

————

Many spokesmen from the slave states, however, did not console themselves about the limits of Northern antislavery. They saw a threat more than the practical limits to the threat. Many were ever on the watch for precedents on which national abolition might be based. The loudest Southern voices called for a moratorium on any discussion in the national councils that bore on slavery, even indirectly. They feared that even the act of debating slavery in the House or Senate implied that Congress had the authority to interfere with the embattled institution. Whether that body chose to act on that authority or not, it was setting a precedent that would allow for future interference. Thus, in 1783, when Quakers petitioned Congress to end the slave trade, and a congressional committee recommended a resolution declaring that each state ought to deal with the slave trade as it saw fit, Southern Congressmen voted against even this apparent vindication of state rights at the hands of Congress.[117] Seven years later, the fact that Congress was debating anti–slave-trade petitions rather than rejecting them outright caused an uproar in Charleston and elsewhere in the South.[118] Seven years after that, in a congressional debate over whether to register black sailors, a representative from South Carolina implored his colleagues to break off the debate and regretted that the subject had ever come up, for it might become "a kind of entering wedge."[119] Such men were determined to see that the Constitution be construed so narrowly and strictly that the federal government would never menace slavery in the South.

The white South, however, was divided when it came to discussion of slavery and the federal government's relation to it. In the debate over the slave trade clause at the Constitutional Convention, for instance, although some Southern delegates declared that all discussion of this purely local issue in that national forum was illegitimate, others readily wrangled over the merits and policy of the slave trade. The same was true for the congressional debates over the slave trade in the 1790s.[120]

Portrait of John Randolph (1773–1833) by John Wesley Jarvis, oil on wood, 1811.
(National Portrait Gallery, Smithsonian Institution)

Those who wished to limit the federal government's power even to discuss slavery carried the day in the South in the 1790s, when Northern Federalists controlled the government. Federalist policies, although hardly abolitionist, included such atrocities in slaveholders' eyes as neglecting slaveholders' property rights in Jay's Treaty with England and encouraging trade with and sending military support to Toussaint L'Ouverture in St. Domingue.[121] But with Jefferson's election in 1800 came a new Southern confidence in the federal government, including among those who had previously been strict constructionists. The Constitution as strictly construed, for instance, gave no authority for the Louisiana Purchase of 1803, or to Jefferson's Embargo and the stern measures required to enforce it. But that did not stop the vast majority of Southern Republicans from supporting these measures.[122] Yet even after 1800, a noisy minority, the "Old Republicans," sought to call their Southern brethren back to limited government and worried about dangerous precedents. One of the leading Old Republicans, John Randolph, spoke with characteristic warmth in the congressional debate over abolishing the slave trade. He objected to a clause in the bill that would regulate the seaborne interstate slave trade in a limited fashion. "If the law went into force as it was," he thundered, "he doubted whether we should ever see another southern delegate on that floor. He, for one, would say, if the Constitution is thus to be violated let us secede, and go home." He warned that the slave trade bill as it stood would serve as an "entering wedge" in the Yankees' supposed drive for universal emancipation.[123]

As divided as the Southern mind may have been on these issues, it was united behind the idea that slavery was and must remain an issue for Southerners alone to deal with. As historian Richard Brown has written, there was "one single compelling idea which virtually united all Southerners," no matter their own stance on the desirability of slavery. "This was that the institution of slavery should not be dealt with from outside the South."[124] Robert Carter, for instance, even as he mulled manumitting his slaves, was alarmed as he read the proposed federal Constitution, for he thought it left the door open to emancipation by the national government.[125] Given the limits of Northern antislavery, this response may seem disproportionate to the actual threat. But in the Revolutionary and early national period, Southern slaveholders felt besieged both from without and from within. As historian Robert Forbes has pointed out, "In order to understand the extreme response of many Southerners to even the most conservative measures to combat slavery, it must be recognized that Americans possessed no model from modern times of peaceful emancipation of a true slave society." Northern states had begun to free their slaves peacefully and gradually, but the North did not qualify as "a true slave society"; not until the abolition of slavery in the British West Indies did such an emancipation take place. Thus St. Domingue was their reigning paradigm for the complete abolition of slavery in a slave society.[126]

The lesson they learned from St. Domingue was that when outside agitators meddled with slavery, as French Revolutionaries had done in the 1790s, they would produce massive slave revolts and even revolution. And slaveholders were not comforted when they read abolitionist voices from the North and elsewhere, both before and after the horrors of St. Domingue, expressing sympathy for slave rebels. These enthusiasts described slaves in rebellion as merely seeking to recover their lost liberty. They blamed slaveholders for turning slaves vicious by their brutality toward them and considered their desire for vengeance justifiable. In a 1794 oration, Connecticut's Theodore Dwight predicted that the St. Domingue uprising would be replicated in the South. But when the Southern slaveholder asked Northerners to assist them in quelling the revolt, he avowed, "No friend to freedom and justice will dare lend him his aid."[127]

In this setting, slaveholders interpreted any attack on anything related to slavery, such as the slave trade or slave representation, as an attack on slavery itself. They were not alone in conflating the slave trade and slavery. Try as many did to separate the two issues, they continued to run together for Northerners and Southerners, abolitionists and slaveholders.[128] Furthermore, Southern delegates to the Philadelphia Convention drew the battle lines on slave representation for all time. They made it clear that without an "express security" in the Constitution "for including slaves in the ratio of Representation," they would consider their human property to be in jeopardy. "Property in slaves," a South Carolinian lectured, "should not be exposed to danger under a Government instituted for the protection of property." Without the vital clause enumerating slaves, Southern delegates suggested, such would be the case with the proposed government.[129] Southern spokesmen thus put their Northern brethren on notice that they would interpret any drive to abolish the sacred three-fifths compromise as an attempt to breach the federal compact and abolish slavery. Their need to defend the citadel of slavery would extend to its outer defenses as well.

———

Although the Revolution made slavery an ideological and sectional issue, it also made it a political one, as politicians and statesmen discovered slavery's usefulness as a partisan weapon. These were related developments, for most of slavery's uses in politics involved painting one's opponents as out of step with constituents who held it in disrepute. A Southern variation on this theme featured accusations that one's antagonists were in league or sympathy with the rising antislavery sentiment that threatened their constituents. The use of slavery as a political tool had been as rare and isolated before the Revolution as attacks on slavery had been.[130] For slavery to be a political weapon of broad application, the stigma attached to it had to be similarly broad. Accordingly, as antislavery sentiment grew, so did slavery's forays into both the international and domestic political arenas. And in turn, these political experiments, no matter their motive, further exposed slavery to scrutiny and raised the stakes surrounding it.

As the controversy between Great Britain and her rebellious colonists grew and became a rivalry between nations, propagandists exploited the newfound squeamishness about slavery on both sides of the Atlantic. Loyal Britons took seemingly endless delight in skewering the patriots for inconsistency in yelping for liberty while holding slaves. The typical American counter to this was the strategy of blaming British greed for foisting slaves on the North American colonists in the first place. This not only parried the English charges of hypocrisy but served as a handy illustration of the home government's abuses of power.[131] For their part, abolitionists in both Britain and America hoped the sting of these barbs would goad their respective countrymen into greater exertion against slavery and the slave trade.

As the American Revolution gave way to the wars of the French Revolution, Britons' concern for world opinion only increased. Locked in a struggle for their national existence and the perpetuity of their monarchical institutions, they needed as many friends as they could get. "The esteem of foreign nations," wrote English statesman and abolitionist James Stephen, "is obviously of consequence to us at all times, and especially at this singular conjuncture." Napoleon Bonaparte was battling Britain for that esteem and seeking to persuade "the world, that [the English] are a sordid, selfish, and unprincipled people, whose gold is their god." Stephen argued that the Atlantic slave trade was the point upon which "we are justly chargeable" with such crimes. He asserted that abolition of the slave trade would go a long way in convincing Americans, whom he hoped would become valued allies, of Britain's good faith.[132] As antislavery activists saw slavery entering politics, they hoped its connection to national interest and reputation would lend a greater urgency to their cause among the otherwise uncommitted.

Slavery also showed signs of usefulness on the domestic political front in America after the Revolution. The political serviceability of slavery in all its variety was on full display in the debates surrounding the drafting and ratification of the United States Constitution between 1787 and 1789. Many historians have posited the centrality of slavery to the Constitutional Convention and the ratification debates that followed. But for most players, slavery constituted a secondary issue that could be used to great advantage in pressing their respective points of view regarding the primary topics at hand.[133]

This was true at the Philadelphia Convention, where discord between the small and large states concerning representation in the new Congress formed the most important divide. The question of whether to count slaves toward each state's congressional presence was contentious, but most often it came into

SLAVERY AND POLITICS TO 1808

play in the context of the larger debate over representation. James Madison

play in the context of the larger debate over representation. James Madison famously asserted in his notes of the Convention's debates that the vital division was not between large and small states, but rather between slave and free states. But a month before he made this characterization, Madison had urged his fellow delegates to set aside the issue of counting slaves for representation, so as not to distract from the real business at hand, proportional representation by population. Indeed, his colleagues agreed that "every thing depended on" whether states would be counted equally or by population. Only after a full month of bruising debate did Madison circle back and suggest that the free state—slave state divergence was the crucial one.[134] This suggests that his famous formulation should be taken more as a diversionary tactic than at face value. Furthermore, New Jersey led the fight against slave representation in Philadelphia, a curious stand for a state with one of the largest slave populations in the North.[135] Apparently, the delegates from this small state thought that by attacking slave representation, they could effectively undermine the principle of popular representation with which it was bound. On the other hand, delegates from the large state of Massachusetts, later the home of slave representation's leading foes, were ambivalent on the issue in Philadelphia. As Northern politicians had done in previous debates over counting slaves, they supported it if it increased the South's tax burden but not if it increased the South's representation. Some Massachusetts delegates did object to counting slaves, but as a whole the Massachusetts delegation compromised on the issue.[136] One's stance on the central question of popular representation strongly colored one's stance on secondary concerns related to slaves.

Similarly, it appears that most participants in the ratification debates made up their minds about the Constitution independent of the issue of slavery, then used its slavery clauses to attack or defend it.[137] Antifederalists accused the defenders of the Constitution of bringing shame on the nation by authorizing the slave trade's continuance.[138] They also cited that clause as "Proof" that the Federalists were "Enemies to the Rights of Mankind." A Kentucky writer fused the abolitionist vision of the tyrannical slaveholder with the Antifederalist vision of the aristocratic Federalist. "Where will ye stop," he demanded of those who sanctioned the continuation of the slave trade. "What security can you give, that, when there shall remain no more black people, ye will not enslave others, white as yourselves?" Truly, the slave trade clause was evidence that the lordly Federalists were "soaring toward the summit of Aristocracy."[139] For his part, Virginia Antifederalist George Mason exaggerated the importance of the slave trade clause by asserting that the Convention would never have agreed to the proposed Constitution without the compromises surrounding the slave trade. As Virginians by and large reprobated the Atlantic slave trade, he hoped this would discredit the Constitution.[140] It was perhaps predictable that astute Antifederalist politicians would make the slave trade clause their weapon of choice, given the fixation of their generation on that feature of slavery.[141]

But the slave trade was not the only weapon they employed. Antifederalists also insisted that the three-fifths clause's "dark" wording was part and parcel of a general mysteriousness and lack of candor in the document.[142] Northern Antifederalists tried to counterbalance the weight George Washington lent to the Federalist side by charging that as a slaveholder his claims to be supporting freedom by means of the Constitution were specious.[143] To illustrate how the Constitution failed to protect liberty of conscience, one writer offered a hypothetical scenario in which Congress ordered freedom-loving Northerners to march to Georgia to put down a slave revolt. This would violate their consciences because their sympathies would lie with the slaves in their "*noble appeal to arms*." This Pennsylvanian summed up the twin prongs of his attack by declaring that the Constitution's "very basis is *despotism* and *slavery*."[144]

Federalists also spun the proposed Constitution in ways dependent more on their audience than on consistency. At the Philadelphia Convention, James Madison lamented the slave trade clause as "dishonorable to the American character" and said that he considered exempting its abolition for twenty years to be worse than saying nothing. But as "Publius" during the ratification struggle in New York, he presented it as "a great point gained in favor of humanity," given that Americans would only have to wait twenty years to abolish the traffic.[145] Northern Federalists followed suit, positing that by dint of the slave trade abolition clause, for the first time "the abolition of slavery is put within the reach of the federal government."[146] Meanwhile, Southern Federalists had to contend with just such arguments from Southern Antifederalists and accordingly assured *their* audience that with the proposed Constitution, "we have a security that the general government can never emancipate."[147] Federalists likewise defended slave representation in the Northern debates, denigrating as so much partisan manipulation the idea that it put slaves and freemen on an equal footing. The Antifederalists were cynically seeking "to excite a jealousy between the inhabitants of the several States," to "mislead" the people and "to avail" themselves "of our strong disapprobation of slavery." Remarks such as these conceded the power of the Antifederalists' tool even as they tried to deprive them of it.[148]

Clearly the Federalists' arguments, as well as the Antifederalists', would have more nearly approximated coherence had their constituencies been more uniform. But consistency regarding slavery was as nothing compared to the overarching goal of securing or blocking the ratification of the Constitution. The scribe for Massachusetts's ratification convention made the telling remark that both sides "deprecated the slave-trade in the most pointed terms."[149] But their mutual deprecation of the slave trade hardly united them behind or against the Constitution, the real issue at hand. Slavery played a supporting role in the political drama of the late 1780s. Nevertheless, the fact that these skilled and dedicated debaters found it such a useful tool spoke to slavery's importance in American life and politics in the wake of the Revolution.

So irresistible was slavery as a tool that it insinuated itself into a wide array of subsequent debates to which it bore no relation. In a congressional debate over how to deal with fraudulent land claims in the Southwest, Virginia's John Randolph had attacked the position and character of the claimants' champion, Matthew Lyon of Vermont. Lyon reminded his peers that "these charges have been brought against me by a person nursed in the bosom of opulence, inheriting the life services of a numerous train of the human species, . . . the original proprietors of which property, in all probability, came no honester by it" than those whose land claims Randolph assailed. To be deemed consistent, Lyon suggested, Randolph should "give up the stolen men in his possession."[150]

Some pamphleteers saw political advantage in decrying their opponents' racism and linking it to slavery. This became apparent in the election of 1800, when Federalist writers attacked Jefferson for his thoughts on African inferiority in *Notes on Virginia*. "Sir," went one exclamation, "we excuse you not! You have degraded the blacks from the rank which God hath given them in the scale of being! You have advanced the strongest argument for their state of slavery! You have insulted human nature!" Jefferson's belief in a separate creation for blacks was of a piece, many Federalists thought, with his bent toward theologically suspect modern philosophy.[151] Such tactics suggested that the late eighteenth and early nineteenth centuries were relatively liberal times in relation to not only slavery but also to race.

Yet even in this atmosphere, slaveholders themselves sometimes boldly brandished slavery in the rough and tumble of unrelated debates. If Jefferson found himself branded a racist by Northern Federalists in 1800, he was targeted by Southern Federalists for being an abolitionist, also based on a reading of *Notes on Virginia*.[152] And in 1807, in support of his opposition to federal interference in a contested election in Maryland, John Randolph pointed out, "particularly to the members of the Southern States, one of the consequences" of federal intervention based on broad construction of the Constitution. What if Northerners insisted on protecting the rights of their black "*citizens*" and "*constituents*" in any federal legislation relative to the franchise? "What was the undeniable inference, the monstrous and abominable conclusion?" Randolph left the answer to his colleagues' imagination, but his question became a running theme in this debate.[153] Some slaveholders apparently had no trouble interjecting slavery into debates to which it was tangential at best, so long as they did so themselves and in defense of their embattled institution.

———

Still, before 1808, early experimenters in the politics of slavery failed to exploit its full potential. Whether on the international or domestic stage, attacks on slavery were most often dissociated from things political, and most political attacks did not incorporate slavery. The issue of slavery never became associated with one particular party's platform or even its bag of tricks; it was for individual use rather than part of any grand political strategy. The salience of slavery in mainstream politics tended to expire with the heated contests that provoked its use.

In the years immediately following the American Revolution, for instance, many Britons did not see American slavery as particularly useful in international politics. This was true in part because the day of antislavery's fashionableness had yet to arrive in Great Britain. In 1783, Quaker abolitionist Anthony Benezet sent several of his antislavery writings to Queen Charlotte of Great Britain, eliciting only a condescending comment on the plain binding of one of the books.[154] When Englishman William Strickland traveled to the United States in the mid-1790s, he depicted Virginia's reliance on slavery as "pernicious." But he was making an agricultural, not a political, point. Strickland also reported British diplomat George Hammond's remarks that the society and "Government of the five Southern States is the worst possible." But Hammond had nothing to say about slavery there.[155] It was not until the War of 1812 that the issue of slavery maintained a consistent presence in Anglo-American disputes.

Neither had Americans fully explored the possibilities of slavery in domestic politics. The Federalists, for instance, made little if any public use of slavery as they combated the nascent Republican Party in the 1790s. In 1793, as the party divisions were forming, leading Massachusetts Federalist Fisher Ames wrote an unpublished screed inveighing against America's Francophile "Jacobins," or Republicans. He enumerated the frauds and hypocrisies of those who pretended to be the friends of liberty and equality, but he did not include slaveholding in his list.[156] As Strickland spoke with a Connecticut Federalist, the Yankee expressed his distrust for Southern Republicans. He was sure that their Anglophobic policies were prompted by their drive to avoid repaying their debts to British merchants. He concluded therefore that dodging debts constituted "the Secret springs of their democracy."[157] Some analysts in later generations, including the next generation of Federalists, proclaimed slaveholding to be "the Secret springs" of their opponents' policies, but this was not a standard Federalist view in the 1790s.

New England's Federalist preachers—mostly Congregationalist clergy composing partisan sermons—attacked Republicans on several grounds in the 1790s, but slaveholding was not one of them. These clergymen were convinced that Republicans' political attachments to Revolutionary France connected the United States to the Antichrist and a whole host of associated sins. They listed specific sins, including Sabbath-breaking, violent anticlericalism, and the subversion of marriage and morality in general, which entailed the plagues of tyranny and violence that Europe was suffering. If Americans were not vigilant against these vices, they would involve the whole country in those plagues and thus destroy it. Thus it was the Republicans' Francophilia, not slavery, that constituted "the greatest danger which, at present, threatens the peace and liberties of our country."[158] Southern slavery was not one of the Federalist clergy's many fears and obsessions in the 1790s. The horrors they perceived following in the Antichrist's train were transpiring abroad—and only potentially in the United States. The American Revolution had alerted them, along with other Americans, of the evils of slavery, of course. But it was hard to recognize slavery as one of this particular Antichrist's sins or plagues, for the French Revolutionaries had abolished slavery in their colonies in 1794, and Napoleon did not reinstate colonial slavery until 1802.[159] For such reasons, the Federalist clergy of the 1790s did not include slavery in their enumeration of sins for which America might be condemned, as many New England clergy had done during the Revolutionary War.

The Federalists' connection to New England sectionalism and a particular brand of antislavery politics was a product of the nineteenth rather than the eighteenth century for at least two other reasons. First, they were in power. As the two parties took shape and commenced hostilities in the 1790s, the Federalists dominated the new national government and espoused obedience to the federal government and loyalty to the Union for which it stood. Fisher Ames wished "to have every American think the union so indissoluble and integral, that the corn would not grow, nor the pot boil, if it should be broken."[160] For his part, preacher David Osgood exhorted his listeners to thank God for the federal government, which was "the greatest, the chief, and, in fact, the basis of . . . all our political blessings."[161] Appeals to sectional interest and sectionalist attacks on Southern slaveholders hardly comported with such a stance.

Second, the parties were national, not sectional. While the Federalist Party's base was in the North, its candidates polled well in parts of the South throughout the 1790s. The Republican Party had its surest footing in the South, but it drew support in the North as well, especially in the Mid-Atlantic. With both parties contending on a national scale, it made no sense for either of them to resort to overt sectionalism, lest they alienate one whole section. As late as 1799, Fisher Ames expressed his hopes that Republican misdeeds would raise the fortunes of Southern Federalists, "for Feds there are even in Virginia."[162]

But when Republican chief Thomas Jefferson gained the presidency in 1801 and took the electoral votes of every Southern state except part of North Carolina, the Federalist leaders' national hopes began to collapse. Fisher Ames, for one, changed his tune. In an 1801 letter to friend Rufus King, he admitted "that on a fair calculation of force, we are weak indeed." Rather than hold out hope for Southern Federalism to revive, he urged that "New England ought to be roused and all our efforts ought to be directed to saving the remnants of federalism." In 1802 this Federalist strategist had given up the idea of "regaining the supreme power," in large part because Federalism was so anemic throughout the South. Under the direction of the likes of Ames, the Federalist leadership would appeal directly "to New England men" and seek to rally them around the specific "interest of the Eastern States," which they charged would not be safe in the hands of the Republicans. They recognized New York and Pennsylvania as hotbeds of Jacobinism, but excoriated above all the rise of "Virginia influence" in the nation upon Republican victory.[163] The Federalists would seek to make their party a sectional powerhouse if they could not regain national power.

After the Louisiana Purchase in 1803, their hopes for a national resurgence faded even further, for by adding Southern and Western territory the Republicans had reduced the Northeast's share of power in the Union. Accordingly, Federalist leaders began to use slavery more frequently in their sectional appeals against the Republicans. They upbraided the Republicans for inconsistency in their avowals of love for liberty and equality, emphasizing that many of the party's leading lights were slaveholders and that much of the Louisiana Purchase would be useless unless cultivated by slaves.[164] The prime evidence of their inconsistency, and the prime grievance of Federalist leaders in reference to the Louisiana Purchase, was the expansion of slave representation that it entailed. Leading Northern Federalists interpreted this southwesterly expansion as a radical redefinition of the Union that would allow unlimited numbers of new states—with slave representation in the Congress and Electoral College— to shift the sectional balance of power away from the Northeast forever. Nothing was more hypocritical, railed Ames, than "the cant of the jacobins" that "the will of the people ought to prevail." For they knew as well as any Federalist that their power rested upon "an avowed inequality," the three-fifths clause. And now they meant to expand that inequality, although "they know that these black votes are given in contempt of the rights of man." Since the Republicans were not disposed to give up slave representation, he hoped that they would at least silence their libertarian rhetoric, "for it's enough to be oppressed, too much to be insulted by our oppressors."[165] The Federalist chieftains did not confine the link between the Louisiana Purchase and slave representation to newspaper barbs. They organized to seek repeal of the three-fifths clause. Some talked of seceding from the Union to form a "Northern Confederacy." In these activities and these attacks on the Republicans were all the elements of their assaults on the power of slaveholders during the War of 1812.

Yet in 1803 and 1804 the Federalists had a hard time persuading average citizens to share their outrage. Agitation against slave representation did not resonate with the majority of voters, even in New England. Aside from Connecticut, no other state accepted Massachusetts's call for an amendment abolishing the "federal ratio." And in 1804 Thomas Jefferson carried every New England state except Connecticut.[166] Although the Federalist leadership had experienced their ouster from national power in 1801 personally and saw the Louisiana Purchase as rendering that ouster irrevocable, such blows fell at a distance from the concerns of most ordinary voters. In July 1804, Ames warned that in the aftermath of the Louisiana Purchase, "if the Middle and Eastern States still retain anything in the union worth possessing, we hold it by a precarious and degrading tenure; not as of right, but by sufferance."[167] But most Americans still found much in the Union worth possessing, and the hardcore Federalists like Ames were left to bemoan what they perceived as "the apathy that benumbs" the citizenry. Indeed, even the Federalist leadership's efforts were lackluster for much of Jefferson's terms in office; for instance, in 1804, no Federalist candidate opposed Jefferson for the presidency in five states.[168]

New England's Federalist clergymen also failed to preach against the Republicans as slaveholders in the first years after Jefferson's election. That event had proven to them that infidelity and all its evils had fastened themselves on the American republic. These "national iniquities" included freethinking, profanity, and Sabbath-breaking. The partisan preachers did not hesitate to fix the responsibility for all this on Jefferson, or to compare him to the worst of biblical rulers. They urged all good Christians to stand against the spiritual influence of the Republican Party, "the greatest danger to which we are at present exposed."[169] The national iniquities and dangers had nothing to do with slavery in these early attacks on Jefferson. The Federalist preachers did not precede the politicians and populace in introducing slavery into their partisan discourses.[170] It was not until after 1808, when Congress enacted Jefferson's Embargo, that the Federalist leadership's hatred of slaveholders and slave representation resonated with preachers as well as voters in New England.

Thus, the American Revolution had created free states and slave states that were drawing sectional battle lines concerning slavery. But the link between sectionalism and slavery had yet to be completed by 1808. For one thing, which states belonged to the North and which to the South was still in doubt. For example, in part because the Upper South had long sided more with the North than with the Deep South on the drive to abolish the Atlantic slave trade, its sectional alignment was fuzzy in many minds.[171] At the Constitutional Convention, a South Carolinian said that he "considered" Virginia to be a "Southern State," but in their ratification conventions Virginians and even North Carolinians tended to speak of "the Southern States" in the third person.[172] Indeed, although Virginia was the largest slaveholding state in the new Union, many foresaw its regional identity aligning with the Mid-Atlantic and especially the Northwest, not with the slaveholding South. Early national Americans tended to conflate the South and the West—including the Northwest—in their calculations of sectional politics.[173] William Henry Harrison, the Virginia-born governor of Ohio Territory, and others like him, saw slaveholding in their future in the Northwest.[174] Their vision only underscored the point that regional identity was not yet fixed.

Furthermore, the contention between North and South over slavery was far from the only, or even the most pressing and obvious, division facing the fragile Union in the early nineteenth century.[175] One fault line that was at least as prominent and threatening as slavery ran between the East and the West. The West was a problem in itself, not because it was the battleground between slavery and freedom. The West was fractured between the Northwest and the Southwest, but in the late eighteenth century that had less to do with slavery than with the Southwest's sense that the Federalist administrations favored the Northwest's interests.[176] The problem of the West's loyalty was apparent, for instance, during the 1789 congressional debate over the location of the national capital; much of the debate centered on better securing the loyalty of Westerners by making the capital accessible to them.[177] Suspicion of both the West and the South mixed in New England Federalists' opposition to the Louisiana Purchase.[178] Fisher Ames typified many Americans' uncertainty. In 1803, he declared his confidence that there would be a civil war in the United States at some point. But "whether that war will be between Virginia and New England, or between the Atlantic and Tramontane [sic] States," or along class lines, he was less sure.[179]

In 1806 and 1807, the slave trade debates in Congress demonstrated anew the seriousness of the growing divide between North and South concerning slavery, but the citizenry riveted its attention on the West rather than on the congressmen's high-flying rhetoric. Specifically, it focused on the Burr Conspiracy, an attempt to detach the aggrieved Southwest from the Union, complete with foreign intrigue. Newspaper coverage and the private papers of politicians bear witness to the fact that these events engrossed Americans more than the slave trade debates did.[180] That the Burr debacle trumped these important congressional debates in the American consciousness confirms historian Peter Onuf's judgment that, before 1815, Americans saw "foreign manipulation of the 'clashing jurisdictions and jarring interests' of widely dispersed and doubtfully loyal frontier settlements" as "the clearest and most present danger to the union." It was only thereafter that it became clear that slavery was the prime threat to the federal compact.[181] This was the result of specific political events and developments, both in partisan politics and with slavery itself, which lay just beyond 1808.

1808, then, proved a vital year for the politics of slavery in America, for more reasons than the abolition of the Atlantic slave trade. The change and agitation of the next decade shaped all future debates over slavery, for they more firmly established and elevated to preeminence the sectional divide over the South's increasingly peculiar institution. The Revolution and its aftermath had forced individuals and regions to make decisions fraught with meaning for the future. For that future was by no means predetermined, or even certain, as the Revolutionary generation's struggle with slavery culminated in 1808.

Federalists, Republicans, and
Slavery during the War of 1812

THE PARTISAN USE of slavery in the early republic reached its peak during the War of 1812. It entered partisan politics well before the war, of course, and the wartime uses of slavery had an impact on the postwar scene. But the New England Federalists' sectionalist strategy and bitter wartime grievances ensured that no period until the 1850s matched the war years in this regard. Between 1812 and 1815, American slavery surfaced in several debates between Federalists and Republicans that on their face bore no relationship to chattel bondage. Some Americans fretted about the introduction of the highly charged issue of slavery into a situation in which the Union was already tenuous. But their concerns only demonstrated just how effective this weapon was. That so many participants in wartime debates, from clergymen to editors to elected officials, resorted to the rhetorical and political firepower of slavery also demonstrates how divisive the War of 1812 was. American slavery was not the central issue of the day—the war was. But those contending over the war capitalized fully on the political value of slavery.

Of course, political manipulation of sectional divisions over slavery was hardly new to the American scene in 1812. Yet the war years, which marked the apex of the struggle between America's first two parties, brought sectionalism and partisanship together in an unprecedented way. The political combatants during the War of 1812 thus pioneered tactics that would surface in later disputes involving slavery. New England Federalists demonstrated the full power of slavery as a political tool in their wartime appeal to Northerners' latent hostility to slaveholders and their power. In turn, Republicans experimented with techniques for parrying the Federalists' sectionalist blows. Their dialectic further attached slavery to North-South sectionalism and began the elevation of that divide over that between the East and the West.

In 1808, Congress passed President Jefferson's Embargo on trade with Great Britain. During the Napoleonic wars, the warring nations, France and especially the great naval power Great Britain, preyed on American commerce in hope of denying its benefits to their enemies. Jefferson and his followers thought trade restrictions would persuade the belligerents to recognize America's maritime rights. The Jeffersonian policy of trade restriction, which the president failed to adequately explain to the public, triggered enormous partisan and sectional rancor. The first Embargo was just one of a series of measures restricting trade with the belligerents. They all seemed to hurt American commerce (vital to the American economy, especially in New England) more than they did the European powers.

In this atmosphere, the Federalist Party increased its efforts and broadened its appeal. It began a series of new newspapers and put up more candidates for office than it had during its doldrums. Those candidates made impressive gains in the elections following the passage of the Embargo in spring 1808. They made the 1808 presidential contest much closer than the one in 1804, retook state governments in New England and New York, and picked up legislative and congressional seats, even in such Republican strongholds as Virginia and Ohio. The negative effects of the Embargo energized voters, creating the highest voter turnout since 1801.[1]

As part of their invigorated opposition to the Jefferson administration, Federalist leaders stepped up their use of slavery to attack the Republicans. Slavery provided a useful metaphor in describing the Embargo's effects, as when Harrison Gray Otis wrote that "unless measures of an explicit and energetic character shall be adopted" to counteract the Embargo, "our people are enslaved and our country ruined."[2] Slavery also provided a useful explanation for the North's plight. For preacher David Osgood, the Constitution's "strange absurdity," slave representation—which gave Southern Republicans "an undue and baneful influence in our national counsels"—had to be repealed in light of Republican atrocities such as the Embargo. Northerners should be ashamed of themselves "if all their parties do not unite in their endeavours to effect this alteration."[3] As the federal government enforced the Embargo, Northern voters became more inclined to listen to attacks on the sectional selfishness of the Southern Republicans than ever before. Even the likes of John Holmes, a staunch Republican from the Massachusetts district of Maine, found it necessary to publicly assault the Embargo in sectional terms. In a memorial that Holmes helped author, the town of Alfred characterized the Embargo as gross tyranny and pointedly reminded the administration that *"oppression did sever us from the British Empire."* "We flatter ourselves," they declared, "that we have as much love of *liberty* and abhorrence of *slavery* as those who oppose us *in the name of republicanism*," or to be more specific, "as our opulent brethren of the South."[4] This sectional characterization of the authors of the Embargo was mild compared to much Federalist rhetoric. But Holmes's support for it suggests that the Embargo brought the evils of the Jeffersonian regime home to Northern voters who had previously seen Republican rule as benign or only potentially dangerous.

Furthermore, in 1811 and 1812 the Republican-controlled 11th Congress admitted Louisiana as a state, authorized the seizure of West Florida, and extended commercial nonintercourse with Great Britain as well as declaring war. For Federalists, as historian Henry Adams wrote, "this series of measures" constituted "a domestic revolution preliminary to foreign war."[5] The War of 1812 thus proved to be the last straw for the New England Federalist leadership and their growing number of Yankee followers, part of the Republican scheme to destroy their section's commerce and political power forever.

The war also deeply offended the moral sensibilities of New England Federalists. They decried the policy of invading Canada, which rendered the war an offensive one. They despised the idea of fighting Britain alongside Napoleon Bonaparte, whom many of them believed was the Antichrist. Massachusetts clergyman Elijah Parish spoke for many New Englanders (albeit in an extreme fashion, as was his wont) when he said that once the United States had entered the war, "all former parties and divisions, compared with the present, were merely the play and sport of children. The contest is no longer between rival candidates for fame, but immediately between Christ and Anti-Christ." Parish also projected that the sufferings his region would incur during the war would far exceed "the little, *the very little*, comparatively, which you have endured by embargo, and non-intercourse laws."[6] As the war dragged on, many New Englanders saw this prophecy fulfilled.

An injury to New Englanders' pocketbooks and an affront to their principles, the War of 1812 produced what even the Louisiana Purchase and the Embargo had failed to produce: a formidable, organized opposition to the federal government in New England. The Hartford Convention, a meeting of representatives from aggrieved New England states in late 1814 to discuss joint defense and political measures in response to the crisis of the war, became emblematic of the New England Federalists' opposition to the war. Since 1803, New England Federalists had talked intermittently of a convention to establish a "Northern

Portrait of Elijah Parish (1762–1825). (American Antiquarian Society)

Confederacy." But not until the waning months of the struggle against Britain did this convention materialize, in response to wartime grievances.

This opposition to the Southern-dominated Republican Party admitted slavery full-force into the polarized politics of the War of 1812. Both Federalist politicians and like-minded preachers explored slavery's possible uses. The clergy added an antislavery moral fervor that much of the lay Federalist leadership lacked. And a strong majority of ordinary New Englanders lent their support to the Federalist campaign and responded to its themes.

In opposing the war, Federalists amplified their traditional arguments in relation to slavery and the Republicans. Drawing on the rhetoric of political slavery, so resonant in American political culture since at least the eighteenth century,[7] they insisted that the Madison administration meant to enslave the people of the North. Josiah Quincy, a leading Federalist from Massachusetts, injected this rhetoric in spectacular fashion into a congressional war debate. During a wrangle over a significant addition to the national army in 1813, Quincy questioned the government's motives in raising this force, given the Republicans' pattern of pursuing their ambitions at all costs. Who knew but what the increased regular army was to be a means of securing the next Virginia president as "President for life"? Quincy observed that this standing army would be deployed largely on the Northern frontier, thus menacing Yankees' liberties at the same time it excluded them permanently from the executive chair of the Union. Duty to his home region and his posterity compelled him to resist such tyranny. "If the people of the Northern and Eastern States," he thundered, "are destined to be hewers of wood and drawers of water, to men who know nothing about their interests, and care nothing about them, I am clear of the great transgression." As for his children, if they were "destined to be slaves, and to yoke in with negroes, chained to the car of a Southern master," their father's resistance would ensure that "they, at least, shall have this sweet consciousness as the consolation of their condition[;] they shall be able to say: '*Our father was guiltless of these chains.*' "[8] Quincy's rhetoric of political slavery was very much in step with other New England Federalists' fears and alarmed slaveholding Republicans. Despite its length, New England newspapers eagerly printed this speech, with commendations attached.[9] In one fleeting reference to the "negroes" of the South, Quincy had brought their slavery to bear on his warning of political slavery; the fact that planters drove black slaves made them more likely to seek to enslave Quincy's constituents. And he had done so in a debate whose origins were as far removed from slavery as imaginable.

The wartime oratory of Elijah Parish teemed with a particularly passionate and vivid version of this call for New Englanders to resist their impending political slavery. In an 1812 sermon, Parish admonished his parishioners to awake to their situation, lest they live to see a scene where "the dead calm of a military despotism soon diffuses silence, solitude, and darkness over the land, interrupted only by the exultation of masters, and the despairing agonies of their slaves."[10] In 1814, Parish spoke at length of the contrast between the ancient children of Israel and the pusillanimous New Englanders of his day. The Israelites' travails in Egypt had at least dispelled "their prejudices in favor of the *union*, under which their fathers had enjoyed repose and prosperity, to *provoke* them to seek a better government; to inflame them to noble darings, in bursting the bonds of oppression; in *dissolving* their connexion with the merciless slave holders of the country." Unless New Englanders severed ties with the South, "you must in obstinate despair bow your necks to the yoke, and with your African brethren drag the chains of Virginia despotism." Nothing but disunion would suffice, for after all their antiwar petitions to the federal government, New Englanders found themselves just as much enslaved as "the stupid African." "Have you learned," he taunted his audience, "to sympathize with [Virginia's] *imported* slaves? Your labors go to the same purse; you virtually support the same masters; you generously lend your help to those miserable beings, who blacken their fields." Would his congregants not resist this bondage? "Bow then to the . . . government, and say to the humble African, 'Thou art my brother.' "[11]

The drive to enslave New England, said the Federalists, could only be expected from an administration dominated by slaveholders, who were natural-born despots. An anonymous newspaper scribbler contended that "the lordly tenants of the Southern palaces and villas, the inexorable masters of hundreds of poor enslaved Africans," were hardly "fit to be entrusted with the guardianship of" Northern freemen's liberty.[12] A Federalist wag suggested that Southern brutality to slaves was of a piece with the Republicans' drive against New England commerce. He imagined a Republican manufacturing enterprise that "had discovered a new item to be manufactured in America" to encourage domestic production rather than foreign commerce: "shoes made of 'biped skin leather' obtained by skinning slaves."[13] After a survey of partisan alignment within Virginia, another writer concluded that "in proportion as federal principles are cherished in Virginia, slavery is less prevalent, and of course where democracy is strongest, slavery is more prevalent."[14] Slavery was the root cause of "the different political views in the Northern and Southern sections of the nation," contended "Cato" in the *Connecticut Courant*. He drew on and expanded Thomas Jefferson's famous characterization of slaveholders as petty tyrants, suggesting that the practice of slaveholding led them to act the autocrat in all spheres. It certainly was the source of the tyrannical tactics and principles of the Republicans at Washington, which "are not found in the text-book from which the northern Farmer teaches his children the principles of civil liberty and free legislation." He charged that Republicans were friendly to libertarian principles only "under certain restrictions in applying them." Just as Napoleon thought liberty "a good thing" only for himself and his friends, Southern Republicans "see the fitness of freedom for themselves and their children, but not for those who till the field, and are most deserving of the reward." "We here trace the reason," he surmised, "why slave-holding politicians, are ready to court French alliances."[15] The idea that slavery was the wellspring of Republican policy deftly reversed the usual Republican characterization of Federalists as closet aristocrats and monarchists.

The War of 1812 also gave Federalists new opportunities, as well as plenty of motivation, to perpetuate assaults on Republican slaveholders as inconsistent. Republicans repeatedly chastised their Federalist opponents for being so unfeeling as to oppose a war to protect the rights of American sailors impressed by Britain's navy. But how could slaveholding Republicans, Federalists asked, have the temerity to claim that their respect for human rights was superior to that of the nonslaveholders of New England? This rhetorical question was one of the Federalists' most effective uses of slavery. "Cato" characteristically offered one of the more vigorous challenges to Republicans' wartime claims to benevolence. In prose dripping with contempt for slaveholders and slavery, he attributed the hand-wringing over impressment entirely to Southern economic self-interest. "The sons of the southern planter" would not go to sea, disdaining seamen's labor. He could not very well entrust his ships to his slaves, for at sea they might "remember that God made them free." Given these limitations, "Cato" argued, the avaricious planters sought to seduce British seamen into their merchant ships' service in order to drive down the wages they would have to pay Yankee tars otherwise. Thus, the profit motive "is at the bottom of all this policy and outcry concerning impressed seamen." The issue obviously did not proceed from "any inbred love of liberty" in the slaveholders' breasts. If it did, "we should not, as we travel in their country, see thousands of slaves, whose path is marked with blood by the drivers' whip. If it was from a love of liberty we should soon" see southern legislatures "giving equal rights and freedom to the blacks as to the whites."[16] Also in character, Elijah Parish used slavery to disprove President Madison's professed compassion for seamen. "If he is so humane," Parish demanded, "why does he continue the lash of oppression on the slaves, which blacken his fields?" He challenged Madison, "in the overflowings of his humanity," to "repair to his hordes of slaves, open the doors of their huts, and bid them go free; let his iron hand wipe away their tears, restore them to their native country; mothers to their children, and children to their homes."[17]

These remarkable passages were unusually powerful indictments of the hypocrisy of white Southerners' libertarian cant, but "Cato" and Parish were far from alone. "An Anti-Party American" from Pennsylvania insisted that the

Republicans should stop trumpeting the natural rights of sailors, for the question of whether Britain could take expatriated Britons from American ships was one "between the English sailor and *his* government." A slave in Virginia, he submitted, had "an unquestionable natural right to his liberty." But should "the slave assert it, and seek refuge under the roof of his neighbour," would not the slaveholder cry foul? "Are not the cases parallel?" Indeed, "if there be a difference," the British had a greater right to recover their fugitives, "in as much as the natural right of a slave to his freedom is *unquestionable*."[18] In such hands, American slavery proved an effective political scourge with which to flog the Republicans when they set themselves up as the friends of humanity. These arguments, although aimed against a quixotic war based on grand principles of natural rights, were full of antislavery implications based on the principles of natural rights. As such they were typical of the Federalist use of slavery during the war: although meant primarily to attack the politics of Republican slaveholders, they focused a brighter light on slavery itself.

———

While the likes of Parish joined lay Federalists in amplifying these traditional uses of slavery against the Republicans during the war, he and other Federalist preachers added their own moral critiques of slavery, which most Federalists— including Federalist preachers—had not pursued before the War of 1812.[19] Many pious Federalists characterized slavery as the sin that had brought the scourge of a disastrous war upon the country. Their vituperation of slaveholders served to fray even further the bonds of Union. For many of them, this was no unintended consequence, for they feared the judgments that came upon those joined to wicked slaveholders.

Disunionism characterized their doctrines better than abolitionism, but they had revivified the rhetoric of their Revolutionary forebears in denouncing slavery as a national sin. Before the embargoes and the war, the Federalist preachers had not condemned Republicans as slaveholders. But with these acts they faced actual, rather than prospective, national evils that cried out for providential explanation, much as their forefathers had during the Revolutionary War. As they rediscovered their progenitors' sense of urgency, they also rediscovered their explanation that slavery was the accursed thing for which God smote their nation with war.

Elijah Parish was a leading exponent of the view that the sin of American slavery incurred God's wrath even on liberty-loving Yankees. In 1814, he added to his call for New England to cut itself loose from the slave South the idea that slavery was a blight on America's moral landscape. "What," he demanded, "is the moral aspect of our nation?" "Are not a million slaves, a million 'souls of men' bought and sold in the markets of the south? Are not the tears and miseries of a million souls daily crying to the God of justice to hasten the day of retribution? Will they cry in vain?" "Must not those States," he asked, "which remain *united* with them [the Southern states], whatever may be their individual character, share in their punishments?"[20] It must be noted that Parish's solution to being yoked with slaveholders, like many of his fellow New Englanders' during this time when the Union hung by a thread, was to abolish not slavery but the federal compact. From the pulpit to the more formally political arena, New England's opposition to the war directly threatened the Union more than it threatened slavery, although slavery added to the weight straining that Union.

The Presbyterian Nathan Strong was, if possible, even clearer than Parish in enjoining his congregants to separate from slaveholders lest they suffer such calamities as the war betokened. In a sermon in Hartford soon after the war broke out, Strong linked Republican slaveholders' support of the war to their ownership of slaves. He said that Christians could rightfully enter into a defensive war, but an offensive war such as this one could only be "congenial to the temper of those who feel not the power of the Gospel; who deal in slaves and the souls of men," even as they hypocritically "cry freedom and rights." Lest his congregation miss the message, Strong identified the slave states as a branch of modern-day Babylon. Its seat was in Catholic Europe, but Babylon's branches could be found in many other places, including "in every State, where the unalienable rights of any intelligent creature in the family of God are denied, and slavery is supported by law." "Christians," Strong commanded, "must refrain from all alliances with this Babylon, whether they may be under the name of policy or religion." And for emphasis he repeated his point concerning the slave South: "Permit me to observe again:—In the enumeration [in Revelation] of these articles in which Babylon deals, we find *slaves and the souls of men*. . . . It can never be safe to depend on the integrity of those who deal in these articles, which are forbidden by the word of God."[21] Although delivered as a spiritual imperative, this plea to separate from slave traders and slave-owners contained a menacing political message for Northern Republicans: alliance with such men is strictly proscribed by the word of God. Strong's spiritual indictment of being in league with slaveholders lent the ultimate support to the New England Federalists' sectionalist strategy.

Nathan Perkins, a Congregationalist preacher in Connecticut, propounded an even more uncompromising moral critique of slavery as part of his providential reading of the war. He listed slaveholding among the "several great transgressions, which must be admitted to be, peculiarly, the Land-defiling crimes of the UNITED STATES" that "have contributed to bring upon us, heavy divine judgments" such as the war. Some Americans "may have *pretended* to excuse, or justify it," but "such as allowedly practice it, or countenance it, are extremely guilty in the sight of God." He rejected slavery on grounds of the brotherhood of man, in light of which "we have no more right to make slaves of others, than they have of us." For all these reasons, he had been "for many years of the opinion" that the whole nation would have "to answer for the sin of slaveholding, at the bar of Providence." While other New Englanders were busy trying to sectionalize the guilt of slavery, Perkins insisted that "not only the slave-holding states, but ALL THE UNION" would suffer under God's punishments for the sin. "And the punishment will not be light," he warned. "It will be proportional to the crime. The crime is the deepest, however common, of any perpetrated in former ages, or the present. Its evils are indeed incalculable. Its enormity awful."[22] What most set Perkins apart was his yearning to see the end not of the Union but of slavery; later in the sermon he urged all people to "be the FRIENDS OF ORDER, AND THE UNION."[23] Perkins looked more to the abolition of slavery than to political separation from America's Babylon as the means of saving New England from divine judgment.

––––––––

What most menaced the Union, however, was not the preachers' renewed emphasis on the sinfulness of human bondage, but the political leaders' renewed emphasis on tried and true issues. Slave representation was the prime issue on which the Federalists intensified their old lines of attack on the Republicans during the war, and it had the broadest resonance among voters. Federalist agitation against the three-fifths clause in New England reached its high-water mark during the War of 1812.[24] As Madison won reelection in 1812 and the war dragged on, New England Federalists increasingly argued that were it not for the added power of slave representation, the Republicans would never have been able to enact commercial restrictions or initiate the war. Many concluded that because of those abuses of power the South had violated the Constitution to such an extent that the Union was practically at an end. During the war, these arguments found broad support in New England, sparking a grassroots movement that helped produce the Hartford Convention.

The outpouring of verbiage from New England's Federalist presses on slave representation during the war repeated a few essential points. These points became conventional Federalist wisdom, as the speeches of legislators and the solemn remonstrances of elected bodies echoed the scribblings of editors and pamphleteers, and vice versa. Because their discussion of the federal ratio focused on a constitutional clause, it forced Federalists to judge the value of the Constitution and the Union it formed.

Most found it wanting. It was a subject of disagreement among Federalists, as some insisted that the Constitution was originally a glorious standard but was now being perverted by Republican slaveholders. But under the stress of their war grievances, the majority of articulate New England Federalists repudiated the Constitution and insisted that the Union was not working as the Founders had hoped. Even as they invoked the Revolutionary example of resistance to tyranny, many Federalists deemed the Founders' spirit of compromise with the South a product of, at best, the earlier generation's political naïveté.

In the year the war broke out, Sereno Edwards Dwight, writing as "Boreas" in a pamphlet entitled *Slave Representation*, argued that slave representation was a glaring defect in the Constitution. Under its influence, griped this son of Yale president Timothy Dwight, Southern oppression was only getting worse with time. "The article authorising the *Southern Negroes* to be represented in Congress," he asserted in language reminiscent of the American Revolution, "*is the rotten part of the Constitution, and must be amputated.*" Its evil only began to be felt in full force upon the ascension of "the *Virginia Faction*" to the presidency. Neither Jefferson nor Madison would have been elected president without it, Dwight submitted, nor would "many of the worst measures" of their administrations have passed in Congress without the "*votes of the Representatives of African Slaves.*" Preparing for the worst in the presidential election that fall, Dwight wanted "it to be distinctly remembered, that if the Scourge of GOD is again to visit this nation in the re-election of Mr. Madison; *it will be solely owing to the black Representation!*" Dwight urged his readers to emulate their fathers' example in resisting despotism, yet he also wondered aloud at the Founders' pusillanimity in granting the federal ratio to "the Slave country" in 1787. How could "the MEN OF THE NORTH, who began, and bore the whole brunt of a war, which was engaged in merely to support two principles: REPRESENTATION WITH TAXATION, —and EQUALITY OF REPRESENTATION," have surrendered those very principles to the slaveholders? He could not believe that men "whose necks were then too stiff to bend beneath the weight of *Ministerial* or even of *Royal* power, would so soon have bent them under the authority of the *Representatives of Negro Slaves!*"[25]

In the turmoil of 1812, the spirit of compromise in the name of Union was lost on this son of the Revolutionary generation.

Several other New England Federalists joined Dwight in simultaneously appealing to the bravery of their Revolutionary ancestors and wondering aloud about their political judgment. "A Citizen of Connecticut," for example, thought that the Union of Yankees and slaveholders was doomed from the start. "It was the misfortune of" the hardy and enterprising men of New England, he said, to be united with men who were "ignorant, effeminate and corrupt, who despise labour," and who were "destitute of every thing which constitutes national or individual wealth except that which is wrung from the pitiful earnings of unwilling slavery. In a moment of unsuspecting generosity, while the wounds were yet bleeding which we had received in their defence, we admitted these men to a share in our councils." But the South had abused the North's magnanimity, and the time had come to "demand an equivalent" for the added power the federal ratio gave the slave states. "Are we afraid to do this? Afraid to follow the example of our fathers? . . . If we dare not do this," he thundered, "let us tear the record of the Revolution from our history. Let us falsify our pedigree, and say we are not descended from the men who fought against oppression—that we have no Yankee blood in our veins."[26]

This thread of disdain for the Founders' acceptance of slave representation as the price of Union ran throughout the New England Federalist literature on slave representation during the war. Even at an 1813 celebration commemorating George Washington's first inaugural, Josiah Quincy talked less of declension from a glorious original standard than of things going from bad to worse. "Bad, and humiliating," he said, "as was the condition of Massachusetts, under the principles of the real constitution, under the principles of the constitution, modified by" the Virginia Dynasty's "usurpation, its condition is a hundred fold worse."[27] A year later, in the Massachusetts state legislature, Federalist Francis Blake could see no reason for the sectional compromises built into the Constitution and did not hesitate to blame the Founders for their posterity's calamities. He referred to slave representation as "an original and radical defect in the form of government and, perhaps, one of the primary causes of our misfortunes."[28] Hartford's *Connecticut Courant* joined in censuring this lack of political wisdom. One editorial concluded patronizingly that New England's Founding Fathers had "expected, honest souls! that under that constitution, they would be protected in the enjoyment of the fruits of their labour." But their descendants were learning the painful lessons of their lack of foresight. "Had what has happened been foreshown to the men of New-England" when they helped draft and ratify the Constitution, this editor concluded, "they would as soon have made *a covenant with death*, as a covenant of union with the states which have thus wantonly and cruelly oppressed them."[29]

Some articulate Federalists thus abandoned hope for the Constitution, but others insisted that the Founders drew up a marvelous system of government that slaveholders were perverting to their malignant ends. These authors argued that the North had granted slave representation to the South in exchange for protection of its commerce, a reasonable compromise. It was only under Jeffersonian misrule that the compact ceased to confer benefits. As agrarians, so the argument went, Republicans were congenitally hostile to commerce and envious of the North's commercial prosperity in the halcyon days of Washington and Adams. This jealousy led them to violate the original agreement, and so flagrant were their abuses of power that they proscribed commerce even as they increased the effect of slave representation by adding new slave states.

The author of one highly influential pamphlet went out of his way to declare his loyalty to the Constitution, even as he railed against the nineteenth-century effects of slave representation. Writing under the pseudonym "Massachusetts," Sidney Edwards Morse insisted that in the 1780s, "the North entered into union with the South on equal terms." Only in the intervening years had an inequality developed, as the addition of new slave states destroyed the original sectional balance of power and gave the South the power to act on its jealousy of New England's enterprise and prosperity. Morse distinguished himself from most of his fellows in protesting his loyalty to the Union, albeit conditionally. In a postscript, he denied rumors that he meant to break up the Union, insisting that if it were dissolved it would be because the South "madly persists in maintaining her present ground."[30] This was, politically speaking, a better stance than most leading New England Federalists took during the war, for it avoided calumniating a Founding generation that the vast majority of Americans still revered.

A picture of abuses of—rather than defects in—the Constitution also resonated more broadly with the Federalist rank and file. This was evident in the petitions of Massachusetts towns to their state legislature in 1814, which produced the Hartford Convention. Almost without exception, the petitioners argued that the Republicans had subverted the original intent of the framers. As Republicans in their "ambition and tyranny" annexed new slave states in addition to the original advantage of slave representation, they had changed the balance and prosperity of the original Union into sectional hegemony and oppression. The Founders surely had not been so unwise as to give the federal government the power to destroy commerce and declare disastrous war at the behest of "the lords of the south and mushroom politicians" of the west. "The concession" of slave representation, one town memorial insisted, "was great; but without questioning its policy, we are entitled" to the benefits of the bargain, not its "subversion" at the hands of the Virginia Dynasty.[31] Likewise, when Federalists outside of Massachusetts gathered at partisan celebrations, they offered such toasts as "*The Federal Constitution*—May its principles be restored" and "*The Integrity of the Union*—In the spirit in which it was formed."[32]

But to whatever source they attributed Southern oppression, New England Federalist writers all accepted it as a fact, and many called on Northerners to shed their partisan allegiances and band together against it. As early as May 1812, New York Federalist Gouverneur Morris privately urged that if the Federalists could agitate the question of slave representation well enough in the states north of Virginia, "this geographical division will terminate the political divisions which now prevail, and give a new object to men's minds." Under such a circumstance, "the Southern States must either submit to what is just or break up the Union."[33] Others called publicly for a Northern anti–slave-representation party. Sereno Dwight insisted that "ALL THE NORTH has one common interest" in manfully resisting the slave states' encroachments on their rights. He called on "all the MEN OF THE NORTH" to lay aside party divisions and "unite *as one man*, and that *a strong man armed*;—to take a solemn view of the magnitude and injustice of the grievance;—and then, *at every hazard*, to apply the needed remedy."[34] "Cato" echoed Dwight, asserting that in the North, "the names of democrat and federalist are now sinking into disuse," for the war had become too awful for Yankees "to indulge in the despicable, tavern play of party politics. They find that northern neighborhood, and northern blood is too precious to be sacrificed to the pleasure of a southern, slave-holding policy."[35] Such Federalist ideologues looked to a sectional party, or at least a sectional movement, to transcend party labels—just the sort of phenomenon that could ruin the Union.

That the New England Federalists chose to focus so heavily on the three-fifths clause brought North-South sectionalism to the forefront of their consciousness and attached slavery ever more firmly to their sectional vision. They identified the Republicans increasingly with the South and slaveholding as one of the Republicans' most distinctive traits. Dwight's *Slave Representation* typified this phenomenon, equating Republicans and Southerners. He did not decry the influence of Western states except as increased by slave representation. Furthermore, he always referred to the South as "THE SLAVE COUNTRY." Rushing new states into the Union, then, was a problem for Dwight because "the Slave country" (the case did vary) thus augmented its power in the Senate.³⁶ Indeed, during the War of 1812, New England Federalists' hatred for slave representation colored their opposition to the addition of new Western states, adding impetus to the traditional Federalist drive to restrain expansion of the Union. For instance, Morse's pamphlet *The New States* was a response to a proposal in Congress to split Mississippi Territory into two states. This was alarming, principally because "the power of the Southern Section is already bloated with the representation of its slaves; and it is now to be still further swollen by the addition of New States." Because of slave representation, Morse added, he would rather make "comparisons between the northern and Southern Sections of the Union, than between the New and Old States."³⁷ Indeed, new states arising in the Northwest did not concern Morse. The centrality of the South and slavery to New England Federalists' analysis of their predicament determined the New England Federalists' wartime sectionalism. And as they elevated North-South over East-West sectionalism in their own rhetoric, they initiated a seismic sectional shift in American politics away from conditions in Aaron Burr's day and before.

Wartime Federalism underwent a subtler shift in emphasis in relation to racial issues. Federalists, while no monolith, traditionally espoused more liberal racial attitudes than Republicans did.³⁸ Yet racist arguments predominated in the Federalists' writings against slave representation. There were exceptions, but the issue of slave representation lent itself to racist appeals that Federalists pursued vigorously. They raised the specter of free Northern whites becoming the equals of degraded Southern blacks. They denounced the idea that the tawny chattel of the South could influence national policy to the detriment of the fair sons of liberty in New England. Most New England Federalists, in this instance at least, were willing to draw on the power of Northern racism to the same degree that New England Republicans were.

Dwight's pamphlet, for instance, brimmed with powerful appeals to racial and regional pride. While castigating their treatment, he suggested that African Americans belonged in bondage. "Let every man of the NORTH call to his remembrance the *condition* of the Southern blacks," he counseled. "Let him recollect that the great body of them are *slaves*; slaves by birth, and by destiny." "Shall Beings, *who cannot testify in a Court of Justice,*" he demanded, "Beings, *who are flogged by the yea*; Beings, to MURDER *whom is a smaller crime than to steal a horse,*" be represented in Congress? Shall they "decide on the question of Peace or War; and thus direct when the MEN OF THE NORTH *shall go forth to battle*?" This horrific prospect had come all too true, and "all those, who fought themselves, or whose fathers fought, for the freedom of America, must now feel the deep disgrace of stooping to become *The Slaves of Slaves.*"[39]

A pseudonymous pamphleteer, "A Friend to Freedom," considered the three-fifths clause not only "oppressive and unjust" as well as "evil" politically, but also obnoxious in principle, for it placed "five slaves on a level with three freemen." "Is that principle just," he demanded, "which equalizes slavery and freedom in any ratio? Is it just that the votes of one hundred slaves (or beasts of burthen) should have the same weight with the votes of sixty freemen?"[40] Notwithstanding this author's pseudonym, he was no friend to the Southern slaves whom he likened to beasts. His argument illustrated how some Federalists could employ racist arguments with the same ease as Republicans.

Sidney Morse found the math—and its racial implications—even more alarming than did "A Friend to Freedom." He warned that if Mississippi Territory were made into two states, its people would acquire inordinate power in the U.S. Senate. After a series of complex calculations, Morse concluded that under such a scenario, "*one slave in* Mississippi" would have "*nearly as much power* in Congress, *as five free men in the State of* New-York." As the slave empire expanded, the voice of millions of Northern "FREEMEN" would in effect be excluded from the national government. Moreover, given the states' power over the amendment process in the Constitution, the slave states might, "agreeably to the letter of the constitution, reduce us to the *most abject* slavery, a *majority* slaves of a *minority*; men, who call themselves *freemen*, the *slaves of slaves.*"[41] Morse thus tapped into his fellow Federalists' accustomed rhetoric of political slavery, to which he added the supreme degradation of enslavement to Southern slaves. The appeal to Yankees' sense of racial superiority was even more vivid in his vision of a future involving more than political slavery. If the present direction continued, Morse foresaw "the sons of New-England" cultivating "the tobacco fields of the South."[42]

Despite the power of this rhetoric, Morse sought to distance himself from the racism of some of his fellow Federalist pamphleteers. He noted that "while these numbers were publishing, several disgraceful attempts were made, in some of the papers, to confound the *negroes* with the *slaves.*" But Morse was eager to clarify that his opposition to slave representation was based on republican rather than racist theory. He believed that only slaves should be excluded from representation, for "*every freeman*, whether *black* or *white*, has a deep interest in the proper administration of Government. Upon such administration depends his liberty, his property, his life, his all." But slaves have none of these privileges, and therefore "they would *gain* by a total destruction of Government. Their only hope of liberty, property, and happiness, would be realized by the success of our enemies. Nay, they are, themselves, our most dangerous enemies."[43]

Despite divisions in the Federalist ranks over race, in their wartime three-fifths campaign, they almost uniformly resorted to vivid descriptions of the affront this clause presented to free white Northerners' racial self-image. Even Morse, who on one level denied the importance of race as a category, provided some of the most striking language of all in his vision of bound New Englanders cultivating tobacco alongside the black slaves of the South. Perhaps such rhetoric helps explain the profound appeal the Federalists' opposition to slave representation had in New England during the war.

Indeed, most of the people who raised a hue and cry about slave representation and expressed their detestation for slaveholders could not be called abolitionists. This was in part a function of the prevailing sentiment among the Federalist leadership. Harrison Gray Otis, for example, the leader of the Hartford Convention movement, had what Samuel Eliot Morison aptly called but "slight moral repugnance for slavery." He seems rarely to have thought about slavery in moralistic terms, generally subordinating the question to other political considerations. After 1800, he came to see slaveholder power as a threat to his party's national ambitions and thus joined the growing chorus of voices decrying that power. His engagement of the issue of slavery, then, almost always came as a function of ulterior motives.[44] The incendiary sectionalist Josiah Quincy had more hatred for the South than Otis, but distaste for slavery did not necessarily drive this hatred. As his biographer has written, Quincy could invoke a "moralistic vocabulary" with the best of them, but he hated slavery first and foremost as "part of a larger antipathy" to Southern Republicans.[45] Quincy himself said later in his life that "my heart has always been much more affected by the slavery to which the Free States have been subjected, than with that of the Negro."[46]

Quincy and Otis typified the Federalist leadership in the early nineteenth century. The electoral debacle of 1800 helped thrust a new generation of leaders to the forefront of the party, who cared more for the power of their party than for any abstract ideals, including antislavery. William Plumer of New Hampshire spoke for these "young Federalists" in 1801 when he called for "a new set of leaders. . . . Let us have men who can relax their principles of morality as occasion may require and adapt themselves to circumstances."[47] Moral antislavery had a place in the Federalist Party, but slavery served mostly as a tool in sectional attacks against Southern Republicans and as a way of reassuring New Englanders of their moral superiority.[48] With significant exceptions —most of whom were clergymen and other members of what might be called the religious wing of the party—New England Federalists' rhetoric during the War of 1812 continued this pattern.

Their agitation against slave representation was certainly consistent with power politics. For one thing, it is doubtful whether New England Federalists thought they could effect an abolition of the three-fifths clause. Some expressed that hope: in 1815, a Connecticut congressman wrote to a constituent that some of his Southern colleagues in Washington had evinced a willingness "to expunge it" in light of the tax burden they might have to carry to pay for the war.[49] But if true, these expressions were not representative of the stance of most white Southerners, who showed no great keenness to tamper with what they saw as one of the Constitution's most sacred and valuable compromises. Thus the New England Federalists were either blinded by acute sectional myopia[50] or had some other object in mind. The burden of the evidence indicates that they had abandoned all hope of appealing to the South, aiming instead to build a sectional party united against slaveholders and their power.

The primacy of the political motive for New England Federalists' campaign against slave representation can also be demonstrated by its timing, which demonstrates that wartime issues and grievances drove the ascent of this pre-existing sectional antagonism to prominence. The focus of most New England Federalist politicians and opinion leaders in the first months of the war was on joining with Federalists and disaffected Republicans in the middle states to elect DeWitt Clinton president of the United States. The hope seems to have been that replacing the current administration would solve New England's problems. New England Federalist papers printed several resolutions from New England towns against the war in the summer and fall of 1812, but these resolutions were silent on the three-fifths clause. Instead they expressed their wish to replace the Madison regime. There were articles and letters railing against Virginia influence and even predicting that Madison would win by virtue of "the slave votes" in the Electoral College, but in general men and measures were the editors' center of attention, not structural reform of the three-fifths clause.[51] The election of Madison by a narrow margin (if not only by the slave votes) signaled the commencement of a veritable flood of slave-representation agitation, as electoral disappointment combined with bitterness over the progress of Mr. Madison's War.

The flood subsided at war's end. The Hartford Convention's resolution against slave representation was still in circulation, but Federalist leaders' resolve to push for it had waned. As the 13th Congress ended, it witnessed half-hearted introductions of the Convention's proposed amendments to the Constitution. On 28 February 1815, Samuel Dana of Connecticut presented to the Senate the Hartford amendments as his state's legislature had directed, and "the resolution and proposed amendments were read." On 2 March, Joseph B. Varnum did the same with a resolution of Massachusetts's legislature to the same effect, and with the same result. There is no evidence of any efforts by Dana or Varnum beyond this perfunctory exercise of duty, or of any further discussion in the Senate. On 3 March (the last day of the session), Timothy Pickering submitted the Hartford amendments to the House of Representatives; they "were read, and ordered to lie on the table." Period.[52] Even the ultra-Federalist Pickering's exertions were feeble in the face of peace and elicited no response from Republicans.

Slave representation proved a powerful impetus for a sectional appeal, but the attention most Federalists paid to it was fleeting. Many Federalists dropped the issue of slave representation for good after the War of 1812. To be sure, there were Federalists who remained engaged with slavery in the postwar years; some Federalist editors, for instance, protested the atrocities associated with the expansion of slavery. These editors, together with some Federalist politicians, stood against slavery and slave representation during the Missouri Crisis. Furthermore, it is impossible to tell how many, like Nathan Perkins, had been "for many years of the opinion" that slavery was wrong, or who retained an unspoken hatred for slavery and slaveholders after the war had alerted their attention to them. But nothing the Federalists did or said about slavery or slave representation, before or after the war, compared to the wartime *expressions* of that opinion.

———

If their credentials as abolitionists were shaky at best, the New England Federalist leadership staked a strong claim to political prowess, for they had found a popular issue with which to wage their opposition to the war. The War of 1812 politicized New England and solidified Federalist control of the region. The Federalists benefited by tapping into deep Northern wells of contempt for the slave South, which had bubbled ever closer to the surface as the war progressed.

The Hartford Convention, that apex and symbol of wartime New England sectionalism, was the result of a grassroots campaign. In the wake of an embargo in 1813 and in the face of the danger of invasion in 1814, Massachusetts towns deluged the state legislature with petitions calling upon their leaders to take strong measures. Most of the town memorials listed their desire to see slave representation abolished as a prime reason for holding a New England convention.[53] Under such pressure, the legislature resolved on 4 February 1814 to call a convention, by a margin of 23–8 in the Senate and 178–43 in the House. The lawmakers acknowledged in their resolutions that they were responding to the town memorials.[54] Although the reasons for support of the Convention were many and although there is no way of equating that support with opposition to the three-fifths clause in the mind of every voter, slave representation and the Hartford Convention became inextricably intertwined from the beginning.

Voters' endorsement for the Convention thus formed a rough measure for the appeal of the campaign against slave representation, and that endorsement was strong in many New England states. Such was the political atmosphere in Massachusetts, for instance, that the Republicans put forth moderate Federalist Samuel Dexter as their gubernatorial candidate in 1814. Dexter was careful to say that although he shared mainstream Federalists' sense of grievance, he differed with them as to "their indiscriminate opposition to the war, especially their convention project." The 1814 election therefore represented a referendum on the proposed Hartford Convention above and beyond the war itself, and Caleb Strong beat Dexter handily, drawing 55 percent of the vote.[55]

The Hartford Convention followed the town memorials in listing the abolition of slave representation first among the constitutional amendments it proposed. A moderate document, given the electric atmosphere that produced the Convention, the Hartford report said its object in proposing amendments was "to strengthen, and if possible to perpetuate, the union of the states, by removing the grounds of exciting jealousies, and providing for a fair and equal representation, and a limitation of powers, which have been misused." The three-fifths clause, it said, "cannot be claimed as a right." It was the product of a sectional compromise and "is therefore merely a subject of agreement, which should be conducted upon principles of mutual interest and accommodation, and upon which no sensibility on either side should be permitted to exist." But then, in a nod to the sensibility on their side, the authors declared that the three-fifths compromise had proven "unjust and unequal in its operation. Had this effect been foreseen, the privilege would probably not have been demanded; certainly not conceded." The report's second proposed amendment required a two-thirds supermajority in Congress to admit new states.[56]

The Hartford Convention report clearly bore the marks of the campaign that had preceded it and was a fair, if moderate, representation of the sentiment of a solid majority in New England. The editor of the *New York Evening Post* noted upon its publication "that the tone of this report, though in our opinion sufficiently high for the occasion, is, I know from the most authentic information, quite inferior to the public feeling in the Eastern States. The people there, *are in advance of their leaders.*"[57] Yet most New England Federalists rallied around this statement of New England grievances. The editor of the *Centinel* printed the Hartford Convention report in its entirety, along with his recommendation that subscribers gather their "families, domestics, and poorer neighbors, and devote one Evening to the careful and thoughtful perusal of [it]."[58]

Perhaps the best evidence of the popularity of the movement against slave representation during the war was the nervousness of the Republicans' response to it. A speaker at a Republican Independence Day celebration in Vermont summed up his party's worries well when he cried that the "torrents of abuse, poured out on the southern states by the factionists of the eastern," were "unjust and treasonable"—for "nothing is better calculated to excite divisions and contentions among the people. Nothing will so readily excite discord and animosity among the different states."[59] This speechmaker spoke to Republican apprehensions that the Federalists had a broadly resonant issue ("nothing is better calculated to excite divisions") in their favor when they inveighed against Southern slaveholders and their power in the Union.

Many influential Republicans shared this Vermont orator's concern. Philadelphia printer Matthew Carey was one. In 1814, Carey, alarmed at the prospects for the Union, published a best-selling work, *The Olive Branch*, as well as excerpts from it in pamphlet form (including one on slave representation). Carey charged that leading New England Federalists sought to revive their political fortunes upon the ruins of a shattered Union, stooping to all manner of demagoguery to accomplish this. Thus Carey's nationwide audience read that the Federalist leaders had raised an outcry against the undue power and influence of the Southern slaveholders, in order "to reconcile the people of the eastern states to the parricidal project of a separation" of such an allegedly unequal Union.[60]

The editors of leading Republican newspapers also demonstrated how popular they considered the slave-representation agitation to be in the North. For instance, Hezekiah Niles, editor of Baltimore's *Weekly Register*, in accusing his political enemies of using the three-fifths clause as a tool in pursuing their ambitions, acknowledged the power of that tool: "They avail themselves, as might be expected, of the popular clamor respecting the representation of slaves."[61] In early 1813, the *National Intelligencer* apprised its readers of "a tissue of false argument . . . woven in a Connecticut loom" in the fall of 1812 and then widely circulated by means of Federalist prints, "the object of which was to inflame the prejudices of the Northern and Eastern people against the Southern states on account of their black population." The language here conceded that Federalists were inflaming *existing* prejudices. The Federalists' manipulation of these sectional antipathies, the editors concluded, "cannot but give pain to every friend of the union, every lover of his country."[62]

———————

In the face of the Federalists' formidable campaign, Republicans cast about for rebuttals. One Republican tactic was to turn the Federalists' attacks on slavery and slave representation against them by appealing to white Americans' racism. Despite the racist arguments that suffused Federalist writings against slave representation, Republicans painted their opponents as *amis des noirs*. Beleaguered New England Republicans employed this tactic with particular urgency. In his satirical narrative of the Hartford Convention, the pseudonymous Vermont wag "Hector Benevolus" described the arrival of "an Ethiopean [*sic*], who said that he had an invitation, and was willing to pray for any thing they desired."[63] In 1812, the editor of the leading Republican sheet in New England, Boston's *Independent Chronicle*, noted that the Federalists were "in the constant habit of abusing the southern States on account of" slave representation. But these Federalists failed to mention that while it took five Southern blacks "to make three '*rateable polls*,' " in the North, "a negroe's *single* vote has full weight." Boston's African American community, he noted, had voted overwhelmingly for Federalist Caleb Strong for governor in the last election. "Whether this was owing to the *donations* from certain federal characters toward the support of their school," the editor sneered, "or the operation of other powerful motives, we do not pretend to say." Yet at Strong's inauguration, "a great number of these federal men of color were driven from the Common" by their pretended white friends—those "who would take them by the arm *on an election day*, (if not give them a fraternal hug) with, 'my good fellow, do take a vote for the federal ticket!' "[64] This account allowed the editor to depict the Federalists as the worst sort of political opportunists. They would stoop to "a fraternal hug," even with black men in order to win an election, and then turn around and abuse those very black men (not to mention the Southerners who came to Washington with only three-fifths of their black population adding to their power) after the polls had closed.

In early 1813, a correspondent of the *Chronicle* submitted a letter that also sought to detract from Federalist support by painting a large part of it black.

Despite what some Federalists would have the people believe, this writer said, "the *truth* is, no slave in" the South "is allowed to vote on any question; while in Massachusetts and the other Eastern States, the vote of a negro is as powerful as any in the ballot box." Far from recommending this state of affairs in New England, he grumbled that at least in the South "none approach the polls but FREE MEN." In Massachusetts, on the other hand, "*the blacks are nearly all Federalists*, and are *directly represented*, both in the State and National Governments." Both the Federalist governor and the likes of Josiah Quincy, he eagerly pointed out, owed their respective positions in part to "the *black* votes of Massachusetts."[65] Republican losses in local elections could produce just as many sour grapes as Federalist losses on the national level, and both parties sought to implicate African Americans in their troubles.

But the *Independent Chronicle* soon retreated from the field of slavery politics. Its attempts to paint the Federalists as Negro-lovers were limited to the first year of the war, and its engagement with the three-fifths clause was similarly short-lived. In December 1812, the editor answered those Federalists who were "continually insulting our brethren of the South as '*slave-holders*,' '*slave-buyers*,' &c.," by reminding them that "it is not only *upon the very labor of these slaves that we subsist, but also that our boasted* COMMERCE *depends*."[66] A May 1813 editorial argued that slave representation in the House of Representatives was meant to balance out the North's disproportionate power in the Senate.[67] But this was a rarity by 1813; the end of 1812 all but signaled the end of this editor's direct contestation of an issue that manifestly was a winning one for the Federalists. For most of 1813 and throughout 1814, this paper resorted to denunciations of Federalists' disloyalty to the Constitution and the memory of George Washington, rather than defenses of slave representation. It was the same with the Massachusetts Republican politicians quoted in its pages: they cast general aspersions on the Federalists but hesitated to openly defend the three-fifths clause. They would assail the timing or policy of the Hartford Convention's proposed amendments but not endorse slave representation in principle. New England Republicans understood all too well the power of the issue in their region during a deeply unpopular war.

They also appreciated the tie between slave representation's salience and New England's wartime grievances, however, for the news of the Treaty of Ghent and the American victory at New Orleans brought some back to directly vindicating slave representation. Upon receiving these tidings, Republican John Holmes, for one, assumed a newly confident tone as the Massachusetts legislature debated the Hartford Convention resolutions. He mocked the Federalist arguments against slave representation that had won over so many New England during the war. One of his opponents had attempted to prove "that the war would not have been declared had it not been for the *slave representation!*" His Federalist nemesis "taxes our gravity" by arguing that Jefferson would not have been elected in 1800 without slave representation. "He then proceeds" thus, Holmes gloated: "Had not Mr. J. been *chosen*, he would not have been *re-chosen*; and had he not been *re-chosen*, Mr. Madison would not have been *chosen*, and *so* there would have been no war—Wonderful! Wonderful!" There was "no proof," Holmes announced, that the votes of the new states brought on the war, and he gleefully pointed to Louisiana's gallant defense of the nation at the Battle of New Orleans to complete his onslaught on what he clearly perceived to be an attenuated Federalist position.[68] Yet the strident tone of this speech belied (or perhaps relieved) the strain of a couple of difficult years for the New England Republicans, in which their opponents had reduced them largely to defensive generalities by using a popular issue against them.[69]

Republicans from Northern states outside of New England employed similar defensive tactics, for agitation against slave representation had put them in a delicate position by ranging them with Southern slaveholders. The delicacy of all the Northern Republicans' position can be seen in the response of Pennsylvania's Republican-controlled state Senate to the Hartford Convention's proposal to abolish the three-fifths clause. "It cannot be concealed," conceded a Senate committee report written by moderate Federalist Nicholas Biddle, "that this subject is surrounded by difficulties, and originally presented important obstacles to the union." In light of these difficulties, these legislators asserted that enumerating slaves for representation, like property qualifications for the franchise in other states, was "a mere municipal regulation, with which the union had no concern."[70] This strained interpretation of the Constitution's intent suited the Northern Republicans' purpose, for by leaving slavery as a local matter, they would not be called upon publicly to side with slaveholders. The Senate committee's members, however, were not prepared to surrender any antislavery credentials to New England Federalists. They remembered that in 1787 many Federalists argued that, at least, the three-fifths clause recognized slaves as more than property. "The states which had always professed to regard slaves as men whose bondage was oppression," they suggested, "should not be the first to degrade them to the rank of mere cattle" by refusing to count them as population.[71] Pennsylvania's Republicans were determined to exclude the issue of slavery from national politics, but they would not allow the Federalists to paint them as soft on slavery.

Northern Republicans offered a few other direct rebuttals to the Federalists on the three-fifths clause. Many emphasized New England's disproportionate power in the Senate as compared to her population. Carey offered this sort of analysis. According to his computations, New England was overrepresented by 14 percent in the Senate. He pointed out that the War of 1812 had passed by a margin of thirty votes in the House of Representatives, while the so-called slave representatives numbered only nineteen. These and other numbers showed that the Federalists' "complaints are to the last degree groundless and factious."[72] Niles did his own calculations to show the extent of New England's preponderance in the Senate. And weight in the Senate, Niles argued, meant more in terms of influence than weight in the House (where, in any event, by his math New England was only short one representative).[73] The Pennsylvania Senate committee's report on the Hartford Convention also referred to New England's disproportionate weight in the Senate, whimpering that "the true sufferers in the confederacy . . . are the large middle states."[74] A legislative committee in New York noted that the Hartford Convention did not propose an amendment "equalizing the representation in the senate, in which the states of Connecticut and Rhode Island are each equally represented with this state, which contains four times as many as the former, and fourteen times as many as the latter."[75] These were able rejoinders to the New England Federalists. But their tone was deliberately measured, and they were exceptions to the rule of nonengagement that most Republicans followed.

Southern Republicans had their own reasons to yearn for slavery and slave representation to be removed from the table. By 1813, when Josiah Quincy complained in Congress about New England's bondage to Southern slaveholders, North Carolina representative Nathaniel Macon had grown alarmed at the exploitation of Southern slavery during war debates. "One of the gentlemen from Massachusetts," Macon complained, "could not miss the opportunity, which this general debate afforded, to mention the negroes in the Southern States. I had supposed, after former debates, they would not have been drawn into questions where there was no necessity for it."[76] This congressional veteran had already seen enough sectional donnybrooks to know the danger of wandering into the territory of slavery. Furthermore, although Quincy had emphasized the impending *political* enslavement of New Englanders, Macon understood that he had implicated Southern chattel slavery in his argument. Although Macon aimed his comments specifically at Quincy, they were a revealing general statement from a slaveholding Republican who would only become more nervous in the future about the injection of slavery into extraneous debates. On the surface, Southern Republicans might have seemed a confident lot, having no need for fiery and detailed defenses of their power in the federal Union.[77] Yet they skirted the issue of slave representation precisely because they were so troubled by the damage any heated or prolonged debate over the federal ratio would inflict on the Union and their party.

Therefore, while Northern Republicans faced peculiar sectional hazards in relation to slave representation, all Republicans regretted that such an explosive and difficult issue should be continually before the public. They recognized their need to preserve their party's national base from the Federalists' powerful appeals. Republicans might hold sway in Washington, but during the domestic crisis of the War of 1812 they were justly afraid that they might soon have no Union over which to preside. For these reasons, their spokesmen's head-on confrontations with the issue of slave representation were infrequent and restrained. Such caution sapped some of the passion and energy from the party line, but this was exactly the point: the party could not stay unified if this issue were to be bandied about endlessly and passionately on both sides.

They did not handle the individual Yankees in question mildly, however. Ad hominem arguments were one area in which Republicans poured forth the passion that was conspicuously absent when they discussed the issues themselves. "Hector Benevolus" assured his readers that the delegates to the Hartford Convention might have had biblical given names but they "were not the ancient prophets, patriarchs and apostles, . . . but only named after them, the same as we sometimes call negro servants after great men, as *Cato, Caesar, Pompey*, &c."[78]

Over time a triumvirate of New England Federalists emerged as lightning rods for Republicans' personal abuse: preachers David Osgood and Elijah Parish and Congressman Josiah Quincy. Osgood, Congregational pastor at Medford, Massachusetts, had been a leading clerical scourge to the Republicans since 1794, and his opposition to the war only increased their ire.[79] Elijah Parish, whose virulent antiwar and antislaveholder rhetoric made him a poster boy for New England sectionalism, got as good as he gave from Republicans. The influential administration organ the *National Intelligencer* was particularly and continually abusive of Parish. Its pages carried numerous articles accusing him of treason, emphasizing how the British admired his sermons and excerpting some of the speeches of "the maniac PARISH, whose infuriate ravings have received so general execration."[80] "Hector Benevolus" described the devil deputizing to the Federalists not only Osgood, "to sanctify your cause with lies," but also the "vile, insolent and frantic" Parish.[81]

The Hartford Convention or *LEAP NO LEAP*.

This 1814 cartoon lampooning the Hartford Convention is of a piece with other Republican attacks emphasizing its treasonable nature. Here the canting, Anglophiliac Hartford men's central dilemma is whether to follow their true desires by flying back to the arms of George III. Timothy Pickering, kneeling in the center, prays: "I, Strongly and most fervently pray for the success of this great leap which will change my vulgar name into that of my Lord of Essex. God save the King." Above, a man representing Massachusetts pulls men representing Rhode Island and Connecticut toward the edge of the precipice, urging: "What a dangerous leap!!! but we must jump Brother Conn." "I cannot Brother Mass," replies Connecticut. "Let me pray and fast some time longer—little Rhode will jump the first." Yet Rhode Island hesitates too, crying: "Poor little I, what will become of me? this leap is of a frightful size—I sink into despondency." George III sits on the right welcoming the men on the cliff. He calls: "O 'tis my Yankey boys! jump in my fine fellows; plenty molasses and Codfish; plenty of goods to Smuggle; Honours, titles and Nobility into the bargain." (Library of Congress)

Josiah Quincy's 1813 address in Congress was but the prime example of his talent for baiting his opponents,[82] and Southern Republicans were quick to revile Quincy and his inflammatory speech. The day after Quincy finished his expostulations, two of his fellow congressmen obliquely accused him of treason. Quincy's sentiments, one insisted, could not help but spark "those flames which it seemed to be his object to enkindle in the Eastern section of the Union."[83] Southern Republican newspapers also went on the offensive against Quincy. It took a Charleston paper seven issues, but it printed the speech in full, denouncing "Mr. Quincy and his speech" at every turn. Its editor admitted that Quincy had shrewdly kept himself within the letter of the law on treason. But "were you to ask the 'Yeomanry' of our Country," he fulminated, "what should be done with that man, . . . what would be their answer? Annihilate him. They would not stop to define the Crime, but would give effect to their indignant feelings."[84] A letter to the editor of Richmond's *Enquirer* resorted to metaphorical rather than actual threats of Southern-style violence against Quincy, as well as a strong dose of irony. That Yankee "never rises but he provokes and is sure to get a severe chastising," the writer fumed. "One would think he had grown callous, but he never waits for his back to get well before he gets it well scored again.— Several have got their whips seasoning for him, and [South Carolina congressman] D. R. Williams will give him as sound a lashing as ever he did any other 'slave.' " "*Quincy admitted that he was a slave in the course of his speech*," the writer pursued, "*which was the only true thing he said.*"[85] Such rhetoric was not calculated to disabuse Yankees of their notion that slaveholding Southerners were violent men who would not scruple to enslave them. Quincy, as with other Federalists, had not championed the enslaved African Americans; indeed, for him, "to yoke in with negroes" was far beneath the rights and dignity of his freeborn white constituents. Nevertheless, slaveholders found his rhetoric sufficiently offensive that he became persona non grata among them, and they took no pains to conceal their personal animus.

Neither were Republicans shy or restrained in wrapping themselves in the flag and in the Constitution, another of their responses to the Federalists' slave representation campaign. The Federalists had allowed the Republicans to pose as the sole defenders of a beleaguered Constitution and of the Union for which it stood, and they were eager to do so. At Republican fetes, authors' speeches and toasts embraced the concept of a perpetual Union in a time when its perpetuity was under threat. An orator at a Republican Fourth of July celebration, for instance, lauded the Union as "the emanation of Divine Beneficence" and thus "stamped with the seal of Heaven."[86] As for the Constitution, one speaker went so far as to call it "perfect."[87] Kentucky's legislature joined him, adding a thinly veiled threat against factious Federalists, when it resolved "that we consider the Constitution of the United States, as the most perfect and stupendous work of human virtue," and that its members would "contribute the last cent of our treasure, and drop of our blood, to support and maintain it against the assault, either of its external or *internal* foes."[88] "On whom does the censure fall," asked a writer for the *National Intelligencer*, if Virginia is

This 1812 caricature of Josiah Quincy lambastes his supposed closet monarchism (down to the scepter in his left hand), as well as his New England sectionalism. He declares: "I Josiah the first do by this my Royal Proclamation announce myself King of New England, Novia Scotia and Passamaquoddy, Grand Master of the noble order of the Two Cod Fishes." (Library of Congress)

overrepresented in the House? "Not on Virginia. She only exercises a right, guaranteed by that Constitution which she is pledged to maintain, and to which it is her sacred duty to conform." Furthermore, this right "was conceded to her by that wise and august assembly," the Constitutional Convention—headed by Washington himself.[89] Let Federalists malign the likes of Washington (whom they affected to reverence); the Republicans would defend the sacred compromises of the Constitution.

As this passage suggests, Republicans found it endlessly useful to invoke the legacy of George Washington, particularly his enormously influential Farewell Address, which warned against the perils of sectionalism. In Hezekiah Niles's general statement of political principles in the prospectus of *The Weekly Register* in 1811, he vowed to "obey the dictate of WASHINGTON, and 'frown indignantly'" on any traitorous wretch "who would create 'geographical discriminations' in the body politic."[90] Niles would find these sentiments from the Farewell Address of enormous value to him in his attacks on Federalists during the war; like so many other Republicans he never tired of reproving the astounding inconsistency of those who feigned fidelity to Washington yet so blatantly violated his warning against sectional divisiveness.[91] "Are those Washington's disciples," asked a Massachusetts orator, "who would persuade you, that the interests and views, habits, and opinions of the different sections of the union are as irreconcilable as the jarring elements; that the North will be enslaved by the South," when Washington himself declared such ideas to be false?[92] Upon the publication of the Hartford Convention report, a Virginia editor responded: "They recommend *political* combinations and *local* associations which Washington denounced! And yet are impudent enough to call themselves the admirers of Washington!"[93] And on it went; grasping for Washington's mantle was a favorite Republican tactic.

So common was it that a Federalist editor lamented "the knavish use made of a paragraph in Washington's Valedictory," complaining that his strictures against sectionalism were "the only piece of advice, or caution, from the pen or from the lips of Washington, which they think proper ever to remind the people of." He catalogued the other clauses of the address that the Republican administrations violated—"And yet the authors of those measures, and their minions, have the impudence to appeal to *him*."[94] Two could play the game of contesting Washington's legacy, and the Federalists did so vigorously. In their Washington Benevolent Societies, they held commemorations of milestones in his life, continuing to maintain, as Fisher Ames had done in years previous, that "Washington's last address to the people is the solemn creed of federalists."[95] But by their blatantly sectionalist stance, New England Federalists had left themselves open to Republican attacks on this score.

The Republicans exposed another Federalist vulnerability when they accused the Federalists of manipulating Northern opposition to slave representation in the service of their political designs and ambitions. Although these accusations carried with them a tacit admission of the widespread repugnance with which Northerners held the federal ratio during the war, they also rang true. A Kentucky Republican submitted that Federalist abuse of white Southerners on account of slavery had precious little moral authority. Referring to the census of 1810, he reminded his readers that Rhode Island and Connecticut still had slaves. Furthermore, he noted that although the United States had outlawed the Atlantic slave trade, "it is notorious that, notwithstanding the many scruples they express," Yankees predominated among those Americans continuing to engage in the traffic. He did not believe that any state governments in New England had taken steps to punish their native offenders on this score, "which shows that their apparent hostility to negro slavery is more the result of a political expedient to decry their sister states of the union than a real philanthropic feeling. In truth, there is a great deal more *ambition* in the argument made use of than of any other sentiment whatever."[96] It underestimated New England's real wartime grievances, but this article did correctly characterize that region's wartime opposition to slavery as much more political than humanitarian. The partisan politics of slavery had come full circle since Federalists had defended the Constitution from Antifederalist attacks by accusing them of manipulating antislavery for political gain.

In the face of the wartime Federalist menace, then, Republicans did not shrink from the fight. But the way they conducted their political battles demonstrated their fear of the slave representation issue. While they tried to maintain a national party, their adversaries pursued an aggressive sectional agenda that they combated as best they could within the constraints that party unity imposed.

———

On the other hand, one important white Southerner was free of such constraints: John Randolph of Roanoke. His response to the New England Federalists was an exception that proved the partisan rule. As an Old Republican whose constituents had voted him out of Congress after his opposition to the war, his position outside the Republican Party—as well as outside elected office—gave him the rhetorical freedom to fight Federalist fire with fire of his own. He published a rejoinder to the Hartford Convention that featured a vigor and directness missing in mainstream Republican publications.

Randolph's indignation against New England sectionalism waxed great only late in the war. During his time in Congress, Randolph had forged an unlikely alliance with Josiah Quincy and for most of the War of 1812 tentatively supported the New England–led opposition to the administration. In 1813, he wrote to Maryland Federalist Francis Scott Key of the need for "union among the parts, however heterogeneous, which compose the opposition. They have time enough to differ among themselves after they shall have put down the common foe."[97] Many Federalists lionized Randolph as a courageous fellow victim of Republican tyranny.[98] For his part, Randolph welcomed the Federalists to the side of state rights and strict construction, and his letters to Quincy asked that his friend remember him kindly to various Federalist leaders. Yet in counseling Quincy on the course they should take in opposition to the administration, the normally loose cannon suddenly sounded like a cautious statesman. He worried about the feasibility of opposition to a popular administration; he said it was inexpedient at the present time to drive for disunion; he denied that New England's grievances were yet sufficient cause for severing the Union. He also warned Quincy not to "expect relief from the *sympathy* of the southern country, the people of which are prepossessed by the daemons of faction and discord with no very favourable opinion of you."[99]

The grievances of New Englanders against the South had never stirred Randolph's sympathy, but by the time of the Hartford Convention, their anti-Southern drumbeat had raised his sectionalist hackles and elicited characteristically caustic rhetoric. In December 1814, Randolph wrote a public letter to James Lloyd of Massachusetts that was reprinted across the nation. In it he declared that when he read "the vile stuff against my country printed and uttered on this subject, by fire-brands" such as those meeting in Hartford, he could not but think that they "ought to be quenched forever." In his passion against the libelers against his "country" of Virginia, Randolph made it clear that he did not assume the "subject" at hand to be limited to slave representation. He reminded these fire-brands' "deluded followers" that "every word of these libels on the planters of Virginia, is as applicable to the father of his country as to any one among us." If present-day Virginians were " 'slave-holders' and 'negro-drivers,' and 'dealers in human flesh,' " so was Washington.[100]

Although most of New England's fire had been focused only on slave representation, Randolph detected an attack on slavery itself. Although Randolph was willing to interject slavery into a variety of ostensibly unrelated debates, it irritated him when Yankees touched on the subject in any way. It was, to his mind as well as to those of other white Southerners, a short step between seeking to abolish slave representation and seeking to remove slavery itself.[101] The relentless focus of the New England Federalists on slaveholders' power had driven a wedge between them and the likes of Randolph, who ever after referred to the Hartford men with disgust.[102] Free of party considerations, Randolph could say so publicly, and with his characteristic animus.

Randolph's rhetoric might be considered out of proportion to the threat Federalists posed to slavery. But it was difficult to separate an attack on slaveholders and their power from an attack on slavery. After all, at the time of the Constitution's ratification, Southern spokesmen had warned Northerners that they would consider the two subjects as inseparable. Furthermore, at times the implications, if not always the intent, of Federalist rhetoric undercut slavery. And during the War of 1812, some New Englanders—notably preachers such as Parish, Strong, and Perkins and laymen such as "Cato"—had sounded something like abolitionists.

––––––––

Indeed, the Federalists' motives in pushing against slave representation were immaterial to their campaign's mark on the politics of slavery in the early republic. That mark was substantial. Their campaign helped ensure that, far from submerging the issue of slavery, the War of 1812 brought it repeatedly to the surface. The Federalists also united regional political interests with a form of opposition to slavery and thus connected two powerful forces that had not been firmly linked for most of the early years of the republic.[103] The Federalists' wartime focus on the South also helped give North-South sectionalism unaccustomed preeminence. After 1815, the Hartford Convention replaced the Burr Conspiracy as the most salient symbol of sectionalism.

Such were the effects of honing in on slave representation for so many years and with such intensity during the deeply divisive war years. The Federalist campaign highlighted yet again how divisive any question related to slavery could be. It gave a strong impetus toward the ultimate fusion of a sort of antislavery and Northern sectionalism (and especially New England regionalism). Furthermore, it showed that some white Southerners were not prepared to make nice distinctions between opposition to slave representation and opposition to slavery. Thus, this time when slavery was not the central issue at hand left its mark on the history of America's sectional conflict over slavery.

Slavery and Partisan Conflict during the Era of Good Feelings

THE FEDERALISTS' WARTIME campaign and rhetoric influenced partisan politics in both the immediate and long terms. By applying the North's vague, self-interested brand of antislavery to politics, the Federalists had revealed the true breadth and depth of Northern resentment of slaveholders and their power. They thus showed the way to all who wished to pursue Northern sectionalism in national politics. Their example did not go unheeded for long.

The postwar political context opened a side door for slavery to reenter American politics soon after New England's Federalists showed it the exit in 1815. The receding power of Federalism gave the Era of Good Feelings its name, but it allowed Republicans the luxury of intraparty dissensions. These divisions proved more dangerous than luxurious, however, for schismatic Northern Republicans had seen the effectiveness with which Federalists had exploited sectional antagonisms over slavery. They thus found it useful to revive Federalist rhetoric in their attacks on the Virginia Dynasty in power in Washington, to which they added their own critique of slaveholders as unrepublican. The return of such tactics to national politics appalled Republicans still loyal to the administration, and they in turn resurrected wartime tactics in defense of party and national unity. The whole process once again revealed the political potency of antislavery sectionalism in the North.

In the months and years following the War of 1812, Federalism was moribund nationally. It had almost no hope of reviving as a national power after the debacle of the Hartford Convention combined with the end of the war and the nationalist spree touched off by American victory at New Orleans. Federalists might lay hold on some few loaves and fishes of government patronage, but only if the Republican rulers of the nation saw fit to distribute them in this way.[1]

Neither was their regional power as secure as it had been during the war; voter turnout and the Federalist margin of victory were much lower in the spring elections for Massachusetts's governor in 1815 than they had been in 1814.[2] Far from organizing a grand sectional party as many thought them poised to do during the war, Federalists would only challenge the Republicans in national politics if they were able to ally with some faction of the Republican Party.

Neither did most of them seem inclined to challenge the Republicans openly. Federalists eager for reconciliation hopefully dubbed the postwar political scene the Era of Good Feelings. Years later, Otis wrote that with the advent of peace, the Federalists' "joy was too engrossing to permit a vindictive recurrence to the causes of" the war. "Every emotion of animosity was permitted to subside."[3] The New England Federalists' sectionalist strategy in politics subsided with their appetite for sectional animosity. In 1816, for instance, a Federalist took up his pen to defend the Hartford Convention—and the Federalist Party more generally—from Matthew Carey's accusations in *The Olive Branch*. This anonymous author could not resist some oblique grumbling about Virginia presidents.[4] But his purpose was to defend the Federalists from charges of sectionalist disunionism. So rather than renewing any sectionalist attack, he defended their record as patriotic and moderate. It was telling that he spoke in generalities reminiscent of the Republicans' tones during the war when they were on the defensive.[5]

In this setting, all organized agitation against slave representation died. Apparently the party leaders judged that further agitation against the three-fifths clause would look too "vindictive." Historian Harlow W. Sheidley has described how, in the Hartford Convention's wake, elite Federalists "needed to restore their credibility as conservatives sincerely wed to the welfare of the nation rather than to the selfish interests of their class and section." This made the abandonment of such issues as slave representation an imperative.[6] Furthermore, their focus, as with that of their constituents, was elsewhere now that their prime danger and grievance had passed. In the first postwar months, Federalist newspapers' domestic lens centered on issues such as Sabbatarianism. There was a noticeable absence of material on slavery and slave representation.[7] Slavery later returned to their columns in response to the horrors and national shame of its expansion, but slave representation did not. New England's disgruntlement with slaveholder power would resurface again in later crises, but New England was concerned with other issues in the first months and years following the war.

But the New England Federalists' retreat from slave representation hardly kept slavery out of national politics. The decline of Federalism reduced the need for Republicans outside of New England to unite against the common threat. Ironically, therefore, Republican postwar national hegemony proved hazardous to party unity. Whenever the need to unify against the Federalists evaporated, a whole series of byzantine internal divisions arose in Republican-controlled states such as Pennsylvania and New York. Some factions remained loyal to the national party, while others manifested more independence. This had been true to some extent during Jefferson's second term, as Federalists were in the doldrums, and was even truer after the war.[8]

The postwar intraparty fissures grew from issues unrelated to slavery, but slavery seeped through them nonetheless. The central issues ranged from the method of nominating presidential candidates to economic policies surrounding banks, tariffs, and internal improvements.[9] But spokesmen for the disaffected factions in the Mid-Atlantic found the rhetoric and existence of slavery of great utility as they attacked mainstream Republicans headed by the Virginian president, James Monroe. Loyal Republicans grew increasingly alarmed as the dissenters' rhetoric grew increasingly strident and rushed to the defense of the South and the Union. The loss of party discipline's restraint on antislavery expression was thus a threatening cloud on the triumphant Republican Party's horizon.[10] Many Republicans who either were not particularly antislavery or who had suppressed their opposition to slavery during the War of 1812 for the purposes of party and national unity found that postwar policy divisions loosened their tongues and unleashed their presses. Outrage at the atrocities associated with slavery's expansion, as well as concern for the nation's image, helped motivate some of them and kept them engaged with slavery after they first came to the issue. But its uses in partisan squabbles were what first elicited their rhetoric against slavery and slaveholders.

Northern Republicans knew all too well how effective the Federalists' wartime campaign against slaveholders and their power had been, and schismatic Republicans soon mastered the Federalist idiom for use in their new situation. Thus abuse of "the *Virginia dynasty*," "*the Virginia succession*," "Virginia influence," and the "nabobs of the south" flourished in the dissenting Republican press.[11] During the war, these same editors and writers had deemed such labels seditious partisan grumbling from New England Federalists. They still sought to distance themselves from the Federalists even as they drew on Federalist rhetoric. Thus, disgruntled Republicans complained of how they gained "little by shaking off the yoke of an Anglo-federal party, if the alternative is to become a province of Virginia, or slaves of the Washington cabinet."[12] Although association with the Federalists was still odious, their rhetoric proved irresistible when Northern Republicans confronted their former allies from the South.

William Duane, whom one Republican loyalist dubbed "the most unblushing apostate that ever wielded a pen or wore a sword,"[13] was the most prominent Republican to become fluent in New England Federalist speech. Duane had been a force in the Republican Party since the late 1790s, often a disruptive one. Although he took part in and caused several rifts within Republican ranks after 1801, he suppressed his grievances with his partisan fellows in the face of the Federalist threat during the War of 1812.[14] But his independent streak resurfaced thereafter as his differences with the Southern-dominated mainstream faction in the party grew. Along with it came a discovery of the malign power of slaveholders. During the war, he had dismissed as so much factiousness the Federalists' campaign against slaveholders' influence in Washington. In 1813, he gibed that if Virginia suddenly joined the Federalist ranks, Americans would no longer hear the New England Federalists inveighing against " 'negro states'—'slave holders'—'Virginia influence,' &c."[15] But he sang their tune when it was his turn to attack the Virginia Dynasty. Duane considered himself consistent in this regard, for to his mind, "the *spirit of despotism*" had "changed sides" after the peace. "Formerly it was foreign influence and the tendency to despotism, holding its *head quarters at Boston*; now it is the intolerance and avarice of the *slave states*, concentrated in the diabolical corruption established in" Washington, where "the nabobs of the south" held sway.[16]

Many of the policies against which the likes of Duane protested were economic, and they echoed the Federalists' old charge that slaveholders posed a threat to Northern prosperity as well as Northern freedom. They charged the Southern Republicans with antipathy to Northern commerce and found slavery to be the root cause of their sectional jealousy. "What do the planters of cotton care about domestic manufacturers, or the shipping interest, or the carrying trade—what is the industry of white men to those who eat the bread of other men's labor," Duane asked. "What do men who know nothing of the earning of wealth, or the value of personal industry—what do they care for those who are not fed by the sweat of slavery?" The administration's economic agenda proved that "the influence of the *negro plantations*" was the "influence prevailing and ruling the government." Meanwhile, "the interests and prosperity of at least six millions of" white Northerners went unheeded.[17] Another Philadelphia editor wondered whether Virginia, "as a slave country," was not "different in its whole moral organization from the free states?" "As the chief power" in the nation, "may it not therefore become dangerous to the liberty, commerce and manufactures of the free states?"[18] Southern slavery encroached upon the interests as well as the liberties of white Northerners: these were the same themes and language that the Federalists had been employing for years.

Nonconformist Northern Republicans injected an important emphasis of their own into partisan politics, however, as they added the charge that slaveholders were aristocratic threats to republican liberty. Federalists had used Virginians' tyranny over slaves as a shield to defend themselves from charges that Federalists were aristocratic much more often than they used it as an offensive weapon in charging that the slaveholders, as aristocrats, were threats to liberty. Despite important exceptions during the War of 1812, more Federalists emphasized that slaveholding Republicans were hypocrites than that they were aristocratic despots. Dissident Northern Republicans, however, coming from a more democratic point on America's ideological spectrum, more fully developed this critique and used it offensively. This characterization of the Southern planters was consistent with the burgeoning view of slavery as threatening to Northern rights.

In pursuing this line of attack, heretical Republicans echoed contemporary abolitionists, who themselves were repeating Revolutionary-era abolitionists' attacks on slaveholders as tyrants. The antirepublican slaveholder was a common character in antislavery tracts in the early nineteenth century. "He who will enslave a black man, or his own, or his son's, nephew's, or fellow-citizen's children begotten on [sic] a black woman," an antislavery man warned, "would not spare you, if he had you legally in his power." He knew slaveholders would object to such rhetoric, but retorted that if slavery "be not *tyranny, monarchy* or *despotism*—I ask, what is?"[19] Abolitionist George Bourne's warning was even direr: "Slave-holders would wade through seas of the blood of white men, as well as black men, to gratify their despotic propensities if they were not restrained." Only fools would trust such men with their liberties, no matter the color of their own skin.[20]

In an era when the peculiar institution seemed to be aggrandizing itself at their expense at every turn, many Northern Republicans took this page from the abolitionist critique of slavery. A Philadelphia newspaper carried a denunciation of the domestic slave trade, which concluded that participants in this traffic were manifestly "lost to all the fine feelings which are the substratum of . . . the love of liberty." The buyers and sellers of human chattel were thus "prepared to elevate" themselves "into the iron chariot of despotism and ride with relentless fury over the neck of millions."[21] In a similar vein, William Duane used the kidnapping of free blacks to lump America's "republican regime" with European tyrants.[22] In 1816–1817, debates within Virginia over regional representation in the statehouse provided Duane further support for the idea that slaveholders were unrepublican. He railed against one Virginian orator in particular for his appeals to "the slavery of the unfortunate blacks, as a reason why liberty should not be extended to the whites." This was evidence of how slavery demeaned all working men in the aristocratic planter's mind—"the blackman labors without estimation and why should not the white!" In light of such attitudes, Duane exhorted the people of the Mid-Atlantic to "watch over your liberties."[23] This had not been his language during the War of 1812. In fact, in an August 1814 letter to Thomas Jefferson, he described American slaves' unique happiness under their benevolent masters. Given their miserable condition in Africa, "the present condition" of African American slaves in "ten thousand cases to one is better than in Africa."[24] According to this accounting, American slaveholders were far from despots. But after the war, Duane and other Northern Republicans both revivified and refined the Federalist allegations that Southern slavery menaced Northern rights and prosperity. Such charges rang true in an era when slavery's forward march seemed forever poised for incursions into the free states.[25]

Loyal Northern Republicans' anxiety for the party and the Union bore witness to the power of this latest round of sectional appeals. They lamented the sectional dangers lurking behind their partisan hegemony in the Era of Good Feelings. They did their best to defend the white South against their erstwhile comrades' contumely. But they knew they could not stand as friends to slavery. So they drew on the general appeal to the value of the Union that they had used against Federalists during the War of 1812. In the process, they again bore unwitting witness to the power of antislavery and sectionalism in the North.

Republican loyalists' own words gave the best indication of how commonplace attacks on slaveholders were becoming in the North after the war. Some tried to dismiss "the flimsy and factious objection" that Monroe was "a *Virginian*" as needing "no other weapons than ridicule and contempt, to put it down."[26] Others could not muster such a game face and repeatedly revealed their perturbation with those "grumbletonians"—some "even styling themselves democratic"—who painted a picture of the North suffering under "Virginia rule."[27] One editor bemoaned the fact that "it certainly has become fashionable for persons to the east of the Delaware" to attack Virginians.[28]

Leading New York writer and Republican James Kirke Paulding, who campaigned tirelessly against sectional divisions within the party and nation, acknowledged that Northerners were "accustomed to stigmatize Virginia and the more southern states, with the imputed guilt of" slavery. He aimed to relieve Yankees of the "pack of prejudices" against the South that they carried into politics.[29] After the Treaty of Ghent, mainstream Republicans heard such prejudices expressed all around them, not just from Federalist quarters.

In light of this new alignment, they feared for the Union. Their angst showed from behind their many postwar affirmations that the federal compact was permanent. They protested this point too much in what was supposed to be the Era of Good Feelings.[30] Others betrayed their doubts even as they denied their fears in the next breath. "What a sublime spectacle will our country present to the world," one surveyor of the expanding Union enthused, "if our Union can be preserved! and preserved, we trust, it will be."[31] In summer 1818, an anonymous correspondent of a New York City paper warned of the "Seeds of Disunion" he saw maturing in the United States—namely, the sectional calumnies he was reading in the newspapers. He encouraged white Northerners and Southerners to mingle together, breaking down the walls of ignorance and distrust that led to the stereotypes of the South "as a land of nabobs and slaves" and the North as brimming with "puritanical tenets" and "narrow bigotry." If Yankees would travel in the South, "they will indeed find slaves and their masters; but this state of things existed previous to our struggle for independence, and should not, at this late day, be made the ground for dangerous and narrow prejudices." He urged editors in particular to guard against illiberal expressions that were making "A DIVISION OF THE UNION" the "most fearful calamity" beclouding the postwar American horizon. In addition to entreaties concerning the value of the Union, he revived the wartime Republicans' appeal to the authority of George Washington's Farewell Address, with its rejection of all partisan and sectional differences that would attenuate the national bonds.[32]

Other Northern Republicans joined this writer in reprising wartime strategies. Some trotted out the tried-and-true tactic of ascribing anti-Southern sentiment to petty partisan plots. All attacks on Virginia's character, a New York editor affirmed, "emanate from *political hostility*."[33] He rendered this analysis more explicit a few months later, charging that the "cry of VIRGINIA INFLUENCE" from the administration's opponents was "the same cry which emanated from their master in 1812, during our national calamity."[34] By suggesting an alliance between Federalists and disgruntled Northern Republicans, such polemicists hoped to tar all their opponents with the brush of the Hartford Convention. The legacy of the politics of slavery during the War of 1812 was thus on full display on both sides of the new partisan controversies in the North.

As vigorously as their delicate situation would permit, some Northern Republicans defended their slaveholding allies as well as the Union in general. "We ought not to envy" the slaveholders for being "the richest men in the country," an Ohio editor pleaded, given their invaluable economic contributions to the nation. Obviously, many people he knew did envy their wealth, but he drew their attention to a not-too-distant future in which Northern industry would earn great profits by adding value to Southern raw materials. He hoped that this process would "establish a bond of interest here, between different parts of the Union, too solid to be dissolved by local and detestable prejudices."[35] In their own attempts to combat such prejudices, others trumpeted Southern planters' essential goodness. A Boston editor, for one, testified to the planters' humanity. The establishment of a Deaf and Dumb Institution in the Deep South, he insisted, proved that "the Southern gentlemen of overgrown fortunes, are constantly distributing the vast proceeds of their invaluable plantations, with a liberality that honours them in the highest degree."[36]

Mainstream Northern Republicans insisted that the South was doing all it could to ameliorate slavery and act against its abuses. They grasped at any supporting evidence of this coming from the slave states.[37] Paulding offered glowing descriptions of the lot of Southern slaves. Their lives "exhibited an appearance of comfort, which, in some measure, served to reconcile me to bondage." It was "gratifying" to see this, "for since their lot is beyond remedy, it was consoling to find it mitigated by kindness and plenty."[38] He decried the domestic slave trade but followed the slaveholders' lead in attaching its odium to the slave trader himself. Indeed, Paulding expressed his certainty that Southern legislators and magistrates would act (in some unspecified way) to mitigate or eliminate the execrable traffic.[39] One ingenious editor even turned the tables on the common wisdom that held that the North was the home of liberty and the South the home of slavery. He related incidents in the slave trade between New Jersey and New Orleans and concluded that the citizens of New Jersey "ought not to have permitted this shocking trade in their vicinity."[40] A few months later, he recounted how, "by the vigilance and humanity of several gentlemen in Virginia, a band of *kidnappers* have been apprehended."[41] Given such facts, he plainly meant to infer, the South was hardly the guilty party when it came to kidnapping and the sale of remaining Northern slaves.

Such reversals of the sectional moral calculus had no hope of popularity in the North, however. The South's allies in the free states understood this, and most of them genuflected to the prevailing aversion to slavery, even as they defended slaveholders. Their protestations that they were not soft on slavery were multitudinous. "We all know," averred a New York editor, "that *slavery* finds no defenders in our country."[42] Paulding certainly seemed like its defender when he offered his rosy picture of Southern slavery and declared that it had reconciled him to bondage. But upon writing that passage, he felt the need to backtrack. "Don't mistake, and suppose that I am the advocate of slavery," he cautioned, "for I hate it."[43] The editor of Boston's *Independent Chronicle*, staunch ally of Southern Republicans, felt the need to include a few antislavery pieces in its columns.[44] Judges who ruled on fugitive slave cases in favor of the masters made sure they declared their state's repugnance for slavery.[45] In 1817, a committee of New York's legislature that recommended a course short of abolition of slavery assured the assembly that they felt "in common with their fellow-citizens the numerous evils which the system of slavery has introduced within this state."[46] Those who advocated inaction on the issue of slavery, and those who defended the South, spoke in terms that suggested how risky such business was in the North.

In the face of such political perils, most loyal Northern Republicans agreed with their Southern brethren that it would be best if slavery were not agitated at all. They had nothing to gain from such agitation, and much to lose. The impulse to preserve the peace was most evident in Paulding's writings. His passion for unity in the country and party added urgency to his response to the domestic slave trade. He exclaimed that when slaveholders allowed "such flagrant and indecent outrages on humanity" as he saw in a passing slave coffle, "in the face of day,—then they disgrace themselves, and the country to which they belong." If the slave trade itself was necessary, this timing was not. "If they must be transported, in this inhuman and indecent manner," Paulding implored, "let it be in the nighttime, and when there is no moon or stars.—Let not the blessed sun see it,—or the traveler carry the news to distant countries."[47] Paulding knew all too well that the outrages of the interstate commerce in slaves would not bear scrutiny, either in the North or beyond. It simply made no political sense to trouble the sectional waters by unnecessarily provocative behavior. If it brought slaveholders political troubles, it did so even more for devoted Northern Republicans, who had to face an antislavery electorate. Such men thus had at least as much reason as other white Northerners to contain slavery to the South, where it might remain out of sight. Their motives added to the complex mixture that impelled Yankees to defend against slavery's seemingly inexorable advance.

————

As the Republican Party fractured in the North, some Southern Republicans fretted for slavery as well as for the Union. True to the pattern set during the War of 1812, they found it more useful to emphasize the second concern than the first. Participation in the war's domestic quarrels gave them experience in such matters, and they trotted out proven tactics once again.

For one, they appealed to the Union in general terms and enlisted George Washington in their cause as often as possible. A Georgia Republican, for instance, alluded to Washington's Farewell Address in his reply to those who opposed James Monroe's candidacy for president because he was yet another Virginian. "Being all Americans," he chided, "all members of the same great family, such local jealousies and geographical distinctions, are extremely illiberal and improper."[48]

The influential Richmond editor Thomas Ritchie made a more explicit appeal to Washington in parrying Northern attacks on Monroe, to which he added other tricks tried in the crisis of the war. An anonymous Philadelphia writer had groused at over twenty years of Virginia dominance of the executive, insisting that the slave states were hostile to the interests of the free states. Would this Philadelphian, Ritchie asked, "have driven Washington from the chair, because he was from Virginia, a slave state? Will he disfranchise all the slave states? . . . Will he draw a line at Pennsylvania, and say to *all* the Southern men, 'We cannot trust you. Ye are either slaves or tyrants.' "[49] Ritchie resisted the idea that any Republicans had joined in the cry of "Virginia influence," still blaming it on the unpopular Federalists.[50] He also protested that those who painted Virginians "as a set of proud nabobs or slave holders" had never traveled south of the Potomac. Much as Southern Republicans had done during the war, he delighted in pointing out Northern Republicans—in this case Paulding and his *Letters from the South*—who truly understood the South and the value of the Union.[51] Such responses to the critics of Southern slaveholders and their power revealed Ritchie's discomfort with any discussion that touched even indirectly on slavery.

The leading Republican sheet, the *National Intelligencer* in Washington, also employed the tactic of oblique responses, for similar reasons. In 1817, it carried a response to "a certain species of injustice which we are sorry to see very often exhibited by the eastern prints against our fellow-citizens south of Delaware." "The subject we refer to," the editors anguished, "is unpleasant to dwell upon at all, and particularly disagreeable, if not improper, for newspaper discussion," but must be dealt with. Such discomfort with any discussion of slavery high- lighted these editors' sense of the divisiveness of slavery. Although they de- fended slavery at some length as a necessary evil, it took continual assaults from the North to draw them into the subject. And in the end, they rebuked North- ern prints who used their vast influence to sow "the seeds of aversion or jealousy between different sections of the union." They wished every American would "conceal from one part of our political family the defects which he might perceive in another."[52] Mainstream Southern Republicans clearly hoped that appeals to the Union would silence discussion of slavery, a discussion from which they had nothing to gain.[53]

Leading Republicans also resorted to ad hominem assaults on dissidents to evade a direct exploration of slavery, much as they had done during the war to the likes of Elijah Parish and Josiah Quincy. Moreover, they sought to identify the dissenters with the political pariahs of the day, the Federalists. Philadelphia editor William Duane was an especial target of their fury. No ordinary apostate, the influential Duane had the capacity to do great harm to the party with his resuscitation of the New England Federalists' barbs. An 1818 piece in a Savan- nah paper abused Duane's character and sought to associate him with the hated Federalists. This article asserted that Duane had not been the same "since he was *deranged* in the army" and denied an office in the navy. Now this insane, disappointed office seeker was "labouring hard to put down the demo- cratic party, by effecting a union between discontented democrats and the federal party."[54] Two years earlier, this same Savannah editor had called Duane "a willing and malicious propagator of odious falsehoods," urged on by "his master, Beelzebub."[55]

Troublemakers like Duane came in for such abuse not only because they threatened the Republican Party, but also because in the process they touched the most sensitive of Southern nerves. Some Southern writers apparently hoped that by displaying just how touchy they could be about almost any mention of slavery, they could shut down all such discussion. They hoped to do so by attacking their opponents rather than defending slavery. For example, in 1816, relatively mild reflections in a Northern newspaper occasioned a bitter response from the editor of the *Savannah Republican*. A Quaker had written to a Philadelphia print to oppose the use of armed force against slave smugglers on the Florida-Georgia border, intimating that greater diligence by government officials and citizens would be sufficient to enforce the ban on the foreign slave trade. It was really a problem of continuing illicit demand more than of supply, he seemed to imply. "This invidious insinuation," the Savannah editor fumed, was an attack on Georgians' "honor and morality." Furthermore, the Quaker's allegations that the South had employed kidnappers in the Northern states showed not only "an absolute unacquaintance with every trait that distinguishes the southern character," but also that "Quakerism breathes a sanguinary spirit of hostility towards us." Quakers also evinced this spirit, he charged, when they "sent amongst us" emissaries "on missions of blood," broadcasting sedition to the slaves "under the cloak of sanctity."[56]

Less than a year later, New York Federalist editor Theodore Dwight, the former secretary of the Hartford Convention, drew the same printer's wrath by opposing the authorization of slavery in the new state of Mississippi. "Not content with his infamous conduct during our late war," the Georgian raged, Dwight "*now* in time of peace endeavors to spread over our land, all the horrors of St. Domingo, and reiterates the old slang of a *division of the nation*. The heart that could originate such poisonous sentiments must be corrupt indeed! *Theodore Dwight*! you are a traitor in politics! a hypocrite in morals! detested be your name while love of country is a virtue."[57] The heat of these replies was out of all proportion to the statements that provoked them. But Southerners committed to the Union and to the Republican Party as well as to slavery saw that the rhetoric proceeding from the North could mean no good for any of the three. They thus hoped to discourage or avoid any engagement with the antislavery North on this issue. They certainly were more eager to engage the Yankees in question than the issues they raised.

––––––––

Dwight notwithstanding, one of the significant facts of the postwar era was that those Yankees hailed from a different party and different states than they had previously. Whereas during the war the epicenter of the politics of slavery had been in New England, after the war those who pressed slavery into their service for redressing ulterior grievances were the Republicans in the middle states. Still, the legacy of the wartime campaigns of the Federalists was perhaps never clearer than in the party struggles of the postwar period. For dissident Republicans played the role and stole the lines of their former enemies, while mainstream Republicans dusted off the responses that they had used to combat the Federalist appeal during the war. Some of the players were different, which alarmed fellow cast members, but the script had been set during the War of 1812.

Slavery in Anglo-American Relations

AMERICAN PARTISANS WERE not the only ones to use American slavery against each other in debates unrelated on the surface to chattel bondage. For slavery permeated the dispute over national superiority between the United States and Great Britain during the War of 1812 and the unstable entente that followed. It suffused the attacks of nationalists in both countries on the national honor, morality, and overall character of their foes. It came into play as both sides claimed the superiority of their respective political institutions.

But neither nation spoke with one voice on slavery. This was particularly true of the United States, where the interjection of British voices magnified the crescendo of sectional dissonance over slavery.[1] The Anglo-American debate sharpened the desire of many Northerners to free themselves from the guilt of American slavery by sectionalizing or removing it. Furthermore, the addition of Britons' influential voices to the chorus of critics drove some white Southerners toward the defense of slavery as a positive good. Slavery's appearance on the Atlantic stage helped to shape America's domestic dispute over the issue.

Slavery had intermittently and fleetingly entered Anglo-American relations beginning with the American Revolution, but the War of 1812 lodged it there more firmly. Prowar Americans from both North and South used the rhetoric of slavery to express their outrage over the British system of impressments. Naval supremacy was vital to Britain's ability to wage its wars with France following the French Revolution, and from their onset the Royal Navy had forcibly boarded American ships to find deserters and press expatriated Englishmen into its service, often taking native-born American citizens along with them. This had long been a diplomatic sticking point between the two nations and had brought them to the brink of war on occasion, such as in 1807 after a particularly egregious impressment in American waters. The American government listed the practice among its grounds for war when it stepped over that brink in 1812. In the postwar years, impressment cast a long shadow over British proposals that the two nations cooperate against the Atlantic slave trade. Having just fought a war in the name of resisting Britain's onboard searches of American ships, nationalist Americans were not prepared to grant a right of search in order to suppress the slave trade.[2] From the British geopolitical perspective, American recalcitrance in cooperating against the slave trade had great utility.

The War of 1812 presented Britain with other irresistible propaganda opportunities as well. Despite their possession of slave islands in the West Indies, Britons' desire to play the liberator on an Atlantic stage led them to offer freedom to American slaves who ran to their lines and then to refuse to return escaped African Americans to their former owners at the end of the war.[3] Americans pushed long and hard for the return of or compensation for these escaped slaves, ensuring that the legacy of the war shaped Anglo-American diplomacy in yet another way.[4] American diplomats' drive for return or compensation, and British stonewalling, were the standard features of these exchanges, regardless of the negotiators' personal stances on or relationship to slavery.

Finally, the War of 1812 seems to have alerted many Britons to the usefulness of American slavery in attacking the character and institutions of the republican upstarts. More travelers were making their way to investigate American conditions, and they did not ignore American slavery, as many prewar visitors had done. Travelers' and literary reviewers' heightened awareness and usages of American slavery coincided with and strengthened the postwar rise in tensions over slavery within the United States. The War of 1812 thus constituted an important milestone in the international as well as the domestic aspects of the politics of slavery.

———

The rhetoric of slavery pervaded American attacks on impressment, the single best example of how slavery entered the debate by a side route. Prowar Americans resorted to the language of slavery in part because its force matched their wrath over the seizure of their fellow citizens. Forcible capture and coerced service on the high seas also presented a natural parallel to the Atlantic slave trade, as well as to the capture and enslavement of whites in North Africa. Moreover, connecting slavery and impressment gave prowar Americans a powerful tool with which to contest Britain's claims to be the world's defender of liberty.

American war hawks drew legions of analogies between the universally execrated slave trade and the impressment they opposed. They repeatedly applied the appellation "man-stealing," so redolent of the Revolutionary generation's campaign against the traffic in Africans, to the seizure of Americans on the Atlantic. Baltimore editor Hezekiah Niles drew this comparison early and often. Impressment "has no parallel," he thundered in a typical editorial, "either for atrocity or extent, in any thing of modern times, but the business of negro-stealing on the coasts of unfortunate Africa."[5] President Madison said of Britain's entire maritime policy that "such an outrage on all decency was never before heard of even on the shores of Africa."[6] Such parallels carried tremendous power, for the Atlantic slave trade had become for the Age of Revolution what the Holocaust has been for the world since World War II: the embodiment of evil.[7] Such rhetoric served further to stoke an already red-hot issue in America.

Another popular parallel to which impressment lent itself was Algerian slavery. Americans in the early republic closely followed stories of whites held in slavery in North Africa, which were at once appalling and fascinating to them, in large part because they involved a reversal of racial roles.[8] Inasmuch as impressment forced white men into labor, it was a natural connection. Niles provided particularly striking, if hardly isolated, examples of this comparison. To the argument that "*Great Britain* wants men for her navy," he replied that "the dey of *Algiers* also wants slaves to build his palaces—one has as much right to *impress* as the other."[9] In late 1814, Niles charged that Britain had delivered impressed American seamen who had "*obstinately refused 'to do duty'*" to be detained in Gibraltar as slaves. As outrageous as this was, however, Niles argued that "their condition might have been bettered by the change. Slavery at *Algiers* is not more severe than on board a *British* vessel of war, and less hazardous."[10] Influential writer Matthew Carey agreed that the plight of those seized by Algerine corsairs "*is far better than that of the Americans impressed by British cruisers.*" Only the impressed sailor, for instance, was compelled to fight against his own country. "Is he not then the most miserable of slaves?"[11]

Antislavery men might well have bristled at the argument that the impressed sailor was in the worst of captivity, for it minimized the plight of African Americans in bondage.[12] Indeed, such rhetoric was eminently safe for American slavery—so long as it stayed within such bounds or used *West Indian* slavery as its benchmark.[13] The editor of the *Savannah Republican*, for example, declared his sympathy for America's "tars, now in the most cruel captivity!" He asserted that "their captivity is worse than the African's." Both suffered coercion, he admitted, "but the African is not compelled as (gracious God!) our tortured citizens are, to fight against their fathers, and become unwilling patricides."[14] This diatribe typified the way white Southern war hawks dealt with the trickiness of employing the rhetoric of slavery. They had to explain why white American captives' liberty was worth fighting for while black Americans' captivity continued.

Yet in whatever form, the rhetoric of slavery as used against impressment was popular, in part because it called into question the vaunted British commitment to liberty. "Does she care about liberty?" demanded one Republican orator. "Is it for liberty's sake, that thousands of men are torn from their homes, their friends, and every thing dear to them, and forced to linger out a miserable existence, in worse than barbarian slavery?"[15] If Britain's general claim to libertarianism could not shield it from such attacks, neither could its specific claim as suppressor of the slave trade. One writer found it outrageous that Great Britain should demonstrate "such zeal for the abolition of the traffic in the barbarous and unbelieving natives of Africa," while it stubbornly adhered to "the practice of impressing American citizens; whose civilization, religion, and blood, so obviously demanded a more favourable distinction."[16] This white Southerner's arguments not only justified or palliated the slave trade, but also showed how impressment could be used to accuse the British of hypocrisy, a favorite American pastime.

Issues surrounding impressment also haunted the slave trade diplomacy of the postwar years. The legacy of the war ensured that for most Americans, resistance to Britain's assertion of control over American seamen took precedence over suppressing the slave trade. John Quincy Adams exemplified this ordering of priorities. As a diplomat during the war, he reflected that "the impressment of seamen is to all intents and purposes a practice as unjust, as immoral, as base, as oppressive and tyrannical as the slave trade." Indeed, he thought that "in some particulars it is more aggravated" than the Atlantic traffic in slaves.[17] For nationalists such as Adams, antislavery took a back seat when Britain asserted its maritime supremacy.

American officials' refusal to cooperate with Britain opened them to the charge of being sympathetic to the African slave trade. Britons, eager to contrast the United States with European monarchies they had helped to restore after defeating Napoleon, seized this opening. At an 1815 county meeting in England, for instance, debate broke out over a resolution commending those who effected the "peace with Americans, the *only free remaining people in the world*." Some in attendance objected to this as a slander on Great Britain. One attendee noted that "he had *considerable reason* for believing that the Congress at

Vienna was now employed in endeavouring to *unrivet the chains of the suffering Africans*; and engaged . . . in so sacred a cause, he could not consent that aspersion . . . should be cast upon them."[18] In a later Parliamentary debate, leading abolitionist William Wilberforce praised American efforts to abolish the execrable commerce, while complaining of the resistance of the Continental European powers. The Marquis of Londonderry, however, pointed out that the United States was the world leader in resisting the mutual right of search to suppress the traffic. He insisted that Wilberforce was "much mistaken, if he supposed that the principal difficulties in effecting this desirable object arose from absolute, and not from free and representative governments."[19] These exchanges revealed what was at stake when anyone commended the regime in Washington. Slavery and the political order were so intertwined that Britain's monarchists took any praise of America on antislavery grounds as an implied criticism of their preferred form of government. In turn, America's refusal to accede to the right of search handed a potent weapon to the anti-republicans.

They also welcomed the propaganda value of freeing American slaves during the War of 1812. While government officials pushed the slave policy largely for military purposes, British scribblers exploited the image of Britons as liberators. A chronicler of the 1814 military campaign in the Chesapeake was typical. He crowed that "perfect freedom—that freedom which the vaunted 'Land of Liberty' denied them—was guaranteed" to slaves running to British lines.[20]

Americans were no more prepared to submit meekly to such barbs than they were to allow the British to carry off their slaves with impunity. British West Indian slavery, as many Americans pointed out, rendered the British slave policy paradoxical at best. Americans expressed disbelief that slaveholding Britain would pursue so reckless a policy as freeing and arming American slaves, as if it had no slaves of its own. A widely reprinted editorial marveled at Britain's offer of freedom to American slaves, whom she "disciplines for our destruction. Does she forget Jamaica and Barbadoes?"[21] There must be some ulterior motive at work, they reasoned.

Such suspicions lent credence to otherwise flimsy American allegations that British officers had sold African American fugitives as slaves in the West Indies. The rumors that the British were selling African Americans as slaves seem first to have surfaced in the summer of 1813 in prowar American newspapers. The Anglophobic Niles was the most prolific in accusations and vehement in rhetoric. His pages brimmed with gleeful outrage at the idea of the British army and navy reviving, in effect, the slave trade to Britain's West Indian possessions, in the form of those African Americans they affected to be liberating. One "gallant admiral," he sniped in a typical passage, " 'delivered' upwards of 100 negroes from their old masters in *Maryland* and *Virginia* to new masters in the *West India* islands, with the common purpose that all her 'deliverances' have: which is, *to make money out of them.*"[22] "But *'religious'* England," he scoffed in another editorial, "has abolished the *slave trade!*"[23] Other papers followed Niles's lead. "One of the People," writing for the *National Intelligencer*, inveighed against Britain's government for "carrying on the slave trade, a traffic which she *pompously* abolished." Moreover, it was doing so "to a much greater advantage than she ever did before, which is by stealing them from their houses in the U. States."[24] The standard American depiction of British cupidity masquerading as humanity reached its height in such indictments.

Partisan newspapers' loose accusations assumed greater gravity early in 1815, when the Madison administration published its own allegations that Britain was trafficking in those black Americans it claimed so publicly to be liberating. It was a weak case based on one letter describing an affidavit from a supposed eyewitness, as well as some newspaper reports of losses sustained by planters; the report did not even include the affidavit.[25] Failing in its own burden of proof, the administration sought in a separate document to shift the burden to Great Britain, calling upon its government to "answer, if it can, the solemn charge against their faith and their humanity."[26] Solemn as these charges were, they rested on precious little proof.

West Indian slavery, however, was the element of plausibility in this contestation of British troops' claims to be liberators. The editors of the *National Intelligencer* developed this theme. Given British soldiers' notorious love of plunder, they asked, and in light of "the galling slavery of their West India Islands," might such men "be expected to undertake a crusade to abolish slavery?"[27] They also published a Jamaican court decision during the war that condemned slaves on board a captured American merchant vessel to be sold into slavery on that island. "The inference is strong," the editors concluded, "that slaves taken from our shores have shared the same fate."[28] They were determined to keep the English from having it both ways, supporting slavery while proclaiming themselves liberators.[29]

Nationalist Americans—both slaveholders and nonslaveholders—also sought to prevail upon the British government to return or pay for the slaves who had fled to their lines. This policy was evident at the talks at Ghent that ended the War of 1812, where the combatants' ambassadors discussed, among other things, the return of American slaves who had run to British lines. As the negotiators dealt with the many issues surrounding slavery and the war, the respective influence of antislavery men in London and of slaveholders in Washington was on full display. The lead defender of Britain's promises of freedom to the American slaves was Henry Goulbourn, the absentee master of over 200 slaves on his Jamaica plantation. It was ironic yet revealing that such as he was the proponent of Whitehall's antislavery stance in this instance.[30]

Meanwhile, the leader of the American call for return or compensation was the nonslaveholding Yankee John Quincy Adams. Adams, as diplomat during the war and then as secretary of state, insisted that Great Britain compensate slaveholders. Time and again he raised the issue with whatever British diplomat he could find, over the course of years.[31] Although this campaign involved a multitude of complex international questions in addition to the issue of property in human beings, on the Anglo-American front Adams sided with slaveholders' claims to property in the escaped African Americans. Abolitionist John Wright dedicated an 1820 pamphlet to Adams, whom he characterized as "a man whose hands have never, either directly or indirectly, been polluted with the crime of slavery."[32] He plainly knew nothing of Adams's negotiations with the British, or of his amicable discussions with John C. Calhoun about the prices the United States should demand from Britain for the slaves of different states.[33] That John Quincy Adams should have been such a bulldog in haggling over compensation for lost human property illustrated the power of American slaveholders in shaping American policy.[34]

It also revealed, as did Adams's stance on the right of search, that some Americans were willing to choose nationalism over antislavery. In a transatlantic debate that involved the very nature and reputation of America's republican institutions, many Americans North and South saw the defense of their country as of primary concern. Their concern along this line only increased after the war as they correctly perceived that discussions of American slavery in the writings of travelers and widely read literary reviewers turned on a debate over which form of government was superior.

Both the enemies and the friends of the North American republic rebuked the Yankees for their slaveholding. Especially after Britain's oligarchic political order prohibited the foreign slave trade in 1807, its proponents used the issue of slavery to face down licentious democrats wherever they found them.[35] They did not hesitate to do so against the United States, especially in the postwar years. One British reviewer, in response to an American writer who had praised America's "free and equal community," eagerly pointed to slavery as the crying contradiction of such a rosy picture. "Among this 'free people,'" he declared, "a negro may be flogged till he expires under the lash, without any violation of the rights of man."[36] English farmer William Faux found that his travels in the United States confirmed his prejudice against American republicanism. "There is, indeed, something in a real upright and downright honest John Bull," he reflected in a letter to an English friend, "that cannot be found in the sly, say-nothing, smiling, deep speculating money-hunting Jonathans of this all-men-are-born-equally-free-and-independent, negro-driving, cow-skin republic." From Americans' democratic individualism and greed, "man-stealing, . . . slavery, whips, gags, chains, and all the black catalogue of monstrous ills proceed." He far preferred the orderly society of oligarchic Britain, where "the poor negro's chains" fell off under a regime that knew what liberty meant and how to preserve it.[37]

American slavery mortified other Britons, for the United States was their model for the reforms they advocated in Britain. They could not avoid the topic, as their counterparts had done before the War of 1812.[38] Like Americans, they approached this problem in a variety of ways. Some sought to defend or downplay the evils of American slavery.[39]

American slavery disillusioned a few others with freedom as practiced in the United States. For example, upon his arrival in New York City from Britain, Henry Fearon publicly toasted America and her free institutions.[40] Yet as he traveled more extensively, Fearon came to see the United States as a place of brutality and hypocrisy. He lamented that those who mercilessly flogged and sold slaves "dare to call themselves democrats, and friends of liberty!—from such democrats, and from such friends of liberty, good Lord deliver us!" Upon his departure from America, he declared that although his love for freedom remained undimmed, "I certainly *have* experienced a most sensible diminution in my love for the *possessors* of freedom" on account of their practice of slaveholding.[41]

Still other British republicans retained their faith in America's example but concluded that the cause of liberty would forever suffer until the sole remaining republic erased the blot of chattel bondage from its landscape. The Scottish radical Frances Wright was one such. Her account of her first visit to the United States concluded with a passionate appeal for emancipation that explicitly linked it to the reputation of free government worldwide. "An awful responsibility," she declared, "has devolved on the American nation; the liberties of mankind are entrusted to their guardianship; the honor of freedom is identified with the honor of their republic." Therefore, she earnestly hoped that the day would soon arrive "when a slave will not be found in America!"[42] Another critic of American slavery offered his remarks in hope that America would abolish it and thus offer an improved model of liberty. "The great curse of America," a writer in the Whig literary journal, the *Edinburgh Review*, proclaimed, "is the institution of Slavery—of itself far more than the foulest blot upon their national character, and an evil which counterbalances the excisemen, licensers, and tax-gatherers of England." He expounded on how slavery blighted all touched by it, drawing on Jefferson's *Notes on Virginia* as well as travelers' descriptions of the domestic slave trade and American racism. "That such feelings and such practices," he concluded, "should exist among men who know the value of liberty, and profess to understand its principles, is the consummation of wickedness. Every American who loves his country, should dedicate his whole life, and every faculty of his soul, to efface this foul stain from its character."[43] He later insisted that he did not "call upon other nations to hate and despise America for" its slavery—"but upon *the Americans themselves* to wipe away this foul blot from their character."[44]

Notwithstanding such disclaimers, many Americans read every British pronouncement on American slavery as aiding monarchists' attacks on the embattled cause of freedom and responded accordingly. As one put it, American slavery should not come between "the friends of freedom, in every country," as they sought to "unite in exposing to the detestation of the world, tyranny and oppression." Indeed, he perceived that "a great contest is going on, in which is involved, the issue of the freedom, or slavery of the world."[45] Another wrote that Americans should not allow "canting hypocrites, bedridden enthusiasts, and sly-booted politicians" to succeed in their drive to identify "our free institutions, as far as possible, with that unhappy system of slavery, which can never be sufficiently lamented."[46] More was at stake than the freedom or slavery of African Americans when Britons attacked American slaveholding.

James Madison shared this nationalist worldview and helped shape the debate from his retirement at Montpelier. Madison read Britons' mounting postwar criticisms of American slavery with indignation, confident that they were nothing more or less than a key element in an absolutist onslaught against republicanism. In 1819, antislavery Philadelphian Robert Walsh asked Madison for information on Virginia slavery for use in his proposed plan to, as Madison put it, "vindicate our Country against misrepresentations propagated abroad." Madison's response argued that the American Revolution had given white Virginians greater respect for human rights and had freed Virginians black and white from the large slaveholdings attributable to aristocratic British property laws. Both increasing humanitarianism and the decreasing size of units of slave property translated into better treatment of slaves. In short, colonial slavery, itself "chargeable in so great degree on the very quarter which has furnished most of the libellers," was much worse than slavery under the enlightened American republic.[47] This interpretation of the Revolution was a necessary function of his tenacity in defending America's experiment with representative government from monarchists' reproach. For Madison, this attack on free government was also personal, for he had staked his entire career on demonstrating to a skeptical world that representative government benefited all who lived under it.[48]

It was one thing for the Virginia slaveholder Madison to whitewash American slavery. It was quite another when Walsh parroted Virginia defenses in his response to British critics. As a patriot as well as a cosmopolitan man of letters, British rebukes of America stung him bitterly.[49] His *Appeal from the Judgments of Great Britain* responded to several British calumniations of the United States, but he devoted particular attention to refuting their claims on slavery and the slave trade. "Our negro slavery," admitted Walsh, was the point "on which we appear most vulnerable, and against which the reviewers have directed their fiercest attacks." He set out to defend against such assaults by any means necessary, for he recognized that issues surrounding slavery "vitally affect national character."[50] In defending America's character, Walsh borrowed heavily from the necessary-evil defense of slavery. He contended that immediate emancipation was impracticable, because of the slaves' *"unfitness for freedom,* no less than the danger to the white inhabitants." American slaves were better prepared for freedom than West Indian slaves who suffered under harsher British slavery, but they were still far from ready. Thus the Southern planters, who happened, "without their own fault, to be afflicted with the curse of negro slavery," had strong pleas of expediency in maintaining it. In fact, said Walsh in a passage that could have been written by any planter, it was true wisdom in America's Founders to leave slavery to be regulated by the states. Otherwise this delicate question "would have been placed at the mercy of men incapable, like the Edinburgh Reviewers, of understanding it thoroughly."[51]

While denying the fault of Americans in the original slave trade, Walsh left no doubt as to whose fault it was. Predictably, it was Britain's. Despite the imperial power's implantation of slavery into North America, Walsh insisted, the Americans since independence had abolished the slave trade—and had done all they could to mitigate an evil they could not eradicate. How, he demanded, could the *Edinburgh Review* castigate the American as *"the murderer and scourger of slaves,"* when the United States' slave population doubled every twenty-six years? "The population of Great Britain, as appears by authentic documents, does not double in less than *eighty years.*"[52] And, again drawing on Madison, Walsh insisted that the American Revolution had produced this amelioration of slavery, so that "the negro has gained nearly as much by our separation from Great Britain as the white."[53] Thus, rebukes for American slavery came with particularly bad grace from the oligarchs of Great Britain, whose rule was disastrous for anyone it touched, of whatever color.

Walsh took a different tack when writing purely for domestic consumption. In advocating the prohibition of slavery in Missouri, he appealed to the British as worthy of emulation and conceded more national guilt over slavery (in the hope that America would atone for it by restriction in Missouri) than he was willing to admit on the Atlantic stage.[54] In short, Walsh drew upon slave-holders' standard defenses of slavery only when he faced Great Britain on the world stage. He would not stand by and let the anti-American oligarchs of Britain malign his country's institutions, even if they said no more from across the Atlantic than he was willing to say for a domestic audience. In this instance, his nationalism trumped his antislavery.

Americans did not always have to choose between antislavery principles and vindicating their nation. For if they spent most of the early nineteenth century on the defensive in relation to slavery, they were sometimes able to go on the attack themselves. Their best opportunity of this sort came with the revival of the African slave trade under the auspices of the French and Iberian monarchies that Britain had restored to power. "The *slave trade*," Hezekiah Niles noted in late 1814, "has been 'restored' by the 'royal Bourbons.' . . . Let *Africa* 'rejoice,' and *humanity* 'repose in the arms of its legitimate sovereign.'"[55] An 1817 article carried Niles's telling headline: " '*Restoration*'—Upwards of six thousand six hundred slaves were imported into the Havanna the first week in the last month."[56] For such authors, the restoration of monarchy and the Atlantic slave trade proved too good a coincidence to be resisted, for it gave them an offensive weapon against this revitalized political menace.

Another offensive tactic of the American nationalists was to appeal to white supremacy by juxtaposing Britain's boasted abolitionism with its oppression of white people. This shifted the focus away from American slavery while simultaneously decrying perceived special treatment for Africans. Philadelphia editor William Duane noted that while Britain's Foreign Secretary, Viscount Castlereagh, was at the Congress of Vienna, he pushed hard for cooperation on slave trade abolition as he carved up Europe among the newly restored monarchies. Thus, "while the *league of despots*" was signing the "treaties which handed over about forty millions of *white men to new masters*," Castlereagh "manifested the

most pious concern for the poor Africans." This, added to the United Kingdom's oppression of the Irish Catholics, meant that Britain's rulers claimed a
sympathy for Africans, who were "a race in a state of nature without religion
or social institutions," while simultaneously subjugating their white Christian
neighbors.[57] "An Enemy of Hypocrisy and Slavery" similarly complained that
the likes of Wilberforce "feel only for the wrongs of Africa, and the distresses of
people with a black skin." For while opposing the slave trade, such "Saints"
supported "every measure of ministerial folly, cupidity, and oppression" that
had gone to suppress the rights of "white slaves" in Poland, Ireland, Spain,
Norway, and England itself. He whined that those "under the misfortune of
being white" received none of the vaunted humanity of the British oligarchs.[58]
Nationalistic Americans spared no tactic, offensive or defensive, to parry the
blows against their cherished system of government, which they detected in
Britons' assorted statements in relation to American slavery.

———————

Nationalists were not the only Americans to join the transatlantic debate,
however. Were all Americans of the persuasion of an Adams or a Walsh, the
international politics of slavery after the War of 1812 might have rescued harmony out of the growing domestic discord over Southern slavery. But this was
not to be. Instead, the British involvement in the politics of slavery deepened
the many fissures within the United States.

One such fissure was the partisan and sectional one between Federalists and
Republicans. Disgruntled Federalists chafing under the Republican yoke found
themselves more in sympathy with Great Britain's abolitionists than with most
of their compatriots. For instance, Federalists gave less credit to the Republican
Congress than to Great Britain for slave trade abolition.[59] In December 1814, a
Federalist newspaper acknowledged the French king's determination to revive
the slave trade in his empire but pointedly remarked that these developments
were "regretted extremely by the philanthropists of England."[60] And in 1818,
the same paper reprinted an article from a French journal that trumpeted "the
suppression of the odious traffic in slaves" by the monarchies of Europe and
drew the moral that "the time is come when nations will be emancipated by the
wisdom of Kings." This notice was part of the French paper's paean to the
progress of "regulated liberty."[61] While the Republicans sought to rebut such
antislavery pretensions from the kings of Europe, Federalists did not feel compelled to do so; after all, "regulated liberty" was something Federalists could
appreciate.

Federalists, even more than most Britons, were accustomed to using Southern slavery to upbraid the hypocritical democrats ruling the United States. They were not about to abandon that stance when the international image of the United States entered the picture—far from it. In 1816, for instance, an anonymous Federalist writer urged his nationalist compatriots to tone down their expressions of national vanity in light of the vicious bondage of and trade in African Americans. "Whatever we may imagine," he lectured the Republicans, "our country is *not* 'the last and only refuge of the oppressed';—we are *not* 'the only free people on earth.' Slavery, degrading slavery, exists in the very heart of our political institutions." While the dictates of humanity had "reached even to the thrones of Kings and compelled them to unite in measures" for the universal abolition of the slave trade, this author cried, the domestic slave trade, and even the kidnapping of free blacks, were carried on in the very capital of the United States. In light of such shameful things, he thundered, "let the boast of equal rights and impartial laws be hushed, or they will be silenced by the cries of the much wronged African.—Let the vaunters of our national glory be stilled!"[62]

The editor of the prominent Boston Federalist organ, the *Columbian Centinel*, tinged his charges of inconsistency with a more specifically partisan edge. He put them in the mouth of an English sailor who saw a slave coffle marching through the streets of Washington. The seaman approached the slave driver and "thus sarcastically addressed him:—'*May it please your honor, Captain, send up you* [*sic*] *signal of* "FREE TRADE AND NO IMPRESSMENT." ' "[63] An 1815 editorial from Philadelphia Federalist Zachariah Poulson railed against North Carolina's governor, who had pardoned a white man who whipped a black man to death. A jury had convicted him, but the majority of the citizens of North Carolina— "one of the States boasting to be the most enlightened in the world"—reveled in the pardon, and surely would hold some "public feast" to celebrate this act of returning the killer "to the bosom of their enlightened society . . ., duly commissioned to whip more negroes to death." "A man of high rank and wealth," Poulson scolded, had recently been "hanged in one of the West India Islands, *under the British Government*, for killing a black under very similar circumstances of cruelty. But Great Britain executes her laws without any regard to the rights of man as understood and practised in the enlightened State of North-Carolina."[64] Sectionalism and partisanship combined with humanity in Federalist diatribes such as this, which could have been written by an English traveler.

Antislavery fervor less mingled with partisanship fired American abolitionists, whose opposition to chattel bondage only increased in the face of British critiques. When this small minority was forced to choose between unquestioning loyalty to America's reputation and opposition to slavery, they chose the latter. They recoiled at the nationalists' palliation of American slavery and preferred to cooperate with and draw strength from British abolitionists. Some such were John Kenrick and George Bourne, both advocates of immediate emancipation. Their writings extracted freely from leading Members of Parliament speaking against the slave trade and slavery, as well as from British abolitionist writings.[65] Other abolitionists used their compatriots' concern with national image to goad them toward antislavery. The antislavery Virginian Edward Coles played this card when walking through the District of Columbia with his boss, President Madison, during the War of 1812. Pointing to slave coffles marching through the nation's capital, he jeered that it was good that no foreign minister from a country "less boastful perhaps of its regard for the rights of man, but more observant of them," was with them to witness such a spectacle.[66] In 1818, a Pennsylvania abolitionist, suing for the release of a group of African Americans from the custody of a slave trader, appealed to the judge's national and state pride. Pointing out that Africans had been free in England for decades, he exclaimed: "Will it not raise the color of your honor's face, to think that personal liberty in Pennsylvania, . . . the bulwark of the liberty of conscience, should be, or is less sacred than it is in England?"[67]

Although it had its uses, on the whole, American abolitionists regarded overweening national pride as harmful to their cause.[68] For when attacks on slavery came from Britons, too many Americans were too busy circling their wagons around the standard of national reputation to see the justice of the attacks. Such was the point of view of a Unitarian minister in the nation's capital, John Wright, who wrote a fiery abolitionist response to American nationalists' arguments in the 1819–1820 pamphlet war touched off by the *Edinburgh Review*'s strictures on American slavery. Whereas the likes of Madison and Walsh extenuated American slavery because they saw the reputation of America's republican experiment as crucial to the cause of human freedom, Wright assigned precedence to emancipation. He complained that the nationalist defenses of American slavery had served to "injure the cause of humanity," for they had "attempted to inflame the minds of the 'American people,' to call forth their worst feelings, and thereby to lead them from the criminal features of slavery." Wright claimed to write "in defence of the unalienable rights of man," seeking to "aid the genuine friends of humanity in their benevolent exertions to drive the *lingering* foe from his last refuge."[69]

In part because Wright saw America as the last refuge not of liberty but of slavery, he would have none of the self-satisfied nationalists' shifting of blame to the British. Diverting attention from the Atlantic slave trade that Americans had so proudly prohibited, he denounced such growing and peculiarly American practices as the domestic slave trade and kidnapping of free blacks, as well as the cruelty of Southern slaveowners.[70] He dismissed the tired argument that Britain somehow forced American colonists to buy slaves, pointing to the Virginia colonial legislature's petitions to the Crown to allow them to tap into the African slave trade.[71] In a final appeal to Americans to live up to their vaunted sense of superiority, Wright asserted that "had the people of England that control over *their* government which the people of this country have over *theirs*, the trade would have been abolished twenty or thirty years before it was abolished by this country."[72] The travelers and reviewers, he suggested, had every right to rebuke a people who controlled their own destiny, yet clung to and even expanded the institution of chattel bondage.

Although the uncompromising vision of Wright was rare, the sense that America must abolish slavery in order to preserve its character in the world spread within the North in the late 1810s. As slavery became a leading issue for some Republicans who had previously suppressed their aversion to slavery for the purposes of partisan unity, some—even some strong nationalists—became increasingly willing to cooperate with Great Britain against slavery, and even to acknowledge the superiority of the British record. Hezekiah Niles, for instance, surely astonished many of his readers when, beginning in 1816, he lauded British efforts against the Atlantic commerce in slaves. While not prepared to entirely suspend his skepticism about their motives, he was willing to give the British the benefit of the doubt, and even to talk of how the right of search was necessary to end the infernal traffic.[73] William Duane also inched toward assent to British condemnation of America's record on slavery. In early 1819, he quoted another paper's plaintive cry in reaction to the internal slave trade: "Have we no magnanimous champion of freedom" in the United States? "No Wilberforce, no Fox, no Sharpe, no Clarkson?"[74] Like a growing number of Northerners, as Duane became increasingly disturbed at the inroads of America's aggressive slave regime, he castigated his country's acquiescence to slavery in terms familiar to its British antagonists.[75]

Yet if some Northern opponents of slavery were willing to talk of national guilt, others evinced a determination to sectionalize that guilt. Britons, usually seeing what they expected and wanted to see, tended to lump all Americans together.[76] This irked Northern sectionalists, who laid the blame for this national blemish at the feet of the South alone. A Fourth of July fete in Massachusetts featured two consecutive toasts meant to separate the Bay State from its Southern neighbors. One was to "*Massachusetts*—Proud of her *freedom*, and proud that she holds no man a *slave*." The next sardonically raised the glass to "*Slavery.*—Her last refuge from persecution is in *Republican America*."[77] One Yankee writer wished that "that section of our country" would "at least forbear to shock the feelings of the world" by continuing the domestic slave trade in broad daylight.[78] A New England literary reviewer complained that Britons' rebukes libeled "the whole nation from north to south." If they had limited their attacks to the Madison administration, this Federalist protested, "we should not have interfered in the quarrel." But the British reviewers' censures on American slavery "carry into every library in England a collected mass of calumny and falsehood against a whole nation."[79]

Yale president Timothy Dwight also pursued this sectionalist strategy. As one who hated to see anything come between the better classes in the United States and Great Britain, Dwight was determined not to let Britons tar his kind with the brush of slavery.[80] He pointed out that "the slave-holding States" had insisted on the constitutional clause that allowed the Atlantic slave trade to continue for at least twenty years. "Blame them for this part of their conduct as much as you please," he wrote. "I shall feel no inducement to refute the charge." He only asked that British critics recognize Northern states' measures against the slave trade.[81] "One of the most extensive kinds of misrepresentation adopted by European travelers in the United States," he complained, "is found in the use of the word *American*." "An inhabitant of New England," he chided careless foreign observers, detested seeing the "characteristics of other states of the union . . . applied to his own." These characteristics included cruelty to slaves.[82]

Nationalists registered their contempt for such sectional selfishness. One grumbled that the only defense of American slavery he had seen from New Englanders consisted "pretty much in an admission of most of the charges, provided an exception is made in favour of New-England." "For ourselves," he lectured, "we know of no such discriminating patriotism as this; and however it may be the fashion in that portion of the union to offer up their brethren as sacrifices to their own interests," he would defend the entire United States.[83] "An Enemy to Slavery and Hypocrisy" was deeply offended by one abolition-ist's dissemination of British criticisms to further the cause of antislavery. "A malignant foreigner," he complained, "had thrown a *bone* among us," and this American enthusiast "caused us all to gather about, and snarl, and bite, and play the dog, and bark away each other's good name."[84]

White Southerners came to expect such abandonment from Yankees, however, and were all the more sensitive to British criticism for it. This was evident in a dramatic episode involving William Faux. In the summer of 1819 while in South Carolina, Faux heard the shocking tale of a slave being whipped to death and wrote of his horror in a letter published in the *Charleston Courier*, among other prints. "A great noise was heard," he noted, when that number of the *Courier* appeared. South Carolina's attorney general admonished Faux that he had "stained the character of South Carolina" and groaned that his letter would be "greedily copied and extensively read to our injury, in the northern and eastern states, and all over Europe." Others confirmed that the letter was offensive largely "because it would make a deep impression to their prejudice in the northern states." John Wright congratulated Faux "on having dared to attack the beast in his temple," but no white Carolinian did so. In fact, the less violently disposed cautioned Faux "against being out late in the evening" in Charleston.[85] He had publicly maligned South Carolina on its tenderest point, and its white inhabitants were confident that Yankees would not come to their aid—indeed, quite the opposite.

As the Faux affair suggested, Britons' forays against American slavery, together with the feeling that Northerners could hardly be trusted as allies, confirmed many white Southerners' sense that their increasingly peculiar institution was under ideological siege. In such a setting, some slaveholders moved toward a full-scale defense of slavery as a positive good. Yet they did so hesitantly, evidently because they knew a principled affirmation of slavery's goodness put them outside the mainstream of thought in the Atlantic world.

In 1819, one beleaguered slaveholder argued that slavery was a positive good and simultaneously denied that he was doing so. In his pseudonymous response to the *Edinburgh Review*'s commentary on American slavery, "An American" complained that British antislavery writings only served to "encourage the zealots and enthusiasts of this country, by affording the sanction of" Britain's "high character" to their wild abolitionist schemes.[86] On first blush, much of his defense against British calumnies on slavery looked familiar. He pointed to the British role in the African slave trade and trumpeted what he presented as America's timely and unanimous action to ban that traffic.[87] Yet even as this essayist sought to contest Britons' exclusive claims to humanitarianism, he was uncomfortable with the philanthropy stalking the Anglophone world. He evinced his ambivalence when he wrote that post-Revolutionary Virginians had been "not only intrepidly, but *rashly* humane" in allowing manumissions on a large scale. He had come to believe that humanitarian zeal was useless. Moralists may declaim against African slavery, he asserted, but "there are moral as well as physical evils in this world, which no human agency can remove. You cannot wash the Ethiop white, nor can you impart to him the active intelligence of the homo sapiens Europaeus."[88]

Although futile, reformist zeal was not harmless. "An American" alleged that it was an insidious threat to order in the world, especially for slaveholders. He maintained that abolitionist agitation had produced slave revolts from St. Domingue to the British West Indies. He raged against antislavery zealots as blithely unaware "that philanthropists were at all responsible for the miseries which they bring upon mankind." It was easy for them to talk of humanity that cost them nothing to effect and that procured for them "distinction as well as profit. But what is sport to one may be death, literally death, to thousands of others."[89]

Antislavery enthusiasts were also simply wrong about slavery, "An American" argued. He allowed that at some future period, African Americans might be emancipated. Yet from this perfunctory nod to eventual emancipation, he proceeded to assert the legitimacy of slavery on grounds of natural and especially biblical law. He contended that, given its sanction of slavery, the Old Testament "must be abandoned as an absolute imposture, if the law authorizing slavery is not of divine" origin. How, then, could the Scottish reviewer "exculpate himself from the charge of blasphemy against the Most High," when he called domestic slavery "the 'consummation of all wickedness?'" Maintaining that neither Christ Himself nor his original disciples condemned slavery, he demanded to know whether "the christians of the present day pretend to be wiser than God Almighty—more merciful than Christ—more humane, more pious, more conscientious, more moral, than the Apostles! Let them beware!"[90]

Yet even as this author ventured into proslavery territory, he hedged his bets. He sought to soften his biblical commentaries by emphasizing that he did not "introduce these quotations from the Old Testament and the new, with a view to justify slavery. Whether they do justify it or not, let every reader decide for himself." He stressed that American slaveholders "do not justify it, but merely tolerate it, to avoid a greater evil."[91] He took a few steps toward proslavery from the antiabolitionist standpoint of most of his predecessors in the Revolutionary generation, but thoroughly advocating slavery was manifestly uncomfortable even for this staunch defender of slavery's embattled citadel.[92]

That discomfort flowed from a justifiable sense that the defense of chattel bondage had become an unconventional position in the Atlantic world. The cultural leaders of that world, the British, leaned decidedly toward antislavery.

There were some exceptions, of course, in Great Britain.[93] But by the end of the eighteenth century, antislavery in its various guises had become undeniably fashionable in Great Britain. The abolitionists' prestige in Britain only waxed as the nineteenth century proceeded.[94] This domestic stature carried over to the Atlantic stage, even in Anglophobic America. Nothing demonstrated their influence on world opinion better than the diplomatic exchanges, cabinet discussions, editorials, and congressional debates in which American officials protested their attachment to suppression of the slave trade while resisting the right of search. Americans would not let the British stigmatize them as backward on slave trade abolition and therefore friendly to slavery.[95]

––––––––––

But if the Atlantic slave trade was still an issue on which Americans enjoyed a broad consensus, Britons' geopolitical usages of American slavery intensified the disagreements among Americans. Some antislavery nationalists, to be sure, subordinated their convictions on Southern bondage to their overriding commitment to the cause and reputation of free government in a world of tyrants. For others, the very issues over which they waged the War of 1812 collided with the slave trade abolition imperative, to the latter's disadvantage. For these reasons, in addition to the sway slaveholders held over the national government, America often played the less-than-heroic role of the slaveholding rebel against British humanity on the Atlantic stage.

Yet the nationalist position was only one of many on the American political spectrum, even when attacked by the hated foreign foe. The internal debate over slavery in the United States was heated enough on its own in the second decade of the nineteenth century, but British assaults tended to raise the temperature even further, contributing to the hardening of positions all along the continuum of American opinion. As a result of their shooting war and war of words with Great Britain, Americans once again saw the bonds of their still-fragile Union attenuated by their disagreements over slavery. Like its domestic American counterparts in the 1810s, the Anglo-American debate about liberty and national institutions proved a catalyst for key developments in competing ideologies and sectional stances toward slavery.

The Political Impact of
African Americans

IF THE DISPUTES of partisan Americans and Britons kept slavery on the national agenda after 1808, so did developments within the institution itself. These included the actions of people subjugated by or recently freed from slavery. Although most had no formal political voice, African Americans nevertheless shaped the politics of slavery in the United States as they pushed against slavery and racism. Their actions did not aim foremost at influencing the debates of white Americans, but rather at securing freedom and equality for themselves. But no matter their motives, slaves' and free blacks' assertiveness helped to ensure that slavery was a delicate political topic between the abolition of the Atlantic slave trade and the Missouri Crisis.

At first glance, that this became a bone of contention was surprising. Most white Americans did not welcome black Americans' aggressiveness, agreeing that slaves and free blacks were a subversive element. Indeed, white Northerners and Southerners shared concerns about the danger black Americans posed, which prompted them to support the American Colonization Society (ACS), an attempt to remove free people of color from the United States. But as with other questions related to slavery, African Americans' behavior, actual and imagined, entered American politics as an agent of discord. It joined other aspects of slavery as a tool in partisan politics. Meanwhile, slaveholders' attempts to control the black population exacerbated North-South sectionalism. Many white Northerners recoiled at the draconian measures slaveholders and their representatives pursued to this end. And when the masters pursued fugitive slaves into the North, sectional tensions only increased. For their part, white Southerners found themselves further alienated from their Northern brethren when some of the latter countenanced slave flight and revolt. This led some of them to reject the ACS as Yankee meddling and to experiment with more thorough defenses of slavery to answer Northerners' reflections on slave revolt.

Thus, African Americans' unwillingness to submit easily to slavery and other abuses helped keep American slavery in the political mix, stimulating the dialectic between North and South. As residents of one section came to believe their rights were under siege, they responded with what they thought of as defensive measures and their counterparts saw as new aggressions. This cycle, set in motion in many instances by black people's actions, helped convince many whites that the Mason-Dixon Line and the Ohio River separated two very different, and perhaps incompatible, regions.

———

Slave rebelliousness boiled over in the second decade of the nineteenth century. As grievances associated with the expansion of slavery grew in the slave quarters, the free black community matured, and Haiti maintained its exemplary force, slaveholders and their allies looked with mounting anxiety upon the United States' restive enslaved population.[1] Masters also knew that their human chattel customarily took advantage of divisions in the white community. And true to form, many slaves exploited the War of 1812 and related conflicts to flee and rebel.[2]

The largest slave revolt in the history of the United States took place in this disordered setting. In January 1811, between 180 and 500 slaves and maroons in southern Louisiana rose up in arms, causing considerable consternation throughout that section of the territory. The insurrection ended after three days, when militia joined with federal troops to vanquish the rebels. Officials reported 66 rebels killed in battle, as well as 21 executed by a hastily convened parish tribunal. The insurgents killed two whites, inflicting mostly property damage.[3] This uprising cast a long shadow over Louisiana's psyche in ensuing years.[4] Chaos and political uncertainty throughout the Gulf of Mexico as Spain and the United States pursued competing territorial claims had formed part of the background to the 1811 rebellion.[5]

The upheaval of the War of 1812 also set many slaves elsewhere in the United States in motion against their bondage. Thousands found flight to British lines the most viable escape route, while others gambled that wartime conditions would aid violent resistance. In both 1812 and 1813, the authorities uncovered large conspiracies in Virginia whose instigators claimed to be counting on British aid. Some plotters told their interrogators that they had heard about the impending war "from the poor people in the neighborhood, and by hearing the newspapers read," while one of their betrayers claimed to have seen British agents circulating among black Virginians.[6] When officials in Frederick, Maryland, uncovered a slave conspiracy in August 1814, they learned that the rebels planned to attack the town "when a large number of the militia was called out."[7]

Such incidents and conditions produced deep insurrection anxiety in the minds of white Southerners during the War of 1812. The private letters of both military and civilian officials in the slave states bore witness to their disquietude.[8] Rumors of slave revolt spread like wildfire when British forces approached slaveholding areas, such as in Washington, D.C., in the summer of 1814.[9] That fateful summer campaign also saw slaveholders in Maryland and Washington "refugeeing" their slaves, driving them inland to keep them from running to the British armies or rising in revolt on their approach.[10] During their second contest with Great Britain, much as during their first, slaveholders were convinced they had much to fear from an internal foe.

Wartime conditions opened opportunities for slaves to flee or rebel, but the Peace of Ghent hardly ended rumors of slave resistance. For instance, two slave plots alarmed many Southern whites in 1816. In March, the inhabitants surrounding Spotsylvania County, Virginia, discovered a plot among slaves there headed by a white man, one George Boxley. This conspiracy, which apparently also involved many slaves and white accomplices in Fredericksburg and Richmond, "agitated the public mind in the neighboring counties" for weeks—in part because Boxley escaped from jail and was never recaptured.[11] "Boxley's insurrection" distressed public officials as far away as South Carolina. It not only raised the specter of slave revolt, but also proved that some white Southerners were unsafe for slavery.[12] White South Carolinians feared insurrection closer to home as well. Bondsmen in and around Camden had set 4 July 1816 as the date to rise up against their masters. Authorities arrested seventeen slaves, convicting seven and executing five. Their action failed, however, to prevent "considerable alarm" in the region roundabout.[13] These two conspiracies were only the most serious of a rash of plots, murders, and other acts of violence attributed to, perpetrated by, or contemplated by slaves throughout the South in the 1810s.[14] Newspaper columns also reported numerous arsons in the South, many of them attributable to slave incendiaries.[15]

No matter how scattered and ineffectual in freeing their perpetrators, acts of violent resistance exacted a heavy toll on the white South's psyche. "The danger to be apprehended to our town from an attack of the enemy," the *Norfolk Herald* lamented during the War of 1812, "is safety to what is to be apprehended from the lurking incendiary. We are always prepared for an open and declared enemy; but no measures can be taken to guard our property against the fell designs of the incendiary."[16] In 1816, citizens in Cumberland County, Virginia, implored their state government to make examples of two slaves convicted of poisoning whites in their neighborhood. These beleaguered people detected a widespread spirit of revolt among America's human chattel. "The slaves in many parts of the United States," they insisted, "have made attempt to make themselves Masters of our Country by rising in arms against us." They saw the poisonings as an adjunct to this general striving for mastery.[17] By 1818, Virginia's state legislators had come to expect a certain level of slave resistance. They forecast that the state's coffers would receive $7,000 for the "Sale of transported slaves" in the upcoming fiscal year.[18]

If violent resistance was not limited to the War of 1812, neither was slave flight. Some fugitives stayed in the South as maroons, and they were relatively numerous in the 1810s.[19] They played a part in such revolts as the Louisiana rebellion of 1811 and in such plots as one in Georgia in 1819.[20] Authorities endeavored to disperse maroon communities in South Carolina and Louisiana.[21] Toward the end of 1816, South Carolina's governor called for renewed efforts in the face of repeated failures to destroy maroon communities in the Low Country's swamps, which had become a magnet for runaways and a menace because of their robberies.[22] Simultaneously, the white citizens in and around Edenton, North Carolina, hoped to break up, "if possible, the numerous camps of runaway negroes, who outrage the peace and quiet of the neighborhood."[23] In the late 1810s, Amelia Island, on the border of Georgia and Florida, hosted a maroon community of well over one hundred fugitive slaves, which weakened the planters' hold on their human property in the region.[24] The largest and most threatening maroon community was "the Negro Fort," a fortified settlement of fugitives on the Apalachicola River in Florida. Runaway slaves had joined forces with Seminole Indians in Florida early in the decade to successfully resist American incursions.[25] These colored guerrillas also received British aid during the War of 1812 and remained in possession of the fort after the war ended. Such was their strength there that this became the largest maroon community in the history of North America before U.S. troops destroyed it in 1816.[26] Planters throughout the South rejoiced at its destruction, for its example had reached much farther than the region from which it attracted runaway slaves. A Mississippi Territory judge, for instance, wrote that its very existence was "highly prejudicial to the interests of the southern states" as a whole.[27]

Neither were the maroon communities within the South the only threat from free African Americans that slaveholders feared. For free black enclaves were growing in Eastern cities, fed not only by manumissions but also by runaway slaves. As the North's commitment to freedom grew, places like Philadelphia beckoned to an increasing number of fugitive slaves who hoped to blend in with the large free black population.[28] In the second decade of the nineteenth century, the city of Baltimore became more than ever a haven for runaways.[29] The growth in the North and at the edge of the Upper South alarmed slaveholders enough. But the number of free blacks also multiplied in the very heart of the most dynamic slave region in the United States—New Orleans. In 1809, a wave of refugees from Haiti doubled the free black population of New Orleans, causing grave concern in the minds of many whites.[30]

Free black communities were also maturing and growing more autonomous. Nothing indicated this better than when Pennsylvania's Supreme Court granted the African Methodist Episcopal (AME) Church its independence in 1816. With strong branches in Philadelphia and Baltimore, the AME quickly extended its reach even to Southern cities such as Charleston. Its very existence as "an independent ecclesiastical organization," whites feared, "gave the idea and produced the sentiment of personal freedom and responsibility in the Negro."[31] Freedmen and freedwomen also proclaimed their individuality by means of "exuberant cultural display" in such places as New York City. The potential and actuality of violence had hastened many a manumission in New York as the uncertain process of gradual emancipation lurched forward after 1799, and the people who emerged into precarious freedom as a result of this process "wanted to be seen" as "assertive and proudly defiant." They got their wish.[32] Free people of color also aggressively maintained their rights in other enclaves from Boston to Baltimore.[33] Where enfranchised, they exerted influence as swing voters in some close elections.[34] They put forward their own interpretations of American history and appropriated white political forms and culture in their celebrations of the abolition of the slave trade. Whites' vicious satires of their abolition celebrations were evidence of how much they irritated the majority, even in the North.[35]

Free African Americans also proved their political acumen as they astutely manipulated Northern whites' pride and prejudice to defend their rights. They spoke from the common ground of shared national pride, speaking of the United States as "our happy country," or as "the most virtuous republic on earth"—at least in theory, which they hoped to see aligned with practice.[36]

They hoped their deeds in the War of 1812, notably the role free black soldiers played in the defense of New Orleans, would reinforce this image of patriotic black Americans.[37] But they also knew their audience's sectional prejudices and heaped special praise on the free states. For instance, when Philadelphian James Forten protested an 1813 proposal to establish a registration system for Pennsylvania's African Americans, he urged the legislators not to imitate the oppression of the slave states. People the world over looked to Pennsylvania for an example of humanity and liberty, he reminded his readers. Therefore, "for the honor and dignity of our native state," he hoped the bill would not pass into law.[38] Other free black leaders in the North found this formula effective; in a growing body of public literature, including resolutions of meetings and sermons, they flattered white Northerners on their emancipationist example and love of liberty, urging them to stand by and even extend them.[39]

African Americans' response to proposals to colonize them to Africa demonstrated their determination to speak for themselves, as well as their proficiency at doing so. The ACS scheme had the appeal of Africa in the African American dual identity, but they put their American foot forward in combating this project, if not always the idea of colonization per se.[40] They might colonize, a meeting of free blacks in Georgetown, D.C., granted, but only if they could settle some "territory within the limits of our beloved Union."[41] A January 1817 meeting of free blacks in Philadelphia, led by James Forten, couched their rejection of the ACS in language that Forten had used so effectively in the past. They resolved "against the contemplated measure, that is to exile us from the land of our nativity." They expressed their "strongest confidence" that the "philanthropy of the free states" would militate against the ACS.[42] But just to be sure, in August 1817, Forten, joined by preacher Russell Parrott, addressed another attack on the ACS "to the humane and benevolent Inhabitants of . . . Philadelphia," hoping to enlist their libertarian pride in preventing the progress of this organization.[43] In resisting colonization they showed just how attached they were to their American homeland and its ideology of freedom and equality.[44]

The essential point for white Americans, however, was not what free blacks said so much as that they were bent on crashing the white preserve of formal politics by expressing their own minds on the subject. That free black people were drawing on American ideology and pushing for inclusion in their respective larger communities was of no comfort to most white Americans. Free black people were entering directly into politics, as well as indirectly, by enabling enslaved black people's flight from slavery. This independent spirit—and the space within which they could act upon it—was exactly what alarmed slave-holders and their allies the most about the growing free black communities in the United States.[45]

Everywhere white Americans looked, then, black people seemed to be asserting themselves in dangerous ways. This created certain baseline assumptions in whites both North and South. These included the belief that slaves universally panted for liberty and would resort to violence to gain it when given the opportunity. A corollary to this doctrine held that free blacks' unity of interest with slaves and general deportment threatened slavery in the South and order in the North.

White Southerners held a common apprehension of the effects of a growing and assertive free black population. It was evident in their legislatures' restrictions on manumission and attempts to drive or keep free African Americans out of their respective states.[46] It was manifest in the memorials of their citizens. In 1817, for example, the citizens of Isle of Wight County petitioned the Virginia legislature for more "efficient laws for the restraint & controul of" free blacks and slaves. In light of "several Murders" committed by blacks in their county within the past year, they declared that "neither the persons, or the property, of the Citizens, can be considered in a state of safety." "Intercourse between slaves and free persons," they concluded, "is calculated to produce crimes of the most serious and dreadful consequences, to promote insubordination & a spirit of disobedience among the slaves, & finally to lead to insurrection & blood."[47] Such notions led the vast majority of Southern whites to agree that removal or restraint of free blacks was imperative.

Many white Northerners shared this fear of free African Americans. Their vicious satires on free blacks provided ample evidence of their racial insecurities. So did their rhetoric when they joined white Southerners to create the ACS in 1816. Concern for safety and order in both North and South was arguably its key founding principle.[48] To be sure, many Northern supporters spoke in terms of the humanity of this philanthropic project to improve the lot of free blacks and render emancipation more likely while also Christianizing Africa. But this concern for Southern slavery mixed in with a drive to rid the North of free blacks.[49]

As for Southern colonizationists, they came in many varieties. Some still held to the Revolutionary formula, admitting slavery to be an evil but pointing to the inevitability of race war unless the freed (but still alienated) black people were removed.[50] But other Southern colonizationists openly welcomed it as a scheme to strengthen the peculiar institution by removing its greatest hazard, the free black population.[51] What held people of such diverse viewpoints together in the ACS was a conviction that free African Americans posed an unacceptable risk to the American social order. In its most public and moderate documents, its leaders depicted free blacks as a degraded, discontented, and thus dangerous "banditti," arguing that colonization was as much an act of self-interested patriotism as of humanity.[52]

Fear of racial convulsions also helped determine that the African coast would be the location of the proposed colony, rather than the American West or Haiti, as some advocates of removal proposed. At the founding of the ACS, its secretary insisted that if located in North America, the colony "would become the asylum of fugitives and runaway slaves."[53] Congressional leaders agreed. Early in 1817, a House committee report rejected the idea of an African American colony in the western territories. Should such a colony "so increase as to become a nation," they averred, "it is not difficult to foresee the quarrels and destructive wars which would ensue, especially if the slavery of people of color should continue, and accompany the whites in their migrations."[54] The United States had not just cleared the Southwest of foreign and Indian threats to create a maroon threat in its place. Neither did most of its citizens wish to see the nation of Haiti strengthened by African American immigrants. Some hoped free blacks would heed the Haitian government's invitation to settle there.[55] But most agreed with a writer who stressed that "every thing tending to the increase of a black population in the West Indies ought to be discouraged in this country." "Surely no American," he lectured, "can wish to see a nation of negroes . . . built up within a few days sail of our southern states."[56] Colonization was in large part built upon and shaped by fear of black assertiveness, and bolstering Haiti's independence was not exactly calculated to assuage that fear. Colonization to West Africa was.

In the form it ended up taking, then, the ACS became a big tent that could accommodate men of a wide variety of viewpoints on slavery and race. This helps to account for its popularity over the course of several decades. A shared fear of free blacks' influence on slaves constituted at least one reason that tent became so capacious.

———

But those who were hoping that the ACS could heal the widening sectional rift over slavery found themselves mistaken. For shared assumptions about the dangers of slaves and free blacks could not stop white Americans from quarrelling among themselves as to the implications of those dangers. Furthermore, that common understanding became a political football in the partisan divisions of the time. Predictably enough, the most virulent partisan usages of the slave threat emerged during the War of 1812. The war's opponents in both sections openly raised the specter of slave revolt if the Republicans provoked British retaliation. Opponents of the war in both North and South presumed that slaves yearned for freedom and itched for the opportunity to seize it. The war, they argued, would provide the slaves just such an opportunity.

Antiwar white Southerners, for obvious reasons, held back while New England Federalists inveighed against slave representation. But they weighed in on the subject of slave revolt, earnestly imploring their prowar brethren to pursue neither the War of 1812 itself, nor harsh tactics in waging that war, lest they incite Britain to tamper with their slave population. As the House of Representatives debated war resolutions in 1811, dissident "Old Republican" John Randolph savaged the war hawks on many fronts but reserved some especially vitriolic passages for the idea of invading Canada and seducing its citizens to rebel against their government. He warned that suborning treason in Canada "might be retorted on the Southern and Western slaveholding states," given "the danger arising from the black population." He assured his audience that he would "touch this subject as tenderly as possible," for it was only "with reluctance" that he addressed it at all. But even without British interference, this witness to Gabriel's revolt admonished, the South had suffered "repeated alarms of insurrection among the slaves—some of them awful indeed." Thus, while others were "talking of taking Canada, some of us were shuddering for our own safety at home." He pointed out that "the night-bell never tolled for fire in Richmond [but] that the mother did not hug her infant more closely to her bosom."[57] Randolph thus marshaled white Southerners' deepest fears against the war.

Randolph had distinguished himself as usual, but he was not alone; other Southern representatives raised the prospect of slave revolt during other wartime debates. In early 1813, Representative Daniel Sheffey, a Virginia Federalist, rose in response to a Georgia congressman's suggestion that the United States seduce British seamen with an offer of immediate naturalization. "I feel astonished," Sheffey protested, "to hear such a proposition made by a gentleman coming from that portion of the Union." White Southerners, he urged, "ought to offer up their daily and nightly prayers to Heaven, to preserve the ocean of life unruffled. They are afloat in a very crazy vessel." For the slaves of the South, he argued, "want nothing but means and opportunity to attempt to break their shackles." If the Republicans invited British retaliation, the invading foe might very well provide both means and opportunity to those slaves. Lest anyone argue that such fears were "visionary," he reminded his audience not only of "the fate of St. Domingo," but also of Gabriel's plot. The conspiracy had convinced him that, like other men, American slaves were "strong, resolute, and ingenious, where liberty is concerned." Therefore, should British forces stir up the slaves, "every man would find in his own family an enemy ready to cut the throats of his wife and children." "Let us keep within the ranks of civilized warfare," Sheffey admonished, "and we may perhaps avoid the danger."[58]

Charges of recklessness against Southern Republicans reverberated outside Congress as well. A writer in the Federalist *Charleston Courier*, for instance, decried the strategy of invading Canada and leaving "this metropolis of the southern states" in a "defenceless situation." Such a course left Carolina "a prey to internal divisions" as well as British invasion.[59] This was typical of the indirection and innuendo with which slaveholders (especially in the Deep South) referred to the prospect of slave insurrection in public, given their fears of what slaves might hear or read. But subtlety aside, these antiwar Southerners indicted the Madison administration's policies in the strongest terms they could think of.

Less subtle were Northern Federalists in Congress, who also used the prospect of slave revolt to question the wisdom of the administration's policies. Many spoke for constituents so alienated from slaveholders that they would rejoice to see the slaves as well as the British visit destruction on them. The bitterness of such rhetoric demonstrated, perhaps better than anything else, how divisive the War of 1812 was.[60] For instance, the Connecticut Federalist Benjamin Tallmadge interjected the threat of slave rebellion into an 1813 debate over establishing an additional military force, which had broadened into an extended dispute over the government's strategy and the war itself. He was particularly opposed to invading Canada, which he said would instigate British reprisal. Given the vulnerability of the slave South, Tallmadge professed to be "astonished at the presumption and rashness with which" Republicans "seem to court the contest." "The hand of the assassin is within their own dwellings," he reminded them. He speculated that "the Providence of God permits this awful delusion" among the Southern Republicans, in order "that vengeance may come on the most ardent authors and abettors of this war to the uttermost. Before these awful judgments shall take place, I conjure gentlemen to pause, and to remember this caution, which is given in the spirit of friendship, before it be too late."[61] Senator William Hunter of Rhode Island displayed a similar tone of mock brotherhood in a speech against the government's proposal to seize and occupy Spanish East Florida.⁶² Southern politicians might be forgiven if they harbored serious doubts about these professions of friendship, obviously meant as indictments of the foolishness of the war policy. Such speeches also confirmed that few congressional debates were safe from intrusion by the issue of slavery.

New England Federalists outside the halls of Congress talked of slave revolt in the South even more freely. Some clergymen envisaged slaves rising to visit God's judgments on their iniquitous owners for advocating the war. Elijah Parish, whose hostility to Southern Republicans knew no bounds, urged his congregants not to shield the slaveholding warmongers from the punishment they so richly deserved. In the most notorious passage of his 1812 fast day sermon, Parish urged New England to "proclaim an honorable neutrality; let the southern *Heroes* fight their own battles, and guard their slumbering pillows against the just vengeance of their lacerated slaves, whose sighs and groans have long since gone up to the court of the Eternal, crying for the full viols of his incensed wrath."⁶³ It requires very little effort to discern that Parish was *hoping* to see the slaves rise in rebellion as a consequence of the war.

Slave rebellion was also among the calamities that many lay New England Federalists not-so-secretly wished upon the warmongers of the South. Boston's *Columbian Centinel*, for example, printed numerous letters from the South reporting widespread insurrection anxiety and slave flight.⁶⁴ These reports not only trumpeted the wartime weakness of slave states, but also struck the editor of the *Centinel* as proof of the visitation of justice upon his domestic enemies. "The Virginians," he wrote in 1813, complained bitterly about the British depredations along their rivers (including stealing slaves), "but they should recollect, that they bellowed loudly for this war, which was declared by their own Rulers. . . . Let them remember . . . that those who delight in war must *expect blows*."⁶⁵ The other leading Federalist print, the *Connecticut Courant*, joined in this barely restrained celebration of the miseries of the slaveholding states. It reprinted troubled letters from the South with the same alacrity as the *Courier*.⁶⁶ In response to the Southern Republicans' hue and cry over British raids in the Chesapeake in 1813, the *Courant* demanded to know whether they would not admit that "almost every thing has not been done" by the Madison administration, "to provoke the enemy to such a barbarous mode of warfare."⁶⁷ Even before these raids began, a Philadelphia Federalist reported that "a considerable degree of alarm exists in Virginia, lest the black slaves should attempt to recover their 'long lost liberties.' " "This oppressed race of men," he recounted, often remarked that *"white man go to Canada, then black man be free."* He concluded with evident delight that some of the "leading democrats must have bad dreams, if not dismal forebodings," as to what they had brought upon themselves and the country by means of *"the present detestable war."*[68]

Neither were the writings of "Cato" in the *Courant* calculated to ease Southern fears about the intentions and sympathies of the North. The first of a series of essays warned that although he regretted the Republican policies that had led the nation to the brink of dissolution and civil war,

> they ought to know that the most bitter consequences of the measure will recoil on themselves. There are circumstances in the nature of their population, which I should tremble to mention, that must produce the event, if a state of national commotion is of long continuance. Their physical strength is so party-colored, that it cannot contain within itself the principles of safety. There can be no long continued peace between the principles of personal liberty and of slavery. There is not a rational creature of God on earth that chooses to be a slave, or that will withhold his hand when opportunity presents to satiate his smothered vengeance on the instruments of his perpetual servitude.—The commotions of war cannot long fail of giving such opportunities. . . . We are therefore amazed to find so many partizans of war in the south.[69]

One wonders what he would have said if he had not "tremble[d] to mention" the slave threat! In any event, "Cato" echoed the Virginian Sheffey in his evaluation of African Americans' inborn longings for liberty. The fourth essay began on a conciliatory note. The writer appealed to white Southerners as a friend who had fought alongside them in the Revolution. But he advised them that, "to tell you the truth, southern brethren, we do not intend to live another year, under the present national measures and administration." And if the Union shattered and they lost Northern protection, "we do not know what you would do, between an external invasion on the one hand, and the internal dread of your slaves on the other."[70] "Heaven save us," one can almost hear white Southerners saying, "from such 'friends!' "

Another theme that accumulated a good deal of partisan mileage was the example of the ex-slaves of Haiti. Many found good partisan reason to laud the Haitians, a course sure to alienate most white Southerners. Northern Federalists insisted that unreasoning racism should not continue to keep the United States from trading profitably with Haiti, whose independence, after all, was a continual finger in the eye of the French. They were apt to draw parallels between the Haitian and American Revolutions. For such men, even black atrocities during Haiti's wars were justifiable, for "there is an inherent principle in man which revolts at oppression in any shape. The worm recoils if you tread upon it, and the most tame of our own species have a keen feeling of retaliation for injury."[71] Such a doctrine could apply to slaves anywhere. Meanwhile, Philadelphia Federalist Zachariah Poulson praised Haiti as "a nation which is asserting its native liberty against" prejudice and other external enemies.[72] The partisan benefits of touting Haiti became clear in a Francophobe Federalist's account of the enlightened policies of "his ebony majesty Christophe." The writer pointedly compared the Haitian monarch's policies to the disarray France's government fostered. "Would not the government of France," he triumphantly concluded, "shrink from a comparison with the government of Haiti!"[73]

As Northern Republicans gave greater voice to their antislavery sentiments after the War of 1812, favorable treatments of Haiti came from their pens and presses as well. While recognizing that "this topic is calculated to give alarm to slaveholders," one New Yorker lauded Haiti's republican constitution, contrasting it with abuses in America's political system he hoped to correct.[74] Some Northern editors also pointed to the standing rebuke an independent Haiti offered to racist theory.[75] To those advocates of slavery who pointed to Haiti's monarchy as proof that blacks would squander the gift of liberty, one writer responded that "the decree is gone forth—and the slave shall shake off his chains. If he makes a bad use of his independence, we cannot help it.—to squander an inheritance, or abuse a privilege, is no new thing."[76] Such expressions demonstrated the gulf that separated Northern partisans' attitudes and concerns from those of the slaveholders of the South. By producing some of the most incendiary treatments of slavery and slave revolt, partisanship continually nurtured sectionalism in the 1810s.

But white Southerners looking for evidence that Yankees could not relate to their fear of their slaves found it beyond the rants of aggrieved Federalists or dissident Republicans. To be sure, slaveholders still had many allies in the free states.[77] And most white Northerners probably did not support the idea of slave rebellion no matter their stance on slavery. But others published provocative views on slave resistance in more than the partisan sphere.

Some espoused the right of slaves to resist their captors. That some New England Federalists and abolitionists advocated slaves' right to resistance was not terribly surprising.[78] But Northern playwrights and novelists, who wrote of Americans in captivity in Northern Africa, had their characters say things that might make any slaveholder squirm and wonder about their domestic application. At the climactic moment of one such narrative, the hero of the piece declares, "A SLAVE has power to strike a TYRANT dead."[79] Republican editor Hezekiah Niles maintained that kidnapped free blacks had the right to kill their abductors. "Who could blame the kidnapped negro," he asked, "for seeking his liberty at any cost, and at every sacrifice?"[80] Such a right of resistance might go well beyond free African Americans kidnapped into slavery—for what slave thought his or her enslavement anything but a forcible denial of their liberty, whether at birth or by sale? Other musings of his applied even more broadly and directly to slave revolt in the South. "Moses, who led the Israelites, slaves of Pharaoh, from Egypt, . . . is regarded as one of the greatest men that ever lived," Niles mused. But "if *Quashi* were to do the same things, and lead our blacks from their task-masters to set up a government for themselves, with similar scenes of war and desolation—what would *we* think of him? how would *our* historians describe him?"[81] Whites in free and slave territory, it seemed, were more apt than ever to answer this question differently.

If such sentiments inevitably rankled slaveholders and their allies, the steps they took to keep their rebellious slaves in check mortified Northerners. This dialectic displayed the dilemma of Union between slave and free states, for while those in the former saw the repression of revolt as imperative, the means they used horrified those in the latter. Poulson manifested his outrage in capital letters when he reported how North Carolina had outlawed five runaway slaves for their "daily depredations." If they did not turn themselves in to "their respective owners," "any person or persons may KILL and DESTROY ALL, or EITHER OF THEM wherever they may be found, WITHOUT INCURRING THE PENALTY OF THE LAW."[82] This dynamic was also evident in 1811 as newspapers reported the brutal violence with which white Louisianans put down and retaliated for the rebellion there. When planters cut off the heads of executed insurgents and placed them on poles, they aimed to terrorize their slaves—but they also appalled many Yankees. Militiamen summarily shot a black prisoner—"for what reason I know not," one reporter commented, "unless to gratify the revengeful feelings of the planters."[83] An editor in Ohio, after reading such accounts, exclaimed that "VILLAINOUS WHITES" in the slaveholding states had "reduced to the level of the *beasts of the field* these unhappy Africans—and are now obliged to sacrifice them like *wild beasts* in self-preservation!" He concluded that "the day of vengeance is coming!"[84] He did not mean the vengeance of whites upon insurgent blacks.

White Northerners' horror and embarrassment at the repressive South extended well beyond the savagery involved in putting down specific revolts. A Boston editor summed up many Yankees' image of the South when he wrote that South Carolina was "*a theatre of crimes and punishments.*"[85] The violent resistance of slaves was no more reprehensible than such punishments as burning slave murderers to death, many reasoned—and at any rate both the crimes and the horrific punishments were by nature "concomitants of Slavery." As for those who would punish slaves in such a way, "away with all their pretence to the name of Christian, or even friend of man." Moreover, "the very assertion, that imperious necessity requires such a horrid example," was "a tacit acknowledgment of [slaves'] natural and unalienable right to freedom," which slaveholders had to use terror to suppress.[86] Under the headline "*abominable*—if true," Boston's *Centinel* reported a Savannah law applying severe penalties to those who would teach a slave to read or write. "For the honor of our country and human nature," the editor groaned, "we hope this is a calumny on the city of Savannah."[87] It was not, and while legislators in slave states deemed such acts to be strictly necessary to keep incendiary materials from the eyes of slaves, they scandalized more than this New England Federalist editor. Niles, for instance, railed at those who would pass such laws and then "rail at the 'degeneracy' and 'brutality' of the blacks!" It was beyond him how they could "produce a *cause* and condemn the *effect*!"[88]

Some white Southerners were deeply sensitive to the impression such laws made,[89] but their racial fears prompted their repeated passage. As one frankly admitted, teaching slaves to read meant that "they will become acquainted with their rights as men. . . . If slavery is to exist, to the disgrace of the country, let ignorance accompany it. Do not, from false humanity, aggravate the wretchedness of slavery, by improving, or refining, the mind."[90] Such comments, despite their apology for slavery, were not likely to impress Northerners. Violent conflicts between slaves and their oppressors revealed potentially irreconcilable sectional dissimilarities.

Slaves' flight to the North also probed weaknesses in the federal Union because of white Northerners' response to it. Although the creation of a free North fostered such conflicts, it is important to remember that the fugitive slaves themselves precipitated them. The free and slave states' laws could coexist peacefully only so long as Southern slaves stayed in the South. When slaves entered free states by flight or otherwise, legal problems arose that tested the very nature and viability of the Union.[91] Slave flight in the years immediately following the War of 1812 produced several controversies between the

states and in Congress. These disputes further alienated Northern and Southern whites from each other.

Concerned for their own rights, Northerners were increasingly unwilling to
allow slaveholders free rein in retrieving their human chattel from their states.
Granted, few whites in the free states actively aided runaways. But sometimes
antislavery activists stymied recovery efforts.[92] And in the 1810s in Ohio, many
joined to petition their legislature to stop the retrieval of fugitive slaves.[93] Such
petitions had effect. Although agreeing to cooperate with Kentucky on the
recovery of its fugitive slaves, Ohio's governor said that in light of "enormities"
such as the kidnapping of free blacks, "the citizens of Kentucky should not
complain that those of Ohio should feel an interest in requiring proof of ownership however inconvenient to the proprietors, before they consent to the removal of negroes against their will." He conjectured that "the want of such
evidence and the violence of attempting to remove them without the warrant of
the constituted authority" had been the main cause of "the difficulty which
actual proprietors have experienced in reclaiming their slaves in Ohio."[94] This
governor's constituents had proclaimed that the rights of free Ohioans—black
and white—were at stake here, and that they should take precedence over any
inconvenience to slaveholders.

The argument that the reclamation of runaway slaves endangered Northern
rights was a common one in these postwar controversies. It was in evidence in
an 1818 congressional debate over strengthening the Fugitive Slave Act of 1793.
Northerners objected that since the original law had proven its potential for
abuse "to the injury of the free citizen," tightening its provisions even further in
favor of slaveholders would oppress the free people of the North.[95] They decried a bill that they claimed would "enable the Southern planters to take and
carry away, not only their own fugitive slaves, but any other person of color,
whether he be a free man or a slave." Moreover, they asserted, "it would enable
them to carry off a free white man."[96] Appointed judges as well as elected
officials gave voice to this sense that they were defending Northern citizens'
rights against Southern encroachment. In 1816, Pennsylvania's Supreme Court
confirmed the freedom of the child of a fugitive slave based on her birth in
Pennsylvania. "We well know the prejudices and jealousies of the southern
parts of the union as to their property in slaves," one justice declared. But he
affirmed the Pennsylvania legislature's right to refuse to enslave anyone born in
this free state. Another justice posited that what was at issue in this case was
"the positive, and artificial rights of the master, over the mother on the one

hand, and, on the other, the natural rights of her child."[97] The assertion of "artificial rights" by slaveholders should never be allowed to abrogate the "natural rights" enjoyed in the free states.

———

Therefore, as slaveholders looked to the North, they perceived a threat to their property—indeed, to their very lives—from a Union that was supposed to protect that property and those lives. Their Northern compatriots agreed with them that slaves and free blacks were a menace. But Yankee partisans and sectionalists evinced more sympathy for slave rebels and fugitives than for those who put or hunted them down. They focused on those Northerners rather than on those who proclaimed their solidarity with the white South in these matters.

From newspapers to statehouses and Congress, slaveholders sounded an alarm upon seeing that many Yankees elevated abstract notions of their rights —which slave hunters theoretically violated—over slaveholders' rights. Safety ranked first in their catalog of rights. In his widely circulated 1810 book, *Arator*, Virginian John Taylor of Caroline was incensed at what he perceived as Northerners' willingness to entice and harbor fugitives. "For what virtuous purpose," he demanded, "are the southern runaway negroes countenanced in the northern states? Do these states wish the southern to try the St. Domingo experiment? If not, why do they keep alive the St. Domingo spirit?" Such meddling would surely "force the slave holders into stricter measures of precaution than they have hitherto adopted" for self-preservation, yet "those who shall have driven them into these measures, by continually exciting their negroes to cut their throats, will accuse them of tyranny."[98] Taylor thus accurately captured (and contributed to) the spiral of mutual sectional recrimination touched off by assertive African Americans, nervous slaveholders, and Northerners opposed to returning fugitives.

If slaveholders feared for their safety, they also valued their property rights above what they saw as "affected railings" from Yankees when Southern agents detained fugitives. One Southern spokesman assured his adversaries that "the free rarely, if ever, suffer" when masters hunted for fugitives. Thus Northerners' complaints were overwrought as well as sanctimonious.[99] Southern legislatures induced their governors to entreat free states' executives to aid them in recovering fugitives. They complained, as did Maryland's House of Delegates, of "the protection given in those states to runaway negroes, by which serious inconvenience is experienced by the owners of slaves." That they customarily did not receive any satisfactory reply surely did not sit well with these slave state officials.[100] In response to the Pennsylvania Supreme Court's ruling in 1816, "a gentleman in Virginia" wrote that the judges' construction of that state's gradual emancipation law of 1780 could only "induce negroes in the neighboring states to runaway from their masters." "The holders of slaves who reside near the borders of Pennsylvania will be seriously injured," he protested, "if their female slaves, by stepping across" the state line to give birth, "may deprive the masters of all claim to their offspring so born." He also affected to decry the inhumanity of a law that would thus separate a child from its parent.[101] In 1818, during the congressional debate over a strengthened federal fugitive slave law, a Georgian rose in the House of Representatives to vindicate "the rights of the holders of that description of property, as secured by the Constitution, as inalienable, and as inviolable on any pretext by those who were averse to the toleration of slavery."[102] The peculiar notions and tender sensitivities of the North, when activated to the benefit of fugitive slaves, violated the Constitution and lessened the value of the Union.

Many slaveholders and their representatives recognized that both the Union and their slave system were at risk when fugitive slaves were the subject. They pled their section's cause with the requisite earnestness, as when Senator William Smith of South Carolina fiercely attacked the 1818 fugitive slave bill's opponents. He mocked their concerns for Northern rights and freedom, telling them that they were "perfectly safe from any such hazard" as being dragged down to work on the South's plantations. "However much we may respect our Northern friends as gentlemen, as lawyers, and as statesmen," he jeered, "we should have no sort of use for them in our cotton fields. Nor should we admire their political instructions to our slaves if they should carry with them their present impressions." Indeed, Smith was convinced "that a general emancipation is intended . . . by the Eastern and Northern States, if they can find means to effect it," for it would be in their economic interests to replace slave capital with commercial and banking capital throughout the United States.[103] Behind the willingness to harbor fugitive slaves, Smith saw mercenary Northerners besieging the very institution of slavery. His speech assured no Yankees that white Southerners had genuine concern for Northern rights. But it demonstrated to his constituents that he was a champion of Southern rights.

It was unsurprising, even natural, that the fugitive slave problem would become so contentious in a federal Union of ever more consciously slave and free states. But this issue was only part of a general atmosphere of sectional hostility exacerbated by slave resistance, and that atmosphere produced suspicions in slaveholders that touched other less naturally divisive issues. Nowhere was this more evident than in some Southern spokesmen's response to the ACS.

Their animus against the ACS was a genuine surprise to many, precisely because its supporters had envisioned it as a rare consensus measure in a polarized sectional climate. One ACS official encapsulated these hopes when he wrote during the Missouri Crisis that it was "consoling and encouraging" in that time of "excitement and agitation" to present a proposal "to the public, in which the humane and intelligent from every part of the United States may unite; and which may tend to heal the divisions which have been excited."[104] Even the moderate ACS, however, failed to live up to such hopes. By 1820, one Richmond editor admitted his reluctance to broach the "delicate theme" of colonization.[105]

It was "delicate" because some slaveholders discerned in the ACS the kind of creeping abolitionism they most dreaded. A Georgia slaveholder, writing in the *National Intelligencer* in 1819 under the pseudonym "Limner," rose in opposition not only to the ACS specifically, but also to the whole humanitarian spirit that it represented. He cited some of the words of ACS supporters to argue that its new object was to emancipate slaves rather than simply to ship free blacks off. If they offered such rhetoric in the South, they would call forth "the ire, not of a mob, but of a people justly concerned for the defence of their peace and safety." He then launched a violent diatribe against enthusiasm under the "cloak" of religion.[106] Some subscribers wrote to protest against his wholesale indictment of philanthropy.[107]

But other white Southerners agreed with "Limner" that do-gooders of this sort endangered the liberties and safety of both whites and blacks. One flatly asserted that the ACS was "an organized conspiracy against the property of the southern country." This cabal was especially threatening because Congress, "which ought to be the natural guardian of that property," was complicit in it, with majorities in both houses poised to lend it aid. "The same spirit which possesses the fanatic in religion, animates the enthusiast in this cause" to advance it by any means, regardless of the consequences. "Is it not time, therefore, for the people of the southern and western states to awake?" They must put Congress on notice that they would "perish in the last defences, rather than submit to the least infraction of these our sacred and indubitable rights." This writer made no apology for such fiery rhetoric, for "infatuation is not to be corrected by *reason,* or even by *ridicule.*" Its devotees must know that "the swords are already sharpening" for "fierce and bloody strife."[108] Faced with such a mentality, even the slaveholding Virginian Charles Fenton Mercer encountered "marked hostility" from some when he traveled in the South to drum up support for the society.[109]

To fully understand this "marked hostility," it must be borne in mind that although the ACS was officially agnostic as to emancipation, it came forward in a time rife with emancipation schemes. Baltimore editor Hezekiah Niles insisted that every reasonable observer knew that slavery would someday be abolished in the United States; the only choice Americans of his generation had was whether it would happen by gradual and peaceful or sudden and violent means. He appealed to an 1819 conspiracy in the Low Country as proof that the case was urgent.[110] The pseudonymous writer "Benjamin Rush" argued that his program of government-sponsored, gradual, compensated emancipation was necessary because slavery "now hangs over us like a black cloud, with threatening and portentous aspect."[111] "Is *safety* an object of importance?" abolitionist John Wright asked the opponents of his push for immediate emancipation. It would not be served by "withhold[ing] emancipation, till the fast increasing coloured population be strong enough to *emancipate themselves*."[112] Similarly, the widely read New England traveler Estwick Evans warned slaveholders that if they rejected his plan, "Heaven's justice may be preparing for us pestilence, famine, and subjugation." No matter how much the proud planters "prate about the inexpediency of giving freedom to the slave," God would ensure that "the cause of the oppressed will not always be unavenged."[113]

Such appeals built on the consensus view that race war in the South was a strong possibility, but they had little chance of swaying slaveholders, coming from men who were hostile to them and their institutions.[114] Many of those slaveholders had a knee-jerk reaction to the ACS because of its association with such men. Launched partly to address insurrection anxiety, therefore, the ACS became controversial partly because of that very anxiety. Slaveholders agreed that African Americans posed a threat, but they divided sharply among themselves as to whether alliance with Yankees in the ACS was the proper way to meet it.[115]

White Southerners also split over how openly to admit the problem their slaves posed, an attitude inextricably bound up with their public stance on the goodness of slavery itself. Some were remarkably forthright about their insurrection anxiety, even in publications the enemies of slavery were sure to read. But others urged that this was dangerous both politically and physically. To divulge their fear, they thought, would encourage the slaves to even greater rebelliousness, for they were certain that their slaves were reading or hearing of such expressions in the public prints. It was also the kind of admission of the op-pressiveness of Southern slavery that some white Southerners were becoming reluctant to make.

Many white Southerners still called slavery an evil and displayed their insur-rection anxiety for all the world to see. Certainly the likes of Randolph and Sheffey had paraded their fears during the congressional war debates, albeit for partisan reasons. Furthermore, in January 1811, during the congressional de-bates over whether to admit Louisiana as a state, Southern representatives argued for statehood based in part on their expectation—vindicated that very month—of a revolt in a region with such a large black population.[116] A few years later, one man in Petersburg, Virginia, told a British traveler in a tavern that he hated to go home in a violent rainstorm, "but was wretched at the thought of his family being for one night without his protection—from his own slaves!" He also told the foreigner that he was still recovering from poison administered to him by a privileged "personal servant."[117] In 1816, an inhabi-tant of Camden, South Carolina, wrote to a friend in Philadelphia to describe the alarm occasioned by the slave plot there. "This is really a dreadful situation to be in," he concluded. "I think it is time for us to leave a country where we cannot go to bed in safety."[118]

Most white Southerners, however, were by no means willing to abandon either slavery or the slave country. They chose instead to defend the institution as best they could in the face of the turbulence of the slaves. This became evident as other Southern writers and spokesmen sought to downplay the gravity and frequency of slave resistance. They used tactics such as avoiding direct reference to slaves when depicting slave flight or arguing that outside agitators had "duped" or "stolen" slaves away from their happy situations. Richmond editor Thomas Ritchie, for one, was a leading practitioner of the tactic of indirection, as when he reported during the War of 1812 that "between 25 and 30 —— eloped from a plantation near Hampton."[119] Ritchie also joined with other editors in reporting the Frederick, Maryland, slave conspiracy of 1814 as "THE LITTLE PLOT."[120]

Even the most serious revolt the United States ever faced, the 1811 uprising in Louisiana, got this treatment in some public communications. One subtle way reporters did this was to describe the insurgents as mere "brigands" or "banditti," thus denying their martial discipline.[121] Governor William C. C. Claiborne of Louisiana admitted the gravity of the revolt privately or when it suited him (such as when applying for federal reimbursement for his expendi-tures in suppressing it).[122] But his public statements were meant to reassure his territory's inhabitants that the situation was well in hand.[123] Louisiana's legislature followed suit, agreeing on the one hand that the insurrection had been "a terrible warning to us all," yet rejoicing on the other that "the disaffection was partial, the effort feeble and it[s] suppression immediate." The legislators emphasized the faithfulness of most slaves, and that "the Blacks have been taught an important lesson—their weakness."[124] Typical of the confusion of the white South in this transitional era, the legislators' arguments at once asserted the beneficence of slavery and confessed the brute force upon which it rested. The latter argument was better suited to impressing eavesdropping slaves of the futility of revolt than to defending the honor of slavery to an outside audience.

Southern spokesmen in that larger forum did what they could to rebut the common wisdom that discontented Southern slaves continually plotted for their liberty. They did so in debates during the War of 1812, but more in defense of the war than of slavery, for they all stopped well short of saying that Southern slaves were happy. Many Southern congressmen rose to refute Randolph's powerful antiwar speech by denying the threat of slave revolt he had raised. "I have no fear of invasion," a North Carolinian protested, "and, therefore, have no fears arising from the black population, which strikes with so much horror on the sensitive mind of the gentleman from Virginia." He went on to say that he thought slavery an evil, and that "most sincerely, sir, do I wish that a second Moses could take them by the hand, and lead them in safety to a distant land, where their cries would never more strike on the ear of sympathy."[125] Distant (and therefore harmless) projections of the emancipation and removal of slaves were the stock-in-trade of the necessary-evil defense of slavery. But this speaker's real point was that prowar white Southerners would not have launched the war if they thought it would bridge that distance.

The young war hawk Calhoun also denied the slave threat as he tore into his Southern opponents, and not on the grounds that slavery was a positive good. After Randolph's description of insurrection anxiety in Richmond, Calhoun offered his mock "regret that such is the dreadful state of his particular part of the country." "In South Carolina," he taunted, "no such fears in any part are felt." That little thrust completed, he granted, only for the sake of argument, that a large revolt was possible. But he insisted that "the precise time of the greatest safety is during a war," for "then the country is most on its guard; our militia the best prepared; and standing force the greatest."[126] In his response to Sheffey's portrayal of the helplessness of the white South, Calhoun added that "if danger indeed existed," Sheffey had "acted with such imprudence as ought to subject him to the censure of any reflecting man." He then abruptly switched subjects, however, unprepared to dispute Sheffey's assertion of blacks' desire for liberation.[127] The young Calhoun was prepared to defend his party more than slavery.

Much as Randolph and Sheffey had incensed Southern Republicans, however, it was the New England Federalists' manifest desire for slave revolt that raised their ire to its heights. Though the Federalists "do not in express terms recommend," groused the editors of the *National Intelligencer*, "yet they very significantly hint to the British commanders the practicability of exciting an insurrection amongst the Southern slave population."[128] "Franklin," writing in the *Richmond Enquirer*, said that you can detect "FEDERALISM OF THE BOSTON STAMP" in a man thus: "Affecting to deplore the danger to which the Southern States are supposed to be obnoxious from a certain class of their population, he excites in that class false ideas of their strength and prompts them to an attempt, which, with whatever horrors its progress might be attended, must inevitably terminate in their ruin."[129] Northern Federalists' malevolence convinced Southern Republicans of their party's righteousness but also helped create a sense that their section was under siege. This perception inflamed all discussion of slavery across sectional lines well beyond the war. In 1819, for instance, one writer blamed a large slave conspiracy in Georgia on Yankee zealots, whose "ultra-humane" effusions were bound to spread among the slaves "doctrines which have produced, and will forever produce, such catastrophes."[130] Northern rhetoric had convinced white Southerners that servile war in the South was, at best, "of little consequence to our Eastern brethren,"[131] and, at worst, their devout wish.

Such indifference and outright hostility provoked in white Southerners not only partisan and sectional bitterness, but also a sense of the need to defend slavery more effectively. The likes of Calhoun were not prepared to travel down that road, but others felt Northerners pushing them toward a thorough repudiation of the idea that Southern slaves were discontented and potentially rebellious. The editors of the *National Intelligencer* insisted that Federalist editors were never known to "betray more ignorance" as when they proclaimed that the slave population was a source of military weakness. "The South," they insisted, "has nothing to fear in that quarter," for "the negroes themselves, on the approach of an invading force, would, if permitted, gladly advance to repel it." They supported this supposition by a benign portrait of Southern slavery. "The slaves in the South," they asserted, were generally "content to do the duty to which they were born, and attached to the families from whom they respectively receive protection and support."[132] From South Carolina came similar arguments. Benjamin Elliott charged that "our blacks have been *used* to appal [*sic*] us" by those who would hinder the war effort. But in reality Southern slaves posed no peril, for they were "the happiest slaves in the world." Indeed, Elliott concluded, they were far happier than they would be wrestling with "the cares of freedom," and far better off than the industrial workers of Britain.[133] The Northern Federalists' expressions concerning slave revolt had impelled these writers to paint a paternalist picture of slavery.

In the 1818 fugitive slave debate in Congress, William Smith joined this proslavery vanguard. His speech against abettors of slave flight branched out into a general discussion of slavery's merits. He posited that runaway slaves found that they had been better off before abolitionists had "seduced" them with fair promises of freedom into running to the racist North. Thus it was common, he claimed, for disillusioned fugitives either to alert their former masters as to their whereabouts or to "run away from these new tyrants . . . back to their former state of slavery, as a better and more desirable con- dition."[134] Northern meddlers had driven Smith to pass off the retrieval of fugitive slaves—and even the kidnapping of the poor free blacks by logical extension—as a rescue operation. None of these were full-blown assertions of the essential rightness of slavery. But it is significant that, in this era in which most white Southerners were still in a twilight zone between necessary-evil and positive-good defenses of slavery, the demands of consistency thrust some pio- neers in that direction.

———

African Americans' struggles for freedom and equality, then, contributed might- ily to the divergence between America's emergent sections. The politics of the 1810s demonstrated that, as one scholar has recently written, "the effort to con- trol the slave population involved every level of political life from the local to the national."[135] Slaveholders' domination of the state at all these levels was of primary importance to maintaining the sway they held over their bondspeople. Yet some Northerners were not prepared to accept the exertion of that sway when it violated their principles or rights. Therefore, African Americans' ac- tions, real and perceived, resounded in politics, from town meetings and news- papers to the deliberations of government officials in all branches and at all levels.

Defending against Slavery

CHANGES IN SOUTHERN slavery wrought by white as well as black Americans helped make the years between the War of 1812 and the Missouri Crisis a seminal period in the development of antislavery Northern sectionalism. During these years, antislavery principles ruled the realms of ethics and rhetoric, but slavery was on the offensive on the ground. Although American slavery had been expanding its territory throughout the early national period, the results of the War of 1812 rendered its growth explosive. Andrew Jackson's wartime career contributed most directly, not only by confirming the United States' possession of the Louisiana Purchase at the Battle of New Orleans, but also by conquering vast Indian territory in the Southwest; in short, Jackson's troops secured the future Cotton Kingdom for the United States. Southern planters could not fill these new lands with slave laborers and cultivate cotton quickly enough.[1]

The aggressiveness of the postwar American slave regime brought slavery home to the Mid-Atlantic and Northwest, whose residents were hardest pressed to keep it at a distance. Whites in these areas who had evinced only nebulous disapproval of black bondage in the South gained a new clarity with the perception that slaveholders were encroaching on their own freedoms. Those who cared only about the rights of white citizens could thus join with those who cared about blacks' rights to oppose the sale and kidnapping of Northern African Americans to servitude in the South, or to resist the threatened spread of slavery to the Northwest. All Northern states hoped to shore up their status as free states by distancing themselves from slavery, but those closest to the South found it the hardest to do so. The vague but latently powerful antislavery impulses of the Revolution thus gained concrete meaning and organized expression in states north of the permeable border with slavery in the postwar years, just as they had in New England during the Embargo and War of 1812.

Thus, slavery's postwar expansion shaped the development of sectional identity, not only in the South, but also in the North. It exacerbated existing resentments against slaveholders. It welded opposition to slavery ever more firmly to the emerging identity of the states who were calling themselves free. These developments proved to many—even before the Missouri Crisis—that the dialectic between slave and free states menaced the Union more than any other domestic division. But these effects spread unevenly through the North, for antislavery sectionalism had become much more urgent and evident in the Mid-Atlantic and Northwest than in New England. Moreover, it had done so for different reasons in these two subregions, for while the Mid-Atlantic sought to repel slave catchers and kidnappers, the Northwest sought to bar the entry of masters and slaves.

————————

In the early nineteenth century, a generic brand of antislavery sentiment continued to pervade the cultural milieu in the United States, especially in the North. Thousands of American schoolchildren pored over the antislavery passages in one of over twenty editions of Caleb Bingham's *Columbian Orator* and read poetry denouncing the slave trade in other readers and anthologies.[2] When these youths' parents went to the theater, they found slavery attacked there, too. *The Padlock*, a play produced for thousands of Americans in the early nineteenth century, ended with a slave character calling on the "sons of Freedom" in the audience to "equalize your laws" and "plead the Negroe's cause."[3] Characters in George Colman's popular play *The Africans*, which dramatized white people's slavery in Northern Africa, insisted that freedom was a boon that "slaves had a right to expect."[4] Opposition to slavery also dominated treatment of the subject in the literature of the period. A character in an 1812 novel depicting Americans in North African slavery demanded: "By what authority, let me ask, does this country, or any other country on the globe, subject any portion of the human species to slavery?" Slaveholding, she answered, was an "assumption of power" that was "in the highest degree, criminal."[5] A large audience read, in Joel Barlow's epic poem "The Columbiad," the standard formula: a firm denunciation of slavery and a vague call for its abolition.[6] The author of a popular captivity narrative also embodied the general tenor of antislavery in this period. Upon his return to the United States after being redeemed from bondage in Africa, James Riley railed against the analogous oppression of Southern slaves. He pledged his life to ridding America of slavery.

But his exceptional experience with African slavery did not make him exceptional in his stand on American slavery. Instead, Riley typified the antislavery of his era, acting against slavery only sporadically and supporting gradual emancipation and colonization when he did exert himself. Furthermore, he worked as an individual, and despite his experiential authority, it is unclear whether he had much of an impact.[7]

While this sort of antislavery sentiment dominated the realm of discourse, it prompted very few Americans to demand the immediate abolition of slavery. From organized abolition societies to individual pamphleteers, slavery's most ardent opponents continued their forebears' gradualism.[8] Even African American leaders, such as Absalom Jones in an 1808 sermon, advocated gradual emancipation.[9]

America's second generation of abolitionists repudiated immediatism, despite the manifest failure of the first generation's hopes that slavery would just fade away after the ban on the Atlantic slave trade. As late as 1815, the biographer of eighteenth-century Quaker abolitionists referred to the antislavery movement in the past tense, rejoicing that its program had "the almost universal consent of mankind." He issued no grand call to emulate the likes of Benjamin Lay, for their work seemed a done deal.[10] But it did not take many long after the War of 1812 to realize, as historian John Ashworth has put it, that "time was not on their side." They grasped, to their horror, "that while the international slave trade had obviously depended on slavery, the converse was not true,"[11] at least for the U.S. slave regime. In this setting, antislavery writers focused particular ire on the "abominable, *internal traffic* in slaves," which had arisen, especially after the war, in place of the foreign traffic.[12] Abolition societies and Quakers funneled their legislative efforts into petitioning for legislative interference with the interstate trade in African Americans.[13] Their legal work centered on protecting free blacks from kidnapping.[14] With little immediate hope of effacing slavery from the United States, they hoped to prevent some of its inroads and ameliorate some of its worst features. Others contributed to a swelling stream of emancipation schemes. All of them proposed gradual abolition, but the sheer volume of such proposals in the 1810s was impressive and revealed abolitionists' sense of the new situation.[15] Although slave trade abolition had fallen short of the promised panacea, abolitionists retained the Revolution's faith in gradualism, even as they proposed new remedies to the growing problem.

There were exceptional souls who issued pioneering appeals for total and instantaneous abolition. Such was George Bourne, a Presbyterian minister who carried on the tradition of his coreligionists, such as Alexander McLeod, who had denounced slavery as a sin. Bourne's great innovation and contribution was to call slavery itself "manstealing," thus applying the language of the slave trade to the maintenance of chattel bondage. Bourne also applied the term "kidnapping" to the practice of slaveholding, arguing that the continual deprivation of liberty to the slave was the daily sin of every slaveholder.[16] The New England philanthropist John Kenrick joined Bourne in the thin ranks of immediatism in the 1810s. "If slavery is 'a violation of the divine laws,'" he demanded, was it not absurd to talk of gradual emancipation? "We might as well talk of gradually leaving off piracy—murder—adultery, or drunkenness."[17] But such radical abolitionists were isolated and disorganized in the early nineteenth century.[18]

None of this, however, is to say that the abolitionists were ineffectual.[19] Despite their conservatism, their efforts to keep African Americans from slavery's reach were significant. Certainly the African Americans whose freedom their legal maneuvering secured did not think abolitionists unimportant. Neither did the would-be masters or kidnappers thwarted by the abolition societies' suits. Furthermore, given the inherent importance of the free black community, the measure of protection abolitionists' activities afforded it was of great political significance.[20] And when abolitionists attacked the domestic slave trade, they dealt a blow to not only a vital economic element of Southern slavery, but also to what both slaves and freedpeople considered the worst aspect of American slavery.[21] Abolitionists of the early nineteenth century also formed an essential bridge between the movements of the Revolutionary and antebellum periods. After the Revolutionary movement reached its apogee in 1808, its successors kept organized, nonpartisan opposition to slavery alive by finding new rallying points such as the interstate slave trade and kidnapping.

Defending against such outrages also had the important advantage of resonating with public opinion in the North. Most white Northerners were not abolitionists cooking up schemes for the extirpation of slavery throughout the United States. But especially after the War of 1812, the South's insatiable demand for African American labor threatened to bridge their cherished distance from slavery by dragging Northern blacks—both free and slave—to work the burgeoning cotton plantations of the Southwest. Thus, more than humanitarianism impelled the white North's outrage at the growing interstate slave trade and the rise of kidnapping.

The horrors of the domestic slave trade increasingly intruded on white Northerners' attention. Northerners read slave sale advertisements in Southern

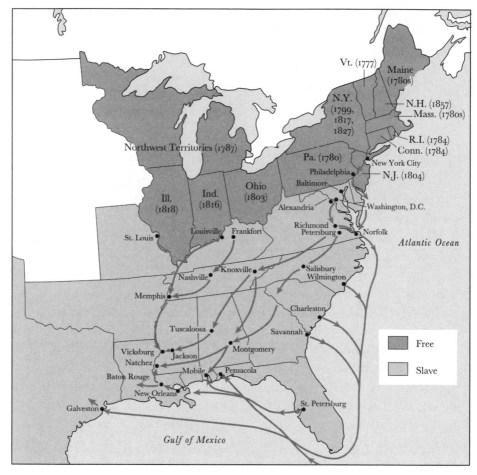

Map 6.1. Northern Abolition and the Slave Trade

Note: Arrows indicate the general direction of the major movements of people through the domestic slave trade. There were very few slaves in New Hampshire after the Revolution, but the legislature did not abolish slavery until 1857. Abolition occurred in Massachusetts not because of legislation but through interpretation of judicial verdicts in the 1780s. In 1799 New York adopted gradual abolition and then in 1817 declared that in 1827 abolition would become final.

papers with a national reach. Yankees visiting the national capital or traveling in the South encountered the traffic firsthand. As they published their impressions in popular travel accounts, they gave many Northern readers their best glimpse of the rising commerce. No matter their personal stances on slavery, they witnessed slave sales and coffles with revulsion. "How deplorable is the condition of our country!" lamented an antislavery New Englander, upon seeing "so many bullocks, so many swine, and so many human beings in our market" daily.[22] The famous architect Benjamin Latrobe, whose opposition to slavery was less fervent, recognized "the difficulty of supressing [sic] the internal Slave trade, without infringing on the rights of private property." But what he saw of the cruelties of the traffic on a journey to New Orleans convinced him that at least the government should desist from supporting it by holding slaves in public jails until they could be shipped.[23] New York writer James Kirke Paulding, whose antislavery was even more tepid, pronounced woes upon "those, who, tempted by avarice, or impelled by vengeance, shall divide the parent from its off-spring, and sell them apart in distant lands!" Although recognizing that "perhaps" this commerce "arises out of the system" of slavery itself, he somewhat incongruously refused to upbraid slaveholders themselves. But he would have liked to see the drivers of slave coffles "hunted by bloodhounds."[24] By means of such accounts, the slave coffle and auction block became the dominant images of slavery in the minds of many Northerners in the early nineteenth century. "I had often heard of Slavery," said one Northerner, "but had never seen it before in its own native colours" until seeing a slave coffle while traveling in the South.[25]

The shock these observations produced found their way into the public prints as far away as New England. "Let anyone possessing one scruple of republican virtue," one New England writer challenged, "read without blushing (if he can)" notices of slave sales printed in such respectable sheets as the *National Intelligencer*. Such practices disgraced the whole country.[26] They also blighted Northerners' hopes for abolition and offended their sense of humanity. One anonymous writer vented his frustration that the Revolutionary generation's hopes had proven delusory. When the Atlantic slave trade "was first abolished," he declared, "I was as happy at the event as others." He now found, however, "that we have had but little relief from that act," for such outrages proved that "the nuisance is as great as ever."[27] In this way, the domestic slave trade offended white Northerners whose physical distance from the trade would have otherwise shielded them from having to deal with it. Thus humanitarianism blended with national shame to gall New Englanders into animadversions on the geographically remote traffic. In this way the domestic slave trade came under nearly universal reproach throughout the North.[28]

But if New Englanders had these reasons to hate the domestic slave trade, it hit closer to home for whites living in the Mid-Atlantic, for some of its points of origin were in their midst. The deliberate pace of slavery's abolition in Mid-Atlantic states left thousands of African Americans trapped in bondage for years. The people caught in this limbo proved an irresistible resource for labor-hungry Southerners, who purchased many of them from disgruntled and greedy Northern masters in the early nineteenth century.[29] Furthermore, in Mid-Atlantic slave states such as Maryland, "term slaves" of another kind— those whose masters promised them freedom at a certain future date—saw slave dealers inducing those masters to renege.[30] Throughout the region, whites did not have to travel or read travel accounts to see these blatant violations of the spirit of gradual emancipation. This traffic implicated their neighborhoods in the worst feature of the very slave system they sought to distance themselves from.

For these reasons, the sale of term slaves provoked an uproar in the Mid-Atlantic after the War of 1812. The harshest denunciations of the interstate slave trade issued from cities like Baltimore and Philadelphia. In the latter city, William Duane's *Aurora* painted a vivid picture of the horrors of the auction block. He printed aspersions on the pretended Christians and republicans who were so "lost to all the fine feelings which are the substratum of philanthropy, patriotism and the love of liberty" as to be involved in such a traffic in any way.[31] No one, however, surpassed Baltimore's Hezekiah Niles in vilifying the trade. "If there is any thing that ought to be supremely hated," he insisted, "it is the present infamous traffic that is carried on in several of the middle states, and especially in *Maryland*, in negroes, for the *Georgia* and *Louisiana* markets."[32] He poured contempt on buyers, sellers, and the drivers of coffles. "We are not friendly to sanguinary or severe punishment," this Quaker editor wrote, "but the business of man-stealing is of so base a character, that we should like to hear that every man engaged in the trade . . . were put to death, or at least, transferred to the tender mercies of a dey of Algiers as a slave for life."[33]

The sale of term slaves provoked more than inflammatory rhetoric. State governments in Maryland, New York, and New Jersey legislated against these southward transfers. Between 1816 and 1819, leading whites formed the Baltimore Protection Society, which successfully lobbied Maryland's legislature to pass a law to protect term slaves from sale to the South.[34] New York's 1817 law hastening its gradual emancipation process included strong prohibitions

Abolitionist Jesse Torrey depicts in this woodcut the slave woman, Anna, who jumped from a tavern in Washington rather than be dragged to the Deep South. Her desperate act helped draw attention to the domestic slave trade, especially in the nation's capital. (From Jesse Torrey, *A Portraiture of Domestic Slavery* [1817], in Rare Book Collection, The University of North Carolina at Chapel Hill)

against transporting term slaves. Yet in 1819, Governor DeWitt Clinton urged the Empire State's legislators to "fortify the existing provisions, on account of the artful evasions which are practised to procure the exportation of servants."[35] In 1818, the discovery of a powerful ring of slave traders operating out of Perth Amboy became a primary issue in New Jersey politics. Grand juries in Middlesex County indicted the traders, who escaped conviction only by leaving the state with their human prizes. Meanwhile, in response to petitions from their constituents, state legislators unanimously passed a law strengthening New Jersey's 1812 act prohibiting transport of slaves and free blacks from the state.[36] The state legislature also instructed New Jersey's U.S. senators to push for federal recognition and support for this law. Late in 1818, a senator and representative from New Jersey introduced resolutions to both houses of Congress calling for a federal abolition of the transportation of slaves or people of color from a state that had outlawed such a trade to any other state. Representative John Linn told the House that this resolution "related to a subject of much interest in his part of the country." But although the measure passed in the Senate, Linn could not persuade enough of his colleagues that they should share New Jersey's interest. It failed by an undisclosed margin on the same day he introduced it, in the face of stern Southern opposition.[37] The escape of the artful slave traders, and the failure of this bill, revealed what Mid-Atlantic Northerners were up against when they sought to defend against slavery's incursions. Yet such obstacles only strengthened the resolve of large numbers of whites in this region, who wanted no part of a traffic many equated with the Atlantic trade.[38]

Yet a related phenomenon alarmed and offended Northern whites even more deeply than the sale of term slaves: the kidnapping of free blacks. Many cotton frontiersmen cared less about the source than the availability of black labor and were willing to buy African Americans whether slave or free. Kidnapping had been a problem since free black communities began developing in the post-Revolutionary North, but after the War of 1812 the dynamic slave system sucked increasing numbers into its insatiate maw.[39] Editors and writers up and down the Northeast coast condemned kidnapping in the strongest terms. Boston's *Columbian Centinel* carried accounts of free African Americans dragged to the plantations of the South. "It is a pity," the editor wrote of the kidnappers, "that some Botanybay [prison colony] could not be found for these children of Beelzebub."[40]

Yet as with the slave trade, kidnapping aroused the Mid-Atlantic states more than it did New England. In both cases, humanitarian outrage joined with the imperative of defending against slavery's encroachment on its northern border. Even the Quakers of the Mid-Atlantic states proved far more active than their brethren elsewhere in remonstrating against the trade in African Americans.[41] No newspaper in these states could avoid the subject of kidnapping. Like loyal Republicans in other parts of the Union, the New England Republicans hoped to avoid dealing with slavery in any form. Unlike their brethren to the south, however, they were able to do so.[42] Mid-Atlantic politicians and editors had to give at least perfunctory nods to the rise of kidnapping and denunciations of the practice.[43] Legions of writers in Pennsylvania and Delaware expressed their alarm at the spread of "this abominable trade."[44] Certain Philadelphia editors brought public opinion to bear against kidnappers by exposing their names to public ridicule and by pressuring fellow editors to join in attacking kidnapping.[45] Marylanders were at least as prolific as their neighbors in execrating kidnapping. "Humanitas," for instance, wrote an exposé of a kidnapping ring for a Maryland newspaper. "Reader," he concluded, "if thou canst peruse the above narrative without feeling the glow of indignation towards the oppressors of innocence, and of pity towards the unfortunate, thou art less than human, and deserve to be banished to the society of beings more ferocious and irrational."[46] Niles was also indignant, decrying the demand created by "planters base enough to purchase *men* without an enquiry as to the manner in which they were obtained." As for the kidnappers themselves, if the death penalty "was ever meritoriously inflicted, these men ought to" suffer it. Niles not only called for laws to abolish the practice, but also declared that the kidnapped African Americans had every right to administer death to their abductors.[47]

Kidnapping also came to the attention of legislatures and courts. In 1816, the U.S. House of Representatives conducted hearings and investigations into kidnapping as well as the slave trade in the District of Columbia. It called prominent abolitionists to testify. The hearings came to little, but demonstrated a broad—if not particularly deep—concern with the issue at the highest levels of the national government.[48] At the local level, states like New Jersey, New York, and Maryland moved the strongest against kidnapping and the sale of term slaves. The margin of the votes in these cases, as one New Jersey resident wrote, demonstrated "the agitation created in the public mind" by kidnapping and the slave trade.[49] Local grand juries and attorneys acted directly on kidnappers by indicting and prosecuting them. Many achieved acquittal, but the prosecutions were telling.[50] So was the jury's verdict in a case trying a black Pennsylvanian who killed his erstwhile master and an accomplice who tried to kidnap him back into slavery. They acquitted him of murdering his former master and convicted him only of manslaughter for the death of the partner in crime. The prosecution had sought the death penalty, but the jury gave him only nine years' imprisonment.[51] In one remarkable case from 1817, the black people aboard the incongruously named schooner *Traveller's Friend*, bound to southern Virginia from Maryland's Eastern Shore, broke their fetters, declared themselves free, put the white men in irons, and brought the boat to Baltimore. With the help of the Maryland Protection Society, they petitioned the court to vindicate their claims to freedom, and in the case of one petitioner, the court ruled in her favor! One headline reporting this case—"SOMETHING SINGULAR"—was apt, but the court's ruling spoke to Marylanders' hatred for kidnapping. As one editor put it, this case was about nothing less than whether "manthieves" could "with impunity violate the laws of Maryland" against kidnapping.[52]

As this concern for the law suggested, Mid-Atlantic whites had reasons beyond basic humanity and decency for opposing kidnapping and the trade in term slaves. For Northerners, such practices threatened their self-image and their nascent view of their section as "the everlasting abode of Liberty."[53] By the 1810s, many were proud that gradual emancipation had disentangled the North from slavery, declaring that "it is our excusable pride that *here* was the cradle of American liberty."[54] Indeed, they looked at the geographical boundary with the slave states as a moral boundary as well, pointing to abundant evidence of "*a defect of humane feeling* in the slave-holding states."[55] Such sectional self-righteousness, however, was more common in New England than in the Mid-Atlantic states after the war. An 1817 editorial in the *Columbian Centinel* was typical. "Notwithstanding all the professions of attachment to the great principles of Liberty and Equality" by the Republicans, the editor crowed, "it is believed to be a fact, that the *Slavery* of a part of God's creation is now permitted *by law*, in all the States of America, excepting Massachusetts and New-Hampshire."[56]

If New Englanders struck a note of complacency, those living closer to the slave states struck one of alarm. The distance from slavery they craved was proving elusive as slave traders and kidnappers stalked their streets. From New York City came the warning that kidnapping, "which has hitherto been principally confined to the southern states, has of late found its way among us."[57] In 1818, a Philadelphia paper reported that a series of kidnappings throughout Delaware and Pennsylvania were "not solitary cases." Of one especially violent kidnapping, the writer lamented: "Fellow citizens, these outrages were committed upon a family of free people in Philadelphia, and on the Sabbath day."[58] This being the case, could the emancipators of the Mid-Atlantic really say they

KIDNAPPING.   Paragraph 63.

The horror and violence of kidnapping, as portrayed in this woodcut, outraged white Northerners. (From Jesse Torrey, *A Portraiture of Domestic Slavery* [1817], in Rare Book Collection, The University of North Carolina at Chapel Hill)

lived in free states? Should they become implicated in the worst abuses of the slave system, white Northerners could bid farewell to their sectional boasts.

Both black and white abolitionists, however, knew they had to convey the evils of kidnapping even more directly to a mainstream audience. A bereaved parent in Delaware published an account of seeing his or her children abducted. "Although I am black," the author concluded, "I have a heart like you, and they have pierced it thro' with sorrow—they have stolen my children!"[59] Powerful as this appeal was, Philadelphia abolitionist Jesse Torrey knew he had to plead for more than sympathy. He pointed out that "the act of depriving a free man of his liberty" was "a violation of the constitution of the United States, and an *overt attack* upon the public liberty." Republican rights and ideals were at stake, he insisted, for the best republic would be "that in which an injury to the meanest member of the community, is esteemed an aggression upon the whole."[60]

No matter what they thought of that "meanest member," many white Northerners agreed that their own rights might be in jeopardy if kidnappers could ply their trade with impunity in the supposedly free states. In early 1819, New York City's mayor insisted that if free states' laws concerning the removal of African Americans were consistently interpreted in favor of slaveholders, "the personal liberty of the most respectable persons, as well as that of the meanest, might be endangered."[61] At the same time, a New Jersey judge wrote an open letter in the press revealing that kidnappers had attempted to bribe him into certifying free people of color to be slaves. When he refused, they tried to blackmail him by spreading rumors that he had in fact helped them.[62] Readers might very well conclude that these blackguards would stop at nothing, including corrupting the justice system, in pursuing their odious line of work. At least one, the editor of the newspaper the *Philanthropist*, made such a conclusion. In a passage that also revealed a fundamental conflict of interest with the South, he asserted that a report of hard times in the slave states was "peculiarly gratifying to the feelings of humanity." Economic hardship in the South, he hoped, would give some relief to the free states by lowering "the price of negroes," thereby abating the "swarm of unfeeling adventurers, who have traversed the Atlantic states, and in the prosecution of their traffic, have trampled on the most sacred privileges and precepts of nature, reason, and religion."[63] Another Pennsylvanian castigated kidnappers and their accomplices more succinctly as "assasins [*sic*] of constitutional liberty."[64]

Although the Northern response to kidnapping and the slave trade was a defense against the most glaring abuses of slavery, to attack slavery's worst features was often to attack the entire system. Thus abolitionists could insist that the slave trade proved not only "the odiousness of [slavery's] features," but that "injustice and cruelty . . . is interwoven with it."[65] Others challenged the very basis of slavery more by implication than directly. For instance, although Hezekiah Niles realized that "we cannot now easily get rid of the slaves," he also asked, "Who could blame the kidnapped negro for seeking his liberty at any cost, and at every sacrifice?"[66] Furthermore, in 1819 Niles thought a Georgia planter's claim to the services of a kidnapped African American ludicrous. He wrote incredulously of how "the *owner* of the *freeman*" claimed "that he held 'the applicant as a slave, by a *bill of sale*,' on which it was contended that he ought to be sent home to his master!!"[67] Most slaveholders would surely have recognized a legal sale as conferring ownership. Niles's incredulous italics and exclamation marks demonstrated that even when the abuses of slavery were the focus, slavery itself could be on indirect trial.

Moreover, appeals to sectional libertarian pride, a hallmark of the opposition to kidnapping and the slave trade, could easily be turned against the remnants of slavery in the North. In 1811 and 1812, respectively, the governors of Pennsylvania and New York implored their respective legislatures, in the name of preserving their "character for humanity," to hasten the "gradual and ultimate extermination from amongst us, of slavery, that reproach of a free people."[68] Neither of these appeals produced fruit. But in the postwar atmosphere, such rhetoric helped move New York's legislature to action against slavery. In January 1817, Governor Daniel D. Tompkins told New York legislators that "the reputation of the state" demanded "that the reproach of slavery be expunged from our statute book." Speeding up the existing process of gradual emancipation would be "consistent with the humanity and justice of a free people."[69] The New York Manumission Society agreed with Tompkins that "the spirit of the times" favored a legislative move to firm up New York's free state credentials. "This one act," they suggested, "is wanting to vindicate and adorn the character of the state."[70] In March 1817, the legislature followed Tompkins' prodding and passed a law expediting gradual emancipation.[71] The bill evinced their desire to protect the state from complicity in kidnapping and the slave trade as well as in slavery itself. It contained stiff fines for the sale or "transfer" of term slaves. Furthermore, it declared the bonds, indentures, or servitude of those held to labor in other states "utterly void" within New York. Sojourning slaveholders could only keep slaves in New York for nine months, after which time they would become apprentices. Finally, the law decreed fines up to $1,000 and prison terms of up to fourteen years for the crime of kidnapping.[72] It passed by the impressive margins of 75–23 in the Assembly and 20–3 in the Senate.[73] This law emphatically declared New York a free state and proclaimed its legislature's determination to defend it against encroachment from the slave states. The two processes were inseparable in the postwar period.

Such laws, and such vote margins, were possible because men and women at nearly all points on the spectrum of racial prejudice supported the drive to keep the North moving toward freedom from the taint of slavery. Many white Northerners who disdained African Americans also hated slavery, precisely because it brought blacks into their midst. A host of observers—from contemporary travelers, abolitionists, and African Americans to modern experts on the subject—have remarked on the virulence of whites' race prejudice in the free states.[74] James Kirke Paulding joined a growing number of voices when he mused in print that "there is much *colour* for the belief" that Africans "must look for their parentage somewhere else" than to the rest of humanity's progenitor, Noah.[75] White Philadelphians displayed their mistrust of black people throughout the 1810s, repeatedly petitioning their state legislature to check the growth of their city's black population and shouting down black Philadelphians' 1818 proposal to create their own fire companies.[76] Governor Clinton requested New York's legislature "to preclude the increase of an unwelcome population" of free blacks in their state and then elaborated at length on why they were so undesirable.[77]

But kidnapping and the term-slave trade offered a way to rid the North of such an "unwelcome population," and Northerners hardly embraced it. This was true in part because racial egalitarianism also had a place in the North.[78] Northern Federalists often propounded antiracist thought, albeit typically leavened with a good deal of condescension. Federalist spokesmen insisted that race should not be the main criterion by which man judged his fellow man; respectability, a stake in society, and even common status as God's children should.[79] Many other white Northerners lifted their voices publicly against racism. "There are prejudices against the race of blacks," the New England traveler Estwick Evans exclaimed, "and I pronounce them vulgar!" He knew some of his fellow Americans would "sneer" at his ideas of equality with blacks, but he declared, "I rejoice in defending this despised and oppressed race of men."[80] Although an eccentric in many ways, Evans was no voice in the wilderness on race in the 1810s. Pennsylvanians such as editor William Duane and congressman John Smilie were two leading Republicans who joined their voices to his.[81] Playwright George Colman propounded a certain racial relativism when he had his characters debate whether white or black men and women were most beautiful.[82] Some Northerners translated sympathy for black people into action. In 1819, the people of Easton, Pennsylvania, discovered that a tin peddler passing through their town had crammed two African American children into his cart so tightly that "one of the little sufferers" had his ear rubbed off. "The people indignantly rose and cut off the [peddler's] ear."[83] African American leaders in the Mid-Atlantic sounded optimistic about race relations in the 1810s. To such men as Philadelphia's Prince Saunders, it seemed a time when white men's "unjust prejudices" were "beginning to subside."[84] Such evidence suggests that a picture of a North full of racists would be overdrawn for this relatively open era.[85]

Mid-Atlantic whites' opposition to kidnapping and the slave trade, taken together with their broad support for the ACS program of removing free blacks from their midst, highlighted the complexity of Northern race relations in this period. Clinton spoke for many white residents of the Mid-Atlantic, who, like their counterparts in the Northwest, were not eager to see their region's black population grow. But there were limits to how that limitation could be accomplished. The ACS spoke to Northerners' desire that emancipation be effected without racial upheaval, whereas the violence of kidnapping raised the prospect of that very sort of disorder. Furthermore, the ACS was a program of voluntary removal, which of course kidnapping and the slave trade were not. Thus it protected the rights of Northern citizens, whereas kidnapping menaced those rights. Finally, there was no way to reconcile the practice of kidnapping with the free states' libertarian professions, whereas for many the ACS fit perfectly with those Northern traits. In short, the forcible removal of black people from the Mid-Atlantic to the South provoked not relief from a region eager to "whiten" itself by any means available, but rather protestation from a region eager to preserve its tranquility, rights, and reputation.

————————

As residents of the Mid-Atlantic states sought to defend their rights and identity against slavery's aggressions in the Era of Good Feelings, so did their neighbors to the west. White Northerners shared an antipathy to such practices as kidnapping, but residents in the states and territories of the Northwest added their own special concerns in relation to slavery. The paramount goal in the Northwest was keeping their locales free of actual slavery rather than its agents, as in the Mid-Atlantic. Most Northwesterners opposed the idea of slavery spreading to their backyard, for a variety of reasons. Some opposed slavery on principle. Others wanted distance not only from slavery but from African Americans. They all believed that the boundary between slavery and freedom should be the Ohio River. Yet slaveholders and would-be slaveholders among them wanted to burst these confines. The drive to take slavery north of the Ohio was not new but seemed especially challenging in the late 1810s, as the plantation complex was on the march elsewhere. Thus Midwesterners were at least as defensive when it came to slavery as their Mid-Atlantic counterparts in the postwar years.

They were defensive in large part because it seemed that slaveholders and their allies were bent on breaking every rule in their rush to expand slavery, including the one that slave and free labor belonged in separate spheres. They also seemed poised to shatter one of the few areas of consensus on slavery in the early republic, an agreement on which states and territories would be free or slave. The bill admitting Louisiana as a state sailed through both the House of Representatives and the Senate in 1812, despite New England Federalists' opposition in 1810 and 1811.[86] That same year, Congress also raised Missouri to the second stage in the U.S. tiered system of territories, with only seventeen votes behind a Pennsylvania representative's motion to prohibit the importation of slaves to the territory.[87] It took many years for the states of Mississippi and Alabama to emerge from the Mississippi Territory. Congress began hearing petitions for statehood from the Mississippi Territory in 1811, but made Mississippi a state only in 1817 and Alabama only in 1819. But the delay was owing to questions about the number of inhabitants the territory held and whether to divide it into two states, not whether to restrict slavery there or exclude from statehood due to the presence of slavery.[88] In February 1819, when Congress addressed Missouri's petitions for statehood, it also debated the government of Arkansas Territory. New York's John Taylor initiated a sharp debate in the House over whether to prohibit slavery from Arkansas. The vote was largely sectional, but Taylor's amendment failed in the House.[89]

To be sure, there were flurries of opposition to new slave states and territory before the Missouri debates. In the period surrounding the War of 1812, many Northern Federalists raised such objections. Federalists in Congress pushed vigorously against not only admitting Louisiana as a state, but also President Madison's 1812 request for authorization to seize West Florida.[90] Many Federalists opposed these acquisitions precisely because they would be slave territory and add political weight to the South. Federalist pamphleteers exclaimed that the rush to add slave states to the Union proved that "the Slave country," not content with its overrepresentation in the House, was determined to put the Senate in a permanent headlock.[91] In 1813, an administration official rued that Northern Federalists had succeeded in painting the West Florida initiative as "a Southern one." It thus disgusted "every man north of Washington." "I know and see every day the extent of geographical feeling," he continued, "and the necessity of prudence if we mean to preserve and invigorate the Union."[92]

But the exact nature of that "geographical feeling" was by no means clear in the debates over new states and territories in the early 1810s. For instance, in January 1811, Josiah Quincy vowed that if Congress granted Louisiana statehood, "it is my deliberate opinion that it is virtually a dissolution of this Union; that it will free the States from their moral obligation, and, as it will be the right of all, so it will be the duty of some, definitely to prepare for a separation, amicably if they can, violently if they must." Quincy denounced the extension of slave representation beyond the original limits of the Union, but this was only one of several complaints he had about admitting Louisiana. His fear and loathing of both the South and the West mingled freely throughout his speech.[93] George Poindexter of Mississippi Territory objected that "political jealousy is inculcated between the Eastern and Western States" by such rhetoric as Quincy's. Poindexter did not address slave representation in his rebuttal.[94] Generally speaking, when the participants in the several debates about geographical expansion referred to Louisiana or Mississippi, it was unclear whether they were referring to them as the West, the South, or both. Most Federalists who objected to expansion did so on grounds of the means of obtaining the territory, or the injustice of vanquishing the Indians, at least as often as they objected to the territory as slave territory. Moreover, Virginia Federalists were among those who opposed the "unholy effort to acquire West Florida." It took the political combat of the War of 1812 to clarify Northern Federalists' primary sectional antagonism.[95] Furthermore, Northern Federalists' object was ultimately to deny statehood to and prevent the accession of slave territories, not to prevent the spread of slavery itself. Thus they were the exception that proved the rule of Northern consent to the expansion of slavery into the Deep South.

Between the War of 1812 and the Missouri Crisis, some Northerners protested against the rapid addition of slave states, but they were lonely voices. In 1817, New York Federalist Theodore Dwight complained of how easily the "wicked tyranny" of slavery was being "permitted in all the states, old and young, lying within the limits of the Potomac, the Ohio, and the Mississippi."[96] That same year, "Northern Republican" wrote for the *Aurora*, expostulating against the division of Mississippi Territory into two states. Such a gratuitous addition to the Southern ranks in the Senate and Electoral College, he wrote, suggested that Northern Republicans were blind to the fact that "there are northern interests, and there are southern ones."[97] Yet the editor, William Duane, welcomed the admission of Mississippi and printed a glowing account that concluded that "the Alabama is an American Canaan."[98]

Thus, despite the young republic's extraordinarily rapid expansion and incorporation of new states in the early nineteenth century, and despite the divisiveness of Southern bondage in many other contemporaneous debates that were of less relevance to slavery, the United States was able to avoid serious sectional feuds over the admission of slave states until 1819. This might have been so in part because slave and free states had entered in balancing numbers —five each between 1790 and 1819. Yet it is unclear how formally national politicians adhered to this equivalence. In 1811, when Congressman Felix Grundy of Tennessee declared that conquering Canada would add weight to the North to counter Louisiana and the Floridas, his frankness was a novelty.[99] Moreover, during the War of 1812 and the years immediately following, Yankee Federalists did not complain that the federal government had failed to seize Canada but had swept to victory in the Southwest; indeed, they opposed the invasion of Canada.[100] North-South sectionalism was simply not the factor in territorial issues that it would become in later years. No wonder a congressman exulted in a letter to his constituents that Mississippi statehood proved that in the United States, "events which shake other nations to the centre, pass with us as an ordinary occurrence!"[101] Although no one would make such a boast about the admission of Missouri, it was easily applied to the entrance of slave states before that imbroglio.

The key reason for this was that the vast majority of Northerners were either oblivious or indifferent to the link between the expansion of slavery and the United States' accumulation of new states and territories in the Deep South. For some, these were events to be celebrated, connected with the growth of the Union but somehow divorced from the growth of slavery. Almost all newspapers in all parts of the North welcomed statehood for Mississippi and Alabama, with nary a comment about their constitutional protections for slavery. They praised these nascent states as engines of American expansion and enterprise—places "pregnant with future greatness."[102] From Baltimore, Hezekiah Niles observed that "the division of the Mississippi territory appears to receive the public approbation."[103]

Others noticed slavery's connection to these new states and territories, but met it with a yawn rather than a cry. Slavery in the Deep South seemed only natural. In 1817, a Washington paper blandly noticed that slavery was "to be allowed" in the state of Mississippi, "as might have been anticipated in that section of the Union."[104] In the 1819 debate over limiting slavery in Arkansas Territory, some Northern congressmen opposed Taylor's amendment because "it applied to a . . . southern Territory." A Southern representative insisted that Arkansas was "a low and warm country, that will not support a laboring white population." Enough Northerners concurred with him that the amendment failed.[105] When a newspaper editor praised Indiana's constitutional prohibition of slavery, "however unsuited to the habits and property of more southern territory," he articulated the broad national consensus. "Where slavery was coeval with settlement," he continued, "we see no prospect of its early or advantageous abolition: where it has not existed heretofore, we hope it will never be permitted to intrude."[106]

Even abolitionists subscribed to the principles underlying separate spheres. In 1819, an antislavery group in Pennsylvania urged the complete abolition of slavery in the Keystone State because "the climate and soil, the moral, religious and political habits of Pennsylvania refute all pretence for the continuance of it among us." Beyond Pennsylvania's borders, they pledged only "to persevere in 'promoting the abolition of slavery' wherever it is found practicable."[107] This attitude may explain abolitionists' general acquiescence in the extension of slavery to the Mississippi and Louisiana territories. They later complained about expansion into Missouri largely because no necessity required it.[108] Jesse

Torrey opposed deporting blacks from the South as part of any emancipation scheme, because without their labor white Southerners would be forced to move to "some latitude more favourable to their *physical* powers, or else perish amidst the desolate cotton and rice fields." He insisted that this only meant that black workers were necessary for staple agriculture in the South, not that they must be enslaved.[109] Other abolitionists demonstrated their belief in the climatic credo even as they turned it against slavery. John Kenrick hoped some Moses could take African Americans from their American Pharaohs into the wilderness of Louisiana, "the southern part of which is well calculated for a settlement of the Africans, and too hot a country for a white population."[110]

There were exceptions to the general assent to these climatic assumptions. A New England literary reviewer insisted that there was "no physical impossibility against" a white population cultivating Louisiana, "as has been absurdly pretended by the advocates of slavery."[111] Princeton's Samuel Stanhope Smith agreed that the idea that Africans "are more capable of enduring heat than the Europeans . . . is confirmed by experience." But he asserted that humans were more adaptable to climate than any other animal. This adaptability not only explained racial differences among the human family, but also held out hope that Europeans could cultivate any climate if they became seasoned to it.[112] But these dissenters from the separate spheres doctrines were few and far between and had no influence on public policy.

In the realm of territorial policy, then, if in no other, the North went from quietude before the Missouri controversy to full-scale agitation with its advent. A key part of the context for that change was a serious challenge to free labor's predominance in the Northwest just prior to the Missouri debates. Many observers perceived slavery's forces massing on the Ohio, and this set off alarms across the North, especially in the Northwest itself. The threatened spread of African American bondage—and of African Americans themselves—into the Northwestern states, particularly into Illinois, offered further proof to Northerners that the gulf between them and slavery might soon be traversed.[113]

The debate over allowing slavery north of the Ohio River exposed deep fissures and great diversity within the white population of the Northwest. The group behind legalizing slavery was one vocal element of this mix. The size and nature of this faction was shadowy, but it seems to have been composed mostly of locals rather than of slaveholders shouting across the Ohio River. For their part, most Southern slaveholders seemed bent on expanding slavery not to the Northwest but to the Southwest. They joined in giving Indiana a unanimous vote for statehood in the House of Representatives, despite its strict prohibition of slavery.[114] The state of Mississippi even freed a slave in 1818 based solely on his residence in free territory, just one example of the slave states' recognition of the legitimacy of free territory in the first two decades of the nineteenth century.[115] It seems, then, to have been settlers in the Northwest who were the main advocates of legalizing slavery there. Many of them were of Southern origin, but not all. In 1818, for instance, an emigrant to Illinois from England wrote of how "if I do not have servants I cannot farm; and there are *no* free labourers here, except a few so worthless, that an English Gentleman can do nothing with them." Other less aristocratic farmers came to a similar conclusion; if they did not have many children as a source of labor, they thought the best solution was to extend the quasi-slavery of indentured servitude there, or to legalize slavery outright.[116]

Whatever the numbers or origins of the advocates of Northwestern slavery, their persistence rendered this contest a serious one. The push for slavery went nowhere in Ohio but was a force to be reckoned with in both Indiana and especially Illinois.[117] From 1810 to 1816, the question of slavery wracked Indiana with divisions as it moved toward statehood. Their defeat notwithstanding, the proslavery faction continued to stir up controversy in Indiana well into the 1820s.[118] In the campaign to elect delegates to a state constitutional convention in Illinois in 1818, such were the numbers and influence of the proslavery faction that slavery became the preeminent issue in the contest.[119] In the end, both the Indiana and the Illinois state constitutions struck something of a compromise, banning chattel slavery but protecting the existing indenture system that kept African Americans in servitude.[120]

Slavery's backers had put a fright into their opponents and extorted some concessions, but in the end they failed to extend slavery to the Northwest.[121] Indiana's 1816 state constitution temporized on indentures, but not on slavery itself. It decreed that the constitution could never be amended to allow slavery or involuntary servitude into Indiana.[122] This outcome demonstrated that those in favor of extending slavery were but a vocal minority whose efforts had stimulated the majority. Keeping the Northwest free from slavery appealed to a cross section of people who craved distance from the peculiar institution for their own particular reasons.

As in the states to the east, antislavery was the majority sentiment in the Northwest. "Holding any part of the human creation in slavery, or involuntary servitude," Indiana's constitution boldly asserted, "can only originate in usurpation and tyranny."[123] In the late 1810s, an Ohioan asserted that "the aversion to slavery is deeprooted and universal" in that state. To advocate slavery would be to "forever ruin" one's "influence."[124] In 1816, when William Henry Harrison ran for Congress for the southern Ohio district, his opponent knew he could gain by charging that this transplanted Virginia planter was "a friend to slavery." His handlers vigorously defended him against this accusation, despite the fact that it may very well have been true.[125] During the 1818 debate over slavery in Illinois, antislavery men relished branding their opponents "the advocates of slavery."[126] Those "advocates" resisted that label, emphasizing the practical benefits rather than the rightness of slavery and even protesting their antislavery feelings. "A Friend to Enquiry" argued that admitting slaves to Illinois and then in time emancipating them would strike a greater blow to American slavery than "the mere act of exclusion." Anticipating the rebuttals this would provoke, he shot back in advance that he was sure he would "have many prejudices to encounter from those whose researches have not been altogether guided by humanity."[127] One of his critics found it easy to characterize such tortured logic as proslavery. "Prudence" wrote that "it is the *dernier resort*" of those who, "finding that the naked hook of *unconditional slavery*, will not be swallowed by the people, have adroitly enough, gilded it over with the form of general humanity."[128] Whether east or west of the Appalachians, it was politically untenable for a Northern man to stand up as "a friend to slavery."

Nevertheless, in the Northwest it was even harder than in the Northeastern states to stand up as a friend to black people. One observer believed that was the lesson of one Ohio candidate's defeat; he had "lost much credit" by his "negro vote," a vote in favor of extending civil rights to African Americans in the state constitution.[129] Many white inhabitants of the Northwest had migrated there from the Upper South, and although some became leaders in the proslavery camp, others had emigrated precisely to escape the plantation system. Article VI of the Northwest Ordinance had attracted these and other opponents of slavery from throughout the Union, as it seemed to promise freedom from slavery in the Northwest. But the Southern emigrants carried with them no great love for African Americans. They hated slavery, but principally because it made slaveholders aristocratic tyrants and limited opportunities for neighboring nonslaveholders.[130]

These Southern migrants helped make the Midwest more inhospitable to African Americans than the Northeast was in the early nineteenth century, although just as inhospitable to slavery. They formed the core of a majority group in the Northwest who feared an influx of former slaves from the South. Laws such as Virginia's 1806 manumission statute, which required freed people to leave the state on pain of re-enslavement, raised the possibility of black migration to the North. Most Midwestern whites joined the ex-Southerners in a determination to hold African Americans—no matter their legal status—at bay. In 1814, the citizens of Harrison County, Indiana, apprised their legislature that they were "opposed to the introduction of Slaves or free negroes in any shape."[131] A letter accompanying the petition complained that "nearly one Hundred" black "wretches" had joined a band of white banditti but appealed for the removal only of the black miscreants. If they were not banished from the county, the writer pledged, either "some lives would be lost" or "the most Respetable Citizens will Remove from the Territory," for their "Parridse will be converted into a Hell, if those Negroes Remains in this Neighborhood."[132] Government officials, eager to maintain both order and their states' or territories' population, kept such petitions in mind. In 1817, Ohio's governor, Thomas Worthington, assured his counterpart in Kentucky that his state's citizens harbored not only "a universal prejudice against the principle of slavery," but also a "universal" wish "to get rid of every species of negro population." These facts were "certain."[133]

For a politician, an overwhelming majority was effectively the same as everyone in his state. But Worthington had exaggerated, for there were others who stood up for the rights of black people, considering them their brothers and sisters. Some actively opposed kidnapping, which would have been a very effective way to "get rid of every species of negro population." In late 1815, near Cincinnati, kidnappers killed a black man and dragged his wife into slavery in Kentucky. In response, some Cincinnatians set out to ensure that "these monsters in human shape may receive merited punishment." They hired an agent to track the woman and her abductors down. He rescued her and detained all but one of the perpetrators. The Cincinnati editor reporting these events rejoiced that this woman had been "restored to freedom, the unalienable right of every member of the human family." An editor in Williamsburgh, Ohio, traced these events to slavery itself and proclaimed his unwillingness to publish fugitive slave advertisements, for "I never will be accessory, in any shape, to redelivering a poor distressed negro, fleeing from bondage to the illegal lash of an unfeeling master."[134] Many migrants from New England carried with them religious beliefs that militated against racism. In 1818, a Yankee settled in Marietta, Ohio, asked his fellow citizens in verse: "*Why* despise the tincture of the skin, / Since all mankind are formed alike within?"[135] In 1819, a British traveler reported an incident in which a black man and a white woman came before a justice of the peace in Indiana to be married. The "squire" reminded them of the Indiana law prohibiting "all sexual intercourse between white and coloured people," but he hinted that "if the woman could be qualified to swear that there was black blood in her, the law would not apply." They took the hint and drew blood from the groom, whereupon "the loving bride drank the blood, made the necessary oath, and his honour joined their hands, to the great satisfaction of all parties."[136] Granted, the applicable law was telling. But so was its evasion in this case. In the early nineteenth century, racial prejudice was ascendant in the Northwest, but it was far from unchallenged.

White Northwesterners' divisions on race relations became apparent when they faced the possibility of freed slaves entering their states in larger numbers after the War of 1812. In late 1816, the legislature of Indiana wrestled with the petition of a Tennessee slaveholder who wanted to free forty of his slaves and set them up in their state. It became a real debate between those who wanted nothing but distance from all black people and those who were inclined to favor the request. The former group won in a special committee that denied entrance to the freedmen, warning darkly that an increase in Indiana's African American population would lead to "a holocast [sic]."[137] In the summer of 1819, Ohioans witnessed the arrival of as many as three hundred freed African Americans from Virginia. A group of Quakers went to minister to the needs of the new arrivals.[138] But for most Ohioans, this influx, plus the possibility that the number might reach five hundred, "produced much agitation and regret." They worried "that we are suffering and likely to suffer many of the evils" of slavery, without "any of the benefits." Much as they might "commiserate the situation of those" who were driven from their state upon emancipation, they hoped their "constitution and laws are not so entirely defective as to suffer us to be overrun by such a wretched population." They deplored "the iniquitous policy pursued by the states of Virginia and Kentucky, in driving their free negroes upon us."[139] It was to avoid just such immigrants that Illinois's first state legislature passed a law requiring anyone bringing ex-slaves into the state to post a thousand-dollar bond for each freed person.[140] For many Northwesterners, draconian Southern manumission laws went hand in hand with the drive to fix slavery's parade of evil consequences on what should be the free, white states of the Northwest.

Although divided by the arrival of free blacks from the South, the racial egalitarians and most white supremacists of the Northwest joined in deploring the threatened encroachment of slavery on their region. Antislavery men knew the diversity of their audience and stressed practical over moral objections to slavery. During the Illinois struggle in 1818, even those who railed against slavery as unjust placed greater emphasis on a standard list of reasons why it was inexpedient to allow slavery in the state constitution. Slavery, went this mantra, would expose Illinois to the threat of insurrection, bring in aristocratic land-monopolizing slaveholders, and discourage white emigration to the fledgling state. Daniel P. Cook, a candidate for Congress, knew this party line by heart. He declared himself unequivocally antislavery, in large part "because I conceive the practice repugnant . . . to the best interests of this territory." Those interests, he continued, were its inhabitants' physical safety, freedom from aristocracy, and ability to attract free white emigrants.[141] So ingrained was the mainstream Northwestern antislavery dogma that "Prudence" mustered an able distillation of it within just days of reading the article by "A Friend to Enquiry." He rejected the influx of black people his opponent's scheme proposed, for "the multiplicity of free negroes, has long been a serious grievance in the Atlantic states," and Northwesterners were not insensible of that. It thus made no sense "to bring in these dusky sons of Africa, to where the citizens do not want them." "Prudence" was no abolitionist, however, for he believed Southern slavery was an issue for Southern states, and thus "we cannot complain if some of them admit slavery."[142]

"Prudence" elucidated the conviction of the clear majority of Midwesterners that both black people and slavery belonged south of the Ohio River. To meddle with Southern slavery would be to presume to dictate morality to distant people, which so many Northwesterners resented when done to them.[143] But neither would they accept the imposition of slavery or its concomitants on their neighborhoods. His opponent's idea of introducing and then freeing slaves would have violated both tenets of this creed. Antislavery men's astuteness in emphasizing the effects of slavery on white people likely saved the day for their cause. It certainly kept their coalition of racists and racial liberals together.

For a variety of reasons, then, most Northwesterners believed the Ohio River should be a firm boundary between freedom and slavery. In 1817, the Supreme Court of Ohio spoke to this belief when ruling on a case in which a Kentucky man claimed as his slave a man who had escaped in Ohio while on his master's business. The court's opinion was *that where a slave was sent into this State to perform services for his master, even for a day, the slave was entitled to his freedom.*[144] These justices hoped to make the Ohio a more secure border than it was in reality. The fact that that border was not so impermeable as they had hoped had political as well as judicial consequences. In early 1819, when Ohio legislators proposed a new state constitutional convention, slavery's opponents raised a hue and cry, declaring the convention movement a key part of a conspiracy to affix slavery on the Northwest. The agitation for slavery in Indiana and Illinois had lost but was still recent and not entirely dormant in early 1819. Thus the slavery issue helped defeat the convention movement, which went down by a margin of five to one.[145] Northwestern voters and lawmakers had repelled the advance of slavery but were still skittish in the immediate aftermath of their victories, for it seemed that slavery never rested.

Others outside the Northwest sought to preserve the Northwest from slavery's restless expansionism. In November 1818, Congressman James Tallmadge of New York opposed admitting Illinois into the Union, because in its constitution "the principle of slavery, if not adopted in the constitution, was at least not sufficiently prohibited." He preferred Indiana's constitution, which upheld the spirit of the Northwest Ordinance by precluding any future allowances for slavery. Those who worried about slavery's encroachments surely were not reassured when Ohio's Harrison responded to Tallmadge by impugning Article VI, which "had shorn the people of their sovereign authority." He hoped to see all Northwesterners "disenthralled from the effect of articles to which they never gave their assent, and to which they were not properly subject." Tallmadge's amendment failed in the House by a 117–34 margin.[146] Thus many Northerners did not share Tallmadge's alarm, although others did. In the summer of 1819, Eastern editors evinced their consternation as they circulated the rumor that Ohio was about to amend its constitution to allow slavery.[147] An Ohio editor sought to reassure them by pointing to "the habits, character, and pursuits of our fellow citizens," as well as "our republican institutions," all of which "tend to preserve a degree of equality among us altogether unfavorable to the toleration of slavery in any shape." To speak of equality of condition was to connect especially with ex-Southerners who hated the aristocracy of slave holding states. To speak of superior habits and character was to connect especially with New England transplants who had long prided themselves on their superiority over inhabitants of the slave states.[148] He was confident that this mix of migrants and motives would secure Ohio for freedom.

Notwithstanding Harrison and Tallmadge, and the nervous Eastern editors and the apparently calm Ohio editor, Northwesterners had more concrete reasons to feel threatened by proposals to expand slavery to the Northwest as well as to the Southwest in the years following the War of 1812. This particular hazard to Northerners' "not-in-my-backyard" brand of antislavery most directly menaced the backyards of Midwesterners.

Yet Tallmadge and those Eastern editors had their reasons for concern. Northeasterners who expected that either they or their children would seek their fortunes in the West believed that the spread of slavery there would blight all their fair hopes. Moreover, especially in the Mid-Atlantic where slavery was breaching the Mason-Dixon Line in search of victims, the thought of slavery spreading to the Northwest reinforced a sense of siege against this expansive institution. It seemed that slavery was on the attack on several fronts. The unruffled Ohio editor sought to allay these fears when he appealed to the climatic creed of almost all Northerners. He argued that "the peculiarities of our soil and climate" formed a barrier to slavery's prosperity in Ohio.[149] His readers might have been more reassured by this recitation of American dogma ten years earlier. Most white Northerners still clung to it, as evidenced by their lack of opposition to the accession of slave states and territories well into 1819. But after the War of 1812 had set slavery in rapid motion, they had had to defend against slavery in territory that their faith in separate spheres had told them was off-limits to slavery: the Mid-Atlantic and the Northwest.

———————

In 1820, the Revolutionary hero Marquis de Lafayette wrote to his friend James Madison concerning slavery. "One is I believe More Struck with the evil," he submitted, "when Looking Upon it from without."[150] Lafayette's insight had great merit, especially given that he was writing to a man who had accommodated to the peculiar institution which surrounded him.[151] Yet no one was more "struck with the evil" than those who sought distance from slavery but could not attain it. Those who truly observed it from a distance might join Lafayette in deprecating it. But for those not inclined to principled antislavery, it was possible to sidestep the issue to some degree, pervasive as it was in the Atlantic world in the early nineteenth century. Another foreign observer, Charles Dickens, captured the psychological roots of the drive for distance when he encountered slavery in America. "Though I was, with respect to it, an innocent man," he wrote, "its presence filled me with a sense of shame and self-reproach."[152] The outrage with slavery and its abuses in the Mid-Atlantic and Northwest after the War of 1812 derived from this sort of unwanted proximity to Southern bondage, not from the relative remoteness the likes of Lafayette and New Englanders enjoyed.

Thus, the postwar expansion of slavery shaped the regional patterns of Northern sectionalism. New Englanders could afford to revel in living in the "cradle of liberty." Thus, although they partook of the antislavery sentiment that suffused the zeitgeist, they did not experience the outrage that pushed Mid-Atlantic Northerners to man the dikes that kept slavery from overflowing into their self-consciously free states. The contours of partisan politics in the Era of Good Feelings only reinforced these regional patterns.[153]

Whether simply sectional or freighted with the baggage of factional politics, the divisions of the late 1810s played an important role in the development and prominence of the divergence between slave and free states.[154] To be sure, the drive to defend against slavery and its various fruits revealed the complexity of Northern race relations, which were often not far removed from racial discrimination in the South. Yet the struggles of these years set threatened states even more firmly on the side of abolition, as Indiana's 1816 constitution and New York's 1817 abolition law demonstrated most clearly. Postwar politics also clarified even further that no sectional rift in the United States was as threatening as that between the North and the South over slavery. Lingering disagreements between the East and the West provoked nothing like the passions of the North-South split over slavery.[155] The confluence of slavery's aggressiveness and its proscription in the realm of ideology had produced a clash pregnant with implications for the North as well as the nation as a whole.

Defending Slavery

IN WHAT WAS becoming a familiar dialectic, the North's defense against slavery in the Era of Good Feelings produced a parallel defensiveness in the South. Limited as was abolitionist activity in the North, slavery's aggressions in the Mid-Atlantic and the Northwest had opened the door to more strident antislavery rhetoric. As the British added their voices to this chorus, and as black people resisted slavery more actively, it became apparent that the general tenor of the times was hostile to slavery even as it expanded its territory. All of this pushed many of slavery's protectors to erect stronger ideological fortifications and abandon exposed positions.

Yet white Southerners did not speak as one on such issues. Indeed, the postwar politics of slavery demonstrated the variety of their opinions and highlighted important new trends in Southern thought. Although most Southern politicos retained great faith in the federal government, a small but important minority sought to convince their peers that strict construction of the Constitution and a firmer commitment to state rights were the only sure safeguards for their increasingly peculiar institution. Many slaveholders and their allies welcomed the philanthropic, evangelizing spirit of the postwar period, in part because they hoped to usher in a pious, paternalistic—and thus more defensible—version of slavery. But others (perhaps a majority of slaveholders, and definitely the loudest group) rejected humanitarianism and missionizing as false humanity that would lead to dangerous meddling with slavery. The roles of government and religion in a slave society were very much up for debate within the South.

The spectrum of thought concerning slavery itself was also wide and contested in the postwar South. White Southerners spoke from various points along a continuum that ran from condemning slavery, through acquiescing in it as permanent if indefensible, to affirming it to be a positive good. In the second decade of the nineteenth century, few occupied either extreme along this spectrum: committed, effective antislavery and strident, unadulterated proslavery found few if any voices. The general trend, however, continued in the direction of recognizing slavery's permanence in the South. And under the pressure of outside attacks, many proponents of slavery fumbled toward a positive-good position. In short, in the second decade of the nineteenth century, leading white Southerners accepted their section's identification with slavery and fought for its interests and reputation with increasing vigor.

––––––––

In a federal union that included the increasingly antislavery North, the question of whether the central government was a reliable bulwark for slavery was of prime importance. A majority of slaveholders still thought the answer to that question was yes. In the 1810s, nationalists and broad constructionists most often carried the day against advocates of state rights and strict construction of the Constitution. When President James Madison ordered an army into West Florida in 1810, he did so without a declaration of war and on the loosest of constructions of the Constitution.[1] Andrew Jackson's invasion of Florida without official authorization from Washington became a bone of contention in 1818 and early 1819 when the likes of Richmond editor Thomas Ritchie rediscovered the virtues of state rights and strict construction. But the majority of whites, particularly in the Deep South, sided with America's hero Jackson, "the protector of *her* soil—the defender of *her* liberties."[2] It was hard for slaveholders and their allies to oppose federal actions that expanded the sphere of their institutions (particularly slavery), no matter those actions' constitutionality. But they also tended to vote in Congress for policies—a national bank, tariffs, and so forth—that most observers believed would benefit the North more than the South. In the late 1810s, future strict constructionists like John C. Calhoun would have preferred to see the federal government extend its reach further, and the politicians were not alone. After gauging public opinion in South Carolina in 1816, Calhoun declared, "I hear not one objection to the bank, Tariff, or taxes."[3] It seems that many Southern Republicans felt secure enough in the driver's seat in Washington that they could afford to be generous to interests that were not their own.[4] Others also may have seen votes for Northern interests as a way of defusing heretical Northern Republicans' challenge to their place in that seat.

At any rate, with slaveholders and their allies in charge of the federal government, their constituents were confident that it would protect and serve both the

South and slavery. In 1812, Virginia's governor, James Barbour, complied with the national government's request to join some of his militia with its regulars in Norfolk. He told his legislature that he would not "indulge . . . in any glowing professions of zeal and ardor in the cause of *state* rights" in order to explain away such a course of action. The Constitution, he insisted, "has most wisely in my opinion, placed the whole physical force of the nation under the control of the national authority."[5] Such a position would have been untenable in Virginia while John Adams was president. Just a few months later, Virginia approved a state army to help the militia defend against slave revolt and the British. At the request of the federal government, however, Virginia agreed to disband this force in exchange for federal troops being stationed in Norfolk.[6] Although these regulars could not protect Virginia's slaveholders from losing thousands of slaves to the British during the war, that hardly shook the state government's faith that Washington would act to protect their property in slaves. The governor recommended that county courts record the slaves lost to the enemy. Then the federal government could press the British for compensation, "or, if the government should deem it wisest with a view to the interest of the whole to forbear to press the point, it will itself indemnify" Virginia's planters.[7] Such was the strength of most leading Virginians' belief that their national government would do right by them.

Slaveholders considered crushing slave resistance a job for the central government in peacetime as well as in wartime. Federal troops helped suppress the slave rebellion in Louisiana in January 1811, and in its aftermath the territory's Legislative Council declared its intention to call on the federal government for one regiment of regular troops to be "permanently stationed at New Orleans." It was counting on this regiment to guard this important American frontier against "external and internal dangers."[8] In 1816, facing depredations from the inhabitants of the Negro Fort, a Georgia editor could "discover no reason why the regular troops, of whom there are more than enough in the nation, should not be ordered" to destroy the Fort "with the least possible delay." It should be enough for Southern state officials to "draw their attention to this subject."[9] Later that year, South Carolina's governor looked to Congress to better supply the state militia in the face of stubborn maroon communities in the swamps and slave insurrection plots. He also freely granted the federal government's authority to nationalize the militia to meet such threats.[10] Such slaveholders expected the central government to act in their interests. They did so with good reason. The personnel and policies of the Republican Congresses and administrations posed no conflict with their local or sectional concerns.[11]

Yet slaveholders were not the only Americans who hoped the federal government would further their aims in relation to slavery. As historian Winthrop
Jordan has written, from its very inception "Congress looked like a magnificent
fulcrum to antislavery organizations."[12] In the early nineteenth century, slavery's opponents continued to look to the national government for aid. The
advocates of abolition repeatedly called for strong government intervention to
effect the emancipation schemes they put forward.[13]

Many of these proposals were advanced as alternatives to the American Colonization Society (ACS), which was the most popular plan and which itself
sought federal funding. "Warburton," for instance, wrote to the *National Intelligencer* of how the ACS plan would never keep pace with the natural increase of
slaves and thus could never remove slavery. But "as slavery is a natural misfortune, the power of the nation ought to be applied to remove it." Specifically, he
urged the government to acquire California, there to establish a multiracial
paradise. If its constitution had no racial proscriptions, freed slaves would
flock there, and "the Californians, under our protection, would become a
distinguished nation, descended from all nations and colors, and, amalgamated
and knit together by a government of perfect equality," would erect a model
of free government.[14] Writers so ill-attuned to Southern sensibilities were
bound to alienate slaveholders from such schemes, and potentially from all
such schemers.

Influential Baltimore editor Hezekiah Niles also envisioned the blurring of
race lines and the intervention of the federal government in achieving abolition. He reluctantly rejected the ACS plan as impracticable.[15] He proposed that
the federal government (by unspecified but supposedly constitutional means)
separate free blacks from slaves, check the increase of the slave population, and
stop the flow of African Americans from the free to the slave states. The
national government would also buy several thousand slave women of child-
bearing age and send them to the North. There, "by *adventitious mixtures, the
effect of common association with the whites, and the operation of climate,*" they would
become lighter in complexion and thus able to be received into American
society. Thus, after long preparation (not to mention magic skin whitening),
many slaves who had been rendered fit for freedom could be liberated, by
national authorities who would not quibble about constitutional questions.[16]

Many other would-be emancipators envisaged bringing the strong arm of
the federal government to bear on their particular projects. Estwick Evans
proposed that Congress buy every slave in the Union and then allow them to
work for self-purchase and full citizenship. This would be cost-free in the long

run for the government, he insisted. Moreover, it was unquestionably "in our power to give freedom to the slaves within our jurisdiction."[17] Such a broad definition of his "jurisdiction" from a Yankee abolitionist surely gave many slaveholders in his audience pause. Another celebrated traveler, James Riley, yearned for some plan of gradual emancipation, "developed and enforced by the general government."[18] Another New England abolitionist, John Kenrick, submitted that it would not "cost the United States more than the expenses of the late war, if so much, to redeem all the slaves, (by making a moderate, but reasonable compensation to the present slave-holders,) and colonize them in South Louisiana." "Whenever the government of the United States shall come to the righteous and consistent determination, that *all the inhabitants shall be free*," he enthused, "it is believed that no insurmountable obstacles will be found in the way of its accomplishment."[19]

In the face of such appeals, a small but influential group of Southern leaders sought to set up just such obstacles against the day when the federal government might reach that determination. State rights and strict construction must hedge in federal power lest the meddlers of the North succeed in hijacking that power. Led by Thomas Ritchie, some postwar Southerners insisted that the expansive projects and proposals of the federal government—a national bank, support for internal improvements, even a national university—amounted to unconstitutional "usurpation."[20] This reversion to the principles of the "Old Republicans" gained momentum especially in the Upper South in the Era of Good Feelings.[21] The revivification of these principles stemmed in part from the need to defend slavery.

No one explained the link between parrying the blows aimed at slavery and limiting the powers of the national government more distinctly than Nathaniel Macon, North Carolina's leader in Congress. He did so in private conversations and in correspondence with younger Southern leaders, hoping to persuade a new generation to carry the Old Republican tradition into a dangerous new world. In March 1818, Macon implored one of his protégés, fellow Carolinian Bartlett Yancey, to "examine the constitution of the U.S.— . . . and then tell me if Congress can establish banks, make roads and canals, whether they cannot free all the Slaves in the U.S." "We have abolition-colonizing bible and peace societies," he reminded Yancey, whose members possessed "a character and spirit of perseverance, bordering on enthusiasm; and if the general government shall continue to stretch their powers, these societies will undoubtedly push them to try the question of emancipation." "The states having no slaves," Macon continued, "may not feel as strongly, as the States having slaves about

stretching the constitution; because no such interest is to be touched by it."
Thus the South must be ever vigilant about assumed powers and broad construction, for "the camp that is not always guarded may be surprised; and the
people which do not always watch their rulers may be enslaved."[22] Yancey was
not entirely convinced, however, so the next month Macon exhorted him to
reexamine the Constitution, whereupon he surely would recognize his error. "If
Congress can make canals," he reiterated, "they can with more propriety
emancipate. Be not deceived, I speak soberly in the fear of God, and the love of
the constitution." The Apostle Paul, he preached, "was not more anxious or
sincere concerning Timothy, than I am for you; your error in this, will injure if
not destroy our beloved mother N. Carolina and all the South country."[23]

Macon's religious and military imagery in these letters spoke volumes. In his
years in Congress he had seen slavery become a sectional and partisan battleground. His confidence in the justice of the South's cause impelled his quest
to inculcate orthodoxy in the rising generation. Only if they repented of their
prodigal search for the wealth and glory of internal improvements and other
distractions would the sons of the South buckle down to man their besieged
section's battlements. Macon understood the attraction of internal improvements and had no objection to states or private ventures funding them. He even
invested in a private canal company. It really was a constitutional question for
Macon, as expressed so frankly in his letters.[24]

Macon failed to convert legions of nationalistic postwar slaveholders to his
cause, but he was not exactly a lone voice in the wilderness. His mission would
continue with less fruit than he hoped well into the 1820s.[25] But he kept the Old
Republican faith alive, and a few Southern spokesmen came around to his
point of view during the Era of Good Feelings. Some Southern spokesmen
linked slavery to Old Republican principles only implicitly. In 1817, Representative John Tyler of Virginia wrote to his constituents to explain his vote against
federal aid for internal improvements. He was not about to "deny the great importance of roads and canals," but he voted against federal funding for specific
constitutional reasons with a sectional twist. "Congress," he announced, had
"no power under the Constitution to interfere with the *police* of the States."[26]

Still others explicitly connected localism and strict construction to the maintenance of slavery. In 1818, when a New Jersey congressman resolved that
Congress restrict the transportation of blacks from free states to slave states,
Mississippi's George Poindexter objected. He argued that every man "had a
right to remove his property from one State to another, and slaves as well as
other property, if not prohibited from doing so by the State laws. With those

laws, whatever they were, the United States . . . had no right to interfere." He raised the specter of the federal government enforcing the proposed ban by "military force," assuring his colleagues that short of such draconian measures such a law would be unenforceable in the South.[27] In an election address in early 1819, Virginia's George Tucker sang the praises of the balance and order of America's federal system, which had kept the confederacy from civil war. The first advantage of this system of limited government, he declared, was that it left states to decide questions related to slavery.[28] Although most prominent Southerners retained a strong faith that the federal government would pro- tect—indeed expand—slavery, an important and slowly growing minority re- verted to the faith of their fathers with a sense of sectional peril.[29]

———

Nathaniel Macon found far more slaveholders in agreement with him on the danger posed by the "enthusiasm" of "abolition-colonizing bible and peace societies." After Napoleon's fall and the return of peace to Europe, many believers in both Britain and America looked to the postwar era as one in which Christianity would diffuse its beneficent rays upon the benighted regions of the entire world. There seemed no limit to what a global extension of America's Second Great Awakening might achieve. The different forms of reform over- lapped, so that temperance men and women embraced missionary work, anti- slavery, and / or a variety of other causes.[30] The boundlessness and zeal of this evangelizing movement, radiating as it did from England and New England, frightened many Southern slaveholders. In response, they rejected the optimis- tic, philanthropic spirit of their age, much as some slaveholders (in smaller numbers and more quietly) were revolting against the unrestrained nationalism of the postwar era.

It became common for slaveholders and their sympathizers to allege that humanitarian zeal produced dire, unintended consequences. An 1818 piece in a Richmond paper used a history of the African slave trade to make this case. The author wondered whether contemporaries so eager to embrace antislavery knew that the hated traffic "had its principal origin in the bosom of one of the most humane enthusiasts that ever lit upon this globe"—the Spanish champion of the aboriginal inhabitants of the New World, Bartolomé de Las Casas. In seeking to protect the Indians from enslavement, he encouraged the importa- tion of Africans as replacement labor. "Las Casas, in the spirit of a false enthusi- asm," thereby "sowed a seed, which has vegetated into a . . . tree of the most frightful dimensions and the most poisonous qualities." It would ever be thus with "men who hurry with headlong impetuosity towards a favorite point."[31]

Other opponents of antislavery humanitarianism drew on this history. In early 1819, the Richmond attorney George Hay, President Monroe's son-in-law, visited Secretary of State John Quincy Adams to voice his opposition to coop-eration with Great Britain against the slave trade. The bans on the Atlantic slave trade, Hay insisted, "had already produced incomparably more mischief than good." For he had "no doubt" that the fatal revolution in St. Domingue was "the legitimate offspring of Mr. Wilberforce's first abolition plans." He concluded his homily by observing that "there was no such absurd reasoner in the world as humanity." For the "slave trade itself was the child of humanity— the contrivance of Las Casas to mitigate the condition of the American In-dians."[32] Hay's diatribe typified a burgeoning Southern argument that the misguided philanthropy of those ignorant of the true nature of slavery was likely to cause infinitely more harm than good. They repeatedly published this warning to abolitionists and their ilk as well as to other slaveholders.[33]

Other Southern spokesmen accused antislavery zealots of being far worse than misguided. They claimed that these so-called philanthropists were so arrogant as to dismiss the light of scripture and the lessons of history in the pursuit of their chimerical theories.[34] Worse, such theories were merely a cloak for self-interest and ambition. "For many years past," asserted one writer, "it has been customary to inveigle or decoy colored servants" away from their masters, allegedly so "that the *poor wretches* might *enjoy* the *benefits* arising from residence in a *Christian* community." But now that Northerners had learned that free blacks were thieves, they wanted to exile them to Africa under the auspices of the ACS. This scheme "redounds but little to the humanity of the people, who enticed them from the guardianship of a provident and benevolent master." Indeed, "it appears that humanity and Christianity, when they affect the pocket, are, too often in the north, a mere rhapsody, a display of words without meaning."[35]

Another astute scribbler branded philanthropists as Federalists and charged them with reverse racism. He claimed that although "the *federal* editors to the eastward, are constantly harping upon the situation of the slaves in the south-ern states," they supported the restoration of Europe's monarchs, "whose busi-ness it ever has been to enslave mankind." "A true philanthropist," he lectured, "views with equal regret and indignation the wrongs of humanity in every quarter of the globe." He groused that "the pens of *federal* editors shed no sympathetic ink for the miserable slaves of European kings," because "the *Africans* have all their sympathy; the slaves in Maryland, Virginia, South Caro-lina and Georgia call forth all their solicitude. . . . Out upon you, ye hypocrites!"[36] This tactic was well placed politically, allowing this writer to sidestep the original issue of slavery and brand all abolitionists as the self-serving imposters that all Republicans knew Federalists to be. Indeed, the legacy of the War of 1812 and its surrounding domestic and international disputes sealed many white Southerners' suspicions against the benevolent movements emanating from New and Old England. These suspicions related to a fear of Northern and British cultural imperialism that ran deep from plain folk to grandees in the postwar South. A Kentuckian summed up this attitude when he inveighed against "northern missionaries whose 'Female Societies, Cent Societies, Mite Societies, Children Societies, and even Negro Societies' gave off the odor of 'the *New England Rat.*' "[37]

Although some white Southerners were enthusiastic in their rejection of enthusiasm, others made their withdrawal from humanitarianism reluctantly, admitting that slavery made such a course necessary.[38] Missions to slaves were one manifestation of the age's spirit of benevolent reform,[39] and many slaveholders saw such endeavors as dangerous. In 1816, in the aftermath of the slave conspiracy in Camden, South Carolina, a local editor noted that "those who were most active in this conspiracy occupied a respectable stand in one of our churches." "Let us borrow from this memorable example of Ethiopian depravity an useful lesson," he recommended, namely that it is dangerous to instruct "the savage mind." "In vain," he warned, "may we attempt to repress a spirit of liberty" once inculcated. As long as they remained slaves, "it is destructive to happiness and incompatible with our interests to improve their understandings."[40] At least twice in the 1810s, South Carolina's legislature received petitions from citizens calling for measures to strengthen the bonds of slavery in the state. They professed to have been initially in favor of ameliorating the slaves' lot, but were now sure "that one of the consequences of softening their condition as slaves has been their forgetting that they were such."[41]

Yet other slaveholders declined to withdraw from the burgeoning empire of benevolence for any reason. Some simply got caught up in the evangelical fervor sweeping the Atlantic.[42] Some thought even the profitable institution of slavery must conform to principles of benevolence to be legitimate. Such was the editor of the *Charleston Courier*, who printed Englishman William Faux's account of a slave whipped to death under the following poetical extract: "*The well taught philanthropic mind, / To all compassion gives, / Casts round the world an equal eye, / And feels for all that lives!*"[43]

These evangelicals tended to become proponents of reform, hoping to render the master-slave relationship holier and more paternalistic, and therefore safer and more permanent. In 1813, Episcopal minister William Meade, later an officer of the ACS, published an appeal in favor of teaching slaves to read. He denied that this course would render slaves more troublesome—indeed, quite the opposite. For masters could control what their slaves read, he implausibly insisted. Furthermore, they would answer to God for their stewardship over their slaves' souls, so it was in their best eternal interests to teach their "people" to read the Bible.[44] John Taylor of Caroline called upon his fellow slaveholders to improve the material circumstances of their slaves, thus "binding his slave to his service, by a ligament stronger than chains."[45] The framers of state constitutions in both Mississippi (1817) and Alabama (1819) aimed to render slavery both permanent and more humane. They severely circumscribed their state assemblies' power to permit manumissions or otherwise act against slavery. But they also allowed for laws restricting the domestic slave trade and punishing cruelty to slaves.[46] A fictional account of a conversation between a Christian slave and his unconverted fellow bond servant also hoped to inculcate a kinder, stronger slavery. The convert preached to his companion against stealing from his master and was a model servant. When his pupil repented and sought his master's forgiveness, the master's generosity and joy in his conversion made the slave "love him for true. I wish every poor negro been have such a good master."[47] The author of this pamphlet, a Baptist minister in South Carolina, clearly hoped to convince masters that evangelizing slaves would greatly strengthen their paternalist credentials.

Some white Southerners sought to stay in the humanitarian mainstream because they hoped to cultivate a better image for the South. They therefore chided their fellow Southrons whose antiphilanthropic stance ceded all claims of humanity to the Yankees and Britons. "A True Virginian" rebuked one such curmudgeon's sweeping denunciation of benevolence, wishing that he had not claimed to represent all Virginians' sentiments. "Surely this is not a sentiment worthy of the intelligence . . . or philanthropy of a *Virginian*. I am a Virginian; but I enter my protest most solemnly against so monstrous an absurdity" as the idea that philanthropy caused more harm than good. He argued that the "*inhuman schemes*" of history had caused the most misery, not the humane ones.[48] Meanwhile, "Colonizer" admonished slaveholders who disgraced the South "in the estimation of the world" by vainly seeking to "arrest the progress of the moral revolution which is evidently working in relation to Africa" and African Americans.[49] Such souls contested all accusations of slavery's systematic cruelty and joined with philanthropists when they could. They were convinced that selective participation in the reform spirit of the age would buttress slavery both institutionally and in appearance.

But it would do so only if the outside world knew the extent to which slaveholders were participating. So these managers of the South's image trumpeted their commitment to the ACS. In 1819, a Virginia paper gave an account of a local ACS meeting, ostentatiously praising Southern support for the "humane scheme."[50] They also asserted that Southerners loathed the kidnapping of free African Americans just as much as Yankees did. They made sure those Northern brethren knew it when officials in the slave states punished kidnapping.[51] They piled up the epithets on the kidnappers, acknowledging that the practice impaired "the honor, the humanity of this nation."[52] They expressed their shock to "discover" that kidnapping existed and insisted that "our Northern brethren may rest assured, that none but the most unworthy of our citizens could participate in, or connive at, a business so infamous."[53] Known kidnappers did indeed suffer obloquy. In 1818, for instance, one Charles Morgan wrote to the *New-Orleans Gazette* contesting "the charge of *kidnapping*," seeking for his sake and that of his family to refute "so foul an imputation."[54]

Slaveholders also knew that the domestic slave trade opened them to censure and sought to minimize that opening. They hoped to preclude Yankee condemnation and intervention in the traffic by assuring the nation that they were acting against it on their own. Thus they ensured that Southern state governments' restrictions of the commerce received publicity in the North.[55] They acknowledged that some evaded these laws but insisted that public opinion in the South was not with the violators. "The evasion or violation of these restrictions does not," a Georgian wrote, "argue a disposition in the majority, in favor of the traffic, any more than the violation of the laws against stealing or murder, or against any fraud or violence, argues a general sentiment against those laws."[56] It was the Virginian John Randolph, in fact, who led the fight in Congress in 1816 to abolish the slave trade within the District of Columbia. This traffic, Randolph asserted, was "a crying sin before God and man" as well as a national embarrassment. He insisted that he did not mean to interfere "in the very delicate subject of the relation between the slave and his master," but slave ownership did not require "that this city should be made a depot of slaves." In fact, it was the slave trade, not his attempts to restrict it in Washington, that interfered with the master-slave relationship, for it tore the slave "from his master, his friends, his wife, his children, or his parents." Thus only "base, hard-hearted masters" in pursuit of high slave prices could participate in

the traffic. Randolph's fellow Virginian Henry St. George Tucker balked at
proposals to refer Randolph's bill to his committee on the District but protested
that he was "no less willing than [Randolph] to cooperate in the measure."[57]
Friendliness to the slave trade was not a tenable position in national politics in
the 1810s, especially if one hoped, as Randolph apparently did, to do public
relations for slavery as a domestic institution.[58]

When Randolph singled out "hard-hearted masters," he pursued a typical
strategy of those who wanted to present Southern slavery as humane. In response to Northern calumny against the South as a whole, slaveholders began
to craft the image of the slave trader as an outcast from Southern society. They
loaded upon these scapegoats all the guilt of the traffic in African Americans.
One writer, with the significant pseudonym of "Philanthropos," decried the
cruelties the slave trade inflicted on blacks merely "to make money for some
pitiless wretch, who has not the spirit or pride to pursue a more honorable
calling."[59] A Georgia editor railed at the open violations of his state's laws
against the domestic commerce "by a set of men, who of all others have least
right to calculate on escaping unpunished"—"the Negro Traders who infest
our State." "The people of this state," he insisted, "*will not* tolerate such vil-
lainy."[60] Charles Ball, who was a victim of the slave trade in the early nineteenth
century, painted a different picture of slave traders' status in society, at least in
the Lower South. A speculator purchased Ball in Maryland, where the citizens
called him "a *negro buyer, or Georgia trader*, sometimes a *negro driver*." But in South
Carolina, he found that "no branch of trade was more honorable than the
traffic in us poor slaves." He later learned that this slave speculator "had
acquired a very respectable fortune—had lately married in a wealthy family"
near Savannah, "and was a great planter."[61] But the realities were less important for Southern exponents than the need to distinguish between mercenary
slave dealers and a virtuous general public led by patriarchal planters. They
recognized that the traffic in slaves highlighted the harshness and commercial
elements of the master-slave relationship. Thus they sought to preserve slavery
itself from condemnation by setting the slave trade apart as a foreign element in
and abuse of the institution.[62] They retained hope that if slavery's worst features
could be shorn or obscured, it might be made to coexist easily with the spirit of
benevolence and reform.

This endeavor was tricky in relation to the economically vital domestic slave
trade, but it was much easier when the Atlantic slave trade resurfaced as a
political issue. Many Southern leaders embraced opportunities to go on record
against the noxious foreign commerce, such as by vilifying foreign nations for

continuing to pursue it.[63] When possible, they categorically denied allegations of smuggling into the Southern states.[64] But credible reports of illicit importations, especially into New Orleans, circulated around the nation.[65] So leading Southern lights joined others in calling for the smugglers' condign punishment.[66] In 1816, Congressman John C. Calhoun spoke warmly against "that odious traffic" and confessed to being "ashamed" that his state's delegates to the Constitutional Convention had been instrumental in securing an allowance for the practice until 1808. Later that year he bought slaves through the domestic slave trade without batting an eye.[67] Upon learning of a Louisiana law probably meant to evade the national slave trade ban, Thomas Ritchie's outrage swept him into advocating a surprising policy. If "such a disgraceful provision" did in fact "exist on the statute book of Louisiana," he demanded, "ought not Congress immediately to counteract it?"[68] Ritchie was so eager to land on the right side of this subject that he championed what one would expect him to execrate as rank nationalism and Yankee interference.

Slaveholders joined with other Americans to bolster the federal ban on the Atlantic slave trade. In late 1818 and early 1819, numerous contraband slaves were sold at auction in Georgia and Louisiana, with the proceeds going to the national treasury, as provided for in the law of 1807. A leading abolitionist rightly observed that these transactions had "excited universal indignation" throughout the United States.[69] The clause of the 1807 law that left the disposal of illegally imported Africans to the local authorities now looked like a monstrous loophole. In May 1819, the ACS made a well-publicized pitch to purchase and colonize some 58 Africans slated to be sold by the government at Milledgeville, Georgia. Its board of managers threw down the gauntlet especially to the philanthropists of the Southern states, arguing that by donating funds to redeem these Africans they could prove "the sincerity of those expressions of detestation so frequently uttered against the slave trade."[70] Many leading Southerners picked it up, then exulted that the contributions of the liberal men of "what are sneeringly called the *slave states*" had outstripped those of "the citizens of the more fortunate states, whose Halls and Temples have so often resounded with eloquent denunciations" of the slave states.[71]

Indeed, leading Southerners gladly embraced this opportunity to safely prove their humanitarianism in relation to slavery. Ritchie argued that the "inhuman and unjust" loopholes in the 1807 law should be closed forthwith. He asked, "What right have we to sell a poor wretch, as a slave, whom we punish another person for attempting to sell?" He recommended that the government free the smuggled Africans and then let municipal laws, such as Virginia's statute requiring free blacks to leave the state, deal with them.[72] This national consensus secured a strengthened slave trade law in 1819, which turned seized contraband over to the ACS for deportation to Africa and defined participation in the Atlantic traffic as piracy, a capital crime. One Virginian rejoiced in the new law. "I do not know that my American pride was ever more highly excited," he cried.[73] Such men spoke to the drive to very publicly accommodate slavery to the humanitarian impulses of the age, even as others loudly spurned them.

––––––––––

White Southerners also took a variety of positions in relation to the moral rightness of slavery and its prospects for perpetuity in America. The early-nineteenth-century South enjoyed freedom of expression, even on the subject of slavery. Southern abolitionists got a chilly reception, but from Kentucky to South Carolina they could still publish their works. They knew they could expect controversy, but they forged ahead and their tracts saw the light of day, if briefly. Antislavery white Southerners understood that the moral uncertainty of slavery's defenders gave them room to operate. The ideals of the American Revolution still led some few slaveholders to antislavery conclusions.[74] Slaveholders knew, wrote Kentucky abolitionist David Barrow, "that the word SLAVE, implies an opposite character, very odious to all true republicans and lovers of the rights of man." Thus white Southerners could flail away at the institution in moralistic terms without having their presses or lives endangered.[75]

Still, there was subtle pressure on the South's remaining abolitionists. In 1818, an anonymous correspondent of a Georgia newspaper lamented that a Southern writer was "so often compelled, from the existing state of society, to suppress his opinions merely on account of their strength and their *liberality*."[76] Although it was possible to maintain a critique of slavery from within the South in 1810s, only the boldest spirits continued to do so, for very few others sincerely held their point of view.

This reaction against the radical principles and heady expressions of the Revolutionary era emerged in large part because of the use to which the enemies of slavery and the South put them. Abolitionists repeatedly quoted Thomas Jefferson's unflattering depiction of the tyrannical commerce between master and slave in *Notes on the State of Virginia*, which had become a standard text for any discussion of slavery in the early republic. They hoped to capitalize on Jefferson's authority as both a spokesman for the Revolution and a slaveholder in the know.[77] These usages convinced some of slavery's defenders to distance themselves from the famous passage and the principles it represented. John Taylor, for one, was determined to disprove Jefferson. "If Mr. Jefferson's assertions are correct," he gibed, "it is better to run the risque of natural extinction, by liberating and fighting the blacks, than to live abhorred of God, and consequently hated of man." But inasmuch as "they are erroneous, they ought not to be admitted as arguments for the emancipating policy." He recoiled at the idea that God would side with the slaves in any contest with their masters. He pointed to Greek and Roman as well as American history to dismiss the notion that slaveholders were tyrants who were not to be trusted with the liberties of the people. "Even the author of the quotation himself," Taylor pointed out, "may be fairly adduced as an instance which refutes every syllable of his chapter on Virginia manners." Finally, he argued that slavery set such a social distance between masters and slaves that it encouraged paternalistic benevolence, not harsh tyranny, between the two classes.[78]

To be sure, under outside scrutiny many slaveholders still wielded the standard Revolutionary necessary-evil defense. After the War of 1812, British traveler Morris Birkbeck spent a rainy afternoon in a Petersburg tavern with several "Virginia farmers." He related that "Negro slavery was the prevailing topic" of conversation—"the beginning, the middle, and the end—an evil uppermost in every man's thoughts; which all deplored, many were anxious to fly, but for which no man can devise a remedy."[79]

By the late 1810s, however, this standard rhetoric was wearing thin, given the persistence and growth of slavery in the South. Briton Henry Fearon insisted that Birkbeck, under the influence of Virginians' hospitality, had been too easily taken in by their antislavery cant. Many slaveholders, Fearon granted, "feel they cannot defend this system by a reference to abstract principles, or the rights of man." Thus, "when they are engaged in argument with an able and enlightened opponent," they "cannot defend the strange inconsistency existing between their *professed* love of political freedom and their actual domestic tyranny." It was natural that "under such circumstances" they would "deplore the evils of slavery." "But that they are *sincere* advocates for its abolition," Fearon concluded, "is what I have not seen the shadow of an evidence to induce me to believe. . . . Let them be judged by their actions;—it is these only that speak the man."[80] "It is not uncommon," reflected another British traveler, "to hear the master, in ill humour" because of the flight or indolence of his slaves, "say that he wishes there was not a slave in the country; but the man who is tenacious of this sort of stock, or who purchases it at a high price, will always find it difficult to convince other people, that his pretensions to humanity towards slaves are in earnest." Indeed, this observer gave abundant evidence of slaveholders' recognition of the permanence of slavery in the South.[81]

Given slavery's durability and expansion in the 1810s, many white Southerners abandoned any idea that it could ever be abolished. These slaveholders were not yet prepared to defend slavery in principle, but they realized that the stock phrases pointing to emancipation, even at some far future day, did not accord with the realities of the times. Both their realism and their ideological perplexity illustrated the transitional nature of this decade. Most stood uncertainly on a middle ground between necessary evil and positive good.

By the 1810s, many who had previously raised their voices against slavery had made their peace with the institution. John Holt Rice, a leading Virginia preacher, educator, and writer, typified what one historian has aptly called "the capitulation" of the white South to slavery. In 1817, Rice called for immediate action against slavery, noting that "it is folly to delay, while the disease is becoming every hour more inveterate." Yet by 1819, he had lost spirit for the struggle, speaking of slavery as "a subject of great delicacy and difficulty."[82] Many other witnesses testified that the sheer force of habit had worked powerfully in favor of slavery, in the practice if not yet the theory of most slaveholders. Edward Coles, who left Virginia for the Northwest to act upon his antislavery convictions, recalled James Madison as one whose "principles were sound, pure, & conscientious" and whose "feelings, were sensitive & tender in the extreme." Yet "the influence of habit & association" with chattel bondage had "lulled in some degree his conscience, without convincing his judgment (for he never justified or approved of it)," so that "he continued to hold Slaves" throughout his life. Coles applied this same description to Jefferson.[83] Other observers echoed Coles's analysis. A British traveler met a white Virginian who seemed to be "a good-natured civil being and by no means wanting in humanity in general; yet custom could make him smile at my expression of abhorrence, when he said there was no law practically for slaves in that State, and that he has *frequently* seen them *flogged to death!*"[84] A native Virginian averred that his fellow citizens were not "barbarians," but that "habit" had made them "forget the situation of these poor wretches, who tremble under their hands, and even reconcile[d] them, in spite of themselves, to the daily horrors which pass under their eyes."[85]

Given such widespread dullness of conscience in the South, many of slavery's opponents despaired of remedying the evil, despite the fact that so few Southerners dared to defend it outright. Northern abolitionists, so eager to notice and promote every inkling of antislavery activity in the slave states, tried in vain to keep their hopes up for much of the 1810s. In 1816, the Methodist General Conference's Committee on Slavery still denounced chattel bondage as a contradiction of "the principles of moral justice." But it threw up its hands on abolition, given "the present, existing circumstances in relation to slavery."[86] By 1819, abolitionists' doubts about the South seeped through the rhetorical facade of a committee report of the American Convention of abolitionist societies. "There are, doubtless, some persons, in almost every district of our country," they insisted, "even in those States where slavery exists in its worst form, who feel the iniquity, and injustice, of holding their fellow creatures, in bondage."[87] This was about as much as one could say, given the decline of antislavery through much of the white South. After 1815, a Presbyterian minister in Virginia moderated his antislavery zeal, seeing how little others had accomplished when they had challenged the peculiar institution from within.[88] In 1816, a leading North Carolina printer declined to publish an oration given before the Manumission Society of North Carolina, pleading that it might get "into the hands of Slaves," and that it would be "of no use to attack the people's prejudices directly in the face."[89]

Yet many outsiders, of course, had none of this editor's scruples about assaulting the peculiar institution, and their broadsides pressured many slaveholders and their allies toward an open embrace of chattel bondage. Tight-lipped accommodation was no longer adequate. None could fully overcome the ideological obstacles to such a stance in an antislavery age, but many moved in that direction. Their arguments may have been half-baked or contradictory, but they perceived clearly the futility of maintaining silence or recycling outdated apologies in the face of incoming fire against slavery.[90]

The replies of slavery's apologists to outside critics in the Era of Good Feelings contained most of the arguments that came to constitute the positive-good canon. Yet time and again, these same apologists stepped backward, refusing to stand by the political implications of their own statements. This pattern was evident in the Upper South. The Richmond writer who used the baneful example of Las Casas's misplaced humanity to rebuke abolitionists also twice reminded readers that Virginia had been "the first to interdict" the slave trade by law.[91] John Taylor insisted that "slaves are docile, useful and happy, if they are well managed." But Quakers and other outside agitators had infused a spirit of revolt in the South that necessitated whatever harshness there was in Southern slavery. He fastened racist descriptions on African Americans that could justify slavery. Yet he also wrote that "negro slavery is an evil which the

United States must look in the face. To whine over it, is cowardly; to aggravate it, criminal; and to forbear to alleviate it, because it cannot be wholly cured, foolish." And after reproving Jefferson's passage on slavery's vices, he pled, "Let it not be supposed that I approve of slavery because I do not aggravate its evils, or prefer a policy which must terminate in a war of extermination." In this passage, Taylor said he hoped to see a gradual emancipation and coloniza-tion of slaves. Taylor's was a strange and contradictory mix of positive good and necessary evil.[92] But this mix was not unusual in the 1810s.

It was no different in the Lower South. An anonymous Georgia penman affirmed that planters put pressure on one another to see that "the negroes should be well fed, well clothed, and be made to do their duty and no more." Such a policy meant that Georgia slaves were much better off than Africans, not to mention British paupers and the free blacks of the North. Indeed, they were the happiest of all Southerners, and would remain so unless officious Yankees continued to meddle in their condition. Good treatment also rein-forced a sentimental attachment between master and slave.[93] But as his glowing report reached its end, he lapsed into the old saw about the British entailing the curse of slavery on America. And he concluded, "I hope you do not now understand me as contending for the moral propriety of *slavery* in its *origin*," for he meant to argue only for the "*political propriety*" of its continuance.[94] Another Georgian argued in one breath that blacks colonized to Africa would be much worse off than under the paternal care of American slaveholders, but in the next proposed his own emancipation scheme.[95] A South Carolinian's play about Americans in Algerian slavery featured a house servant back in Carolina declaring, "To be sure I slave for true; but poor folks must work every where." If he was a poor white man, he would be fired when he got "sick, or lame, or old too much to work." As a slave in Carolina he had plenty to eat, was cared for when ill by his kind mistress, and so forth.[96] This was an early critique of free labor. But aside from this entirely gratuitous little speech, this playwright failed to directly engage slavery. She even left the contrast between American and Algerian slavery unspoken, single-mindedly pursuing her melodramatic story. These efforts were weak compared to the antislavery authors of Algerian plays and novels, who more ably mingled their message with their melodrama. Tepid and vague as Northern antislavery usually was in the early republic, it often put the pioneers of proslavery in the shade.

In fact, the weak commitment of slavery's defenders to their own argu-ments only emboldened the institution's assailants. Abolitionist John Wright at-tacked his opponent's obvious inconsistency in defending yet not defending slavery.[97] David Barrow gloated that slavery's proponents wished they could silence rather than engage abolitionists because they found themselves "on very unequal ground, with those who espouse the 'Rights of Man.' "[98] The African American minister Daniel Coker composed a fictional dialogue between a preacher like himself and a proslavery Virginian. The Virginian ran through the full complement of his arguments for Southern slavery, from property rights to biblical justifications. In short order, however, the minister was able to force his companion to retreat, first to a necessary-evil defense and then to a desire to free his and all other slaves. This bludgeoning of his fictional opponent served obvious rhetorical purposes for Coker, but his portrait was accurate in two important ways. The white Virginian presented the full panoply of assertions that comprised the proslavery argument. But he was neither consistent nor confident.[99] As with his nonfictional counterparts, both the arguments this Virginian advanced and the uncertainty with which he advanced them illustrated the pressures slavery was under from the world at large.

———

The confusion of the proslavery pioneers of the 1810s mirrored the divisions within the ranks of all defenders of slavery in the United States. They disputed the appropriate powers the Constitution should bestow on the federal government. They took a variety of stances toward the benevolent spirit stalking the Atlantic world. They occupied various places along the spectrum of thought relating to slavery itself, often not sure themselves where they stood.

But if the general picture within the South was muddy, the trends were clear. Manning the ramparts of slavery in a dangerous age moved important Southern spokesmen to advocate limited government, hard-headed realism rather than wild-eyed philanthropy, and perpetual slavery for African Americans. The proponents of all these positions moved outside the mainstream of the age and found themselves at odds with their Revolutionary inheritance. But they deemed such reactionary positions necessary to the maintenance of a way of life that provoked enormous protest elsewhere even as it spread itself into new territory.

8

Commencement Exercises:
The Missouri Crisis

THE MISSOURI DEBATES of 1819–1821 convulsed the United States. When Missouri Territory applied for statehood in February 1819, legions of Americans joined in the contention sparked by an amendment to the statehood bill offered by Congressman James Tallmadge of New York. The Tallmadge Amendment framed the first round of the controversy, which lasted until February 1820. It would have restricted slavery in Missouri by halting the importation of slaves and gradually liberating those already in bondage there. This phase of the crisis passed with the first Missouri Compromise, which authorized Missouri to come in without a restriction on slavery, but also admitted the free state of Maine. It also drew a line through the rest of the Louisiana Purchase territories at Missouri's southern border, restricting slavery north of that line but allowing it below it. Thus authorized to draft a state constitution, Missourians proceeded to guarantee slavery and—most provocatively—bar free people of color from entering their state. These clauses revived the crisis in late 1820 and early 1821, as Congress and the nation debated the acceptability of the Missouri state constitution's exclusion of free blacks. Another congressional compromise ended the second round, and a presidential proclamation in August 1821 recognized Missouri's admission with the opprobrious clauses intact.

Though ending in compromises, these debates' shock waves reverberated throughout American politics. Missouri dominated the business of Congress for weeks at a time and followed congressmen to their places of lodging. Speaker of the House Henry Clay observed that the Missouri question "monopolizes all our conversation, all our thoughts and . . . all our time. No body seems to think or care about any thing else."[1] Clay also lamented that in congressional circles as in public speeches, "the topic of disunion is frequently discussed and with as little emotion as an ordinary piece of legislation."[2] Reading of the controversy

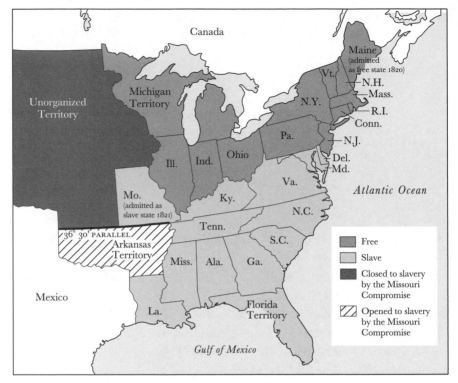

Map 8.1. The Missouri Compromise

from Monticello, Thomas Jefferson agonized that the Missouri conflict was "the most portentous one which ever yet threatened our union. In the gloomiest moments of the revolutionary war, I never had any apprehensions equal to that I feel from this source."[3]

This dispute inflamed more than America's elite. Editor Thomas Ritchie commented that other newspapers he read were "full of it. The whole country appears agitated by this question."[4] Even those printers who tried to eschew the quarrel found it impossible to do so. For instance, in December 1819 the editors of the *National Intelligencer* pledged twice to cease giving their columns over to this dangerous debate—and violated both vows in short order.[5] Some citizens did more than read about the Missouri dispute. In both North and South, town meetings and celebrations vehemently declared local sentiments, and mob behavior punctuated a few such gatherings. At a public dinner in 1820, Pennsylvanians drank a menacing toast to "*Missouri and the slave states—May they be as ready and willing to protect themselves against their slaves, without the aid of the north, as they have been willing to increase their danger" by extending slavery.[6] Southerners responded with threats of their own, and proslavery Missourians mobbed and otherwise intimidated dissenters.[7] Townsmen in Carlisle, Pennsylvania, gathered to burn in effigy their representative in Congress, David Fullerton, who had voted against restricting slavery in Missouri. They ignited his likeness in front of a large transparency reading "FULLERTON AND SLAVERY."[8] A mob in Hartford, Connecticut, did the same to an effigy of their own representative.[9] No wonder one Northern politician asserted that "for a member of either house" of Congress "from a non slave-holding State to tolerate slavery beyond its present limits, is political suicide."[10]

With their constituents' voices ringing in their ears, politicians found it necessary to put themselves on record on the question. This made for numbingly long and repetitive debates in Congress. One senator began a three-hour speech pledging to "speak with laudable brevity"![11] Congressmen delivered lengthy orations even after admitting that they had no new light to shed on the question.[12] Hezekiah Niles, whose columns groaned under the volume of the speeches, groused about congressional discourses that were "made without the hope that they will have any effect on the members of congress—with the *sole* view of being read in the newspapers." "Is it necessary," he wailed, "that every person, blessed with the gift of speech, and qualified to talk a couple of hours at a time, should speak on it?"[13] Anyone who has waded through the printed speeches feels Niles's pain. He also made an important point: the newspapers were a means to the end of reaching the voters, who read and responded to the debates.

These politicians and citizens did not come suddenly to such deep-seated convictions about the extension of slavery to Missouri. In fact, voters and officeholders in both North and South brought existing grievances to the Missouri debates. Missouri exposed and exacerbated but did not create those sectional tensions. Likewise, it prompted moderates to return to tactics they had employed in earlier controversies. The legacy of a decade's worth of political combat involving slavery was thus on full display. Missouri was, however, an unusually sustained and intense treatment of slavery. Some antagonists found that their previous positions could not withstand the scrutiny of their opponents, so they advanced to new territory. Thus the Missouri Crisis was at once a culmination and a new beginning.

———

Many inhabitants of the free states entered the Missouri controversy with anxieties about slavery's infringements on their liberties. These fears fueled many Northerners' exertions. Many Yankees took their horror of the internal slave trade and kidnapping of free blacks into the Missouri debates and argued that opening the vast new state to slavery would only increase these twin evils.[14] As with their previous opposition to the slave trade and kidnapping, their expressions mixed humanitarianism with concern for their own rights as citizens. Nothing made the connection between these practices and white people's liberties better than a tale of a North Carolina man who was dragged by kidnappers from his dying wife's bedside. A slave trader refused to buy him because he was "a perfect white man," so his captors cut his face and hands repeatedly and "poured aquafortis into the wounds" so as to change his color. "Such," the narrator concluded, "is the abominable sin and iniquity of slavery," a sin and iniquity that must not spread to Missouri.[15]

The doctrines Southern representatives advanced during the Missouri debates did not reassure Northerners trying to keep their distance from slavery. The antirestrictionists argued that diffusing the slave population would be a benefit to both white and black, but many Northerners thought the implications of this dictum horrifying. Pennsylvania's John Sergeant implored in Congress: "Has any one seriously considered the scope of this doctrine?" He continued: "It leads directly to the establishment of slavery throughout the world. The same reasoning that will justify the extension of slavery into one region of the country, will justify its extension to another." For these reasons, Sergeant submitted, compromise was "out of the question."[16] The representative of a state that had fought to distance itself from slavery, Sergeant was not about to sanction precepts or practices that only brought it nearer to the North.

Neither were many Northerners' fears for their own liberties assuaged by Missouri's state constitution. In the summer of 1820, reports wended their way eastward alleging that "a few designing men" hoped to secure certain antidemocratic features for the new state government. "The friends of Democracy should be on the alert," the reporter exhorted, "and keep a watchful eye on those who wish to make a constitution for *nabobs* only."[17] Upon the constitution's publication, its clause barring free people of color from the state alarmed Northerners, and not necessarily because of any love for black people. A New York City printer insisted that the question now before Congress was nothing less than whether a state had "THE RIGHT OF RESTRICTING FREEMEN." If Congress sanctioned the charter with this provision, he asked, "WHAT SECURITY WOULD THERE HEREAFTER BE FOR . . . THE LIBERTIES OF THE PEOPLE?"[18] Another New Yorker looked forward to the second round of the Missouri debates as "one more opportunity" for "the free states to regain their rights."[19]

It was no coincidence that those who emphasized extension's threat to Northern liberties hailed mostly from the Mid-Atlantic states. This resonated with their region's chief concerns about slavery after the War of 1812. Indeed, citizens and representatives of the Mid-Atlantic, especially New York and Pennsylvania, constituted antislavery's vanguard during the Missouri controversy. New York representatives Tallmadge and John Taylor and Senator Rufus King were leading lights in instigating and prosecuting the campaign for restriction.[20] Their state's legislature resolved "nearly unanimously" in favor of restriction, declaring that the Missouri question was "a subject of deep concern among the people of this state."[21] In his 1820 address to his legislature, New York governor DeWitt Clinton defined "the interdiction of the extension of slavery" as "a paramount consideration" for his administration.[22] Meanwhile, Pennsylvania offered several proofs of its devotion to the Tallmadge Amendment, including its legislature's resolutions in its favor. These resolves, which asserted that extension to Missouri "would open a new and steady market for the lawless venders of human flesh," passed *unanimously*.[23] Citizens of the Keystone State knew the slave traders' and kidnappers' lawlessness all too well and sought to deprive their enterprises of a new impetus.

New England compiled a more uneven record during the Missouri debates. The region contributed several important restrictionists, but it also produced more than its share of "doughfaces," or Northerners who voted with the South. Contemporary and modern observers have attributed this to a variety of causes, from local distractions such as Massachusetts's constitutional convention of 1821, to New England Federalists' need to maintain a low profile lest the Hartford Convention's associations taint restrictionism or harm their agenda in Washington.[24] There is truth in all of these explanations, but there are two more whose roots were in the period immediately preceding the Missouri Crisis. First, after the War of 1812, New England Republicans were the only members of their party who still had to compete with a vigorous Federalist Party. They needed the aid and comfort—and patronage—of the Southern Republicans who dominated in Washington. Second, and perhaps most important, if New Englanders were inclined to avoid a strong antislavery stance, they were better able to do so than those of the border free states. Their geographical position enabled them to achieve without much effort the distance from slavery for which other Northerners had to strive. Accordingly, they were less responsive— as a general pattern with many exceptions—to the urgency of restriction. It was telling, for instance, that Federalist preacher Elijah Parish reentered the headlines with a vigorous set of letters in spring 1820—on religious, not political, questions, having nothing to do with the Missouri Crisis.[25] In 1821, he spoke at a Boston convention of Congregationalist ministers. His subject was abolition—but of war, not of slavery.[26] Other New England Federalists remained engaged in slavery politics, but for the likes of Parish the old urgency on the wickedness of slaveholders had gone south.

Northwestern states also sent fewer doughfaces and stronger restrictionists to Congress than New England did, in part because of Missouri's location. The furor of 1819–1821 showed how much had changed since 1812 when Missouri quietly advanced within the system of territorial grades. The contrast owed itself in large part to the feeling of defensiveness that the free states, especially in the Northwest, took into the Missouri controversy. Extending slavery there typified the postwar threat to Northerners' distance from slavery.

The prospect of planting slavery in Missouri violated white Northerners' notions about slavery's proper sphere and confirmed their fears of the slave regime's boundless aggressiveness. Concerns about the potential march of slavery and African Americans into the Northwest echoed in the Missouri debates. King articulated the apprehension of many Northerners when he alleged that the slave states wished to do more than "fill the fertile regions W. of the Mississippi with slaves." For "a hot controversy" also existed "in Illinois, & Indiana and even in Ohio, to break down the restraints which . . . prevent the introduction of slaves into their extensive, fertile and happy States; and great & continued and (if the Missouri question be carried without restrictions) successful exertions will be made to effect this object."[27] In early 1820, an Ohio politician wrote that the recently agitated question of slavery "with regard to our own Constitution" in the Buckeye State had "aroused" Ohioans against slavery's expansion. Therefore, "no detail of the [Missouri] question will now pass them unheeded."[28]

In particular, the South's position that states possessed unlimited sovereignty over slavery seemed calculated to abet slavery's transgression of its traditional bounds. Many Northerners realized that these arguments negated the Northwest Ordinance, which they believed was meant to fix "a perpetual incapacity to permit slavery" upon Ohio, Indiana, and Illinois.[29] An Indiana congressman deplored such challenges to the Northwest Ordinance, to which "we, northwest of the Ohio river, are indebted for our happiest institutions—our freedom from slavery."[30] Given slaveholders' mania for state sovereignty, Representative Daniel P. Cook of Illinois doubted whether they would honor the proscription of slavery north of the Missouri Compromise line. "Are we to understand gentlemen as conceding the point," he queried his colleagues, "that Congress has the power to make that restriction or territorial prohibition perpetual and binding on the States hereafter?" At this, William Lowndes of South Carolina "smiled and shook his head." Whereupon Cook exclaimed, "Away with your compromise. Let Missouri in, and the predominance of slave influence is settled, and the whole country will be overrun with it."[31]

Northern angst at the prospect of African Americans themselves exceeding their proper sphere also had to be reckoned with in the Missouri debates. As Congress debated Missouri's ban on free blacks, both sides appealed to the Northwest's powerful desire for separation from African Americans. The dispute over Missouri's constitution, an Ohio congressman wrote to his constituents, had "perfectly convinced" him "of what I have long suspected, that the southern states are taking measures to throw their worthless black population into Ohio, Indiana, and Illinois." Should such states as Missouri prohibit the entrance of free blacks, "all the worthless slaves, which are vicious, intractable and unprofitable to their masters, will be liberated and forced across the Ohio, to the injury of our country."[32] On the other side of the question, Senator John Holmes of Maine, the quintessential Northern man with Southern principles, warned the Northwest of the consequences should they force free blacks on Missouri. Missouri had good reasons for excluding them, and "if a State does not possess this power, the condition of the non-slaveholding States is most alarming." The free African American population of the South was growing rapidly, he cautioned, and thus if the doctrine of free emigration for blacks gained purchase, the South could foist them on the North. "The New England States are probably in little danger from this principle," Holmes averred. "It is the States bordering on the slaveholding States which will experience its tendency and effect." To see the North's border states "forced . . . to receive free blacks from the slaveholding States," he concluded, "is a doctrine that I, as a northern man, do not . . . fully relish."[33] Holmes was thus able to pose as "a northern man" for a change and draw on Northerners'—particularly Northwesterners'—fears. The feebleness of other Northerners' replies to Holmes's admonition demonstrated its power.[34]

No matter their uses, the Northwest's proto-Free-Soil principles were palpable in the Missouri controversy. If its congressmen did not honor their constituents' desire for distance from slavery, they paid a price. In early 1819, Representative John McLean of Illinois joined with his state's senators in opposing the Tallmadge Amendment. Many believed this demonstrated Illinois's Southern sympathies. But in the ensuing election, Cook, an ardent restrictionist, soundly defeated McLean. Cook's margin of victory only increased in his reelection in 1820.[35] A Detroit editor was the exception that proved the rule in the Northwest. He was generally indifferent to the question of restriction, except as its agitation menaced the Union or impeded the work of Michigan's delegate in Congress, who was seeking to accomplish other business more "essential to" his constituents' "individual and general interests." Whereas one of the essential objects in Ohio, Indiana, or Illinois was keeping clear of slavery, Michiganians lived too far north to worry much about slavery coming their way. Their main interest was in increasing the territory's population so as to become a state. Thus slavery in Missouri entered his paper only when he invited Northern emigrants to come to Michigan rather than Missouri.[36] The pattern of restrictionism in the Northwest, then, confirmed the general Northern principle that whites mobilized against slavery only when it affected them. And when it did, the representatives who appeared to abet slavery typically suffered.

Of course, Northern politicians had paid no political price for supporting the entrance of other states in which slavery was legal, including Alabama in 1819. The nerves of Northerners bordering the slave states were highly sensitive in that year, but only Missouri touched them. This was because of Missouri's geographical position and attributes. Although migrants from the South made up the bulk of its population, it lay too far north to enter quietly as a slave state. Slavery seemed less necessary in Missouri than in the Deep South. In the years prior to Missouri's petition for statehood, even some Southern observers lumped Missouri with Michigan as territories likely to enter the Union only with "an eternal prohibition" against "the introduction of involuntary slaves." These analysts remarked that "an experiment is making in the West," as to whether free or slave labor was superior. "The *Ohio* river is the line, which exactly defines the boundaries of the experiment." And Missouri fell on the northern side of this great laboratory.[37]

The notion that the extension of slavery to Missouri shattered the previous limits on chattel bondage surfaced repeatedly in the Missouri controversy. Tallmadge declined to propose the prohibition of slavery in Alabama, because it was too rooted there to be removed without placing a sizeable free black population near slave populations. "Willingly, therefore, will I submit to an evil which we cannot safely remedy." But this need for caution did not apply to Missouri.[38] Restrictionist Robert Walsh argued that Congress had allowed slavery in Louisiana and other new slave states only because it there "appeared, from the number of negroes, and the inveterate habits and dispositions of the considerable white population, to be a necessary evil. . . . Is this the case as to the slavery existing in Missouri? It cannot be pretended."[39] The Yankee scribbler "Freemen" captured the North's anxieties well when he wrote that the defeat of restriction would eventually lead to the "illimitable extension and perpetual duration of domestic slavery" in the United States "under latitudes as far north as these New-England States."[40]

If slavery in Missouri violated notions of its sphere, as the debates wore on some on both sides lost patience with the whole notion of separate spheres for slavery and freedom. In the midst of a diatribe against the Missouri Compromise of 1820 drawing a line between slave and free territory, Ritchie mocked the idea that the land north of that line "is not fit for slaves—the climate is too cold! Not fit! why then is Virginia, or Maryland, inhabited by slaves?"[41] Likewise, the Missouri Crisis tested some Northerners' acceptance of the old doctrine, even as they advanced it as an objection to slavery in Missouri. In January 1820, Senator Jonathan Roberts of Pennsylvania granted that Congress had allowed the Deep South states into the Union with slavery, but "on what grounds I know not." "I am bound to believe," he continued doubtfully, that it was "from what was understood to have been uncontrollable necessity. If so, it can avail Missouri nothing, as no such necessity exists in this case."[42]

Many Yankees' willingness to admit even Deep South territories as slave states expired with the struggle over Missouri. The encroachments of slavery had convinced them that sectional warfare—political and ultimately otherwise —would mark all future territorial questions. Their enemies had sallied forth into the realm of freedom, and they would now contest what they had previously ceded as the domain of slavery. In this setting, the acquisition of Florida changed from a consensus to a controversial measure. Before the Missouri question spread its poison throughout national politics, most people in both sections viewed Florida as a national security problem rather than as slave territory.[43] Newspapers in both sections treated the Seminole War, the incursion into Florida led by Andrew Jackson, not as a war to expand slavery, but as "the Indian War."[44] As for Jackson's high-handed tactics in that war, which some—mostly Virginians, not Yankees—questioned, Niles claimed that "ninety nine hundredths of the people believe that general Jackson acted on every occasion for the good of his country."[45] Jackson had the staunch support of the likes of Tallmadge and John Quincy Adams, while some of his harshest critics were Southerners, including Secretary of War John C. Calhoun.[46] These would have been strange political bedfellows indeed had Florida involved a question of slavery.

With the advent of the Missouri Crisis, however, many Northerners came to view Florida through the lens of slavery's expansion. In a December 1819 conversation with Adams, Lowndes predicted that "the course of the Missouri slave question might materially affect the disposition of the Northern people in regard to the acquisition of Florida."[47] He was correct. One Northerner posed the questions: "Will not the population of Florida probably be a slave population? Have not the slave states already obtained a great ascendancy in this country"?[48] An anonymous Philadelphia writer protested against the federal government's apparent intention to annex Florida and Texas, showing how far the Missouri issue had raised the stakes. "If all future acquired territory," he complained, "is destined merely as a market for Slaves, and admitted into the Union on this condition, then, the less we acquire the better." This would not only increase the evil of slavery, but also abet "the southern states," who "appear to be grasping after power, and aspiring to become a more priviledged [sic] order than what they are at present." Allowing these petty despots such power "will, perhaps, at some future day, overthrow the liberty of this country."[49] In Congress, New York's Taylor declaimed just as bitterly against Southern expansionism. He had watched the South annex slave territories and states with great dispatch in recent years, and now it aimed for Missouri. "Where will it end?" he demanded. "Your lust of acquiring is not yet satisfied. You must have the Floridas. Your ambition rises. You covet Cuba, and obtain it. You stretch your arms to the other islands in the Gulf of Mexico, and they become yours." Such a course would "justify extreme measures" from the North in response.[50]

Taylor's eye, jaundiced by Missouri, took in far more than Florida, and others followed suit. In late 1819, public meetings in Philadelphia and Boston resolved that *all* future states should be subject to slavery restriction.[51] In February 1820, Senator Roberts of Pennsylvania framed the Missouri question as "whether freedom or slavery is to be the lot of the regions beyond the Mississippi"—not just of Missouri itself.[52] Given Northern bitterness over new slave states, President Monroe decided not to reach for Texas in 1820, judging that slaveholders should be "content with Florida for the present."[53] In short, the Missouri Crisis had irrevocably politicized many Northerners' view of new slave states and territories.

Nevertheless, there were many others who still viewed the acquisition of Florida mainly in terms of removing "an assylum" [sic] for criminals or "foreign foes."[54] And in February 1821, during the second round of Missouri debates, the Senate ratified the annexation of Florida with only four dissenting votes. Perhaps lingering climatic notions, and certainly the national security issues Florida presented, had won the day for the treaty with Spain.[55]

Furthermore, with the aid of Northern votes, Congress passed the Missouri Compromise of 1820, which allowed Missouri to come in as a slave state and then drew a line at its southern boundary below which slavery would be permitted in territories and states. In the end, when seeking to end the controversy, the compromisers fell back on the tried-and-true principle of separate spheres.[56] At the moment when this doctrine was under its greatest stress, Southern and Northern moderates joined to codify it. The location of the line they drew was a tacit admission that Missouri was indeed north of slavery's natural orbit, and they clearly hoped to placate angry Northerners by declaring that Missouri would thus be an aberration. The same precept that had helped to spark the Missouri Crisis was called in to settle it.

For some observers, however, such a settlement was more alarming than the Crisis itself. The term "Mason-Dixon Line" had gained currency for the first time after John Randolph's usages of it during the Missouri debates,[57] and now it seemed destined to become official and extend across the continent. Jefferson famously deplored the compromise, for "a geographical line, coinciding with a marked principle, moral and political, once conceived and held up to the angry passions of men, will never be obliterated; and every new irritation will mark it deeper and deeper."[58] "What," asked John Taylor of Caroline, "is the political attitude of nations towards each other, supposed by a balance of power" between the North and the South? "Hostility," he answered. And "what is the effect of hostility? War. A balance of power is therefore the most complete invention imaginable for involving one combination of states, in a war with another."[59] By this logic, a compromise meant to avert secession and war may actually help bring it on. What troubled such observers was that the Missouri Compromise of 1820 not only recognized but also formalized the very fact that its authors wished to legislate away: the sectional divide over slavery was the primary fissure in the Union, and was well nigh irreconcilable.

By the time of the Missouri Crisis, testimonials to slavery's political preeminence were legion. Congressman Charles Pinckney of South Carolina confessed that he could not see "any question, but the one which respects slavery, that can ever divide us" as a nation.[60] Three important Johns agreed with him. John Quincy Adams stated flatly that "a dissolution, at least temporary, of the Union . . . must be upon a point involving the question of slavery, and no other."[61] John Taylor of Caroline asserted that only on the slavery issue could

Maine unite with Ohio, or Missouri with Maryland. It was the only "natural, instead of . . . unnatural geographical division."[62] John C. Calhoun told a friend that he could "scarcely conceive of a cause of sufficient power to divide this Union, unless a belief in the slave-holding States, that it is the intention of the other States gradually to undermine their property in their slaves."[63] At the time of the Burr Conspiracy, Americans had no problem conceiving of another cause that might destroy the Union. They could well imagine the West breaking off from the East. Much had changed, then, between 1807 and 1820.

Tensions between the East and the West had not disappeared completely, but they had subsided while the clamor between the North and the South rose. During the Missouri debates, some antirestrictionists tried to pass off the antislavery campaign as an Eastern plot to restrict the growth of the West. This spoke to the mixture of Western and Southern elements in the sectional identity of places like Missouri.[64] Yet most commentators agreed with Rufus King that the old and new states were "becoming fast bound together by a band 'stronger than hooks of steel.' " To support this assertion, King pointed to the West's staunch wartime support for America's rights, which "must be regarded as generous tokens of national attachment."[65] During the War of 1812, the West eagerly demonstrated its attachment to the United States.[66] The War of 1812 therefore did wonders for the West's image in the East.[67] The postwar period also produced another harbinger of East-West unity: internal improvements. Many observers were confident that such projects as the Erie Canal would bind East and West "with the strong bond of interest and affection, giving stability and perpetuity to the Union."[68]

This was an assurance that no one could claim when it came to the yawning gap between the North and the South. The bridges between the East and the West could be measured,[69] whereas those between the North and the South were afire. The West was no longer the main concern in and of itself; it was now the site upon which the free and slave states waged their own contest. Even traditional notions concerning the West that had created common ground— namely that nature and circumstances had rendered it obvious where one's dominion ended and the other's began—had come under tremendous pressure during the Missouri Crisis.

———

Republican unity also came under enormous strain as politicos from the Northwest and Mid-Atlantic who had previously allied with the South under the Republican umbrella embraced restrictionism to continue their defensive war against slavery. During the clash over Missouri, sectionalists across the

North repeatedly echoed the rhetoric that had in past conflicts proven so useful aimed against Southern Republicans and so threatening to Republican and national harmony. Some Federalists harked back to the invectives against slave-holders that had mobilized so many New Englanders during the War of 1812. The likes of King easily lapsed into denunciations of the ambitions and tyranny of "the slave Legion" in Washington and elsewhere. "It is not enough," he glowered, "that we shd. be in fact slaves in this great Confederacy," but the slaveholders wished to fix slavery—and slave representation—in the West. By this means "we must be made the slaves of Slaves."[70] In 1820, Connecticut Federalist James Hillhouse published a caustic parody of "the Royal State of Virginia" issuing decrees to the North, "given at our imperial City of Rich-mond, the first year of the crusade for unlimited slavery!"[71]

More significantly, many Northern Republicans drew on such rhetoric dur-ing the Missouri controversy, just as some had during the Era of Good Feelings. Indeed, the leading postwar practitioner of Federalist-style attacks on Southern Republicans, William Duane, only increased his publications in this vein dur-ing the Missouri debates. In late 1819, "Mene Tekel" wrote for Duane's sheet denouncing slave representation, which the North originally "submitted to as a temporary evil, which a wise policy would in a few years correct." But now that slaveholders evinced a desire to extend slavery west of the Mississippi, the evil promised to be far from temporary.[72] For his part, Duane branded slave repre-sentation the "most odious of all the *aristocracies* that human cupidity had ever devised." The existence and extension of slavery and slave representation sacri-ficed "the rights of the free people of this union." This potent mix of opposition to both slavery and the three-fifths clause abounded in Duane's sheet during the Missouri Crisis.[73] Many other Northern Republicans echoed the wartime Federalists. In the resolutions of their town meeting in favor of restriction, New York City's citizens adverted to the "injustice of further extending *that* principle of representation, . . . by which freemen are legislated for through votes de-rived from the possession of slaves."[74] New Jersey's legislature spoke in similar terms.[75] So did Northern Republicans in Congress.[76] In the press, "A Republi-can of '98" sounded more like a Federalist of 1812 when he deprecated the nation's "vassalage to an aristocracy of nabobs and slaveholders."[77] By 1820, so common was this rhetoric from Northerners of all stripes that Randolph cracked that "Virginia Influence" had become the "999th stave of the Yankee doodle doo."[78]

Dissident Republicans had practiced that particular stave all through the Era of Good Feelings. But during the Missouri Crisis, many mainstream

Northern Republicans also joined forces with Federalists and spoke in their idiom. From within Monroe's Cabinet, Adams wrote in New England Federalist in his journal. "With the Declaration of Independence on their lips, and the merciless scourge of slavery in their hands," he seethed, "a more flagrant image of human inconsistency can scarcely be conceived than one of our Southern slave-holding republicans."[79] Upon hearing of the Missouri Compromise, Adams ascribed the fault of it to "the Constitution of the United States, which has sanctioned a dishonorable compromise with slavery." Rather than accommodate the South, Adams reflected, the North should have insisted on restriction until the South seceded and "a new Union of thirteen or fourteen States unpolluted with slavery" could emerge. The slave states might reenter, but on the free states' terms.[80] From his description of the problem to his proposed solution, Adams sounded less like a Republican in Monroe's camp than a wartime ultra-Federalist. Adams wrote in private, but other Northern Republicans publicly defected from their Southern brethren. This was evident even in Boston, where Republicans had nursed grudges against Federalists through years of defeat. In December 1819, William Eustis, who had been secretary of war under Madison, chaired Boston's restrictionist meeting, joining such Federalist luminaries as Daniel Webster and Josiah Quincy on the stand.[81] Even the editor of the *Independent Chronicle*, Boston's proadministration organ, flirted with restriction for a time.[82]

If Federalist rhetoric proved influential during the Missouri Crisis, so did the postwar dissident Republicans' critique of slaveholders as enemies to liberty. In an 1820 pamphlet, a Massachusetts minister declared that "the phrase *republican slave holder* is a solecism. The Emperor Nero whose despotism and cruelty have long been proverbial . . . had as good a claim to be called a republican, as any man who traffics in slaves or unnecessarily holds them in bondage."[83] Duane questioned "the mental capacity" of a candidate for office in Missouri who claimed to be both "*a republican*, and an enemy to the *restriction of slavery*."[84] "Wilberforce" insisted that "the personal freedom of no human being is safe, when the shield of justice no longer opposes a barrier to the tyrannical exercise of power." Thus he insisted that the doughfaces had become "the successful advocates of SLAVERY AND SOUTHERN ARISTOCRACY."[85] "Spirit of Penn" wrote that whereas slavery made slaveholders tyrants, "every citizen, who regards his own liberty," must "summon all his energy to extirpate Slavery."[86] Northern officeholders joined editors and anonymous scribblers in reading slaveholders out of the republican ranks. A senator from New Hampshire argued that the Constitution's guarantee of republican government to new states mandated restriction, because "slavery is incompatible with a pure democracy. . . . It degenerates to aristocracy, monarchy, and perhaps, despotism itself."[87] In a May 1820 address to his legislature, Connecticut's governor Oliver Wolcott warned that "a diversity of habits and principles of government" was growing in the United States, and that slavery's expansion augmented the sway of an ascendant "aristocratical order." Congress must prohibit slavery in Missouri, then, to "protect the people against the masked-batteries of aristocracy."[88]

The spread of slavery also menaced liberty's reputation in a monarchical world. Americans were all too acquainted with the uses to which Britons hostile to their country and institutions had previously put American slavery. The prospect of extending slavery to Missouri gave America's critics even more ammunition.[89] The need to preserve America's republican example fired Northern sectionalists' antislavery zeal and proved a potent argument in favor of restriction. Tallmadge attributed his desire to contain slavery to his solicitude for America's good name. In his speech demanding a stronger barrier against slavery in Illinois, he recounted the abuse Americans took for boasting of freedom but conniving at slavery. "He desired, above all things," the report of his address read, "to cast back this odious aspersion from ourselves upon those who were forward to accuse us of it, though they were themselves guilty of the original sin." An article like the one in Indiana's constitution prohibiting slavery forever would "preclude the possibility of future abuse" by America's enemies.[90] British criticism also pushed Tallmadge to prominence in the fight over Missouri. He declared that it would be damaging even to discuss "the moral right of slavery," for "how gladly would the 'legitimates of Europe chuckle' to find an American Congress in debate on such a question!" Extension of slavery to Missouri would only give further aid and comfort to the antirepublicans of Europe.[91]

Sensitivity to foreign criticism inspired other restrictionists. "We have attempted to set an example to the world of the capacity of man to govern himself, and of securing to all the enjoyment of equal rights," Illinois's Cook lectured. "But, alas! the brilliancy of this example abroad is too much darkened by the gloom which slavery spreads over it, and while we continue to spread that gloom, the happy influence of republican government will continue to be weakened" and eventually even be "entirely lost." Therefore, Congress must "show the world that slavery only exists in the bosom of our Republic from uncontrollable necessity."[92] The restrictionist call to preserve America's exemplary force and integrity also echoed in state legislatures and constitutional conventions.[93] It found its way into toasts at public celebrations.[94] Newspapers teemed with it. "We talk of the tyranny and despotism of the Old world," an anonymous correspondent of a New York City sheet anguished, "but will any man in his senses say, that England or France would permit a slave population of millions to be held in grinding servitude in the bosom of their empires?" If Americans allowed slavery to take root in Missouri, "then may we confess the charge of hypocrisy, and subscribe to the doctrine, that FREEDOM AND SLAVERY ARE PROPER COMPANIONS."[95]

Even Robert Walsh, one of America's staunchest defenders in the war of words with Great Britain, argued that Britain's antislavery reputation would eclipse America's should his countrymen sanction slavery beyond the Mississippi. In one sense, this line of argument was consistent with his response to the *Edinburgh Review*, for confining slavery where it existed would back up his plea that Americans were doing all they could to mitigate and gradually remove the evil. Yet when making this purely domestic appeal, Walsh admitted what he was unwilling to confess when addressing the British. He acknowledged, for instance, that the twenty-year continuation of the slave trade under the Constitution "might" have been worthy of reproach. Doing the right thing in relation to Missouri, then, would enable Americans "to make amends for our remissness, to use the softest term." Therefore, Walsh exhorted his compatriots to "eagerly seize the opportunity as one graciously afforded by Providence, for . . . proving to the world the sincerity of our past professions, and the validity of our pleas, on the subject of negro-slavery."[96] In his direct response to British critics, Walsh never admitted such national guilt, never disclosed an uncertainty about American sincerity. Neither did he point to Britain's antislavery actions as a model for America as he did in his remarks on Missouri.[97]

In short, in the Missouri debates, Northern restrictionists catalogued how Southern slavery impinged on the free states. Both Federalist and Republican accents staged this recital of why Yankees should care about chattel bondage to their south. And Northerners both east and west spoke in this language. For years, Northerners had complained about the slave regime's assaults on their liberties and national honor. The Missouri controversy focused all of these accusations on one point and thus produced a compendium of existing Northern grievances. It was a potent mixture whose appeal in the North highlighted the fragility of the Union and the Republican Party, one of the few national institutions in the United States.

———

By 1819, moderate Republicans in both sections knew how to defend their political position. They knew their task was to change the subject, by making the restrictionists out to be the sort of power-hungry manipulators who would rather rule over the ruins of the Union than be ruled under it. The middle-of-the-roaders not only believed this to be true, but also knew from previous experience that this charge could be an effective strategy. Indeed, charging ulterior motives was one of several tactics that they imported into the Missouri controversy from the War of 1812 and the Era of Good Feelings. Only those slaveholders who were prepared to fully embrace a proslavery position were comfortable when slavery was discussed, so the moderate line was also most slaveholders' line. Neither did those who hoped to hold the Union and the Republican Party together have anything to gain from stoking the fire of the slavery controversy, so they hoped to cool it by proven means.

The idea that the agitation for restriction was a Federalist plot thus flourished in the arguments of antirestrictionists. This had several advantages. One was that many people truly believed it. They said as much in private letters.[98] Another was that it downplayed popular support in the North for restriction, portraying it as the manufacture of a few schemers.[99] The main advantage, however, was that it might attach the stigma of the Hartford Convention to the restrictionist campaign. Antirestrictionists could thus tar antislavery with the stain of treason. Moreover, they might detach loyal Northern Republicans from the movement. A St. Louis editor surmised that Missouri's firm stand against restriction would "prostrate those Hartford convention men who now predominate in the north, and give the victory to the friends of the union and to the republicans of the Jeffersonian school."[100] Congressman Benjamin Hardin from Kentucky admonished his Northern Republican colleagues that the restrictionists sought to organize a sectional party in the hope that "Federalism, not of the honest and patriotic kind, but of that description which wished success to Great Britain during the last war, shall again raise its head."[101] Other writers and speakers appealed even more explicitly to both Northern Republicans and Unionists of all stripes, warning them that Federalists were once again exploiting the sectional "divisions of the country" over slavery. These schemers did so because they knew that these "may aid more powerfully in the work of disunion than any other circumstance."[102] Moderate Republicans reminded their erstwhile comrades of when they had all rejected the Hartford Convention's proposals to abolish slave representation and protested that the Hartford men "ought not to be forgiven in this generation."[103]

This was a powerful plea, given the freshness of Americans' memories of the war. Accordingly, many Republican restrictionists felt the need to consciously distance themselves from Federalists. They often did so by trying to switch the

Hartford Convention label from themselves to their foes. Duane, for instance, railed against Southern attempts to carry the Missouri Compromise "by *menace*" of civil war and disunion. "The *Hartford Convention*," he concluded, "finds its counterpart in crime and contempt, in this case."[104] A Western sheet published a roster of the doughfaces, whose "names will be recorded on the same black page with those of the members of the Hartford Convention."[105]

Moderates nurtured partisanship as sectionalism eclipsed it because they recognized that sectional parties posed a greater danger to the health of the Union than traditional parties. Senator James Barbour of Virginia argued that heretofore the political parties had been "comparatively harmless. Such will not be the case when you divide by latitudes." In the "collisions" of such parties, "the Union will shake to its foundations."[106] In 1820, James Madison hoped for a heated tariff debate in Congress, for it would "divide the nation in so checkered a manner, that its issue" could not be as "serious" as the Missouri scare.[107] Southern Republicans fretted most about sectional parties,[108] knowing a solely Southern party would be a minority. So dominant were the warnings against a Northern sectional party that a Massachusetts Republican complained that no one seemed to consider the South's unity threatening. "In the South," he pointed out, "you behold eleven states, all contiguous, some proud and aspiring, all united to a man. In this unanimity there seems to be perceived no danger."[109] Preserving the Union at all costs was the cry of moderates, but the costs seemed always to be billed to Northerners. Another Bay Stater noted that the South voted unanimously for extension, "and then are struck with horror at our giving this question a geographical distinction."[110]

Even as mainstream Republican Unionists capitalized on the Hartford Convention, they also revisited the tactics they had used to counter the Federalists' assault on slave representation in the years leading up to the Hartford meeting. During the Missouri controversy, as during the War of 1812, few directly defended the three-fifths clause.[111] Instead, they exploited Washington's Farewell Address. In 1820, for instance, a Savannah printer issued an editorial admonishing restrictionists that "to sow the seeds of jealousy and disunion" was "but little better than *treason*." "All good citizens," he preached, must " 'frown indignantly' upon" the instigators of strife, "so long as they reverence the warning voice of . . . Washington."[112] Boston's *Independent Chronicle* printed a rebuke to the fomenters of sectional discord under the headline "Washington's Farewell Address."[113] As they had during the war, those seeking to parry blows against slavery also invoked the blessings of the Union.[114] This was an effective tactic that restrictionists felt their vulnerability to.[115]

Another common strategy of moderates was to insist that slavery was not the question in the Missouri debates. The sheer volume of these protestations suggests how desperately the moderates were seeking to make the contest one they could win. Northern doughfaces, who faced an irate constituency, had the greatest need to define the subject in this fashion. But Southern representatives who were not yet willing to defend slavery to the fullest, and all those who knew the divisive power of slavery in politics, had strong incentives to try to remove chattel bondage from the discussion.

The antirestrictionists repeatedly pled that the crux of the matter was not the existence of American slavery, but whether to bottle slaves up in the Southeast. The editor of the *Independent Chronicle* grew exasperated with polemicists who made as if the debate was over whether slavery would increase in the United States. "Once for all," he groaned, "no such question is presented. . . . The question concerns only the *diffusion* or the *concentration* of the slaves now in the country." No one—least of all this printer—was advocating slavery or its aggrandizement.[116]

Another antirestrictionist argument was that the real issue was equal rights and freedom of choice for white Missourians and migrating slaveholders. No matter how much he abhorred slavery, the plea went, he could not countenance this usurpation of free citizens' rights. "If congress can . . . trammel or control the powers of a territory in the formation of a state government," proclaimed Kentucky's state legislature, it "may, on the same principles, reduce its powers to little more than those possessed by the people of the District of Columbia, and whilst professing to make it a sovereign state may bind it in perpetual vassalage." The legislators specifically refrained "from expressing any opinion either in favor or against the principles of slavery." They acted merely "to support and maintain state rights."[117] A Massachusetts doughface assured his constituents that his vote against restriction was an antislavery measure. He asserted that "if congress has the power of *limiting* the exercise of sovereignty in a *new state*, what shall prevent it from stretching its prerogative over the sovereignty of an *old one?*" Would Massachusetts "have borne to have had congress say to her, '*you shall not abolish slavery*'"? He, for one, could not have, for he detested "*slavery*, in any form, as much as any man."[118]

The sum and substance of the creed of the doughface and Southern moderate, then, was that they stood not for slavery, but for the Constitution and Union, whose maintenance was the heart of the Missouri matter. "Slavery would be a less evil," a Boston editor pronounced, "than would be a spirit of acrimony and hostility between different sections of the Union."[119] John

Holmes swore that he and his fellow doughfaces were "not the advocates or the abettors of slavery. For one, sir, I would rejoice if there was not a slave on earth." Yet if "my feelings are strong for the abolition of slavery, they are yet stronger for the Constitution of my country. And, if I am reduced to the sad alternative to tolerate the holding of slaves in Missouri, or violate the Constitution of my country, I will not admit a doubt to cloud my choice." For without the Constitution there would be no liberty in the United States, and much as he wished otherwise, he could not find the power to restrict slavery in a state in that sacred charter.[120] Congressman Louis McLane of Delaware also declared that he "would yield to no gentleman in the House, in his love of freedom, or in his abhorrence of slavery in its mildest form." "At the same time," however, he "would yield to no gentleman in the House in his regard for the Constitution of his country, and for the peace, safety, and preservation of the Union of these States."[121]

The problem for moderates, of course, was that slavery *was* the central issue of the Missouri debates, as their colleagues and constituents repeatedly reminded them. The restrictionists knew what their opponents were up to and drew the issue as starkly as they could. So indefensible was slavery, wrote one, that to carry the question of extension, "every artifice is used to draw off the attention of the people . . ., and to brow-beat the opponents of Slavery." He listed all the devices used against restrictionists and cut through every one of them to clarify "this question of Slavery."[122] "Freedom and slavery are the parties which stand this day before the Senate," King affirmed.[123] An Indiana editor reported that David Fullerton had been burned in effigy "for voting in favor of Slavery on the Missouri question."[124] A Maine printer drove home slavery's centrality when he branded Holmes—that "doughface of doughfaces" —an "unblushing advocate of domestic slavery."[125] This sort of clarity plagued doughfaces in particular, who suffered vilification in the North. They claimed to be saving the Union but were branded traitors. They claimed to be making an independent stand but were depicted as the South's submissive lap dogs. They had to wonder about the pseudonym of one "Humanitus," who execrated Northern antirestrictionists in verse: "Curst be the wretch who sells his vote for pelf, / Let him, like Judas, go and hang himself."[126] Doughfaces also paid a heavy political price in their home districts for their support of the Southern position on Missouri.[127] The best hope for Northern men of Southern principles was that Missouri would prohibit the growth of slavery on its own, thus removing black servitude from discussion altogether.[128]

However, even some of those who alleged slavery to be extraneous to the debate could not resist engaging the issue. In February 1820, Senator Richard M. Johnson of Kentucky rose on one of the fiercest days of debate to reiterate that the dispute was not about chattel bondage. He assured his colleagues on both sides that their opponents did not mean what they said in the heat of debate; surely Northerners would not meddle with slavery, and Southerners were not the advocates of slavery in the abstract. Johnson then launched into a paean on Southern slavery, including an assertion that it was superior to free labor in the North![129]

————

Johnson's instinct to defend slavery was well placed, for more than the Republican Party was at stake for white Southerners in the Missouri Crisis. They also read it as a threat to their peculiar institution. This was less a revelation to many slaveholders than a confirmation of existing suspicions or convictions, and accordingly it intensified trends already under way in their thought and tactics. The Northern attempt to use the federal government to halt the spread of slavery vindicated the small but growing movement back to state rights and strict construction of the Constitution. It convinced many Southerners to emphasize the Constitution, narrowly construed, at the expense of the Declaration of Independence and the liberal principles it enshrined. More and more slaveholders also waxed stronger in their suspicion of the philanthropic zeal they thought restrictionists embodied. Thus, the slaveholders posted their own anthology of extant defensive doctrines in response to the North's voluminous collection.

Although white Southerners still differed on the respective bounds of state and federal authority, the Missouri controversy pushed Southern opinion toward state rights. To be sure, some slaveholders and their allies still favored a vigorous federal government, in part because they believed it was still safe for slavery. The Missouri Crisis failed to convince Calhoun, for one, that the North was about to capture the federal government with the intent to turn it against slavery.[130] Others looked to preserve or augment Southern influence within a strong national government. For a Virginia editor, the first round of the Missouri controversy had proven that the Senate's weight in Washington must be maintained or increased, for it had proven itself "*the bulwark of southern rights and interests* against the *domineering and encroaching spirit of the north.*"[131] The pseudonymous "A Southerner" placed less trust in either house of Congress, convinced that "in both branches of our national assembly combined, the northern interest has the superiority in number. It is therefore of vital importance," he urged, "that the Executive chair be filled with a man from the slaveholding states, who, in case of extremity, can prevent by his veto any permanent evil from being entailed on us."[132]

Most Southern spokesmen, however, painted the state governments as the best ramparts of Southern rights. Since the end of the War of 1812, they had espied the growth of latitudinarian constitutional principles in both Congress and especially the Supreme Court. The Congress had reestablished a national bank, for instance, and then John Marshall's Court had declared the rights of that bank superior to those of the states in which it operated. They also saw Northerners calling in print for federal intervention to prevent sanguinary punishments of slaves after Georgia burned two slaves who murdered their master. The Yankees pled for Congress or the president to remove the local officials who authorized these sentences, declaring that the Eighth Amendment gave the federal government authority to override the states in this way.[133] The restrictionists' drive was the last straw. Both rounds of the Missouri debates centered on dictating the behavior of a state, after all, and Northerners interpreted the Constitution broadly to justify their position.

Slaveholding Virginians led the way in the revival of state rights doctrine. In late 1819, Judge Spencer Roane of the Virginia Supreme Court attested that "a revival of the spirit and principles of 1799" had taken place in Richmond, in reaction to the U.S. Supreme Court's nationalism, as well as the Missouri question.[134] The Old Dominion's legislature circulated their exposition on the proper powers of the states to the other states' legislatures. Virginia's legislators also voted 142–38 to make their resolutions on this head binding as instructions to their U.S. senators.[135] State rights men in Richmond hated the first Missouri Compromise, which recognized Congress's right to restrict slavery in the northern trans-Mississippi territories. Virginian supporters of the compact found themselves on the defensive, obliged to explain their actions just like doughfaces were having to do in the North. Virginia's representatives in Washington took notice, providing by far the most Southern votes—seventeen out of the state's delegation of twenty-two in the House of Representatives—against the compromise.[136] For the first time in the nineteenth century, John Taylor of Caroline, who wrote an extended paean to state rights and strict construction at the height of the Missouri Crisis, found that he spoke for the majority of slaveholding Virginians.[137] In the House, Virginia's James Pindall pushed state rights theory to its extremes. He characterized the Union as "a national, or rather an international compact, in which the relations of sovereignty between the respective States and between those States and the General Government are prescribed, adjusted, and limited."[138]

That Virginia rather than the Deep South was the hotbed of the state rights revival was in part the legacy of its years at the head of the Union in the early nineteenth century. For two decades, Virginia had been the target of partisan Northern sectionalists, who complained not generally about Southern domination but specifically about Virginia domination. This created a sense of defensiveness in Virginia, a sense that sectional politics was a zero-sum game in which the winners lorded mercilessly over the losers. During the Missouri Crisis, when an alliance of Northern Republicans and Federalists looked likely to sweep into power in Washington, many leading Virginians expected the consequences to be dire. From Thomas Ritchie came the warning: "If we yield now, beware.—they will ride us forever."[139] He knew it would be so, based on the behavior of past winners of this game. Indeed, Ritchie echoed Thomas Jefferson, who wrote in 1798 that "we are completely under the saddle of Massachusetts and Connecticut. They ride us very hard."[140] In February 1820, a resident of Richmond told Senator Barbour that the public there believed that to countenance the Compromise would be "to yield the interest of the Southern States, together with the constitution itself, to the domination of the East." This was "too horrible to be tolerated."[141] Another letter from Richmond decried any bargain that "would lead directly to a dissolution of the Union, by giving an unjust influence in the National Councils, by which the Southern people would become the 'hewers of wood and drawers of water' for those of the North."[142] Talk of "the domination of the East" and "an unjust influence" in Washington inverted decades of attacks from Northern Federalists and schismatic Republicans. Thus the years preceding the Missouri debates went a long way toward determining what part of both the North and the South led out for and against restriction.

Southern opponents of restriction also advanced strict construction as a companion doctrine to state rights. They argued that the idea of proscribing slavery in Missouri rested on a dangerously loose reading of the Constitution. Kentucky's Hardin expressed these sentiments as forcefully as anyone. He challenged those who would tamper with the South's property in slaves "to lay your finger upon that part of the Constitution which will sustain you in the high ground you assume." He meant a specific clause that would assign the authority directly, for he had grown weary of Northerners wresting various passages to their ends. In particular, he groaned, "I am heartily tired with the continued and repeated claims of this General Welfare" clause from the Preamble. "When he was but a youth," he quipped, "we made him considerable presents from time to time, at the expense of State rights: when he grew to be a man, we provided him a handsome marriage portion by giving him a bank of thirty-five millions! . . . It is time we should resist his claims and stop him in his high career of universal dominion."[143] Although many saw the first Missouri Compromise as a Southern victory, strict constructionists loathed it for recognizing the right of Congress to restrict slavery north of the compromise line. Thomas W. Cobb of Georgia, for one, spoke "very warmly, against all restriction whatever, as tending to universal emancipation"[144] Some leading Virginians had become so doctrinaire that they tried to dissuade Monroe from giving an inaugural address in 1821, considering the practice "anti-republican and not authorized by the Constitution."[145]

As slaveholders and their allies sought to elevate the efficacy of the Constitution as strictly construed, they backed away from the Declaration of Independence's doctrines of universal liberty and equality. They found this necessary because throughout the Missouri debates, Northern restrictionists appealed to those doctrines. They did so in Congress.[146] They did so in the solemn resolutions of state legislatures.[147] They did so in Cabinet discussions, where Adams argued that since "a power for one part of the people to make slaves of the other can never be derived from consent," the Declaration proved that the power of enslavement was, "therefore, not a just power."[148] They did so in the press, where one writer asserted that "the declaration of Independence being anterior to the constitution, ought to be considered as the basis of the union."[149] An abolitionist even raised the Declaration to a par with the Bible. Even "if there were nothing in the scriptures which necessarily implied a prohibition of slavery," he wrote, "yet the declaration of American Independence, stands as a perpetual standard against it: and every man who believes that declaration true, believes slavery to be a moral evil."[150]

Most slaveholders preferred to see the Declaration as a human proclamation rather than a divine document, limited in its scope at the time it was issued and in its application to the question at hand in 1819–1821. "As to that clause of the Declaration of Independence in which Congress stated their *opinion* that men were created equal, and that liberty was an inalienable right," Representative Alexander Smyth of Virginia averred, "it has the same force and effect" as any other proclamation of opinion, "having no political power."[151] Kentucky's Hardin argued that the document's "efficient parts" were those alone that declared the United States' sovereignty. "The balance of the declaration," he insisted, "is nothing but a manifesto to the world." The North's absurdly high estimate and strained interpretation of this passage only showed slaveholders the weakness of "the tenure by which they hold their slave property, should the non-slaveholding States obtain a decided ascendancy in the Congress and councils of the nation."[152] Nathaniel Macon tried to exclude the Declaration from the debate no matter its construction, for it affirmed " 'that all men are created equal;' follow that sentiment, and does it not lead to universal emancipation?"[153] Other Southerners answered that it did not, for only in the wildest flights of abstraction could anyone believe that those statements had reference to any social group but white men.[154]

Their choice of the Constitution over the Declaration put slaveholders in the uncomfortable position of rejecting or qualifying one of their country's basic texts. They even placed the Constitution ahead of majority rule and the wishes of constituents. Undemocratic on their face, such maxims only confirmed Northerners' image of slaveholders as enemies to liberty.[155] But although this meant swimming against the tide of progress in an optimistic age, so powerful was the need to do so during the Missouri Crisis that Jefferson himself backed away from his own document's implications. He wrote that if Congress could meddle with slavery based on the Declaration, it might "declare that the condition of all men within the United States shall be that of freedom; in which case all the whites south of the Potomac and Ohio must evacuate their States, and most fortunate those who can do it first."[156]

Slaveholders also found it necessary to abrogate another of Jefferson's Revolutionary-era effusions, his indictment of slavery's effects in his *Notes on Virginia*. Antislavery men repeatedly bludgeoned slaveholders with this passage, as well as with the antislavery sentiments of other Revolutionary-era Virginians.[157] Little wonder, then, that a letter in a Georgia newspaper complained that such writings as Jefferson's "have undoubtedly had very considerable agency in producing the dangerous ferment which has prevailed in the north" against slavery and slaveholders.[158] Similarly, Southern congressmen disavowed the *Notes*, insisting that Jefferson was swept up with the "enthusiasm" of the Revolution when he wrote them.[159]

Moreover, slaveholders left no doubt that "enthusiasm" had become a dirty word for most of them. They saw in restrictionism just that brand of humanitarian zeal that they had long feared would destroy their world. Some retained their faith in philanthropy, hoping to contest their enemies' exclusive claims by trumpeting their own beneficence. They proclaimed that allowing the diffusion of slavery was the only way to prepare for future emancipation and keep the sacred ties of masters and slaves intact among a mobile people.[160] They reminded the nation of their support for the humane ACS scheme, hoping that their cooperation with Northern philanthropists on this endeavor would "go far to moderate the clamors against the south" from Yankees.[161] They welcomed chances to execrate kidnapping and legislate against the Atlantic slave trade at the height of the Missouri Crisis to prove their benevolence.[162] But for every slaveholder still clinging to the dream of staying in the mainstream of the liberal and benevolent milieu of the age, there were more than one who saw do-gooders as public enemies. They saw meddlesome Yankees and Britons as hopelessly ignorant of the true conditions of slavery, which robbed their pre-scriptions of the authority that comes from practicability. Southern spokesmen reminded them of the unintended consequences of benevolence, arguing that halting slavery's expansion would "kill with kindness" by "humanely starving" slaves "to death by confining them to limits which cannot yield them a sup-port; to secure them from slavery, they give them up to the gradual annihilation of hunger."[163]

Others portrayed the effects of misguided zeal as more insidious than lu-dicrous. White Southerners' insurrection anxiety spawned their suspicion of outside agitators, and the Missouri debates demonstrated the connection be-tween these two concerns. A Louisianan wrote to Calhoun about "the spread-ing influence of the new born black colored sympathy of our Northern and Eastern brethren," who were sponsoring black preachers and otherwise med-dling with Southern African Americans.[164] Ritchie wrote of restrictionists with bitter sarcasm, growing out of a decade in which many Yankees had demon-strated their indifference or worse to the prospect of a slave insurrection. Curb-ing the number of slave states would render the South "weaker as to foreign and domestic dangers; and more dependent on" the free states "for help in the hour of need." "Should we ask their help," Ritchie railed, "they would say, it is mighty bad; they are mighty sorry; they will come and help us presently, but they must say their prayers first, which prayers would begin and end (when the mischief was all over) like the Pharisee's with thanking God that they are not as the wicked odious southern men are."[165] Other slaveholders fumed that they expected objections to Missouri's exclusion of free blacks from the starry-eyed Yankee, who inflicted his philanthropic principles on others—unconcerned that free blacks were "firebrands to the other class of their own color"—but not on himself.[166] Jefferson expected "our Holy Alliance of restrictionists" to offer slaves "freedom and a dagger."[167] Early in the Missouri debates, a Southern representative accused a Northern colleague of "speaking to the galleries" where African Americans sat and by his rhetorical flights "endeavoring to excite a servile war." Slaveholders feared that the restrictionists' effusions might convince African Americans that they had friends in the North.[168]

Many Southern spokesmen pointed to the example of Haiti for proof that zeal without knowledge could kill. Alexander Smyth told the House that the blind, infatuated philosophy of French radicals and British abolitionists had produced the revolution in St. Domingue and revolts in the British West Indies. If they kept up their meetings and pamphlets, "our philanthropists may acquire as good a title to the execrations of the Southern people as Robespierre and Gregoire acquired to the execration of the French people of St. Domingo." If white Southerners escaped a similar fate, Smyth assured his audience, it would be owing to their own "strength, foresight, and vigilance, and not to the good will of our philanthropists."[169] Another Virginian drew similar lessons from St. Domingue, but sighed, "Where or when has it been known that fanaticism has paused to reflect on consequences?"[170] Still another Virginian, John Taylor of Caroline, granted that the "friends of the blacks in France disavowed at first the design of emancipation," but he maintained that "their speeches and writings gradually awakened the discontents of the slaves" anyway. "This awful history," he concluded, "engraves in the moral code the consequences of a legislation exercised by those who are ignorant of local circumstances."[171]

Besides being dangerous, Southern spokesmen argued, the alleged humanity of restrictionist agitation was false, a mask for political schemes. It had always been so, for throughout history "Ambition" had wrought horrors "in the name of humanity, and under the pretext of devotion to religion!"[172] Taking a page from refutations of Great Britain's antislavery pretensions, they contended that true humanity would consider the plight of whites as well as blacks. A congressman from Virginia confessed that he found it "somewhat singular that the passion of humanity should, at the same instant of time, have seized so strongly upon New England and Old England," and had focused so narrowly on "the black slaves in the United States. Slavery on every other portion of the globe seems to have had no effect on the sympathies of these philanthropists. They have not been excited by the condition of the white slaves of Europe; nor by the sufferings of the white, black, and party-colored slaves of the Indies," for whose sufferings, of course, Britain was responsible. They honed in on the black slaves of the South because these were politically useful to them.[173]

During the previous decade, slaveholders had come to believe that the pretended philanthropists of the North and Britain would use Southern slavery to obtain power, careless at best of the slave resistance they were fomenting. Slaveholders thus found it necessary to do all in their power to defend their peculiar institution against them. The Missouri Crisis was not exactly a wake-up call for slaveholders and their allies, but it did steel their resolve by confirming their suspicions about the intentions of slavery's opponents.

———

Participants in the Missouri debates thus rehearsed all the arguments that previous controversies had rendered standard. But antagonists on both sides also pressed their opponents to examine many of their customary theses. In the name of consistency, many in both North and South began to abandon untenable positions.[174] Thus, as old ideas and arguments passed through the refiner's fire of Missouri, many participants grasped at new and unalloyed principles, even as others still clung to the dross.

The Missouri debates pushed many of slavery's guardians toward a fuller defense of Southern bondage. The South still had room for a variety of thought on slavery. Indeed, in 1819, Tennessee abolitionist Elihu Embree founded a periodical devoted entirely to the abolition of slavery. He soon expanded his subscription list past 2,000, despite opposition and obstruction.[175] Some few white Southerners openly supported restriction.[176] Nevertheless, the Missouri debates moved Southern slaveholders toward greater unity behind the peculiar institution. For the most part, they put aside partisan differences and embraced an antirestrictionist orthodoxy.[177] If state rights, strict construction, and suspicion of outside agitators were firm tenets in this creed, by 1821 many of its framers wanted to add a positive-good defense of slavery.

The positive-good doctrine became more attractive to many slaveholders because Northerners exposed the flaws of other defenses of slavery. Many Southern spokesmen attempted to apply the old necessary-evil creed to Missouri through the doctrine of diffusion. Only by spreading the slave population extensively, and thus reducing its proportion to the white population, could Southerners safely consider emancipation. "What enabled New York, Pennsylvania, and other States, to adopt the language of universal emancipation," said Virginia's John Tyler in one of the more persuasive presentations of diffusionism, was "nothing but the paucity of the numbers of their slaves. That which it would have been criminal in those States not to have done, would be an act of political suicide in Georgia or South Carolina to do."[178] The problem with such an argument was that it implied that it was "criminal" for Upper South states with a lesser concentration of slaves to hold on to them. Moreover, Tyler's logic cut against the legality of slavery in Missouri, for in 1819 its slave population was not dense.

Furthermore, Northerners repeatedly demonstrated the illogic of diffusionism. One Northern penman declared it "fallacious." "It is not true that emigration from a State will permanently diminish its population. Does any man suppose that the population of Great Britain is less at the present day, because of the emigration of our ancestors?" One of the great evils of slavery was that "taking it away does not remove it. The spread of our negro population, is like the spread of a plague; it will afford no relief to impart the malady to others: we may give the infection to the whole world and the virulence of our own disease will be unabated."[179]

For many Northerners, the drive for expansion to Missouri revealed the slaveholders' traditional apologies to be worse than "fallacious": they were a fraud. Slaveholders had long blamed Great Britain for fixing the curse of slavery upon them but now evinced their desire to fix that curse upon the people of Missouri, without a legitimate plea of necessity. A congressman from Pennsylvania asked, "why should we make Missouri a slaveholding State? As the climate imposes no necessity, wherein does any excuse exist?"[180] "Necessity" was starting to look more like an "excuse" for further aggressions by the plantation complex. Congressmen tended to accuse the Southerners of fraud as gently as such an explosive charge could be made. To give slavery "new root," Illinois's Cook submitted, "and spread it beyond its ancient borders," showed "that it exists, at least in a part of our empire, from choice."[181] Contributors to Northern newspapers were usually less subtle. Niles contended that Missouri was "a portion of country in which there is no excuse for" slavery, "save that of avarice and a desire of living on the labor of others."[182] "The people of Virginia and all the other southern states *profess* to abhor slavery," ran another diatribe. "All this appears well on paper," but the slave states' stance on Missouri proved how hollow such professions really were.[183] A correspondent of a Philadelphia sheet claimed to "write from the conviction of my understanding, forced reluctantly upon me, when I say I do not believe that the Southern States mean anything more than to blind and deceive the citizens of the free States, when they make their high professions of their sense of the evils of Slavery."[184] "The discussion of this Missouri question," John Quincy Adams reflected, "has betrayed the secret of their souls." They were, despite their professions, ardently attached to slaveholding.[185]

If the necessary-evil argument did not fare well at the hands of such Northern assaults, neither did the hesitance with which some of slavery's champions had ventured into the territory of positive good. As they had in the debates over slavery in the decade leading up to Missouri, many of the peculiar institution's champions advanced full justifications for it but then backed away. In the

Senate, James Barbour demonstrated the confusions of this position. He appealed to ancient as well as American history to prove that slavery had no ill effects on the moral or political virtue of slaveholders. But he took no position on the morality of slavery. "Whether slavery was ordained by God himself in a particular revelation to his chosen people," Barbour hedged, "or whether it be merely permitted as a part of that moral evil which seems to be the inevitable portion of men, are questions I will not approach: I leave them to the casuists and the divines." Although he hoped to disprove the notion that slavery made tyrants of slaveholders, he did not want it to be "supposed, that in the abstract I am advocating slavery."[186] Many of slavery's defenders in the Missouri debates joined Barbour in his muddle. One asserted that slavery was justified by the laws of nature and of God, that the most civilized nations in history had practiced it, that slaves were legitimate property, and that "Negroes have no right to object to Slavery" because they had put each other in worse captivity in Africa. But then he protested that "I am no friend to slavery; I wish from my soul it were abolished."[187]

The restrictionists made such dilatory souls pay for their uncertainty, pushing them to own up to the logical implications of their arguments. A representative from New York, for instance, paraded the perplexity of the hesitant proslavery men's stance before the House. "Why is it," he wondered, "that gentlemen, after denouncing slavery as an evil, proceed immediately to treat us with palliatives and excuses for the practice?" He called Randolph on the carpet for declaring that slavery "is an awful and tremendous judgment" and then "in the next breath" telling his colleagues of "the dangers of emancipation; of the happy condition of the slaves; of their affectionate attachment to their masters, and of the cruelty of the restriction."[188]

No wonder Randolph groused that "these Yankees have almost reconciled me to negro slavery."[189] He and others like him had seen how untenable their position in no man's land was proving to be, and they advanced to a more decisive stance. "An American" asked, "Will any Christian say that slavery must necessarily be excluded" from Missouri, "when it was *expressly* sanctioned by the old, and recognized without censure by the new, testament?" To restrict slavery was "a plain, palpable, reversal of the decree of the Almighty."[190] He offered no apology for this assertion, none of the standard disclaimers that he was no advocate of slavery. Members of Congress joined him in defending slavery without excuse. Senator William Smith of South Carolina delivered the strongest proslavery speech of the whole Missouri controversy, in response to Northerners whom he accused of fomenting servile rebellion in the South.

Smith was "happy to say" that they were mistaken in their assumption that the South lived "in a constant state of alarm" and "a constant danger, from an insurrection of this part of our population. This people are so domesticated, or so kindly treated by their masters, and their situations so improved," that ill-disposed Yankees "cannot excite one among twenty to insurrection." Smith's whole speech was an unmitigated tribute to the virtues of slavery, on a variety of both religious and secular grounds.[191] Nathaniel Macon of North Carolina and South Carolina's Charles Pinckney added their own undiluted proslavery speeches.[192]

Contemporaries recognized the novelty of this principled and unapologetic defense of slavery. A senator from Ohio responded with shock to Smith's speech. "That gentleman justified slavery on the broadest principles, without qualification or reserve," he marveled. "This was taking entirely new ground; it was going farther than he had ever heard any gentleman go before."[193] So did a Philadelphia writer, who expressed his amazement at reading that some Southern congressmen had "pronounced some extraordinary doctrines" in relation to slavery and freedom.[194] But if Yankees recoiled at such doctrines, it was their own assault on the slaveholders' previous defenses that had elicited the new ones.

By the same token, the Missouri Crisis forced Northerners to examine their positions on slavery and race. Much like Southerners who took two steps forward and one step back on their road to proslavery, some restrictionists took up very advanced antislavery positions, only to retreat to traditional assurances that they meant no harm to slavery where it existed. It was one thing to propound radical antislavery precepts in the newspapers, or in private reflections.[195] But it was quite another to proclaim such principles—and then publicly stand by them—from responsible positions in the government.

Various members of Congress embodied this strength of conviction mixed with hesitance in the application. Senator Jonathan Roberts of Pennsylvania, a leading restrictionist, denied "that there is any power in a State to make slaves, or to introduce slavery where it has been abolished, or where it never existed, or even to permit its existence only as an evil admitting of no immediate remedy." In its origins, he declared, slavery was founded on "the frauds and crimes of the man-stealer." Such statements menaced slavery in old as well as new slave states. But Roberts "most readily" admitted that "a sudden and general emancipation . . . would be the frenzy of madness" and could only hope for its eventual demise "in the fulness [*sic*] of God's providence."[196] New Hampshire's William Plumer Jr. argued that "what is morally wrong can never be politically right." He was not content to reprobate slavery "as an evil merely," for it was also "a crime" that "outrages every principle of justice and of humanity, and can rest for its defense on no grounds which do not equally support the tyrant." But Plumer was anxious not to be "misunderstood" on this point, for slave-holders may have "a present qualified right" to its continuance in the old slave states, if not its establishment in Missouri.[197]

Senator Rufus King made the best-known rhetorical sortie against slavery—and beat an equally public retreat. In a speech on the Senate floor, King asserted that he had "yet to learn that one man can make a slave of another. If one man cannot do so, no number of individuals can have any better right to do it." He therefore maintained that "all laws or compacts imposing any such condition upon any human being, are absolutely void, because contrary to the law of nature, which is the law of God," and which "is paramount to all human control."[198] King immediately stepped back from the radical implications of these precepts. He told the antislavery group publishing the notes from this and another speech on Missouri that he was "particularly anxious not to be mis-understood on this subject, never having thought myself at liberty to encour-age, or to assent to, any measure that would affect the security of property in slaves, or to disturb the political adjustment which the Constitution has estab-lished respecting them." Thus, "the observations, which I send you, should be constructed to refer, and be confined, to the prohibition of slavery in the new States."[199] King, Plumer, and Roberts typified the advanced doctrines and conservative conclusions of many Northern politicians.[200]

Slaveholders and their allies exploited this incongruity in their opponents' position. They suggested that restrictionists must have been driven by base motives given their inability to stand by their professed principles. "If you are not in pursuit of power and influence," Virginia's Smyth demanded of North-erners, "if the future freedom of the blacks is your real object, and not a mere pretence, why do you not begin" in Congress's own backyard, the District of Columbia, where "you have undoubted power" to legislate? He was sure his opponents would not pursue abolition in the District, "and yet you will impose on others an obligation to do and suffer an act of injustice which you dare not attempt to do yourselves."[201] Senator William Pinkney of Maryland argued that the Tallmadge Amendment itself proved restrictionists' inconsistency. For although they had execrated slavery as evil and unrepublican, they failed to propose the immediate emancipation of slaves living in Missouri.[202] Some doughfaces urged their tormenters to set the example of abolition in their own states before they "undertake to prescribe to others."[203]

Some restrictionists essayed to do both. They pushed for a firmer commitment to abolitionism in the North as well as restriction in Missouri. This was
evident in New York. In late 1820, a court of common pleas in Onandaga
County ruled against a master seeking damages for the loss of a slave. The
ruling rather extravagantly declared that "SLAVERY CANNOT EXIST UNDER OUR
CONSTITUTION."[204] In September 1821, in the convention drafting a new constitution for New York, Tallmadge sought to make it truly so. He proposed a
clause engrafting the 1817 abolition law onto the new charter, hoping to give
abolition the constitutional sanction necessary to prevent the kind of de facto
slavery practiced in the Northwest.[205]

Pennsylvania restrictionists also joined in the drive for consistency. In 1820,
the Keystone State's Senate considered a bill freeing the state's remaining
slaves. Whereas their citizens' "anxious wish to break the shackles" of slaves
was "well known," the bill read, it would be "in accordance both with the
honor and interest of this commonwealth to efface so foul a blot, wholly and
irrevocably, from her statute books." The bill failed, suggesting most legislators'
satisfaction that the "honor and interest" of the state was not in need of track-
ing down and freeing a few hundred slaves.[206] But the proposal itself, and its
timing, spoke to some Northerners' drive for consistency as a result of the
Missouri debates. So did the suggestion of "A Citizen of Philadelphia," who
was shocked to learn from a speech on Missouri that Virginia's law code
punished kidnapping much more severely than did Pennsylvania's. He urged
the state's legislature to make its laws agree with its restrictionist stance, for they
would not "whilst she suffers . . . *Slavery*, in whatever shape or form it may
present itself, to exist within her borders."[207] Throughout the late 1810s, the
legislature had debated strengthening the state's kidnapping law by increasing
its penalties. But it did not finally pass a law until 1820. Significantly, supporters
of the new law styled it "a supplement to the act, entitled, an act for the gradual
emancipation of slavery." The title spoke to "A Citizen of Philadelphia's" concern for completing the work of gradual abolition.[208] In Pennsylvania's 1820
campaign for governor, challengers to the incumbent, William Findlay, dug up
his past slaveholding and posited that he was still a slaveholder. They could not
believe "that a people who held the slavery of the human species in such
abhorrence as do the people of Pennsylvania, could possibly be induced to *make
choice of a slave holder for their chief magistrate*."[209] Although most white Northerners hardly became raving abolitionists following Missouri, the national debate abetted the process by which they declared their states unequivocally free,
especially in the Mid-Atlantic.

The Missouri controversy also reverberated throughout the North on the subject of race. This was particularly true of part two of the debate, which focused on Missouri's exclusion of free blacks. White Yankees still demonstrated a range of opinions concerning the rights and abilities of African Americans. Many evinced their solicitude for the rights of African American citizens and proclaimed that they would do their constitutional duties "even to the black man."[210] Others affirmed that they were "not only averse to a slave population, but also to any population composed of blacks, and of the infinite and motley confusion of colors between the black and the white." Thus they opposed inflicting such a people on Missouri by extending slavery there.[211]

Southern representatives mockingly suggested that their Northern counterparts make up their mind about black people's equality. Until they did, they would be open to charges of hypocrisy. Most Northern representatives insisted on free blacks' right to emigrate to Missouri, but not on their rights once in the state.[212] This allowed Southerners to contend that Northerners could not object that Missouri's constitution infringed on the rights of citizens. So did the free states' discrimination against their own black people. Even in "the State of Massachusetts, always foremost in the work of liberty," Smyth jeered, "the free negro is under considerable disabilities."[213]

These were devastating critiques, and some Yankees preferred to turn them aside by asserting that African Americans already enjoyed full citizenship rights in the North. They argued that free blacks in their states were not deprived of any of "the broad and essential rights of citizens": they had the right to hold property, to be tried by jury, to be granted habeas corpus, and to vote in some states. As for alleged restrictions on their rights, prohibitions on interracial marriage acted against both whites and blacks and not being required to serve in the militia was a blessing, not a curse.[214] For other Northern whites, however, the Missouri debates forced an examination of their racial attitudes and the rights that African Americans should enjoy.

Some found that they agreed with the most racist of white Southerners. At New York's 1821 constitutional convention, many delegates supported disenfranchising African Americans. "They are a peculiar people," declared one, "incapable, in my judgment, of exercising" the franchise "with any sort of discretion, prudence, or independence." New York was not about to let women, aliens, or Indians vote, so why should it allow blacks to vote? Most states, both free and slave, were wise enough to deny them the ballot. Therefore, this question could not possibly have "any connection at all with the question of slavery."[215] The Buck-tail faction of New York Republicans hoped to profit from such racism. Its candidates and spokesmen noted how hard the Clintonian faction was working to get out the African American vote in the gubernatorial elections of 1819 and 1820. "Affairs look *black* indeed," one editor gibed, "when such a call is considered indispensible." This was the worst sort of demagoguery, they argued.[216]

But courting black votes in these elections did not spell defeat for the Clintonians, in part because many New Yorkers, like other white Northerners, retained liberal racial views. The Missouri debates only clarified those views, at least in the short term. In fact, the Clintonian faction made political hay out of the Buck-tails' acknowledged "*hostility to blacks.*" Their adversaries' racial attitudes, plus their doughfacism in the Missouri debates, added up to a picture of Buck-tails as the Southern slaveholders' lackeys. "What sort of republicans are these," a Clintonian scribbler demanded, who would vote to extend slavery and then decry black voters' exercise of their voting rights?[217] Constitutional convention delegates warned their racist colleagues that if they stripped blacks of the ballot, they would "hear a shout of triumph and a hiss of scorn from the southern part of the union," given that New York had taken such "high ground against slavery." More specifically, during phase two of the Missouri controversy, the legislature had nearly unanimously instructed its senators in Washington to fight against Missouri's exclusion of free blacks. Could the framers of the new constitution brook such inconsistency?[218] Perhaps for similar reasons, in their respective constitutions drafted after Maine achieved statehood, Massachusetts (1821) and Maine (1820) both granted the franchise to "every male citizen" over the age of twenty-one.[219] Thus the Missouri controversy had shaped the constitution of more than the new state of Missouri. It influenced the course of state and national politics, the identity of the free and slave states, and their relations with each other.

In short, the Missouri Crisis had ushered in a new clarity in the sectional politics of the United States and moved each section toward greater coherence on the slavery issue. It did not do so because of the novelty of the issue of slavery. The participants' sense of the threat the Missouri imbroglio posed—whether to their nation's reputation, their party, or the interests and rights of their section—was a product of the international, partisan, and sectional contests that had preceded it. Furthermore, to meet these perceived challenges, they drew on tactics they had found useful in the past. But the length and intensity of the controversy over Missouri had forced its participants to confront the implications of their—and their opponents'—positions. Even the black citizens of

Philadelphia, who needed little education about their white countrymen's racial attitudes, found that the Missouri debates had unmasked the purveyors of the necessary-evil panacea, the ACS. At a November 1819 meeting, they declared that "the recent attempt to introduce slavery, in all its objectionable features, into the new states" only "confirms us in the belief" that the ACS was part of Southerners' scheme to "completely and permanently fix slavery in our common country."[220]

Maryland's Pinkncy thus spoke for both sides when he admitted that an adversary's stated principles "were not, perhaps, entirely new. Perhaps I had seen them before in some shadowy and doubtful shape. . . . But in the honorable gentleman's speech they were shadowy and doubtful no more," and thus truly alarming.[221] Given this increased definition, both extremists and moderates found that some of their previous positions and tactics served them well but that others needed to be discarded. Thus, while the Missouri Crisis represented the climax of the politics of slavery in the early republic, it also pointed to new directions in the antebellum era. The politicians and citizens who shaped the contest over Missouri might well have been told what newly minted high school and college graduates have heard from time immemorial: although this seemed like the end of a long road, it was also the start of a new one.

Antebellum Legacies

THE MISSOURI COMPROMISES, meant like so many other compacts before and after them to put the issue of slavery to rest, failed to do so. It was clear that this would be the case even as Congress hammered them out. Many Northerners conceded defeat in the battle but not the war after restriction in Missouri was lost, vowing to work even harder against slavery in the future.[1] From the South came the observation in August 1821 that "the Missouri question is settled, but the excitement is not allayed."[2] Far from ending the struggle over slavery in the United States, the Missouri Compromises set the stage for a new phase of that contest that would lead to civil war. Missouri and other antebellum conflicts pushed many Americans in new directions, creating more extremists on both sides. Yet old antipathies still resonated, and old ideas and tactics persisted. Both Northerners and Southerners had found some early national arguments and tools wanting, but they found more of them useful even in their changed circumstances.

The Missouri imbroglio cast a long shadow over American politics, threatening to turn national questions into sectional ones. Presidential politics was an especially prominent arena that contestants turned even more overtly sectional in Missouri's wake. In October 1820, a Pennsylvania restrictionist made a last-second plea not to reelect Monroe. He queried whether the president "of a free people" should be one "who, in addition to the act of holding his fellow creatures in bondage, enforces, with all his official influence, the pernicious doctrine of the extension of Slavery."[3] The 1820 election came too soon after Missouri's first round for disaffected Northerners to organize opposition to Monroe, but they quickly turned their attention to 1824 as their chance to elect a president from the free states. Meanwhile, Southerners backed self-consciously pro-

Southern candidates. The presidential campaign of 1828 also lasted about four years, and rivalry between the North and South loomed large there, too. Division over slavery was not the only issue in these contests, of course. A Northern congressman pinpointed Missouri's effect on national politics when he said that "the same feeling" it had produced still prevailed, "but other considerations mix with the old controversy, & give it a different aspect."[4]

No matter how mixed, the specter of a sectional alignment in national politics haunted those committed to the Union's preservation and the national reach of the sole remaining national party, the Republican. This menace also hung over the Second Party System of Whigs and Democrats that succeeded the years of one-party rule. The Federalists' sectional appeal during the War of 1812 and the Missouri Crisis taught antebellum partisans that nationwide parties and the Union were safest when they could keep slavery off the table. Avoidance of slavery was thus the creed of moderates in both sections throughout the antebellum period. They showed their commitment to it by using less than moderate means, including mob violence, to repress agitation of the issue.[5] But they also relied on cross-sectional partisan alliances. In 1827, Martin Van Buren, the principal architect of the Second Party System, held that parties must be organized around issues other than slavery. He wrote that "if the old" party loyalties that bound "the planters of the South and the plain Republicans of the north" receded, "geographical divisions founded on local interests or, what is worse[,] prejudices between free and slave holding states will inevitably take their place." "Party attachment in former times," he explained, "furnished a complete antidote for sectional prejudices by producing counteracting feelings. It was not until that defence had been broken down" after the War of 1812 "that the clamour agt. Southern Influence and African Slavery could be made effectual in the North." Thus, Van Buren argued, party spirit "can & ought to be revived."[6]

If previous crises illustrated the threat that sectional parties posed, they also suggested how moderates might defuse it. Thus, appeals to the value and permanence of the Union never went out of style for moderates. In 1842, when Congressman John Quincy Adams of Massachusetts presented a petition from his constituents praying Congress to look into measures to dissolve the Union, slave state representatives jumped at the chance to defend the Union instead of slavery. They moved to censure Adams, declaring that "the Federal Constitution is a permanent form of government, and of perpetual obligation." Therefore, Adams and the petitioners had struck a blow against all lovers of the Constitution.[7] A Virginian reminded Adams of the strictures against sectionalism in George Washington's Farewell Address.[8] Much as Federalists had done three decades earlier in response to these same rebukes, Adams insisted that Washington's "voice had been to him . . . next to the Holy Scriptures."[9]

Another common tactic moderates used was to connect agitators, whether proslavery or antislavery, with the fallen Federalists and their Hartford Convention. For decades after it had disbanded in 1815, that Convention retained its salience in partisan politics both nationally and especially in New England.[10] It was a sword that cut many ways. In the late 1820s and early 1830s, South Carolinian proponents of nullifying a federal tariff branded their in-state opponents soft on Yankee tyranny. But the antinullifiers knew how to combat fire-eaters and linked them to New England Federalists. "The worst days of the 'Hartford convention,'" went one attack on the nullifiers, "presented us with no paper so disreputable" as their ravings.[11] This hiss and byword, however, was most commonly used to attack antislavery men and movements. The idea that Federalists inspired antislavery agitation was both a comfort and a tool for antebellum moderates; although expressed mostly for public consumption, it also appeared in private letters. It also persisted for a long time. In the late 1830s, a Democratic congressman cried that to effect their long-standing "purpose of humbling and degrading the Democracy," "the Federal party have joined the Abolitionists." In 1840, former president Andrew Jackson charged that "the federal party" had used the abolitionists for their malign partisan purposes. Other Democrats made this linkage as late as 1849.[12] An Ohio politician said it best when he groused that "although the former division of parties does not in fact exist," it was still far too easy "for a demagogue to blast the prospects of the finest man in the world, by crying out Federalist."[13]

By such means, national parties did become agents of national unity, restraining agitation of the slavery issue for decades. The loyalties of the Second Party System took hold on both Northerners and Southerners. Those acting as sectionalists were few and far between, and they often came to that position only after a long struggle with fealty to party. The parties were uneasy alliances between like-minded men from both sections, but alliances nonetheless. It took a great deal of provocation to move most opponents or defenders of slavery out of their parties.[14]

Provocations were not wanting in the antebellum era, so on occasion sectionalism broke through all the impediments to its expression in national politics. The Republican Party that arose in the superheated atmosphere of the 1850s was the most successful descendant of the Federalist sectionalists of the 1810s. Like the Federalists, the Republicans essentially gave up on winning votes in the South and felt a burning sense of sectional grievance. The Federalists and dissident Republicans of the 1810s found that antislavery appeals worked best when Southern slavery affected white Northerners. Similarly, the slowly rising popularity of Northern sectionalism from the Liberty to the Free Soil to the Republican parties illustrated the rising sense that Southern slavery threatened the rights and interests of white men. From the 1830s to the 1850s, as slaveholders and their allies sought to silence antislavery agitation, more and more white Northerners came to feel their own rights—especially free speech rights, such as the right to petition Congress and freedom of the press—under siege. And as slaveholders endeavored to spread slavery to western territories, they seemed poised to deprive the free men of the North and their posterity of the opportunity the West represented.

These specific events and issues all helped convert vague antislavery feeling to organized action. Before Congress's 1835 passage of the Gag Rule rejecting all antislavery petitions, a Republican remembered in 1854, "Abolitionism was but a sentiment, and a mere sentiment is not a sufficient basis for a formidable political organization," unlike "when great principles of constitutional right are violated." The achievement of the Republican Party was to use similar turning points to mobilize that "sentiment" into a truly "formidable political organization."[15] Party leaders created a diverse coalition under the banner not of abolitionism but of resistance to the encroachments and demands of the South. A New York antiabolitionist, for one, converted to the Republicans because he could not stand to see the North "bullied, whipped and '*kicked*,' into any course or policy which they may please to dictate to us." Northerners must stop "acting under the lash of the Slave Power."[16] Just as New England Federalists had argued that Southern Republicans had usurped the government in order to enslave and rule over Yankees, the later Republicans warned that the "Slave Power" of the South was conspiring with its Northern auxiliaries to enslave and rule over the North.[17] Taking a sectionalist stance freed the Republicans of the 1850s to say so, just as the Federalists' regional strategy had a half century earlier. Although the Republican Party was much more potent than any Northern sectionalist party that preceded it—including the Federalists during the War of 1812—it was not unprecedented.

Not surprisingly, the Federalists' anti-Southern rhetoric echoed in that of antebellum Northern sectionalists. Recoiling at the South's opposition to the administration of John Quincy Adams, Yankee politicos urged New England to "stand forth in the manliness of her united strength," lest the South "govern the East, now and forever."[18] Josiah Quincy had contributed to the Federalist lexicon back in the 1810s, and during the crisis of the 1850s he revived it. He endorsed Republican John Fremont for president in 1856, believing that "the question to be decided, at the ensuing Presidential election, is, Who shall henceforth rule this nation,—the Slave States, or the Free States?" Fremont would "restore the Constitution to its original purity," reversing the slave states' perversions of it over the course of fifty years in which they had "subjugated the Free States." He warned that if the free states did not rouse and unite themselves, "nothing is left to them but to yoke in with the negro, and take the lash, submissively, at the caprice of their masters."[19] Such language was as well suited to the 1850s as it had been to the 1810s.

At least one Federalist policy also resurfaced when Yankees again called for the abolition of slave representation. The three-fifths clause had enjoyed a low profile after the Missouri Crisis, in part because Northern sectionalists ascribed Southern power more to doughfaces than to this constitutional provision. As the North's population growth exceeded the South's, even with slave representation the South needed Northern cooperation to get anything done. Adams, for one, feared not "the power of the South, which can effect nothing by itself," but rather "the treachery of the Northern representation, both to Northern interests and principles."[20]

Yet Adams was also instrumental in an offensive against slave representation in the 1840s. This campaign, like the one thirty years earlier, originated in a sense of sectional oppression and emanated from Massachusetts. The setting was what Adams called "the degradation of the free and especially the eastern portion of the Union."[21] As a congressman, Adams had seen the South and its allies impose the infamous Gag Rule in 1835 and renew it every year since. He saw the executive branch leading the charge to annex Texas and the Supreme Court striking down the Northern states' laws protecting fugitive slaves from recapture. In 1843, revolting at "the transcendent omnipotence of slavery in these United States," Adams resolved to call "the whole freedom of this Union" forth "in its own defence."[22]

He soon got his chance, as it was his honor to introduce resolutions from Massachusetts's legislature urging the repeal of the federal ratio. Adams was a logical choice to do so, and not just because of his prominence as a former president. He had personal reasons for hating slave representation. Both his father in 1800 and Adams himself in 1828 had narrowly lost their reelection bids to candidates who carried the South and its extra electoral votes.[23] In Congress in the 1830s and 1840s, he was a nominal Whig but at heart a sectionalist, "acknowledging no party communion," he said, "with the Whigs of the slave representation." His popularity and notoriety were on sectional terms.[24] This standing freed him to act for Northern interests in ways loyal partisans could not. Adams brought the Massachusetts resolves forth, significantly enough, on the same day he resumed his annual fight against that emblem of Southern tyranny, the Gag Rule. These resolutions gave rise to what Adams somewhat fantastically called "the most memorable debate ever entertained in the House," which resulted in both a select committee and the main body of Congress rejecting them by wide margins.[25]

Despite their voting advantage, Southern representatives did not combat these resolutions only with calm obstructionism in committee. They declared that when Yankees "come to this House, and deny us even the right of representation on this floor," it was yet another offensive in the North's "war" on the South. "The day of battle must come," one thundered, and Southern men must "gird up your loins; put on your armor, and prepare for it."[26] Another saw in Adams's agitation of this issue a parallel with instigators of revolt in Haiti, "who shed the blood of a sleeping infant and stuck a pole through its warm and quivering body, and under that standard marched with torch in one hand and sword in another."[27] Such remarks were a reminder that slave representation was inextricably bound up with slavery itself. Indeed, the dispute over these resolutions continually wandered into the subjects of slavery and abolition.[28]

Both Northerners and Southerners also made it clear that they regarded slave representation as integrally woven into the fabric of the Constitution. In the House, a Kentuckian cautioned that even receiving Massachusetts's resolves would violate the Constitution, as the three-fifths clause was a "solemn guaranty to the slave States."[29] One of Massachusetts's senators dutifully presented his state's proposal but declared that he opposed it, as "he was not for disturbing the foundations of the government."[30] Bay State legislators also circulated their proposed amendment to other state legislatures, and the assemblies of Georgia, Alabama, and Virginia all branded it an attempt to dissolve the Union. An Alabama official dubbed it "the Hartford convention amendment," and another pledged never to "relinquish this right."[31] Virginia's legislature remonstrated that the three-fifths compromise was the one "upon which the federal union of the states was formed," and which was still "essential to the peace, welfare and continuance of the slaveholding states in this Union."[32] This clause was sacred indeed if it could never be abolished even by the established amendment process.

These exchanges in the mid-1840s bore many similarities to the conflict over slave representation during the War of 1812. The previous debate was longer.

The antebellum revival featured more Southerners willing to defend slave representation.[33] But the heat of that defense illustrated an older truth: whether in the 1780s or the 1810s or the 1840s, to touch slave representation was to touch the open nerve of slavery. And even in the 1840s, more debaters preferred wrapping themselves in the Constitution and brandishing the stigma of the Hartford Convention to directly discussing the federal ratio. That made for better politics, enabling more Northerners to resist Massachusetts's call even in a time of sectional tension.

The representation of Southern African Americans remained controversial even after the Thirteenth Amendment abolished slavery, as Northerners again wrestled with the South's weight in Washington. Yankee politicians worried that the Southern states might actually benefit politically from emancipation, for all of their black people, not just three-fifths, would now be counted for representation. If they could not vote, their liberation would actually benefit the white Democrats who could. Ohio's senator John Sherman spoke for many when he decreed that "never by my consent shall these rebels gain by this war increased political power and come back here to wield that power . . . against the safety and integrity of the country." Congressional Reconstruction —notably Section Two of the Fourteenth Amendment—thus ensured that only once black men could vote would each rebel state's congressional representation be restored.[34] Throughout the life of slavery and even beyond, then, many Northerners shared the Federalists' concerns about the South's power. The Federalists had demonstrated the political possibilities of exploiting those concerns, and thus they hold a significant place in the history of the politics of slavery. The Republicans of the 1850s and 1860s brought these potentialities to fruition, but the Federalists had shown the way.[35] No wonder they haunted antebellum moderates.

———

Another constant that plagued defenders of slavery and other American institutions was the criticism of British observers and officials. American slavery was of continual geopolitical usefulness to British enemies of republicanism, especially after Britain's abolition of slavery in its colonies in 1833. Queen Victoria refused all compromise with Americans on the subject of slavery and granted fifty acres of Canadian land to black fugitives from the United States. This enabled one bold runaway slave to write to his master with the taunt that he had left "the land of bondage" and entered "a land of liberty" in Canada, ending with "God save Queen Victoria."[36] The monarch knew the value of such expressions, as she revealed in her speech from the throne in 1866. She granted that the abolition of slavery in the United States was a worthy act, but pointedly noted that Britain in particular rejoiced, having "always been foremost in showing its Abhorrence of an Institution repugnant to every feeling of Justice and Humanity."[37] Other enemies of republicanism upbraided Americans for actions in relation to slavery no matter what they were. This was evident during the Civil War, when British conservatives first criticized Abraham Lincoln's administration for failing to act against slavery, then denounced the Emancipation Proclamation as an encouragement to slave revolt. As English reformer John Stuart Mill put it to an American correspondent, there were British Tories "who so hate your democratic institutions that they would be sure to inveigh against you whatever you did, and are enraged at no longer being able to taunt you with being false to your own principles."[38] For such people as for their counterparts earlier in the century, the two countries' rival political systems were the real issue when American slavery came up.

Reformist Britons, too, still railed against American slavery because they hated to see America's example impaired. Charles Dickens was the most famous of these, visiting America in 1842 and writing two books about his experience. Like Henry Fearon before him, he traveled to the United States as its professed friend and left thoroughly disillusioned. In his nonfictional travel account, he attended to regional differences in a way that would have pleased Timothy Dwight, positing that slavery was the key distinction between the slovenly, brutal South and the praiseworthy North. Indeed, slavery was the only American atrocity significant enough to merit a chapter of its own.[39] In it and elsewhere he derided slaveholders and others who joined in subjugating black people. He knew how best to jab those professed republicans "whose inalienable rights can only have their growth in negro wrongs"; he continually branded them the authors and beneficiaries of a racial aristocracy.[40] Dickens also included some American scenes in his next novel, *Martin Chuzzlewit*. The characters in this book find the United States a dreadful place in every respect and rejoice when they return to Old England. The American characters defend "nigger slavery" as one of their country's cherished institutions.[41] In the tradition of the *Edinburgh Review* from 1819, Dickens insisted that these criticisms were a mark of true friendship. America's "best friends" hoped to see it reform itself, he wrote, rather than "reducing their own country to the ebb of honest men's contempt," thereby putting "in hazard the rights of nations unborn, and very progress of the human race."[42]

Antebellum Americans took no more kindly to such animadversions, whether from professed friends or enemies, than their predecessors had. Dickens's self-appointment as America's instructor, as well as the content of his lectures, grated on his vast American audience.[43] Nationalists' conviction that the British aimed to overthrow American liberty colored their response to British abolitionists and gave them a weapon with which to attack the American abolitionists who cooperated with them. In the turbulent 1830s, for instance, Boston's establishment feared that American abolitionists were collaborators with a British plot to overthrow order in America.[44] From the 1820s through the Civil War era, white Southerners in particular were convinced that the British plotted against their institutions and interests. In 1831, when Nat Turner rose in revolt, some of his white neighbors—like many black people—were convinced that British troops had entered Virginia to support the insurgents. Even those who resisted such wild notions believed that the British were doing everything they could to undermine both American slavery and American freedom.[45]

Believing that republican institutions were still Britons' true target, nationalists brought out the same responses they had used earlier. Antiabolitionists eagerly painted American abolitionists' ties with Englishmen as treasonable. They also pointed out that "the enemies of liberty in Europe" called the most loudly for American—but not for French, Spanish, or Portuguese—abolition. Their attempt to extinguish the beacon of liberty was only too obvious.[46] James Kirke Paulding continued his writings in this vein. In 1822, he questioned the motives behind Britons' prolific "declamation" on the subject of slavery. Raising the ever-useful charge that Britain tyrannized and acquiesced in the oppression of all other people but American slaves, Paulding lectured that "to oppress one people, and at the same time affect great commiseration for another, is not humanity, but hypocrisy. It is assuming a cloak for some interested purpose." That purpose was plain: if they could paint "the miseries of the negro in the most exaggerated colours"—especially in America—"honest John Bull may in some degree be reconciled to his own sufferings."[47] In 1836, Paulding repeated many of these same arguments, insisting that the real issue was the threat the American example of liberty posed to the Old World's tyrants.[48]

But even antislavery Americans still suspected the motives of Britons, especially royal officials making an antislavery stand. Adams, for one, treated the issue of slavery very differently when raised by the British than in a purely domestic context. In the face of persistent British importunity to grant the right of search to suppress the Atlantic slave trade, Adams as secretary of state repeatedly refused. In 1822, a British diplomat asked him whether he "could conceive of a greater and more atrocious evil than this slave-trade." He said he could, for "admitting the right of search by foreign officers of our vessels upon the seas in time of peace . . . would be making slaves of ourselves."[49] Adams was far from alone in this, as antislavery Northerners such as Rufus King urged the Monroe administration not to yield on a point that America had fought the War of 1812 to maintain.[50]

Other antebellum Northerners' concerns for the cause of liberty in the world actuated not nationalism but antislavery zeal. A delegate to New York's 1821 constitutional convention warned that racial restrictions on the franchise would hand "the proud English critic" an opportunity to boast of England's superior commitment to liberty.[51] Concern for the reputation of human liberty, as Greeks and Latin Americans moved in the direction of independence, was at least part of why some Ohioans embraced their state legislature's call for the abolition of slavery in the United States.[52] Black abolitionist David Walker touched white Americans' sensitivities when he chided them that "the English are the best friends the coloured people have upon the earth."[53] White abolitionists followed suit, contrasting European abolitionism and American support for slavery in order to goad their countrymen toward abolition.[54] Improving democracy's reputation also motivated Republicans in the 1850s. As Lincoln put it in 1854, slavery "deprives our republican example of its just influence in the world—enables the enemies of free institutions to taunt us as hypocrites."[55]

British criticism stung slavery's defenders even more. Nineteenth-century Southern planters assiduously pursued the ideal of the English country gentleman, and in general were so influenced by English culture that reproaches from that source hurt. Antebellum Southern spokesmen tried to strike an independent pose, as when a South Carolina legislator declared that "the opinion . . . of the outside world on slavery is entitled to less weight than upon almost any other subject."[56] But this was the essence of protesting too much, for on no other subject did white Southerners care *so much* about world opinion! In actuality they had a love-hate relationship with the outside world. Dickens offered a compelling portrait of white Southerners' "impotent indignation" at British censures mixed with an anxiousness that they think well of the South. As he traveled among them, Dickens testified that "they won't let you be silent" on slavery. "They *will* ask you what you think of it."[57]

When offering their own thoughts, apologists for slavery went in new directions even as they repeated past responses to the British. British colonial emancipation threw down the gauntlet to those who said slavery could never be abolished peacefully in true slave societies. In response, Southerners emphasized the miseries of free *British* laborers more than they might have otherwise and denigrated the newly free societies in the West Indies as failures.[58] But they also rehearsed tried-and-true rejoinders from past conflicts. In 1857, for instance, proslavery firebrand George Fitzhugh admitted to the domestic slave trade in the United States. "But," he roared back, "we have no law of impressments in the South to sever the family ties of either blacks or whites. Nor have we any slavery half so cruel as that to which the impressed English seaman is subjected." Continuing aspersions that had been cast five decades earlier, Fitzhugh noted that the adversities of men "torn from their wives and children, to suffer and to perish in every clime and on every sea, excite not the sympathies of" Britons bent on rebuking American slaveholders; "they are all reserved for imaginary cases of distress" in the South.[59]

In short, from the early nineteenth century to the Civil War, the British presence in American life intensified the sectional strain over slavery. Conflicts with the British also had a way of acting as microcosms of the domestic strife. The controversy over Southern states' Negro Seamen Acts, which began in 1822 and continued for decades, encapsulated the effect the British had. Responding to Denmark Vesey's conspiracy in Charleston, the Southeastern states passed laws detaining all black sailors while their ships were in their docks. The British protested, for this involved the seizure of black British mariners. White Northerners also disapproved, in part because this dispute gave Britons occasion to throw out the kinds of barbs that had for so long mortified Northerners. "These Yankees may kidnap one another," a British official jabbed, "but they must not kidnap British subjects in violation of the law of nations." The broad use of "Yankees," lumping all Americans together as kidnappers, was the very thing that had outraged Northern sectionalists in the past. The Southern states' defiance of federal law also offended Northerners, for federal courts had ruled the laws unconstitutional but they continued to enforce them. This raised the question, as a Supreme Court justice put it, of whether there was a "right in each state to throw off the federal Constitution at its will and pleasure?" There had to be, Southern spokesmen responded, if meddlesome Yankees sought to make white Southerners "victims of a successful rebellion, or the slaves of a great consolidated Government." For them, this issue involved the "necessity of self-preservation." As with previous Anglo-American conflicts involving slavery, this dispute tested rather than strengthened the bonds of the federal Union. At least one British minister knew that it would be so, predicting that agitation of the Negro Seamen question by his government would "lead to great excitement between the parties already at issue" in the United States "on the question of slavery."[60]

Neither did African American assertiveness end up uniting the North and the South. Often vicious racism ruled the day in the North, to be sure. But slave resistance continued to evoke different responses from North and South. Black people thus continued their influence on politics despite being almost entirely disenfranchised.

The four decades between the Missouri Crisis and the Civil War were dark ones for race relations in the United States. White Northerners by and large stepped back from the racial openness that had characterized the Revolutionary and early national periods. Pressed by Southerners to realize a clearer position on black people's status, white Yankees' answer did not do them credit. Racist doctrine surfaced repeatedly in New York's 1821 constitutional convention, for instance, which enfranchised all white men but retained property qualifications for black men. White New Yorkers retained these racial restrictions until after the Civil War, when the Fifteenth Amendment forced them to abandon them.[61]

Such proscriptions only increased free blacks' assertiveness, which in turn exacerbated white Northerners' racism. Antebellum black Northerners' typical response to discrimination was to call for greater unity, self-reliance, and militancy in the black community.[62] Drawing on writings of early national black leaders, antebellum black thinkers nurtured militant abolitionism among both whites and blacks.[63] Free blacks in the North continued to be a thorn in the side of the white South—as runaway magnets and unfortunate symbols in the antebellum period, and then even more directly as Union soldiers in the Civil War.[64] But even as they contributed to antislavery on the one hand, on the other their behavior and rhetoric engendered greater hostility in white people throughout the country.[65] The drive to remove black people from the United States continued to resonate with those seeking distance from such brazen African Americans. In 1824, a New Jersey ACS meeting stigmatized free people of color as "a moral and political pestilence" and an "enormous mass of revolting wretchedness and deadly pollution."[66]

But if the ACS represented continuity, other developments signaled change. Riots against black communities and their white champions became a new hallmark of race relations. A Cleveland editor looked back on "liberal sentiments" expressed in the Ohio press during the 1810s, "which, had they appeared twenty years later, would have produced a bonfire of the offending newspaper's press and types."[67] In 1812, African American leader Paul Cuffee met with President Madison at the White House, but such a meeting would soon become unheard-of, so that when Lincoln invited Frederick Douglass to the White House, the meeting itself was a highly significant event.[68] Indeed, so strong was race discrimination in the federal government that the United States did not recognize Haiti's independence until 1862, in part to avoid the awkwardness of a black ambassador in Washington.[69] Surely Southern domination of the federal government helped make this so. But as historian Don E. Fehrenbacher suggested, after the Missouri Crisis most white Northerners acquiesced in Southern racial doctrines for the purpose of "maintaining sectional peace."[70] Most of them also agreed with those doctrines.

Nevertheless, "sectional peace" was fleeting in the antebellum period, in part because some white Northerners still expressed their sympathy for slaves resisting their masters. In times of crisis, slaveholders focused on their effusions rather than the racial solidarity that most white Northerners manifested most of the time. Yankees' troublemaking began with their influence on black rebels, white Southerners argued. Vesey, for instance, read many antislavery tracts, including speeches by the likes of King during the Missouri controversy. These gave him the sense that slave insurgents might have friends in the North and both inspired him and gave him a recruiting tool. "Mr. King was the black man's friend," Vesey told one of his recruits.[71] Union with the antislavery North opened the South to dangerous outside influences.

Then when Southern authorities put down insurrectionists, queasy Northerners cried out against the violence involved in doing so. To be sure, many were more horrified by the revolts than by their suppression.[72] But these did not garner Southern attention as much as Theodore Dwight did, who said that no Americans, "who boast of freedom themselves," should be surprised at plots and revolts among slaves, for "white men" would do the same in the position of "these miserable children of Africa."[73] Or the Ohio judge who wished "the slaves would rise up and cut the throats of their masters."[74] Or the antislavery poet John Greenleaf Whittier, who announced to white Virginians: "We leave ye with your bondmen, to wrestle, while ye can, / With the strong upward tendencies and God-like soul of man!"[75] Similarly, try as Republican leaders might to distance themselves from John Brown's 1859 attempt to instigate slave rebellion at Harpers Ferry, Southerners took Henry David Thoreau as the emblematic Yankee. Thoreau insisted that Brown "could not have been tried by a jury of his peers, because his peers did not exist." "It was his peculiar doctrine," he continued, "that a man has a perfect right to interfere by force with the slaveholder, in order to rescue the slave. I agree with him." He concluded by comparing Brown to Christ and pronouncing that "he is not Old

Brown any longer; he is an angel of light."[76] It was this sort of extravagance that caught Southern attention.

White Southerners remained divided over how best to deal with the slave threat but united against such Yankees.[77] Slaveholders had unbounded hatred especially for abolitionists and expressed it in extreme rhetoric. In the august halls of Congress, for instance, Southern spokesmen branded abolitionists "murderers, foul murderers, accessories before the fact, and they know it, of murder, robbery, rape, infanticide." Even the term "blood-hounds" was "too mild," one Southron said. "I call them *fiends of hell*." As such "it would be an offense against heaven not to kill any available abolitionist."[78]

The idea of outside agitators was both a useful and a strongly held belief. It was useful to Southern spokesmen who portrayed slavery as a benevolent institution. Southern slaves were happy, they insisted, and therefore their masters stood in danger only if outsiders contrived to render them discontented. This argument distinguished them from their early national predecessors, most of whom freely admitted the danger of revolt. In fact, the antebellum champions of slavery set out to refute the nervous expressions of that earlier generation.[79] As James Henry Hammond put it, "Our slaves are the happiest three millions of beings on whom the sun shines." But "into their Eden is coming Satan in the guise of an abolitionist."[80] In January 1861, Senator Jefferson Davis solemnly declared that "history does not chronicle a case of" a true "negro insurrection," for only when whites stirred blacks up did they want liberty.[81]

In short, black Americans' actions set off sectional divisions rather than unity. Fugitive slaves in particular became a bone of contention, especially during the 1850s. Northerners argued then, as they had four decades earlier, that having to tolerate and even assist slave hunters threatened their rights and their identity as residents of the free states.[82] For white Southerners, it was a question of self-defense as well as interest when Yankees encouraged slave flight or revolt. Such conflicting imperatives were as difficult to compromise in the antebellum period as when they first surfaced in the early national era.

By contrast, questions surrounding the expansion of slavery became *more* intractable in the decades after the Missouri Crisis. To be sure, the United States annexed new slave territory after the Louisiana Purchase and the acquisition of Florida, and Northern opposition to new slave states failed by wide margins in Congress.[83] But the votes did not tell the whole story, for every expansion of slave territory was now controversial.[84] In 1837, Vermont's legislature encapsulated this new spirit of resistance when protesting against annexing Texas. The members remonstrated against "the admission into this Union, of any State whose constitution tolerates domestic slavery."[85] Texas's southerly location and climate no longer entitled it to the free pass it would have received in the early national period. Indeed, spokesmen for the doctrine that southern latitudes were reserved for slavery now hailed only from the South.[86] So did the boosters for acquiring Cuba, or Central America, or all of Mexico. The Missouri debates began the sectionalization of American expansionism, a process brought to fruition in the 1850s.[87]

But if the antebellum West was a—in fact, *the*—theater for sectional conflict in a way it never was before 1819, it was so for familiar reasons. In particular, Northerners still craved distance from slavery. Over 51,000 citizens of Massachusetts said it all in 1843 when they petitioned Congress to enact such laws and initiate such constitutional amendments "as may forever separate the people of Massachusetts from all connexion with slavery."[88] But if it could expand to the West, that distance was in question. Particularly if slavery spread to places like Kansas or Nebraska or California, to whence many Northerners saw themselves or their children migrating, it would rob them of their future prospects.

The motive of distance from slavery still set definite limits on most Northerners' antislavery. It had its bright side, as when Yankees resisted the capture of fugitive slaves, which would have implicated them in slavery.[89] They also joined black people in resisting the twin evil of kidnapping as late as the Gettysburg campaign of 1863.[90] But the dark side of the drive for distance, the desire to be rid of African Americans, became more prominent in the antebellum period as race relations soured. In 1861, fugitive slave Harriet Jacobs, who settled in New York City, described being treated by some whites "as if my presence were a contamination."[91]

The Northwest continued to manifest the strongest opposition to black people's presence. In 1824, Ohio's General Assembly passed what came to be known as the Ohio Resolves, calling for emancipation throughout the Union. But they made abolition conditional upon the freed people's emigration abroad (rather than to Ohio). They also reprinted the state's 1804 Black Laws, as if to drive the point home.[92] In 1846, the exodus of over five hundred black people freed by John Randolph's will captured national attention. They intended to settle in northwestern Ohio, but townsmen along the Miami and Erie Canal would not let them disembark, much less move in. Finally a town brought them food, but even these people opposed their settlement en masse, whereupon the black refugees dispersed to various locations in western Ohio. The scare led residents in one county to meet and call for "the expulsion of all blacks from the county." Abolitionists organized against this resolution, and it failed, for it went too far for most white Ohioans, even in the 1840s. But racial liberals were still in the minority.[93] In 1850, delegates to Indiana's convention revising the state constitution argued that keeping free blacks out of the state was consistent with their hatred of slavery. Allowing slaveholders to dump the sick and old slaves on the Northwest, they reasoned, would strengthen slavery in the South.[94] But in reality what most Northerners, especially in the Midwest, meant by antislavery still had little to do with the South. In fact, some feared that abolition there would send hordes of black people north. During the Civil War, some of their fears were realized. Even the upper Midwest—Wisconsin, Minnesota, and especially Iowa—saw its previously tiny black population explode. Race riots were part of the response in Ohio and Illinois. The Democrats made great bales of political hay out of this issue, putting the Republicans on the defensive.[95] Antislavery that emphasized the rights and interests of white people, inconsistent and limited as it was, retained a superior political appeal.

———

Nevertheless, the continued expansion of slavery stimulated the rise of an abolitionist movement that stood against slavery because of its impact on black as well as white people. The recognition of slavery in Missouri pounded the final nail into the coffin of the Revolutionary generation's faith that cutting off the slave trade would lead to American slavery's natural death. It also revealed slaveholders' intransigent commitment to slavery. The resulting sense of urgency helped spawn the Ohio Resolutions, which eight other Northern states endorsed. Their authors declared that they were "predicated upon the principle that the evil of slavery is a national one, and that the people and the states of this Union ought mutually to participate in the duties and burthens of removing it" before it got even worse.[96] The slaveholders' defiance of such calls for gradual emancipation helped pave the way for an even more strident antislavery stance in the North, convincing abolitionists that slavery would only increase unless they did something immediately. "To some degree," as David Brion Davis has written, "immediatism was the creation of the . . . slaveholders themselves."[97]

In many ways, the abolitionist movement heralded by William Lloyd Garrison's emergence as an immediatist and founding of the newspaper the *Liberator* in 1831 was a new thing under the sun. It no longer featured the gradual emancipation schemes that had characterized abolitionism from the Revolution forward. Indeed, it might be said that the new abolitionism had *no* program, other than calling upholders of slavery to repentance. It included a concern for black people that was missing in most white Northerners' antislavery. Garrison's antislavery, for instance, contrasted in several ways with the political antislavery the Federalists had pioneered. For him, slave representation was evil because it enabled the slaveholder "to perpetuate his oppression" of black people as well as white.[98] Moreover, while the New England Federalists had trained their ire specifically on the three-fifths clause, Garrison pointed to *several* clauses in the Constitution to prove that it was a proslavery document. And for him, the Union was problematic because it was proslavery, not because it facilitated bad policies.[99] His was a much broader-ranging critique of slavery's place in the nation, undertaken from different motives.

But for all their novelty, antebellum abolitionists owed much to the abolitionism and political antislavery of the preceding generations. As unlikely as it may seem, many of these radical agitators drew much from the conservative Federalists. In his formative years, Garrison worked for the Federalist printer Ephraim Allen, from whom he inherited a commitment to reform, a religious and sectionalist vision of the South and slavery, an ambivalence about the Constitution and Union, and some strident language in which to express this worldview.[100] Many other white abolitionists had deep roots in New England Federalism and the religious and political culture for which it stood. Some had family connections to orthodox Congregationalism, as the very names of two important abolitionists proclaimed. The "P." in Elijah P. Lovejoy stood for "Parish," his name being a memorial to the fiery minister Elijah Parish.[101] Theodore Dwight Weld's namesake was Theodore Dwight, the prominent Federalist sectionalist and advocate of immediate abolition.[102]

New England Federalism did not automatically create abolitionists in the next generation. Garrison's emergence as a radical abolitionist placed him at odds with Allen and others of his Federalist mentors and heroes. Federalism warned against fanaticism, and many remnants and inheritors of the Federalist persuasion far preferred the moderate ACS to radical abolitionism. Garrison's hero Harrison Gray Otis and War of 1812–era sectionalist Sidney Edwards Morse, among others, entered the ranks of abolitionism's enemies.[103] Moreover, the old Federalist rants against the rule of slaves could just as easily be turned to racist as to antislavery purposes. New Yorkers opposed to black suffrage complained in 1821 about how the votes of "a few hundred Negroes of

"Virginian Luxuries," artist unknown, probably New England, ca. 1825. This pointed association of slavery's physical and sexual brutality with Virginia—rather than the South more generally—hints at the continuing influence of New England Federalist rhetoric and rivalries. (Abby Aldrich Rockefeller Folk Art Museum, Colonial Williamsburg Foundation, Williamsburg, Va.)

the city of New York" could "change the political condition of the whole state," and in 1846 about how "we want no masters and least of all no Negro masters, to reign over us."[104]

Despite the limits and ambiguities of its influence, however, Federalism echoed in the program and rhetoric of antebellum abolitionists. Both groups debated the merits of the Constitution in light of its clauses empowering slave-holders. Like the Federalists he had read as a teenager, Garrison branded the Constitution a "covenant with death" and an "agreement with hell."[105] His opponents, like some of the Federalists before them, insisted that the Constitution was originally antislavery in spirit, and that the government took a pro-slavery stance because the Slave Power had subverted it. They called for political action to restore the original balance of power and spirit of freedom the Constitution was meant to enshrine.[106]

Both political and Garrisonian abolitionists summoned the Federalists' spirit of resistance to the South. The New England Federalist idiom was Garrison's native tongue, and he employed it in challenging Yankees to combat slavery. "Where is our Northern manhood?" he demanded. "Do we always mean to cower under the Southern lash?"[107] In 1859, Wendell Phillips urged his fellow New Englanders to activate the "element in Yankee blood" that would steel them to successfully "grapple with the Slave Power."[108] The political abolitionists who supported free-soil political action harnessed the power of Federalist-style sectional agitation by showing Northerners how slavery affected them directly. Such was its force that even Garrison, who had foresworn politics as morally tainted, was attracted as well as repulsed by the growth of free soil's appeal.[109] Political abolitionists knew their audience and told it that "we must all be free, or all slaves together," for the South meant to deprive the North of "those liberties brought to Massachusetts by the Pilgrims and cherished by their descendants."[110] Whittier repeatedly wrote in these tones. In 1835, after an antiabolitionist meeting in Boston, he demanded to know whether, in "this the land our fathers loved," their sons would "yoke in with marked and branded slaves," and "speak but as our masters please."[111] Antebellum opponents of slavery did not need a new language to rally Northerners against the South; the old Federalist dialect did fine.

Neither was the Garrisonians' characterization of slavery as a sin an innovation. In this they were in line with the religious branch of Federalism, which itself had carried on and refined the Revolutionary-era Congregationalist tradition. Antebellum abolitionists also channeled the likes of Parish when they welcomed the prospect of slave revolt visiting God's wrath on the South. Even Garrison was ambivalent—any use of force violated his pacifist principles, but this form of violence visited God's judgments on his nemesis the Southern slaveholder.[112]

Early national evangelicals, who had also carried forward the tradition of castigating slaveholding as a sin, influenced the antebellum abolitionists as well. Garrison, for instance, had a long association with the Baptist abolitionist George Bourne, who taught him to call slavery itself "manstealing" and "kidnapping," a daily deprivation of freedom whose guilt could not be shifted from any slaveholder's shoulders.[113] Bourne therefore carried the evangelical antislavery legacy to a new generation, even as the likes of Alexander McLeod supported the ACS.[114]

Other earlier abolitionists and antislavery traditions also helped shape the antebellum movement. Whittier grew up in the Society of Friends and lionized antislavery Quaker fathers like Anthony Benezet.[115] Garrison attributed his "conversion to abolitionism" to a chance meeting and subsequent partnership with Quaker abolitionist Benjamin Lundy, who like Bourne had continued an earlier tradition.[116] David Walker acknowledged his debt to Jesse Torrey in his 1829 pamphlet.[117] Furthermore, antebellum abolitionists directed much of their energy against the domestic slave trade, thus following their predecessors in the 1810s and 1820s. From 1831 to 1850, for instance, the masthead of the *Liberator* featured a scene from an auction block pointedly set in Washington.[118] This message, as with so much else in their program and rhetoric, echoed earlier controversies, although they applied it more consistently and directly.

————

This sort of sustained pressure against slavery led some of its antebellum defenders into new territory. As they had started to do in the Missouri debates, opponents of slavery pushed its advocates toward more consistent stands. Abolitionists skewered the inconsistency of Southerners who claimed that slavery was a good thing but also proclaimed their hatred of the slave trade that brought Africans into this supposed blessing.[119] They never quit holding up the writings of Jefferson, whether in the *Notes on Virginia* or in the Declaration of Independence, as evidence of slavery's evil and incompatibility with republicanism.[120]

Southern leaders were all too aware of this practice. Virginia governor John Floyd's file of abolitionist literature included a free black newspaper that quoted Jefferson's *Notes* ("I tremble for my country when I reflect that God is just") on its masthead.[121] The Declaration could scarcely be avoided, of course, and some proslavery men systematically refuted its claims for the inherent rights and equality of all men. "No man was ever born free," countered one, and "no two men were ever born equal." Rather, "man is born to subjection."[122] "To talk of equality of rights is absurd," wrote another, and "to talk of inalienable rights seems not much better." For the only right mankind had without the effort of acquiring it was breathing the common air![123] It would be hard to imagine a more circumscribed notion of natural rights.

Some of slavery's defenders went well beyond denying the validity of the Declaration. They declared slavery a positive good and believed that calling it anything less would not be enough to counter the abolitionists. To continue earlier generations' "apologetical whine" would not meet the challenge and would reveal "the false compunctions of an uninformed conscience."[124] The new proslavery men would not yield an inch in their paeans to the peculiar institution. One considered the defense of slavery "the defence of human civilization" itself. He praised the African slave trade, which "has given, and will give, the boon of existence to millions and millions in our country."[125] Another launched a campaign to revive the Atlantic slave trade in 1853 in the name of consistency. "We have been too long governed by Psalm-singing School masters from the North," he said. *"It is time to think for ourselves."* This notion of reopening the trade eventually came before Congress—which condemned it by a 152–57 vote, quantifying proslavery's progress since the 113–5 margin in 1807—and retained momentum into the Civil War.[126] Such advanced arguments grabbed headlines at the time, as they have since.[127]

But even in the antebellum decades, the South was hardly unified on slavery. Divided between Upper and Deep South, mountains and cotton belts, it contained a multiplicity of subregions whose inhabitants' commitment to slavery varied.[128] And whatever the region, full-scale advocates of slavery remained a minority. Many white Southerners considered the idea of reviving the Atlantic slave trade "monstrous," and they won the day when the Confederate Constitution banned the traffic. For as much attention as the proslavery push to reopen the commerce garnered, it showed how divided and complex the South remained.[129]

Furthermore, the necessary-evil school proved tenacious, even as its premise that slavery would someday disappear from America wore terribly thin. The Upper South, in particular, clung to necessary-evil notions, which fostered continued debate over slavery and rendered the region a battleground for hearts and minds between Southern fire-eaters and antislavery Northerners.[130] But it was some time before the Lower South itself stopped talking of slavery as an evil. In 1824, South Carolina's governor rehashed the tried-and-true charge that "the evils of slavery have been visited upon us by the cupidity of" the British, "who are now the champions of universal emancipation."[131] In 1831, a Georgia planter told Alexis de Tocqueville that slavery was "the one great plague of America," but that the prospect of race war posed an insuperable barrier to emancipation. A prominent South Carolinian also told Tocqueville that slavery was "a great evil," but that abolition was impracticable. He vaguely hoped that "the natural course of things will rid us of the slaves."[132] These three men could have said and written all these things fifty years earlier and from hundreds of miles northward. While the Nullification Crisis pushed many South Carolinians to a more uncompromising position on slavery, most public argument proceeded along necessary-evil lines, even in Carolina, until the mid-1830s.[133]

Other champions of slavery remained in the no-man's-land between necessary evil and positive good that had been so thickly populated in the early national period. Indeed, for all the pressures for consistency after the Missouri Crisis, most of slavery's ardent advocates did the traditional back-step into disclaimers that they were not defending slavery in the abstract. In 1822, for instance, South Carolinian Edwin Holland concocted an eclectic mixture of defenses for slavery. Southern bondsmen, he insisted, were "perfectly happy and contented with their situation," certainly more so than working people in the North or in England. But he calumniated the Atlantic slave trade as a curse to all involved. He granted that both historically and in 1822, the slaves presented a constant threat of resistance. And he was eager to fix the blame for all this evil on the British and on "the NORTHERN and EASTERN Sections of our Empire."[134] The next year, another Palmetto State man, Frederick Dalcho, trumpeted the beneficence and holiness of Southern slavery. But he also declared that "we deprecate the evil which attends it. It has descended to us; we have not produced it. We would most willingly apply the remedy, if we knew what it was." He even promised that if the Northern states would foot the bill, very few planters would oppose compensated emancipation and colonization.[135] Another contemporary Carolinian, Baptist minister Richard Furman, performed the 1810s-style flip-flop in a matter of three pages in his pamphlet.[136] Yet another, writing in the mid-1830s, paused in his paean to Southern slavery to denounce the African slave trade.[137]

Writers from farther north followed the same pattern as these Carolinians. An 1836 tome published in Philadelphia vindicated slavery as biblical, natural, and probably eternal. "The divine will," the author pronounced, "has been distinctly and actively expressed in its favor." God ordained it because it had always "tended to ameliorate and elevate the character of mankind." But he denounced the African slave trade, even as he proclaimed its consequences a great blessing to both black people and the nation as a whole. The slaves were more comfortable and civilized than they would have been in savage Africa, but the British were to blame for this "inhuman traffic"![138] In pamphlets published in 1838 and 1845, Marylander John Carey also glorified Southern slavery and then declared himself unready to do so. He wrote that the slave trade had introduced Africans into a humane institution. But it was also "an evil," albeit one necessary to provide the tutelage that would eventually qualify Africans for freedom.[139] Carey and many others demonstrated the ongoing confusion of the Southern middle ground—advancing proslavery arguments yet not ready to follow their logical conclusions.

These writers had their reasons for lingering in the twilight zone. Many of them snatched at any available defense, jumping into the fray rather than waiting until they had perfectly honed their philosophy. But they also continued to live in a world in which slavery was proscribed ethically. In 1830, as abolition societies struggled, abolitionists nevertheless believed that "the spirit of the times" was in favor of liberty worldwide.[140] British abolition in 1833 seemed to confirm this, even as abolitionists remained a tiny minority in the North. In 1837, Catherine Beecher declared "the tendencies of the age" hostile to slavery. Thereafter, the rising numbers of Americans who belonged to antislavery organizations, as well as the increasing salience of slavery in American politics, seemed to bear her out.[141]

Most Southern spokesmen sought to stay in the mainstream of Western thought, even as they defended an institution that was taking a beating in that realm.[142] Their obsessions with British opinions of Southern slavery spoke to this. The Southerners Dickens met mingled necessary-evil apologies for slavery with high praise for the institution. They garnered more of his sympathy than the full-blown advocates of slavery he had read, despite his awareness that slavery's expansion had made some of their professions ludicrous.[143]

Dickens's response confirmed the wisdom of retaining the older defenses for slavery; they held less water but were better calculated to attract agreement in the wider world. Indeed, the audience mattered. For instance, when speaking in South Carolina, James Henry Hammond blessed the name of "the wise and good Las Casas," who "first introduced into America the institution of African slavery."[144] However, in public letters responding to British abolitionists, he proclaimed Southern slavery "a moral and humane institution" but refused to defend the African slave trade. He also claimed to be defending slavery not in the abstract but as it was practiced in the South, although he proceeded to justify slavery in general from the Bible and other sources.[145] He was sure of his course when in front of his proslavery constituents but double-minded on a larger stage. His letters were far more representative of the white Southerner in the national and international sphere than were the consistent extremists who have received so much attention. The latter group's effusions highlighted what had changed since the early national period, even as those in continuity with it were greater in number.

Given the antislavery spirit stalking the Western world and influencing governments like Britain's toward emancipation, more slaveholders than ever before sought to combat liberal constructions of the central government's power. The federal government still acted largely at the behest of the white South. But more and more Southern spokesmen refused to take the kind of chances in the second quarter of the nineteenth century that they had taken in the first. They could not toy with a strong central government because they believed that the North—whose population advantage was growing with every census—swarmed with zealots scheming to use the government to enact their nefarious projects of false philanthropy.

Much as older traditions nourished a new generation of Northern antislavery activists, the Old Republicans aided in the conversion of a new generation of Southern leaders to the doctrines of state rights and strict construction. John Randolph of Roanoke's faithfulness to the old dogmas showed wayward nationalists the way home to the old creeds. He would give no latitude to the Yankees' "meddling, obtrusive, intrusive, restless, self-dissatisfied spirit," which broke out "in Sunday Schools, Missionary Societies, subscriptions to Colonization Societies—taking care of the Sandwich Islanders, free negroes, and God knows who." In the mid-1820s, Calhoun, acting under Randolph's influence, awoke to the dangers of the federal government.[146] Nathaniel Macon was another Old Republican determined to inculcate true principles in the rising generation. In 1824, he was still sending epistles to Bartlett Yancey reiterating his earlier preachments. "If Congress can make banks, roads and canals under the constitution," he repeated, "they can free any slave in the United States, so I long since have told you, and so I formerly told Calhoun, and often I believe in your presence and that of others." He again warned him that "the spirit of emancipating with those who have no slaves, never dies." His experiences early in his congressional career had taught him of the Yankees' restless "desire to meddle with the conditions of the slaves, and every debate since, in which they have been mentioned stronger and stronger ground has been taken" on the antislavery side. He therefore urged Yancey to keep Congress within limits, repeating these pleas in 1825.[147]

The Ohio Resolutions, agitated throughout 1824 and 1825, were Macon's best evidence that abolitionism had run amok in the North. They were alarming because they featured a state legislature taking on the role of the emancipation schemer, calling on Congress to act against slavery. Such "officious and impertinent intermeddlings with our domestic concerns," Georgia's governor proclaimed in 1825, presaged the day when the federal government might "openly lend itself to a combination of fanatics for the destruction of everything valuable in the Southern country." He entreated white Southerners "to step forth, and, having exhausted the argument, to stand by your arms," for "one movement of the Congress, unresisted by you," would spell disaster. The

Deep Southern states and Missouri heard him, vehemently rejecting these resolutions.[148]

The geographic distribution of these official responses demonstrated what had changed in the South since Virginia led the state rights crusade during the Missouri Crisis. Missouri had not been enough to convince the Lower South of the virtues of state rights and strict construction; the 1820s proved the pivotal decade for that development. Nationalism was still the order of the day there in the early 1820s. The Vesey plot, the Negro Seamen controversies, the Ohio Resolutions, and finally debates over the tariff turned especially South Carolinians to this faith.[149] Theirs was all the zeal of the convert, and they soon surpassed the Virginians.[150] Thereafter the Carolinians stood at the extreme of a growing commitment to limited government involvement in slavery, at least in theory.[151] Thus the rise of Garrisonian abolitionism in the 1830s, and the rising influence of political antislavery thereafter, deepened but did not initiate the localist commitment of the South. And Randolph's and Macon's roles in initiating it exemplified the fact that the 1820s witnessed merely another intensification of a trend under way during and even before the Missouri Crisis.

––––––––

The story of the rise of state rights in the South mirrored the general story of the link between the politics of slavery in the early national and antebellum periods. Given the exigencies of the antebellum strife, radicals in both the North and the South took new advanced positions, attacking or defending slavery in ways that had previously been very rare. Yet the zealots on both sides remained minorities, and the rest of Americans spoke and wrote in ways that would have been familiar in the 1810s. Most white Northerners still acted against slavery only when it impinged on their rights, interests, or self-image. The expansion of slavery remained the most common way it did so. Politicians used slavery to best advantage when they kept the nature of Northern antislavery in mind, as Federalists and others had previously. Most white Southerners remained committed to slavery in practice but confused about how far to press defending it. Moderates fell back on old tactics to try to defuse the growing controversy, insisting that the Union was what was really at danger from enemies both domestic and foreign. The 1810s were not the 1850s. But antebellum strife over slavery took the shape it did in large part because of developments and lessons learned in that crucial decade.

Notes

ABBREVIATIONS

AC   *Annals of the Congress of the United States*, 9th Cong., 1st sess.–17th Cong., 2d sess.
          (Washington, D.C.: Gales and Seaton, 1852–55)
Centinel *Columbian Centinel* (Boston)
Courant   *Connecticut Courant* (Hartford)
Enquirer *Enquirer* (Richmond) / *Richmond Enquirer*
NI   *National Intelligencer* (Washington, D.C.)
NWR   *Niles' Weekly Register* (Baltimore)
PADA   *Poulson's American Daily Advertiser* (Philadelphia)
WR   *The Weekly Register* (Baltimore)

INTRODUCTION

1. *PADA*, 21 Jan. 1820, 17 Aug. 1820.
2. *PADA*, 18 Feb. 1820; see also 8 Mar. 1820, 22 Mar. 1820.
3. *PADA*, 22 Feb. 1820.
4. *PADA*, 27 June 1820.
5. *NWR* 18 (1 Apr. 1820): 88–89. For similar rhetoric from Charlton upon receiving a donation from Philadelphia, see *PADA*, 24 Apr. 1820.
6. *Enquirer*, 18 Apr. 1820; *Savannah Republican*, 2, 25, 28 Mar. 1820.
7. *NWR* 18 (1 Apr. 1820): 88–89.
8. Ibid.; *Newburyport Herald*, 24 Mar. 1820.
9. *Centinel*, 4 Mar. 1820; see also 15, 18 Mar. 1820.
10. Embree, *Emancipator*, 8–9. See also *Newburyport Herald*, 17 Mar. 1820; *PADA*, 28 June 1820, 14 July 1820. For a Northern editor more uncomfortable with New York officials' actions than Savannah's reply, see *National Advocate*, 8, 10, 14, 17 Mar. 1820.
11. *NWR* 18 (1 Apr. 1820): 89.
12. *NWR* 19 (18 Nov. 1820): 177; Moore, *Missouri Controversy*, 152–53; Adams, *Memoirs of John Quincy Adams*, 5:122–23.
13. Adams, *Memoirs of John Quincy Adams*, 5:91.
14. Gamaliel Bradford, "A Letter to the Hon. Harrison Gray Otis, Peleg Sprague, and Richard Fletcher, Esq." (Boston, 2 Sept. 1835), in *Legal and Moral Aspects of Slavery*, 12, 25.
15. See, e.g., Locke, *Anti-Slavery in America*, 3–6, 155; Adams, *Neglected Period of Anti-Slavery*, 30; Jenkins, *Pro-Slavery Thought*, 48–58; Jordan, *White over Black*, 331; Peterson, *Thomas*

Jefferson and the New Nation, 995; Fehrenbacher, *Dred Scott Case*, 100–101, 111; Greenberg, *Masters and Statesmen*, 88; Nash, *Forging Freedom*, 185; Wright, *African Americans in the Early Republic*, 180–85; Ashworth, *Commerce and Compromise*, 192–93.

16. See, e.g., Dangerfield, *Awakening of American Nationalism*, 107. Duncan J. MacLeod paid attention to the 1810s and tried to connect Missouri with previous concerns but confessed his inability to do so; see *Slavery, Race, and the American Revolution*, 62–108, 198n100. Robert Pierce Forbes has rightly complained that "historians have tended to present the Missouri crisis as a full-dress debate over slavery that sprang up out of nowhere and then submerged just as rapidly." He has made striking arguments about the years before Missouri and paid more attention to those years than most other writers have. Yet he has generalized about the impact of the War of 1812 on thinking about race and slavery on the basis of scanty evidence; Forbes, "Slavery and the Meaning of America," 39–40, 59–65, 89–121, 123 (quotation). For his part, Larry E. Tise labels the decades between 1790 and 1820 as "the most important era for the shaping of American proslavery ideology"; see Tise, *Proslavery*, 42–74; quotation on 42. He does so for the wrong reasons, for he defines proslavery too broadly and misunderstands the ultimate purpose of the Anglo-American debates involving slavery—which was to use slavery to attack the opponents' political institutions. But he at least attends to disputes involving slavery in this period.

17. Fehrenbacher, *Slaveholding Republic*, 262–63. This oversight contrasts with his sensitivity elsewhere in this volume to "minor but illuminating episodes in the great American struggle over slavery" in the 1820s, "an ostensibly quiet decade"; 3–13; quotations on 10, 3.

18. *PADA*, 8 Dec. 1819.

19. Although seeking to avoid being overly cynical, I question the value of Richard Buel Jr.'s argument that, given the importance of persuasion rather than coercion as a tool of government in the early republic, we should take early national "political eloquence" at something like face value. "Today," he continues, "we approach what politicians say skeptically, expecting much of it to be 'spin.' During the early Republican era rhetoric was far more highly esteemed, especially in national politics, and often proved determinative"; *America on the Brink*, 6–9; quotations on 7. I am not sure I see the fundamental difference between early and modern political rhetoric, for "spin" is meant to persuade. I therefore maintain that early national political leaders' instrumental efforts at persuasion should be open to skepticism.

20. For instance, Donald L. Robinson has maintained that black resistance to slavery was "of marginal importance" to the central political events of America's founding era; *Slavery in the Structure of American Politics*, 7–8.

21. Freehling, *Reintegration of American History*, esp. vii–x, 82–104, 253–74. David Brion Davis has also recently regretted that, with some few exceptions, "the specialists on abolition and the specialists on slavery and the slave trade live in entirely different worlds"; "Looking at Slavery from Broader Perspectives," 465. Two recent books highlight this weakness in the historiography (or historiographies). James Sidbury has argued that our understanding of Virginia between the American Revolution and the War of 1812 would be far different if we called it "Gabriel's Virginia" rather than "Jefferson's Virginia"; see *Ploughshares into Swords*, esp. 256–57. But the proper formulation might be "Gabriel's and Jefferson's Virginia," which would emphasize the inextri-

cable links between whites and blacks in both the South and the nation as a whole. Ira Berlin has reminded us recently that political power was of the utmost importance to slaveholders; indeed, it was what transformed "societies with slaves into slave societies"; see *Many Thousands Gone*, 10. Despite the value of this insight, this volume does not discuss politics beyond the struggles between masters and slaves in any significant way.

22. Link, *Roots of Secession*, esp. xiii, 1–10, 80–96; quotation on 1. See also Freehling, *Road to Disunion*; Oakes, "Political Significance of Slave Resistance"; Berlin et al., *Slaves No More*, esp. xv, 75. Ashworth boldly declares that "it is not too much to say that behind every event in the history of the sectional controversy, lurked the consequences of black resistance to slavery." It was therefore "a necessary condition of the struggle" that led to the Civil War, "a *sine qua non*"; see *Commerce and Compromise*, 1–10, 496–97; quotations on 6. But in the end it is an underdeveloped theme, propounded only in his introduction and conclusion. John R. McKivigan and Stanley Harrold have also pointed out that the best examples of historians who have linked insurrection anxiety and politics have treated antebellum controversies; see *Antislavery Violence*, 8–9. For other treatments of blacks' impact on politics, see Blackburn, *Overthrow of Colonial Slavery*, esp. 27–28, 530; Rothman, "Expansion of Slavery"; Schwarz, *Migrants against Slavery*, 40; Gudmestad, *Troublesome Commerce*, chap. 2; Condit and Lucaites, *Crafting Equality*.

23. Hahn, *Nation under Our Feet*, 1–7, 13–61; quotations on 3, 53.

24. A note about how I have attempted to deal with the complexities of terminology when referring to Southerners is in order here. Throughout the text, I have distinguished between white and black Southerners rather than assuming that "Southerners" refers to whites. As for Southern spokesmen in national politics, however, the presumption of this work is that they were white men, and more specifically slaveholders. Southern state governments largely served slaveholders' interests, and the South's national representatives either were slaveholders themselves or represented their interests. Although slaveholders and nonslaveholders disagreed over many issues, nonslaveholding white Southerners did not set a separate agenda in the national arena. For these reasons I present the slaveholders as voices for the South in national politics, even for all the variety of those voices. Thus, although I have tried to be as specific as possible in identifying the speakers, such phrases as "Southern spokesmen" refer to white slaveholders or their allies.

25. Foner, *Politics and Ideology*, 22–23, 37–40; quotations on 38, 37. See also Moore, *Missouri Controversy*, 175.

26. Fischer, *Revolution of American Conservatism*, esp. 91–109, 187–91. For more recent calculations of voter participation in this period, see Pasley et al., *Beyond the Founders*, 48, 73–74.

27. Waldstreicher, *In the Midst of Perpetual Fetes*; Pasley, *"Tyranny of the Printers."*

CHAPTER ONE

1. Davis, *Problem of Slavery in Western Culture*; quotation on viii.

2. Ibid., 93 (quotation), 111, 168, 190, 196.

3. Ibid., 118–21, 125–64, 170; quotation on 121. For literary confirmation of Davis's

interpretation of pre-Revolutionary antislavery, see Basker, *Amazing Grace*, esp. xxxvii–xl, 5–8, 84.

4. Greene, *Negro in Colonial New England*, 18.

5. My interpretation of the oft-told Georgia story accords with and follows Davis, *Problem of Slavery in Western Culture*, 144–50.

6. McManus, *Black Bondage in the North*, 1–35. See also Greene, *Negro in Colonial New England*, 22–31, 57–71.

7. Berlin, *Many Thousands Gone*, chap. 7, esp. 181, 187. For New York's attachment to slavery, see White, *Somewhat More Independent*, esp. chap. 1.

8. Peterson, "Selling of Joseph," 1–22, does an excellent job of putting this pamphlet into the context of the extraneous concerns about social disorder that produced it. See also Davis, *Problem of Slavery in Western Culture*, 342–48. James J. Allegro has argued that concerns about slavery and the slave trade in early eighteenth-century Massachusetts constituted a "movement" that produced not only "a pamphlet war" but also "antislavery legislation"; see "Increasing and Strengthening the Country," quotations on 8, 14. But it seems to me that such rhetoric is overinflated. The "pamphlet war" seems more of a skirmish, whereas the "movement" was not only fleeting but also successful only in securing legislation to restrict the slave trade.

9. For instance, see Sandoz, *Political Sermons*, 25–50 and passim; Hodges, *Root and Branch*, esp. 119–26.

10. Bruns, *Am I Not a Man and a Brother*, 3–5; quotation on 5. David Brion Davis has pointed out that these Quakers' desire—and failure—to compromise away or ignore the issue of slavery foreshadowed later attempts in the United States to do the same; *Problem of Slavery in Western Culture*, 316.

11. See Hodges, *Root and Branch*, 124–25, for a good discussion of the variations among Quakers and their individual meetings. This should modify the popular image of the Quakers, summed up well by Mary Stoughton Locke, who wrote of the Friends as "uniformly sincere and unworldly and single-minded" in the pursuit of abolition; see *Anti-Slavery in America*, 21.

12. Bruns, *Am I Not a Man and a Brother*, 34–36, 41–44, 59, 61–63. For the almost continual agitation of the issue of slavery among the Quakers for nearly a century, see ibid., 3–99 passim; Nash and Soderlund, *Freedom by Degrees*, chap. 2; Locke, *Anti-Slavery in America*, 21–45.

13. Vaux, *Memoirs of the Lives of Benjamin Lay and Ralph Sandiford*, passim; quotation on 23.

14. Essig, *Bonds of Wickedness*, esp. chap. 2; Davis, *Problem of Slavery in Western Culture*, 213–14, 308.

15. Essig, *Bonds of Wickedness*, 3–5, 10–14. Throughout this fine book, Essig is careful to note that evangelism did not necessarily equal antislavery. Virginia planter Robert Carter demonstrated this truth. After his conversion to the Baptist church, he sent a young man to school in Philadelphia to study to become a Baptist preacher. To reimburse his family for the loss of a future breadwinner, he gave his parents a slave. See Morton, *Robert Carter*, 238.

16. Davis, *Problem of Slavery in Western Culture*, 150–52; quotation on 151. See also chap. 13.

17. Bruns, *Am I Not a Man and a Brother*, 278–90.

18. Sandoz, *Political Sermons*, 240.

19. Schmidt and Wilhelm, "Early Proslavery Petitions," 136, 138–46; quotation on 139. For

other examples of the emphasis on property rights in early national defenses of slavery, see Price, *Freedom Not Far Distant*, 58–61; Jan Lewis, "The Problem of Slavery in Southern Political Discourse," in Konig, *Devising Liberty*, 265–97. For others who sought to tie abolitionists to the British, see Greenberg, *Masters and Statesmen*, 111; Gellman and Quigley, *Jim Crow New York*, 35.

20. Davis, *Problem of Slavery in Western Culture*, 370, 438–45, 482–93.

21. Benjamin Quarles, "The Revolutionary War as a Black Declaration of Independence," in Berlin and Hoffman, *Slavery and Freedom*, 283. For the very different experiences of other slaves, see Price, *Freedom Not Far Distant*, 63–67, 71–73.

22. Rush to Granville Sharp, in Bruns, *Am I Not a Man and a Brother*, 270.

23. William Dunlap, quoted in McManus, *Black Bondage in the North*, 175.

24. For a sense of how antislavery dominated Anglo-American literature and theater in this period, see Basker, *Amazing Grace*, passim, esp. xlvii, 183–86, 216, 289, 353. Generations of schoolboys read Caleb Bingham's collection of exemplary oratory and literature, including its strongly antislavery passages; see *Columbian Orator*, esp. 88–104, 207–12, 256–57. Those same schoolboys read Jedidiah Morse's enormously influential geography book, in which he put forth a tepid antislavery sentiment that lamented slavery's effect on white people as part of his presentation of New England and the North as superior to the South; see *American Geography*, 65–68, 140, 144–48, 219, 352–53, 388–89, 432–33. Popular playwright Royall Tyler's novel, *The Algerine Captive*, went beyond decrying slavery just for white men, taking a strong, principled antislavery stance in its story of an American taken into captivity in Northern Africa. Meanwhile, an English anti–slave-trade song, "I Sold A Guiltless Negro Boy," enjoyed "substantial but not spectacular popularity" in the United States; Schrader, "Singing SHEAR History." A play written by a Philadelphian, John Murdock, despite its manifest ambivalence on the wisdom of emancipation, featured a slave being immediately freed; see *Triumphs of Love*, 19, 52–53, 67–69, 81.

25. Bruns, *Am I Not a Man and a Brother*, 321, 325–27, 344–48, 358–65, 374–76, 397–400, 423–26, 432–40, 456–61; quotations on 326, 435. Achan was an Israelite who brought God's judgment upon Israel during the conquest of Palestine under Joshua by taking an "accursed thing" from defeated Jericho. The presence and concealment of this unauthorized contraband of war in Israel's camp led to its defeat in a subsequent battle. See Joshua 7.

26. Quoted in Locke, *Anti-Slavery in America*, 61. Locke points out that this pamphlet had wide circulation and was found in George Washington's library; ibid., 62. At any rate, its author (presumed to be John Dickinson of Pennsylvania) was far from alone in this argument; for a sense of its prevalence, see Bruns, *Am I Not a Man and a Brother*, passim.

27. Essig, *Bonds of Wickedness*, esp. chap. 5; Stout and Minkema, "Edwardsean Tradition."

28. Fladeland, *Men and Brothers*.

29. Berlin and Hoffman, *Slavery and Freedom*, ix (quotation); Bruns, *Am I Not a Man and a Brother*, 104, 223–24, 402, 412–13, 458–59; McLeod, *Negro Slavery Unjustifiable*, 18; Branagan, *Serious Remonstrances*, 56–59.

30. For just one example, see McLeod, *Negro Slavery Unjustifiable*, 15–16, 42.

31. Ibid., 18, 34–36 (first quotation on 35); Bruns, *Am I Not a Man and a Brother*, 188, 414–16, 421–22 (second quotation on 415).

32. Davis, "Emergence of Immediatism," 210–19.

33. Hinks, "It Is at the Extremest Risque"; Bruns, *Am I Not a Man and a Brother*, 456–59.
34. McLeod, *Negro Slavery Unjustifiable*, 40–41.
35. Wesley, *Thoughts upon Slavery*, 34–35, 39n–43n, 49–57.
36. Wiecek, *Sources of Antislavery Constitutionalism*, 150–52; quotation on 151.
37. See Bruns, *Am I Not a Man and a Brother*, 268, 274–77, 305, 365–76, 439–40; Kaminski, *A Necessary Evil*, 4–5, 10–11, 24.
38. Davis, *Problem of Slavery in Western Culture*, 399–400; Davis, *Problem of Slavery in the Age of Revolution*, esp. 257–59.
39. Locke, *Anti-Slavery in America*, 188–95.
40. Zilversmit, *First Emancipation*; Nash and Soderlund, *Freedom by Degrees*; White, *Somewhat More Independent*; Horton and Horton, *In Hope of Liberty*; Melish, *Disowning Slavery*; Hodges, *Root and Branch*.
41. For a history of this bill and the debates surrounding it, see Mason, "Slavery Overshadowed," 59–81. For Macon's statement, see *AC*, 9th Cong., 2d sess., 225.
42. See Anthony Benezet in Bruns, *Am I Not a Man and a Brother*, 268–69. For more on this focus on the Atlantic slave trade, see ibid., esp. pts. 2 and 3; Locke, *Anti-Slavery in America*, passim; MacLeod, *Slavery, Race, and the American Revolution*, 36–47.
43. Bruns, *Am I Not a Man and a Brother*, 270.
44. A point made by MacLeod, in *Slavery, Race, and the American Revolution*, 198–99n100.
45. Kaminski, *A Necessary Evil*, 59–60, 87, 135, 137–38; quotation on 87.
46. Sandoz, *Political Sermons*, 1161–62. For more optimism in New York, see Strickland, *Journal of a Tour*, 77. Shane White has argued persuasively that complacency helped delay gradual emancipation in New York; *Somewhat More Independent*, 32, 80–87.
47. *Aurora*, 13 Dec. 1806. For other examples of this optimism in 1808, see Basker, *Amazing Grace*, 636–38, 645–46, 665–66, 671–73, 681–83. For a more pessimistic view, see 647–59.
48. Porter, *Early Negro Writing*, 338 (first quotation), 372; *PADA*, 1 Jan. 1808 (second quotation). Twenty years earlier, on 4 July 1788, the black inhabitants of Providence, Rhode Island, had met to celebrate the fact that the Constitution even held out the prospect of the abolition of the slave trade; see Kaminski, *A Necessary Evil*, 114.
49. For fears of a rival imperial power turning British North America's slaves against their masters, see Hodges, *Root and Branch*, 132; McManus, *Black Bondage in the North*, 110, 123, 126–27; Mullin, *Flight and Rebellion*, 130–31; Wood, *Black Majority*, esp. 304–7. In the 1780s, George Mason of Virginia recalled that seventeenth-century English protector Oliver Cromwell had instructed his commissioners to the colonies to use servant and slave revolt to subjugate Virginia if nothing else worked; see Kaminski, *A Necessary Evil*, 59.
50. The most recent and authoritative treatment of slave flight during the Revolutionary War is Pybus, "Jefferson's Faulty Math."
51. Philip D. Morgan, "Black Society in the Lowcountry, 1760–1810," in Berlin and Hoffman, *Slavery and Freedom*, 111–12, 138–39.
52. For excellent discussions of the nature of the challenge revolutionary Haiti posed to slaveholders, see Davis, *Problem of Slavery in the Age of Revolution*, 562–63; Davis, "Impact of the French and Haitian Revolutions," in Geggus, *Impact of the Haitian Revolution*, 3–8; Berlin, *Many Thousands Gone*, 4, 222.

53. Egerton, *Gabriel's Rebellion*.
54. McColley, *Slavery and Jeffersonian Virginia*, 108–9. See also Scott, "Common Wind"; Hunt, *Haiti's Influence on Antebellum America*; Sidbury, "Saint Domingue in Virginia."
55. See Hodges, *Root and Branch*, 171–75; Nash and Soderlund, *Freedom by Degrees*, 75–77, 94–95, 140–41; White, *Somewhat More Independent*, 143–49.
56. Meaders, *Advertisements*; quotation on 191.
57. Kaminski, *A Necessary Evil*, 268. Ironically, Madison had allowed Billey to stay in Philadelphia because he was afraid that Billey was so infected with the contagion of liberty that he would be a malign influence on his slaves in Virginia.
58. Kaminski, *A Necessary Evil*, 199.
59. Schmidt and Wilhelm, "Early Proslavery Petitions," 134, 139 (quotation), 141, 143, 146.
60. *AC*, 9th Cong., 2d sess., 174.
61. Iaccarino, "Virginia and the National Contest over Slavery," 37–40.
62. James A. McMillin's upward revision of the number of slaves imported between the Revolution and the 1808 ban is persuasive. He demonstrates that around 170,000—rather than the 92,000 in the previous best estimate by Philip D. Curtin—Africans entered the United States in that period, suggesting that they had a greater impact for a longer time than previously thought; see *Final Victims*, esp. 119. For starters, in 1810 Africans "composed more than one-fifth of the slaves in South Carolina"; Berlin, *Many Thousands Gone*, 314.
63. Lachance, "Politics of Fear"; Mason, "Labor Supply in the Age of Toussaint."
64. For the Great Migration's effects on slave family life, see Morgan, "Black Society in the Lowcountry," in Berlin and Hoffman, *Slavery and Freedom*, 124; and Allan Kulikoff, "Uprooted Peoples: Black Migrants in the Age of the American Revolution, 1790–1820," in Berlin and Hoffman, *Slavery and Freedom*, 143–71, esp. 143, 153–67. James Sidbury has demonstrated just how "Virginian" in loyalty and identity black Virginians were in the early republic; see *Ploughshares into Swords*, esp. chap. 1–3.
65. Steven F. Miller, "Plantation Labor Organization and Slave Life on the Cotton Frontier: The Alabama-Mississippi Black Belt, 1815–1840," in Berlin and Morgan, *Cultivation and Culture*, 156–58, 165–69; quotation on 157. For the notion of customary rights and obligations worked out in a dialectic between master and slave, see Genovese, *Roll, Jordan, Roll*. For accounts of slavery from the early republic that highlight these themes, see Steward, *Twenty-two Years a Slave*; Ball, *Fifty Years in Chains*.
66. Aptheker, *American Negro Slave Revolts*, 235–38; quotation on 235. For a similar sentiment from James Monroe, Virginia's governor in 1800, see Ammon, *James Monroe*, 189.
67. Mullin, *Flight and Rebellion*, 127; Berlin, *Slaves without Masters*, pt. 1.
68. Mary Beth Norton, Herbert G. Gutman, and Ira Berlin, "The Afro-American Family in the Age of Revolution," in Berlin and Hoffman, *Slavery and Freedom*, 190–91.
69. Locke, *Anti-Slavery in America*, 109–10.
70. Points made persuasively by McColley, *Slavery and Jeffersonian Virginia*, chap. 2, 4, 6–7. David Brion Davis has also effectively asked whether, in light of most Virginia planters' behavior, Jeffersonian necessary-evil cant can "be termed 'antislavery' without diluting the concept of any meaning." See Davis, *Problem of Slavery in the Age of Revolution*, 164–84; quotation on 170. Consider also William M. Wiecek's observation that "by making emancipation turn on unlikely, not to say fantastic, conditions," early national "Virgin-

ians committed themselves to maintaining slavery indefinitely"; see *Sources of Antislavery Constitutionalism*, 91. For a fascinating and telling account of one white Georgian's rejection, then quick embrace, of slavery, see Kaminski, *A Necessary Evil*, 164–65.

71. Dillon, *Slavery Attacked*, 65.

72. Bruns, *Am I Not a Man and a Brother*, xxviii; see also 264.

73. Kaminski, *A Necessary Evil*, 203.

74. Rogers, *Evolution of a Federalist*, 373. See also Finnie, "Antislavery Movement in the South," 160–63.

75. Finnie, "Antislavery Movement in the South," 343–546; Schwarz, *Migrants against Slavery*.

76. Schmidt and Wilhelm, "Early Proslavery Petitions."

77. Morton, *Robert Carter*, 251–70. In 1793, Carter left Virginia to live in Baltimore. Methodist leaders spreading their rule of excommunication for unrepentant slaveholders in Virginia in 1785 faced more overt persecution, including from one "high-headed Lady" who offered a mob fifty pounds if they would give one Methodist leader a hundred lashes. The Methodists repealed their rule in 1785. See Bruns, *Am I Not a Man and a Brother*, 502.

78. Meaders, *Advertisements*, 175, 191.

79. See Kennedy, *Mr. Jefferson's Lost Cause*, 73, for a perceptive discussion of what was politically possible for opponents of slavery in early national Virginia.

80. Mathews, *Slavery and Methodism*, 20–61. The Methodists were key registrars of public opinion, for "no nonpolitical organization touched the lives of more people" than this largest of Protestant denominations, and "none reflected the social attitudes of millions of Americans more accurately." Methodist ministers had "learned to make only those decisions which they could enforce," and thus, "as indicators of public opinion, ministers were almost as reliable as politicians"; ibid., vii. James Essig provides a valuable description and analysis of the retreat from antislavery by Southern evangelicals more generally, although he dates it beginning in the 1790s; *Bonds of Wickedness*, chap. 3, 4, 6. For another, more general, account, see Mathews, *Religion and the Old South*.

81. Hamilton, "Revolutionary Principles and Family Loyalties," 531–56; Finnie, "Antislavery Movement in the South," 40–46; McColley, *Slavery and Jeffersonian Virginia*; Douglas Ambrose, "Of Stations and Relations: Proslavery Christianity in Early National Virginia," in McKivigan and Snay, *Religion and the Antebellum Debate*, 35–67. Alice Dana Adams was able to document much antislavery activity in the South in the early republic in *Neglected Period of Anti-Slavery*. Yet she often exaggerated its extent by confusing those who wished to reform (and hence strengthen) slavery with true opponents of the institution. For the 1806 law, and the hostile climate toward manumissions in general, see Berlin, *Slaves without Masters*, chap. 3, 6, 10. Alison Goodyear Freehling posited that this law was in keeping with Virginia's brand of antislavery, which had always been accompanied by the desire to remove free blacks rather than incorporate them; see *Drift towards Dissolution*, 117. But this law was obviously meant to cool, not encourage, manumissions and in any event stands in stark contrast to the 1782 law.

82. See Finnie, "Antislavery Movement in the South," 143, 212–309. See also Allen, "Debate over Slavery," chap. 2, esp. 66–70; Davis, *Problem of Slavery in the Age of Revolution*, 196–212.

83. Papenfuse, *Evils of Necessity*, esp. 2–38, does a good job of describing this struggle for one influential white Southerner.
84. Quoted in Locke, *Anti-Slavery in America*, 128; for the date, see 202.
85. See, e.g., Bruns, *Am I Not a Man and a Brother*, 279, 285–86.
86. Ibid., 221–22.
87. Schmidt and Wilhelm, "Early Proslavery Petitions," 138–46; quotations on 139, 143, 144. Aside from this one, however, and contrary to Schmidt and Wilhelm's reading, these petitions are better described as anti-emancipation than as proslavery.
88. Kaminski, *A Necessary Evil*, 167.
89. Ibid., 206.
90. Ibid., 216–18, 222–23; quotations on 218, 222.
91. Ibid., 226.
92. Ibid., 60.
93. *AC*, 9th Cong., 2d sess., 240, 238.
94. See *Virginia Gazette or, Norfolk Intelligencer*, 9 June 1774. This and many other ads can be accessed at a valuable searchable database, "Virginia Runaways: Runaway Slave Advertisements from 18th-Century Virginia Newspapers," <http://people.uvawise.edu/runaways> (accessed 10 Feb. 2006). I am indebted to Professor Thomas Costa, who operates this site, for the reference to the 1774 advertisement, which predates by over two decades the earliest reference that Mullin makes to such an icon; see Mullin, *Flight and Rebellion*, 114–16. Mullin recognizes that many slaveholders had long preferred to think of outside agitators as principally responsible for slave flight but emphasizes the spread of this argument in the 1790s as antislavery waned. See also Kaminski, *A Necessary Evil*, 220–21; Meaders, *Advertisements*, 18, 211.
95. Schmidt and Wilhelm, "Early Proslavery Petitions," 141 (quotation), 143, 145.
96. Schweninger, *Petitions to Southern Legislatures*, 21–23. See also Essig, *Bonds of Wickedness*, chap. 6.
97. See Finkelman, "Slavery and the Northwest Ordinance," esp. 346; Finkelman, "Evading the Ordinance," 21–51, esp. 22; Robinson, *Slavery in the Structure of American Politics*.
98. Finkelman, "Evading the Ordinance," 22–34; quotation on 23. Thus Finkelman, a leading proponent of the idea that the initiative shown by proslavery men demonstrates that the early republic was essentially proslavery, is at times confounded by his own evidence. For some of the petitions and Congress's response, see *AC*, 10th Cong., 1st sess., 22–27, 31, 501, 1331. For the antislavery tenor of the intellectual climate in the early nineteenth century, see also Forbes, "Slavery and the Meaning of America," esp. 89–121; Dangerfield, *Era of Good Feelings*, 216.
99. Kaminski, *A Necessary Evil*, 137.
100. See Preyer, "Congressional Fight over the Admission," 1–51.
101. Robinson, *Slavery in the Structure of American Politics*, 313, 362, 386–92, 406–8; Rothman, "Expansion of Slavery," 31–54.
102. Robinson, *Slavery in the Structure of American Politics*, 269–71; Simpson, "Political Significance of Slave Representation," 329–34; Brown, *Constitutional History*, 107–20, 213–26; Gannon, "Escaping 'Mr. Jefferson's Plan of Destruction,'" 413–43.
103. My interpretation here, and in chap. 6, clashes with that of Roger G. Kennedy, who portrays territorial debates throughout the early national period as serious and ex-

tended (*Mr. Jefferson's Lost Cause*, esp. 1–3, 210–16), and agrees with that of Don E. Fehrenbacher (*Dred Scott Case, Slaveholding Republic*, chap. 9) and William M. Wiecek (*Sources of Antislavery Constitutionalism*), who emphasize the consensus over what Fehrenbacher calls the doctrine of "nonintervention" with slavery in the territories.

104. Fehrenbacher, *Dred Scott Case*, 74–100; Onuf, *Statehood and Union*, 110–13.

105. Wesley, *Thoughts upon Slavery*, 39–44; Locke, *Anti-Slavery in America*, 183–84; Bruns, *Am I Not a Man and a Brother*, 183, 382. For George Whitefield's resort to the climatic justification, see ibid., 379. For South Carolinians' long-standing belief in this stereotype, see Wood, *Black Majority*, chap. 3. Its origins appear to have been in Portuguese Brazil in the seventeenth century; see Curtin, *Rise and Fall*, 80. For most Revolutionary-era whites' acceptance of this "climatic logic," see Jordan, *White over Black*, 526–27; quotation on 526.

106. Brown, *Constitutional History*, 107–20, 213–26; quotation on 107–8.

107. See Melish, *Disowning Slavery*. Melish exaggerates Northern racism for the early nineteenth century but otherwise provides a very useful portrait.

108. Branagan, *Serious Remonstrances*, 32–34, 92–93 passim; quotations on 32, 92. Branagan anticipated the charge that these arguments were racist and denied it; 87. For a brief biographical sketch of this "God-intoxicated man" and analysis of his writings, see Essig, *Bonds of Wickedness*, 152–56; quotation on 152.

109. Morse, *American Geography*, 249.

110. Strickland, *Journal of a Tour*, 163, 77. This resonates with Melish's description of efforts both actual and imaginative to remove African Americans from the Northern landscape; see *Disowning Slavery*, chap. 5 ("To Abolish the Black Man").

111. Berwanger, *Frontier against Slavery*; Litwack, *North of Slavery*. That such restrictive laws were more prevalent in the Northwest than in the Northeast may have something to do with economics. Free blacks' labor was more in demand in the households and docks of the Northeastern cities than it was on the family farms of the Northwest. Certainly Branagan expected that "many rich men will reprobate my plan" of emancipation and colonization "because they suppose black persons will suit them better as servants, than poor white people"; *Serious Remonstrances*, 19. I am indebted to one of the participants in the Newberry Library Early American History Seminar for this insight.

112. Kaminski, *A Necessary Evil*, 125 (quotation), 146.

113. Ibid., 108, 110–11.

114. Banner, *To the Hartford Convention*, 84–99; quotation on 85. This was part of a general vision of New England's cultural superiority to the South and West; see Stephen Nissenbaum, "New England as Region and Nation," in Ayers et al., *All over the Map*, 38–52.

115. Tyler, *Algerine Captive*, 1:81–82, 135–40, 162–70, 177, quotation on 138; 2:26–27, 50, 188.

116. Bruns, *Am I Not a Man and a Brother*, 452.

117. Ibid., 493–502.

118. Kaminski, *A Necessary Evil*, 203.

119. McColley, *Slavery and Jeffersonian Virginia*, 99. For more on Southern fears of "entering wedges," see Robinson, *Slavery in the Structure of American Politics*, 287, 335.

120. Kaminski, *A Necessary Evil*, 60, 205–6, 214–24.

121. Wills, *Negro President*, 33–46; Iaccarino, "Virginia and the National Contest over Slavery," 55–79.

122. See Cooper, *Liberty and Slavery*, 99–106; Robinson, *Slavery in the Structure of American Politics*, 392–97; Abernethy, *South in the New Nation*, 312; Brown, *Constitutional History*. Even the leading strict constructionist, Nathaniel Macon of North Carolina, supported the Louisiana Purchase without reservation; see Battle, *Letters of Nathaniel Macon*, 40, 46. His colleague John Taylor of Caroline was uneasy about the Purchase on constitutional grounds but supported it on other grounds; see Taylor, *Arator*, 24–25. This inconsistency of constitutional stances was not lost on contemporaries; see, e.g., Ames, *Works of Fisher Ames*, 1478. "In Jefferson's day," Richard H. Brown has written, "the tie between slavery, strict construction of the Constitution, and the Republican party was implicit, not explicit." But in Jefferson's day—not to mention Madison's and Monroe's—this tie was not so much implicit as it was violated, and that by the very Republicans who had previously opposed an aggressive federal government. See Brown, "Missouri Crisis," 58. Forrest McDonald is closer to the mark when he writes that, especially in the early republic, "the striking of constitutional stances would remain as much a function of tactics as of genuine conviction. The rule of thumb seemed to be, when one's rivals or enemies were in control of the central government, one was prone to savor state rights, but when one's own faction was in control, the doctrine lost its zest"; *States' Rights and the Union*, 47–48; quotation on 48. This constitutional functionalism cut both ways, however, and chap. 3 of McDonald's work gives a nice overview of the Federalists' and Republicans' mutual flip-flop on state rights and strict construction between 1800 and 1815.

123. *AC*, 9th Cong., 2d sess., 636; *Phenix*, 14 Mar. 1807; *Centinel*, 11 Mar. 1807; *Balance*, 17 Mar. 1807; *Republican and Savannah Evening Ledger*, 19 Mar. 1807.

124. Brown, "Missouri Crisis," 55–56; quotation on 55.

125. Morton, *Robert Carter*, 60–61.

126. Forbes, "Slavery and the Meaning of America," 342 (quotation), 599–602. For the distinction between a slave society and a society with slaves, see Berlin, *Many Thousands Gone*.

127. Essig, *Bonds of Wickedness*, 112 (quotation); see also Wesley, *Thoughts upon Slavery*, 25, 30n–31n, 49; Bruns, *Am I Not a Man and a Brother*, 121, 126; Branagan, *Serious Remonstrances*, 15–19, 39–55; Dillon, *Slavery Attacked*, 47–49, 61–62. Such language came from at least one abolitionist in the South, Presbyterian minister David Rice of Kentucky. In 1792, writing as "Philanthropos," he expressed full sympathy with the slaves in the "perpetual war" that was slavery, including "the brave sons of Africa engaged in a noble conflict" with their oppressors in St. Domingue; McColley, *Slavery and Jeffersonian Virginia*, 197.

128. Mason, "Slavery Overshadowed," 72–73.

129. Kaminski, *A Necessary Evil*, 52–53; quotations on 53.

130. For exceptions, see Davis, *Problem of Slavery in Western Culture*, 310; Minkema, "Jonathan Edwards' Defense of Slavery," esp. 31–35; Allegro, "Increasing and Strengthening the Country," esp. 13.

131. Kaminski, *A Necessary Evil*, 3, 7, 13, 59; Bruns, *Am I Not a Man and a Brother*, 385–86.

132. [Stephen], *Dangers of the Country*, 106–11; quotations on 106.

133. My interpretations here accord in many respects with those of Fehrenbacher, *Slave-holding Republic*, chap. 2, and Jordan, *White over Black*, 325. For leading examples on the other side of this historiographical debate, see Paul Finkelman, "Slavery and the Constitutional Convention: Making a Covenant with Death," in Beeman et al., *Beyond Confederation*, 188–225; Kaminski, *A Necessary Evil*, vii; Morgan, "Slavery and the Debate over Ratification." Morgan's notes cite even more voices from his (the majority) side of this debate.

134. Kaminski, *A Necessary Evil*, 44, 46 (quotation), 47.

135. Ibid., 46, 48, 54, 57, 58.

136. Ibid., 46, 50–51, 56. During the debates in Congress in 1783 that established the precedent of counting three-fifths of all slaves, the question was whether to count them for purposes of assessing taxes to each state. In this debate, Northern congressmen accepted the three-fifths ratio readily, their only reservation being that it was not five-fifths; 20–22. This, of course, contrasts to their opposition to it when it became an issue of representation in Philadelphia in 1787, mild as that opposition was. During the ratification debates, likewise, Northern campaigners either decried three-fifths as too high or too low a ratio, depending on whether they spoke of representation or taxation, respectively; 77–79, 85, 88, 92–94, 102. In short, the reader of these debates can easily be excused for cynicism and for concluding that slave representation was a versatile tool rather than a core concern.

137. For exceptions, especially from New England Quakers, see ibid., 72–74, 90, 95.

138. Ibid., 126, 133, 148.

139. Ibid., 130, 179–80.

140. Ibid., 184. Despite the fact that Mason had attended the Philadelphia Convention, these were far from pure eyewitness recollections. They were manifestly part of his and Patrick Henry's drive to besmirch the Constitution by any means necessary, for they attacked both the continuation of the slave trade *and* the alleged insecurity of slave property under the new federal government. Their opponents did not hesitate to point out this apparent inconsistency, although in turn these Federalists were using slavery however they could to secure ratification; see 185–86, 189–92.

141. Particularly in the North, the Antifederalists consistently set their sights on the slave trade clause; see ibid., 96–97, 99–100, 102–8, 111, 122–33. By contrast, few paid attention to the fugitive slave clause, either in Philadelphia or during ratification; see 65. That the Antifederalists made use of the clause most likely to provoke controversy in their day seems further evidence that their opposition to it was good politics.

142. Ibid., 136 (quotation), 146.

143. Ibid., 89, 95, 107–8, 149.

144. Ibid., 134.

145. Ibid., 62–63, 141–42; quotations on 63, 141. He declared protests against this clause—much like the ones he had advanced in Philadelphia—to be factious attempts "to pervert this clause into an objection against the Constitution"; 142.

146. Ibid., 121, 135 (quotation), 138, 181.

147. Ibid., 170 (quotation), 178–79. For a prime example of a Southern Antifederalist (Patrick Henry) drawing on Northern Federalists' broad construction of the Constitution's power for emancipation, see ibid., 191–95.

148. Ibid., 79–88, 100; quotations on 79, 82. "MARK ANTONY," the writer quoted, insisted that he himself was no less antislavery than any Antifederalist.
149. Ibid., 89.
150. McColley, *Slavery and Jeffersonian Virginia*, 122.
151. Dain, *Hideous Monster of the Mind*, 56–57; quotation on 56. See also Sandoz, *Political Sermons*, 1457–60; Kerber, *Federalists in Dissent*, 18–22, chap. 3–4.
152. Robinson, *Slavery in the Structure of American Politics*, 266–67.
153. *AC*, 10th Cong., 1st sess., 883, 888–89, 908–9, 919; quotations on 883, 888–89.
154. Bruns, *Am I Not a Man and a Brother*, 491.
155. For Strickland and slave agriculture, see *Journal of a Tour*, 19–27, 31–34; quotation on 31. For Hammond, see 52–54; quotation on 52.
156. Ames, *Works of Fisher Ames*, 974–84.
157. Strickland, *Journal of a Tour*, 203–4.
158. Osgood, *Wonderful Works of GOD*, 22 (quotation); [Osgood], *Devil Let Loose*, 5–14; Dwight, *Duty of Americans*, 8–32; Morse, *Sermon, . . . April 25, 1799*, 3–50; Parish, *Oration Delivered at Byfield, July 4, 1799*, 3–18; Prince, *Discourse, . . . May 9, 1798*, 5–44; Strong, *Sermon, . . . November 16, 1797*, 9–15; Strong, *Political Instruction from the Prophecies of God's Word*, 3–24.
159. Davis, *Problem of Slavery in the Age of Revolution*, 29, 30.
160. Ames, *Works of Fisher Ames*, 695.
161. Osgood, *Wonderful Works of GOD*, 16. For the New England Federalist clergy's loyalty to and celebration of the national government throughout the 1780s and 1790s, see Sassi, *Republic of Righteousness*, chap. 2, esp. 34–51.
162. Ames, *Works of Fisher Ames*, 1307; see also 1337 for his hopes for the South in 1799.
163. Ibid., 9–10, 16–17, 120–82, 209–23, 1418, 1429, 1449–55; quotations on 1418, 1450, 16, 17, 130. See also Wills, *Negro President*, 2–3, 106–13.
164. See Basker, *Amazing Grace*, 568–78, 607–9; Shugerman, "Louisiana Purchase," 273–74.
165. Ames, *Works of Fisher Ames*, 264–68; see also 328.
166. Adams, *New England in the Republic*, 183–203, 235–40; Gannon, "Escaping 'Mr. Jefferson's Plan of Destruction,'" 413–43. Indeed, as Gary Wills has pointed out, when the 1803–1804 secession plot was revealed in 1828, even the descendants of those implicated said they had no knowledge of it. The plotters had kept it quiet, knowing it would be unpopular absent some new provocation—such as the Republicans leading the nation to war with England. See *Negro President*, 127–39.
167. Ames, *Works of Fisher Ames*, 86–92; quotation on 87.
168. Ibid., 1456–60, 1472–76, 1525, 1543, 1553–54; quotation on 1457; Lampi, "Embargo Reaction," 2–3.
169. Emmons, *Discourse, . . . April 9, 1801*, 1–38; quotations on 35, 34. See also Cumings, *Sermon, . . . April 9th, 1801*, 20–29; Sassi, *Republic of Righteousness*, 84–105.
170. Most of them did not do so even after the Embargo; the War of 1812 is what provoked almost every Federalist preacher, who assailed the Republicans as slaveholders. For example, Elijah Parish, who became remarkable for his use of slavery in his assaults on the War of 1812 and its authors, said nothing about slavery even in his harshest partisan sermons; see *Ruin or Separation from Anti-Christ*; *Sermon, . . . May 30, 1810*; *Sermon, . . . April 11, 1811*.

171. For the indeterminacy of sectional alignment in the early national period, see Peter S. Onuf, "Federalism, Republicanism, and the Origins of American Sectionalism," in Ayers et al., *All over the Map*, 15–24; Berlin, *Many Thousands Gone*, 228; Fehrenbacher, *Slaveholding Republic*, 58; Jordan, *White over Black*, 315–16. Such confusion belies John Alden's assertion that the South was a unified section even as early as 1789; *First South*, 4–12. This section builds on the excellent insight of Howard Albert Ohline, who wrote that the abolition of the Atlantic slave trade "helped to increase slavery as a sectional issue, because antislavery interests no longer had an issue which cut across sectional lines"; "Politics and Slavery," 401.

172. Kaminski, *A Necessary Evil*, 49 (quotation), 194, 198. See also Strickland, *Journal of a Tour*, 52–54; quotations on 52, 53.

173. See Robinson, *Slavery in the Structure of American Politics*, 186–97, 203–5; Peter S. Onuf, "Federalism, Republicanism, and the Origins of American Sectionalism," in Ayers et al., *All over the Map*, 15–24. In 1804, the Methodist General Conference decided to print two *Disciplines* in order to accommodate sectional differences regarding slavery. The Conference included Virginia in the one printed for the North; Mathews, *Slavery and Methodism*, 26.

174. Adams, *History of the United States*, 349–50.

175. For good recent treatments of how tenuous the Union was in its first decades, see John M. Murrin, "A Roof without Walls: The Dilemma of American National Identity," in Beeman et al., *Beyond Confederation*, 333–48; McDonald, *States' Rights and the Union*, chap. 2–3; Sharp, *American Politics in the Early Republic*.

176. Cayton, " 'Separate Interests' and the Nation-State," 39–67.

177. Ames, *Works of Fisher Ames*, 698–712.

178. Gannon, "Escaping 'Mr. Jefferson's Plan of Destruction,' " 423–25, 434.

179. Ames to Christopher Gore, 3 Oct. 1803, in Ames, *Works of Fisher Ames*, 1463.

180. Mason, "Slavery Overshadowed," 74–81. Observers from across the Atlantic noticed this disparity in coverage and mirrored it. London's leading print, the *Courier*, noted that the American papers were "almost entirely filled" with reports and opinions on the Burr Conspiracy; 28 Feb. 1807. Then, throughout the spring of 1807, the *Courier* reported on Burr but took no notice of the United States' debates over the slave trade ban.

181. Onuf, "The Expanding Union," 78. For similar judgments on the Western threat, see Waldstreicher, *In the Midst of Perpetual Fetes*, 246–93; Drew McCoy, "James Madison and Visions of American Nationality in the Confederation Period: A Regional Perspective," in Beeman et al., *Beyond Confederation*, 226–30, 236, 249–56.

For Thomas Perkins Abernethy, the Burr Conspiracy's "potentialities were so portentous that it seems reasonable to say that next to the Confederate War it posed the greatest threat of dismemberment which the American Union has ever faced"; *Burr Conspiracy*, 274–75. Abernethy may have succumbed to a strong temptation for American historians in studying something other than the Civil War—that of believing that one's particular crisis is the second most serious the nation has ever faced. Still, the alarm that Burr's plot caused cannot be overlooked. For more on Burr's popularity in the West and the commonness of threats of Western secession in the early national period, see Remini, *Course of American Empire*, 47–50, 71–72, 144–64; Abernethy, *South in the New Nation*, 122–23.

CHAPTER TWO

1. See Fischer, *Revolution of American Conservatism*, 84–86, 115–19; Ratcliffe, *Party Spirit in a Frontier Republic*, 85–86, 122–23, 136–67; Pasley, *"Tyranny of the Printers,"* 235–36, 350, 404–5; and esp. Lampi, "Embargo Reaction." For Jefferson's political blunders in rolling out and then enforcing the Embargo, see Peterson, *Thomas Jefferson and the New Nation*, 883–91.

2. Otis to Roger Griswold, 4 Jan. 1809, quoted in Banner, *To the Hartford Convention*, 354.

3. Osgood, *Discourse, . . . May 31, 1809*, 26–27.

4. Quoted in *PADA*, 29 Apr. 1814. This article compared this earlier stance of Holmes's with his steadfast support for the War of 1812 in order to make him look inconsistent.

5. Adams, *History of the United States*, 247. For a good general account of the animosity stirred up by the Embargo measures, see Stagg, *Mr. Madison's War*, 14–47.

6. Parish, *Protest against the War*, 10, 12.

7. See Bailyn, *Ideological Origins of the American Revolution*, esp. 232–46.

8. *AC*, 12th Cong., 2d sess., 569–70.

9. See *Courant*, 19 Jan. 1813; *Centinel*, 13 Jan. 1813, 30 Jan.–6 Feb. 1813.

10. Parish, *Protest against the War*, 13.

11. Parish, *Discourse, . . . April 7, 1814*, 7–18; quotations on 14, 16, 12, 13, 17, 18.

12. *PADA*, 15 Dec. 1814.

13. *United States Gazette*, 17 Aug. 1814; quoted in Peskin, "How the Republicans Learned to Love Manufacturing," 249.

14. *Newburyport Herald*, 10 Sept. 1813.

15. *Courant*, 21 July 1812. Sidney Morse warned that slaveholders, given too much power within the government, might change its very form: "They can destroy the present form of Government altogether, and establish on its ruins an aristocracy, or a monarchy. They possess in short the *supreme* power." See "Massachusetts" [Morse], *New States*, 6–15; quotation on 13.

16. *Courant*, 28 July 1812.

17. Parish, *Discourse, . . . April 8, 1813*, 13–14. As he bid Madison and his kind to "restore" African Americans "to their native country," Parish demonstrated how much he wanted to see not only slavery, but also African Americans, disappear from America. He spoke for multitudes of New Englanders; see Melish, *Disowning Slavery*.

18. *PADA*, 27 Apr. 1813. See also 1 May 1813, 4 Dec. 1814. For another among the many examples of this rhetorical stance, see for instance the toast offered at a Washington Benevolent Society meeting: "The Southern Slave-Drivers,—bawling 'Sailors' Rights' with a whip in one hand and Paine's Rights of Man in the other—too contemptible to merit execration"; quoted in Adams, *New England in the Republic*, 280.

On the other hand, for some Federalists, slaveholding represented not the antithesis but the fullest expression of the kind of self-interested, wide-open democracy they feared. Massachusetts cleric John Popkin, for instance, drew a stark contrast between true Christian liberty and secular notions of liberty, which was really license. Only a recognition of God's sovereignty, Popkin insisted, "teaches us to respect all the true rights of man." Thus the spread of the gospel "has had a great tendency, and a great effect, 'to loose the bands of wickedness, to undo the heavy burdens, to let the oppressed go free, and to break every yoke;' to abolish or mitigate slavery." Popkin saw slaveholding as indicative of the licentiousness of individualistic, materialistic America. This made slaveholding unrepublican in the sense that it violated classical notions of ordered liberty. See Popkin, *Sermon*, . . . *November 25, 1813*, 17–18.

19. To be sure, even staunchly antiwar preachers often failed to use slavery in their condemnations of the war and its authors; slavery was about the only punch they pulled. See Osgood, *Solemn Protest against the Late Declaration of War*; Emmons, *Discourse, Delivered November 25, 1813*; Emmons, *Discourse, . . . April 13, 1815*. But whereas Federalist preachers had almost uniformly failed to preach against slaveholders before the war, during the war this became one of their most prominent themes.

20. Parish, *A Discourse, . . . April 7, 1814*, 20.

21. Strong, *Fast Sermon, . . . July 23, 1812*, 15–18.

22. Perkins, *National Sins, and National Punishment*, 3–17; quotations on 13, 14, 16–17.

23. Ibid., 28.

24. Albert Simpson has identified the War of 1812 as one of three occasions on which opposition to slave representation spiked in the North. The other two were at the time of the Louisiana Purchase and during the Missouri controversy; "Political Significance of Slave Representation," 315–42. The relative lack of popular fervor over the federal ratio in 1803–1804, however, places the Louisiana Purchase controversy behind the War of 1812. And the three-fifths clause was only one of many arguments put forth against the expansion of slavery to Missouri.

25. [Dwight], *Slave Representation*, 3, 21, 19. For biographical details, see Malone and Johnson, *Dictionary of American Biography*, 5:569.

26. *Courant*, 20 Dec. 1814.

27. Quincy, *Oration Delivered before the Washington Benevolent Society*, 13–17; quotation on 15.

28. *Centinel*, 16 Nov. 1814.

29. *Courant*, 15 Feb. 1814; emphasis added. A Washington Benevolent Society meeting in 1814 featured a toast with similar language: "The present Misrulers of our Country— ye have made a covenant with death and with hell are we at agreement"; quoted in Adams, *New England in the Republic*, 280. I am indebted to Professor Lewis Perry for pointing out that Federalists drew this vivid language from the Bible; see Isaiah 28:15.

30. "Massachusetts" [Morse], *New States*, 33–34, 36. This was a classic ploy used by most nineteenth-century Americans who threatened disunion, one meant to place the blame on the other side. The editor of the *Centinel*, for instance, warned that if disunion "in fact takes place, *it will be the work of the present Cabinet*"; 13 Jan. 1813. Sidney Edwards Morse was the second son of influential geographer Jedidiah Morse and brother of Samuel F. B. Morse. See Malone and Johnson, *Dictionary of American Biography*, 13:251–52.

31. Senate Documents 4820, Massachusetts Archives; quotations from documents 4820/ 17, 4820/13, 4820/33. The townsmen of Southampton were an exception, urging repeal of the three-fifths clause and complaining of the addition of new states. Both added "to the fatal preponderance of southern influence, in our national Councils." Unless checked, they urged, these defects would "pave the way for a dissolution of the Union, an event which however much they may deprecate, they do not consider as the greatest of all *possible* evils"; 4820/20.

32. *PADA*, 18 Aug. 1813; see also 20 July 1812, 10 July 1813, 28 Feb. 1814.

33. Morris to DeWitt Clinton, cited in Morison, *Life and Letters of Harrison Gray Otis*, 2:82–83.

34. [Dwight], *Slave Representation*, 3, 22.
35. *Courant*, 28 July 1812.
36. [Dwight], *Slave Representation*, 4–18; quotation on 6.
37. "Massachusetts" [Morse], *New States*, 3.
38. For a fine treatment of Federalist racial openness, see Paul Finkelman, "The Problem of Slavery in the Age of Federalism," in Ben-Atar and Oberg, *Federalists Reconsidered*, chap. 7.
39. [Dwight], *Slave Representation*, 4, 22. In such passages, Dwight echoed Elijah Parish, whose sermons evinced no racially egalitarian sympathy for the slaves of the South— indeed, quite the opposite. If New Englanders allowed themselves to be reduced to political slavery, they would deserve the same contempt in which he held "the stupid African" who "blacken[ed] the fields" of Virginia. Sympathy in its truest sense for Virginia's slaves was for Parish a disgrace.
40. "Friend to Freedom," *Southern Oppression*, 3, 11–15. The language of Francis Blake on the floor of the Massachusetts legislature paralleled this pamphleteer's rhetoric. "The slave of a southern planter," he insisted, "is as much a political nonentity, as the black cattle or merino sheep of a New-England farmer; and there is no more reason for a representation of the one than the other"; *Centinel*, 16 Nov. 1814. Although this refers only to the political rights of chattel slaves, the analogy echoed that of "A Friend to Freedom." Beyond that, it echoed the rhetoric of some New England Antifederalists who had opposed the three-fifths clause in the 1780s; see Kaminski, *A Necessary Evil*, 79, 93, 166.
41. "Massachusetts" [Morse], *New States*, 6–15, 28; quotations on 6, 13, 28. For similar arguments, see "Northern States," *Centinel*, 27 Apr. 1814, 28 May 1814.
42. "Massachusetts" [Morse], *New States*, 33–34.
43. Ibid., 32–33.
44. Morison, *Life and Letters of Harrison Gray Otis*, 2:219–23; quotation on 219.
45. McCaughey, *Josiah Quincy*, 202–15; quotation on 205.
46. Quincy, *Address . . . Power of the Slave States*, 4.
47. Fischer, *Revolution of American Conservatism*; quotation on 29.
48. Banner, *To the Hartford Convention*, 99–109.
49. Lewis Burr Sturges to Roger Minott Sherman, 1 Jan. 1815, in Morison, *Life and Letters of Harrison Gray Otis*, 2:192.
50. As suggested by Morison, *Life and Letters of Harrison Gray Otis*, 2:264; and Adams, *New England in the Republic*, 295.
51. *Centinel*, July–Dec. 1812; *Courant*, Aug.–Dec. 1812; *PADA*, 6 Oct. 1812.
52. *AC*, 13th Cong., 3d sess., 280–81, 284, 1269–70; quotations on 281, 1269.
53. Morison, *Life and Letters of Harrison Gray Otis*, 2:85–101, 153–54. The wartime crisis of defense was the immediate cause of the Convention; see Hickey, "New England's Defense Problem," 587–604. But slave representation was the principal political griev- ance they urged the Convention to redress. Only a minority of the town petitioners called for any specific political remedy to their plight, but of those who went beyond a vague call for aid, the abolition of slave representation was the leading remedy pre- scribed. The memorials are collected in Senate Documents 4820, Massachusetts Ar- chives. For some of them, see *Centinel*, 9 and 16 Feb. 1814.
54. Dwight, *History of the Hartford Convention*, 341–42.

55. Morison, *Life and Letters of Harrison Gray Otis*, 2:93–94; quotation on 93. For Dexter's letter explaining his grounds for reluctantly running as a Republican, see *Courant*, 1 Mar. 1814.
56. *NWR* 7 (14 Jan. 1815): 311.
57. Quoted in *Centinel*, 11 Jan. 1815. In his recent book, Richard Buel Jr. contests the idea that the Hartford Convention was moderate, as part of his allegations of the overall irresponsibility of the Federalists; see *America on the Brink*, esp. 226–27.
58. *Centinel*, 11 Jan. 1815.
59. Mallary, *Oration, Addressed to Republicans*, 13.
60. See [Carey], *Calm Address to the People of the Eastern States*, 23.
61. *NWR* 7 (11 Feb. 1815): 371.
62. *NI*, 15 Jan. 1813.
63. "Benevolus, Hector," *Hartford Convention in an Uproar*, 8.
64. *Independent Chronicle*, 4 June 1812.
65. Ibid., 11 Jan. 1813. The editor repeated this jab in response to Quincy's agitation of the slave representation question in his Washington Benevolent Society speech, 24 May 1813. The two articles shared the same headline: "BLACK FACTS." For the impact and contentiousness of black men's votes, see Fox, "Negro Vote in Old New York," 252–75.
66. *Independent Chronicle*, 21 Dec. 1812.
67. Ibid., 24 May 1813.
68. Ibid., 20 Feb. 1815. Up to this point Holmes had responded only indirectly to Federalist arguments on slave representation and rebuked Federalist disunionism, etc. See ibid., 10 Mar. 1814, 27 Oct. 1814. Compare his mocking tone with that of "Hector Benevolus," also writing after the crisis had passed; "Benevolus, Hector," *Hartford Convention in an Uproar*.
69. Years later, a correspondent of the *Independent Chronicle* looked back in anger on when the advocates of the Embargo and War of 1812 were "stigmatized as enemies to the commerce of the Northern States" by New England Federalists: "Reflections most derogatory were bestowed upon the Southern States," and by extension their allies in New England. "'*Virginia Influence*,' became the general watch-word, and every republican at the northward who supported this system, was exposed to every species of calumny and personal insult"; 20 June 1818.
70. *NWR* 8 (1 Apr. 1815): 65–67. In arguing against the Hartford amendments in the Massachusetts House, Holmes argued along similar lines, although he applied his point to slavery itself. The right of "holding slaves," he insisted, was "a *municipal regulation* with which we had no concern"; *NWR* 7, suppl., [Feb. or March 1815]: 49–50.
71. *NWR* 8 (1 Apr. 1815): 65–67. As "Publius" and thereafter, James Madison employed this ingenious spin on the three-fifths ratio; see McCoy, *Last of the Fathers*, 244–47.
72. Carey, *Olive Branch*, 346–53; quotation on 353.
73. *NWR* 6 (21 May 1814): 187–88; 7 (24 Dec. 1814): 253.
74. *NWR* 8 (1 Apr. 1815): 67.
75. *NWR* 8 (8 Apr. 1815): 100. See also "HOSMER," in *NI*, 7 Dec. 1814.
76. *AC*, 12th Cong., 2d sess., 755.
77. Albert Simpson has written that the Missouri Crisis marked the first time the South "defended slave representation against the attacks delivered upon it by the North." Before 1819, the South, in command of the federal government, "ignored the at-

tacks, ... standing firmly on the Constitution" and displaying "a calm and dispassionate temper in the face of many provocative denunciations and attacks"; "Political Significance of Slave Representation," 340–41.

78. "Benevolus, Hector," *Hartford Convention in an Uproar*, 6.

79. Sandoz, *Political Sermons*, 1218–34.

80. *NI*, 15 Jan. 1813; see also 8 Oct. 1812, 21 and 24 Nov. 1812, 19 Jan. 1813, 8 Mar. 1813, 21 and 29 May 1813, 21 Feb. 1814, 9 May 1814, 22 and 25 June 1814. Parish's enemies printed extracts of his sermons in the hope that readers would contrast his ranting with the sentiments of loyal Americans. See Carey, *Olive Branch*, 309; Van Pelt, *Goodness of God*, 3–4; *Independent Chronicle*, 17 Dec. 1812.

81. "Benevolus, Hector," *Hartford Convention in an Uproar*, 15. For another author who assaulted Osgood and Parish together, see [Plumer], *Address to the Clergy of New-England*, 5–28, esp. 17.

82. After it became clear to him that the Federalists were to remain a minority nationally, Quincy gloried in provoking the Republicans. "Denied power," Robert McCaughey has written, "Quincy learned to make notoriety suffice." His speeches were interrupted by objections more often than any other congressmen's besides John Randolph's. "Like a lawyer confronting a hopelessly hostile jury, ... Quincy seems already to have been preparing his appeal to the higher courts—posterity." (Indeed, he said so himself in his 1813 speech against the augmented army.) His status as a lightning rod was only increased by his knack for uttering a remarkable number of catchphrases that became infamous nationwide; see *Josiah Quincy*, 51–57, 78–84; quotations on 53, 55.

83. *AC*, 12th Cong., 2d sess., 593–96, 605; quotation on 594.

84. *Investigator*, 4 Feb.–13 Feb. 1813.

85. *Enquirer*, 14 Jan. 1813. On 2 and 4 Feb. 1813, this paper printed Quincy's speech.

86. *NI*, 4 Aug. 1813, quoted in Stampp, "Concept of a Perpetual Union," 24–25. See also *WR* 5 (11 Dec. 1813): 249; *WR* 5 (12 Feb. 1814): 398–99; Carter, *Oration, Delivered before the Republicans of Portland*, 13–15. Such rhetoric calls into question Kenneth M. Stampp's assertion that New England Federalists' threats to the Union called forth "mild responses" from Republicans in defense of the Union. It is true, as he argues, that they did not necessarily craft a coherent case for the perpetuity of the Union, but the fact that their case was not fully formed does not mean that their repeated appeals to Union were unimportant; see "Concept of a Perpetual Union," 23–36; quotation on 24. Similarly, Paul C. Nagel wrote that "in the uncertain years after 1776, Union was generally accepted as a hopeful experiment," but "barely a generation" later, "unity was enshrined as an Absolute." Yet his "generation" was about fifty years long, if I have read his uncertain chronology correctly. But in his prologue he dealt at length with an 1815 lecture that trumpeted all of Unionism's central themes and attacked its challengers as traitors. And he recognized that "the idea of Absolute Union expanded with the severity of sectional crises"; see *One Nation Indivisible*, 4–31, 110; quotations on 11, 110.

87. Kidder, *Oration, Pronounced at Bloomfield*, 6.

88. *Newburyport Herald*, 10 Jan. 1815.

89. *NI*, 17 Feb. 1813; reprinted in *Enquirer*, 26 Feb. 1813.

90. *WR* 1 (7 Sept. 1811): 8.

91. *WR* 3 (13 Feb. 1813): 379; *NWR* 6 (5 Mar. 1814): 1; *NWR* 7 (3 Dec. 1814): 197. Paul C.

Nagel aptly wrote that, during the War of 1812, "the shade of Mount Vernon was habitually on call" and that the likes of Niles were instrumental "in elevating the Farewell Address to inspired station"—although he did not explain why as fully as I attempt to do in this chapter. *One Nation Indivisible*, 224–30; quotations on 226.

92. Bangs, *Oration, Pronounced at Sutton*, 11.

93. *Enquirer*, 14 Jan. 1815. See also "Benevolus, Hector," *Hartford Convention in an Uproar*, 27–46.

94. *Courant*, reprinted in *PADA*, 22 July 1813.

95. Ames, *Works of Fisher Ames*, 301.

96. *NI*, 7 May 1813. See also *Aurora*, 29 Mar. 1813.

97. Randolph to Key, 12 Sept. 1813, in Risjord, *Old Republicans*, 147.

98. Under the headline "Legislative Foolery," *PADA* noted that Georgia's legislature, "in resentment at the political integrity of JOHN RANDOLPH, have changed the name of a county in that state, from RANDOLPH to Jasper"; 12 Jan. 1813. See also 20 July 1812, 4 Dec. 1812, 19 Feb. 1813.

99. Letters of John Randolph of Roanoke to Josiah Quincy, 1812–1826, in John Randolph Collection, Library of Congress, 16 Aug. 1812, 19 Apr. 1813, 23 May 1813 (quotation), 20 June 1813, 29 Jan. 1814, 1 Mar. 1814.

100. In Kirk, *John Randolph of Roanoke*, 266–67. See also *NWR* 7 (24 Dec. 1814): 258–62; *Centinel*, 24 Dec. 1814. It was noticed and reprinted in many other papers.

101. See Ohline, "Politics and Slavery," 467, for a brief discussion of the link between slavery and slave representation.

102. Kirk, *John Randolph of Roanoke*, 273–75. For their part, Randolph's erstwhile Federalist admirers were put off by this letter; see, e.g., *Boston Palladium*, quoted in *PADA*, 2 Jan. 1815.

103. Howard Ohline made many of these points in his dissertation. Although his research was thin for the period after about 1808, he drew some important conclusions about the period leading up to 1815. The Federalist drumbeat against the slave representation, he argued, resulted "in the wide distribution of anti-southern propaganda in which slavery became the major symbol of sectionalism." Far from a distraction from slavery, he correctly concluded, the war marked a high point in the distribution of this propaganda. The War of 1812 thus served to make slavery the focus of sectional struggle, he argued, and therefore "the roots of political sectionalism based upon the issue of slavery were in opposition politics"; see "Politics and Slavery," 439–67; quotations on 454, 467.

CHAPTER THREE

1. A good example of Good Feelings strictly on Republican terms came in 1818, when Federalist Harrison Gray Otis wrote to Secretary of War John C. Calhoun recommending a fellow Bostonian for a military appointment, in part because he had "never taken a part in political controversy"; see Meriwether et al., *Papers of John C. Calhoun*, 2:249.

2. *Centinel*, 15 Apr. 1815.

3. Adams, *Documents Relating to New-England Federalism*, 90.

4. [McKean?], *An Answer*, 21, 139.

5. Ibid., esp. 88–172.

6. Sheidley, *Sectional Nationalism*, 17–21; quotation on 19.

7. *Centinel*, 25 Feb.–15 Apr. 1815; *Courant*, 14 Feb.–28 June 1815.

8. For a brief guide to the schism in Pennsylvania, see Phillips, "William Duane." For New York's complex divisions, see Hanyan, "DeWitt Clinton and Partisanship."

9. For a recent treatment of the heated economic issues, see Dupre, "Panic of 1819." For an overview of the politics of the period, see two standard works by George Dangerfield, *Era of Good Feelings* and *Awakening of American Nationalism.*

10. This chapter builds on the insights of Brown, "Missouri Crisis."

11. *Columbian*, 5 July 1816; *Aurora*, 11 Nov. 1816, 4 June 1819.

12. *Columbian*, 22 Apr. 1816; see also 5 July 1816.

13. *National Advocate*, 20 Apr. 1818.

14. For a lively picture, from Duane's point of view, of the feuds within the Republican Party, especially beginning in Jefferson's second term, see Duane, "Letters," 257–394. For useful secondary accounts of the fractious Duane's importance in Republican schisms early in the nineteenth century, see Phillips, "William Duane"; Pasley, *"Tyranny of the Printers,"* chap. 8, 12.

15. See *Aurora*, 1812–1815, esp. 29 Mar. 1813 (quotation).

16. Ibid., 4 June 1819; see also 11 Nov. 1816, 29 July 1819, 20 Sept. 1819. For a similar line of attack, see *Albany (New York) Register*, quoted in *Reporter*, 19 June 1816.

17. *Aurora*, 23 Feb. 1818; see also 13 Feb. 1818, 13 Apr. 1818.

18. Philadelphia *Union*, quoted in *Enquirer*, 19 May 1818.

19. Barrow, *Involuntary . . . Slavery*, 21–27; quotations on 21, 22n.

20. Christie and Dumond, *George Bourne*, 108, 128 (quotation), 163–64, 181–82. See also Torrey, *Portraiture of Domestic Slavery*, 10–11, 50n; Evans, *Pedestrious Tour*, 277–78; Winch, *Gentleman of Color*, 159.

21. *Philadelphia Gazette*, reprinted in *Aurora*, 14 Jan. 1819.

22. *Aurora*, 1 June 1819.

23. Ibid., 1 Feb. 1817; see also 25 July 1816, 10 Aug. 1816. The speaker in question had argued against the unrestricted "spirit of innovation" in representation that could lead to such despotism as "a curly-headed, thick-lipped, flat-nosed African" voting or even being elected; see *Enquirer*, 28 Jan. 1817. A flippant public remark from a slaveholder in the District of Columbia did nothing to assuage such concerns, even as he mocked them. He complained of the District's restrictions on slaveholders from outside of Maryland and said that if Congress meant to "exclude slaves from the District of Columbia, let them pass a general law to that effect" so that it would at least operate equally. The elite in the nation's capital, he jested, "would be delighted to receive a white colony from Massachusetts and Connecticut, to supply in the menial offices, the place of the sable colored race." The Yankees' "steady habits and obedient tempers" would be more than welcome; see "JUSTICE AND EQUALITY," in *NI*, 11 Apr. 1816. Neither did a Norfolk printer do much to dispel grumblings about "Virginia influence." In fact, he documented and boasted about it, noting that of the 190 members of the House of Representatives, 78 were natives of Virginia. "The number representing Virginia being only 23," he gushed, "it would hence appear that she has supplied the southern and western sections of the Union with 55 statesmen"; *Norfolk Herald*, quoted in *Charleston Courier*, 2 Mar. 1818.

NOTES TO PAGES 80–85

24. Duane, "Letters," 373–75; quotations on 374.
25. See chap. 6 for slavery's encroachment on free states.
26. *Independent Chronicle*, 8 Feb. 1816.
27. *National Advocate*, 13 Sept. 1816.
28. Ibid., 21 May 1818. See also ibid., 7 Dec. 1816; *Columbian*, 22 May 1818.
29. [Paulding], *Letters from the South*, 1:20–36; quotations on 26, 30. For more on Paulding's nationalist and partisan project, see Ratner, *James Kirke Paulding*.
30. See, e.g., *NWR* 9 (27 Jan. 1816): 388; *NWR* 12 (7 June 1817): 228–30; *Aurora*, 2 Dec. 1817. For other quotes from the immediate postwar period asserting that partisan and sectional fervor had subsided, see Skeen, *1816*, 17–33, 125–33. As I read these quotes, Skeen is too willing to accept them at face value, as descriptive of goodwill reigning briefly in 1816 rather than prescriptive.
31. *Independent Chronicle*, 1 Aug. 1816.
32. *Columbian*, 16 June 1818.
33. *National Advocate*, 21 May 1818.
34. Ibid., 10 Sept. 1818; see also 28–30 Apr. 1818.
35. *Western American*, 26 Nov. 1815; see also 13 Jan. 1816, 9 Mar. 1816.
36. *Independent Chronicle*, 2 Sept. 1818.
37. Ibid., 24 Oct. 1816, 31 Oct. 1816, 9 Jan. 1817; *Columbian*, 8 July 1818; Walsh, *Appeal*, 415–21.
38. [Paulding], *Letters from the South*, 1:20–36; quotation on 24.
39. Ibid., 1:120–31. For the white South's tendency to blame the slave trader for the ills of the slave trade, see Bancroft, *Slave Trading in the Old South*; Tadman, *Speculators and Slaves*; Gudmestad, *Troublesome Commerce*.
40. *Columbian*, 3 Aug. 1818.
41. Ibid., 12 Dec. 1818.
42. Ibid., 26 June 1818.
43. [Paulding], *Letters from the South*, 1:117–20; quotation on 119.
44. *Independent Chronicle*, 15 Aug. 1816, 6 Feb. 1817, 22 May 1817. The scarcity and perfunctory tone of these scraps suggest this interpretation of them.
45. Finkelman, *Imperfect Union*, 89.
46. *Journal of the Assembly of the State of New-York*, 239.
47. [Paulding], *Letters from the South*, 1:130. Paulding's solicitude, along with other evidence in this chapter, belies Albert F. Simpson's statement that the Missouri controversy "revived and intensified the old sectional animosities which had been so happily quiet since the arrival of the news of the Treaty of Ghent"; see "Political Significance of Slave Representation," 315–42.
48. *Georgia Journal*, 24 Jan. 1816.
49. *Enquirer*, 19 May 1818.
50. Ibid., 2 May 1817; see also 5 Apr. 1817, 27 May 1817.
51. Ibid., 15 May 1818.
52. *NI*, 14 Aug. 1817; see also 5 Mar. 1818, 1 Apr. 1819.
53. Neither did the few remaining Southern Federalists see anything to gain from a thorough sectional discussion of slavery. This was apparent in the pages of the *Charleston Courier* during the Era of Good Feelings, in which the weakness of the editorial voice suggested that this editor had lost his way politically. He put himself on record, feebly

and perfunctorily, against the kidnapping of free blacks; 9 July 1817, 30 July 1817, 24 Jan. 1818. He watched with some detachment, and through the prism of partisanship rather than sectionalism, the splintering of the Republican Party to the North, with all its implications for slavery; 28 Aug. 1816. He printed accounts of tensions between the South and the West produced by Henry Clay's presidential ambitions; 21 Apr. 1818. But he was content to ignore the mounting evidence of North-South sectionalism attached to slavery in the postwar years.

54. *Savannah Republican*, 30 Nov. 1818.
55. Ibid., 3 Oct. 1816; see also 8 Oct. 1816, 15 Oct. 1816, 19 Oct. 1816, 28 June 1819.
56. Ibid., 9 Nov. 1816.
57. Ibid., 21 Oct. 1817.

CHAPTER FOUR

1. This point is at odds with Don E. Fehrenbacher's recent argument about America's stance on the world stage. "At home," he wrote, "the American nation was a house divided by the slavery question, but in the conduct of foreign affairs it appeared consistently as a slaveholding republic"; *Slaveholding Republic*, 91. This statement, developed in chap. 4 of Fehrenbacher's masterly book, applies best to the U.S. government's diplomatic activities.
2. Soulsby, *Right of Search*, remains the place to start for negotiations on slave trade cooperation.
3. Many scholars have discussed British policies toward American slaves during the War of 1812 and their effects. See especially Cassell, "Slaves of the Chesapeake Bay"; Owsley, *Struggle for the Gulf Borderlands*; Bullard, *Black Emancipation*; Altoff, *Amongst My Best Men*; George, "Mirage of Freedom"; Mason, "Battle of the Slaveholding Liberators," esp. 671–73.
4. See Lindsay, "Diplomatic Relations."
5. *WR* 2 (18 Apr. 1812): 119. Matthew Carey quoted this passage in *Olive Branch*, 181.
6. Madison to Albert Gallatin, 28 July 1809, quoted in Adams, *History of the United States*, 81.
7. See Davis, *Problem of Slavery in the Age of Revolution*, 549.
8. See Melish, *Disowning Slavery*, 137–61; Baepler, *White Slaves*, 1–2, 24–31, 45–48, 303–10, for evidence of these accounts' vast popularity.
9. *WR* 3 (9 Jan. 1813): 303.
10. *NWR* 7 (27 Oct. 1814): 110.
11. Carey, *Olive Branch*, 210. At least some American slaves in North Africa agreed that even the theory of impressment was worse than what they suffered. According to one account, a British consul offered them freedom, "but a large majority of our patriotic tars" declared "that they would not be released by a government which they detested, on account of its tolerating the impressment of seamen, and swearing that they would sooner remain under the Bashaw than George the third"; see Baepler, *White Slaves*, 197.
12. Alexander McLeod, an antislavery Presbyterian minister, favored the war and compared impressment to enslavement of a kind but left African slavery out of the question. The hypothetical he used for an analogy was one in which Britain's government entered English subjects' homes and sold the fathers into slavery. If the king had no

right to do this, he asserted, neither could he drag expatriated Englishmen from American ships into "servitude"; *Scriptural View*, 163–65; quotation on 164. The abolitionist McLeod was not one to follow some of his fellow Republicans in branding American tars' plight as worse than American slaves'.

13. The grandiloquence often burst these boundaries, especially in the North. For instance, Pennsylvania governor Simon Snyder's oratory featured graphic descriptions of the lashing that the "enslaved" American tars endured, something no white Southern speaker ventured to do; *WR* 1 (21 Dec. 1811): 281. Hezekiah Niles asked his readers to imagine that "a gang of those fellows known in the middle states by the name of 'Georgia traders,' were to seize on a parcel of free *negroes* and carry them off." If the stolen blacks "were to rise upon them and destroy every one of them—who is there that could call this a 'mutiny'?" As Niles pursued his point, the implications of his analogy hardly became less threatening to slavery, as he hoped that Congress would "by premiums or some other means, excite and promote a spirit in the American seamen to hew their way to freedom, if enslaved; or to destroy all who shall attempt to fetter them"; *WR* 1 (2 Nov. 1811): 147–48; see also *WR* (14 Nov. 1812): 174. Niles later avowed his intention to "bring the case nearer home" by having his audience imagine Southern planters kidnapping white Northerners to stock their plantations; *WR* 3 (9 Jan. 1813): 303. This certainly brought it home, being the kind of scenario many Northern Federalists were also conjuring up. Far preferable from the planters' perspective were the more distant analogies to Africa, Algiers, and especially the British West Indies. Niles acted more in this spirit after the war began, as when he posed another analogy for impressment, in which a robber took a farmer's child and had it "transported to *Turkey* and sold as a slave"; *WR* 2 (25 July 1812): 247–49. Still later, he used West Indian planters as the counterparts to the Royal Navy, as when he wrote that "the British recruit their navy upon the same principle that a West-Indian planter obtains his slaves, which is power"; *WR* 4 (20 Mar. 1813): 53; see also *WR* (25 July 1812): 349.

14. Quoted in *Investigator*, 2 Nov. 1812. Another white Southerner scribbled that impressed tars suffered the "worst of slavery, *to fight for their oppressors!" NI*, 10 Mar. 1812.

15. Van Ness, *Oration . . . , July 4th, 1812*, 22–23.

16. *Enquirer*, 24 Nov. 1812.

17. Adams, *Memoirs of John Quincy Adams*, 2:422.

18. *Cobbett's Weekly Register*, reprinted in *Western American*, 10 June 1815.

19. *Parliamentary Debates*, 2d ser., 5:1327–28, 1335; quotation on 1335. Londonderry inexplicably grouped the recalcitrant monarchies ruling Spain and France under the rubric of representative governments.

20. Quoted in Altoff, *Amongst My Best Men*, 125.

21. *Independent Chronicle*, 2 Jan. 1815; see also *United States' Gazette*, quoted in *NWR* 7 (24 Dec. 1814): 262.

22. *WR* 5 (2 Oct. 1813): 84.

23. *NWR* 7 (31 Dec. 1814): 284. The sheer volume and persistence of his charges on this score are impressive. See *WR* 4 (7 Aug. 1813): 376; *WR* 4 (21 Aug. 1813): 407; *WR* 5 (11 Sept. 1813): 30–31; *WR* 5 (18 Sept. 1813): 46; *WR* 5 (16 Oct. 1813): 119; *WR* 5 (15 Jan. 1814): 330; *NWR* 7 (6 Oct. 1814): 54.

24. *NI*, 24 Oct. 1814. See also *Enquirer*, 16 Dec. 1813; *Western American*, 27 May 1815, 10 June 1815.

25. *AC*, 13th Cong., 3d sess., 287–91.
26. "An Exposition of the Causes and Character of the Late War with Great Britain," in *NWR* 8 (8 Apr. 1815): 72–99; quotation on 95.
27. *NI*, 21 June 1815.
28. *NI*, 24 June 1815.
29. For their part, the British fully understood the seriousness of these charges as touching their national honor and launched a full investigation into the matter, which exonerated British soldiers and other officials; see Mason, "Battle of the Slaveholding Liberators," 674–75.
30. For a fuller discussion of Goulbourn and other unlikely implementers of British policy toward American slaves, see ibid., 675–76.
31. See Adams, *Memoirs of John Quincy Adams*, 3:204, 234, 255–59, 293–95, 398–400; 4:430–31; 6:39. As late as 1822, well past his personal antislavery epiphany at the time of the Missouri debates, Adams doggedly denied Great Britain's right to liberate American slaves.
32. Wright, *Refutation of the Sophisms*, iii.
33. Adams, *Memoirs of John Quincy Adams*, 6:69. For other revealing exchanges over slaves between Adams and British ministers, see Fehrenbacher, *Slaveholding Republic*, 94, 102.
34. His stance also suggests how much had changed since the Federalists were in power in the 1780s and 1790s. Negotiating with Britain on behalf of the federal government in those decades, John Jay was inclined to agree with British arguments in favor of the liberty of American slaves who had run to the British during the Revolutionary War. He was eager to accept compensation for the slaves as a compromise between slaveholders' property claims and the African Americans' personal claims for freedom. His disinclination to push as hard as Adams later did on this issue is all the more remarkable because, unlike the nonslaveholder Adams, Jay was a slaveholder, and one of his slaves appears to have gone from New York with the British at the close of the war; see Littlefield, "John Jay," 109–10, 125.
35. See Colley, *Britons*, 350–63, for a discussion of how abolition of the slave trade became a key part of the national self-image and a key weapon in putting French and American republicans in their place, for Britons of many ranks.
36. *Quarterly Review* 10 (Jan. 1814): 518–19; see also 19 (Apr. 1818): 57; 21 (Jan. 1819): 129–32; 29 (July 1823): 343.
37. Faux, *Memorable Days in America*, 2:90, 1:100.
38. See Cuming, *Sketches of a Tour*, in which slaves throughout are shadowy parts of the landscape, barely mentioned by the author; Bradbury, *Travels in the Interior of America*, in which the author travels extensively through slave country with nary a comment on slavery; Melish, *Travels in the United States of America*, in which the author discusses slavery mostly for its effects on the white population and relies on Jefferson's *Notes on Virginia* for most of his moral commentary on the institution. For an enemy of American institutions who made little use of slavery in his prewar travel account, see Ashe, *Travels in America*.
39. See Mason, "Battle of the Slaveholding Liberators," 680.
40. *NWR* 12 (23 Aug. 1817): 416.
41. Fearon, *Sketches of America*, 97, 270–71, 288–91, 430; quotations on 291, 430.
42. Wright, *Views of Society and Manners in America*, 267–70; quotations on 267–68, 270. See

also Birkbeck, *Letters from Illinois*, esp. 22, 32, 66, 70; Birkbeck, *Notes on a Journey in America*, 10–14, 21–24, 28.

43. *Edinburgh Review* 31 (Dec. 1818): 146–50; quotation on 146.
44. Ibid. 33 (May 1820): 395–431; quotation on 420.
45. *Enquirer*, 22 Sept. 1820.
46. *National Advocate*, 30 Oct. 1818.
47. [Rives and Fendall], *Letters and Other Writings of James Madison*, 3:121–24; quotations on 121, 122. In 1818, the editor of Baltimore's *Maryland Censor* made a similar argument. He pointed to the amelioration of American slaves' conditions since the Revolution as proof of the "happy effects of a mild and free government"; quoted in *NWR* 15 (29 Aug. 1818): 5–6.
48. See Drew McCoy's insightful discussion in *Last of the Fathers*, 105–13, 236–40, 262–65. Although recognizing Madison's inaction on slavery (and even his accommodation to it), McCoy also argues that to his last days, Madison's concern for the reputation of his country steeled his "determination to end slavery in America"; ibid., 262. Yet it might be better said that by the time of his retirement, Madison's concern for the reputation of his country pushed him to a determination to *palliate* slavery in America and continually shift the blame back to Britain.
49. Lochemes, *Robert Walsh*, 31–48 and passim.
50. Walsh, *Appeal*, 306, 309.
51. Ibid., 383–90.
52. Ibid., 413–15. Such passages call historian Larry E. Tise's interpretation of Walsh into question. Tise portrays Walsh's *Appeal* as "the most formidable defense of slavery prior to the rise of abolition." Worse, he sees this book's author as typical of many early national Northerners who, in their contest with Great Britain over slavery, "began, almost unthinkingly, to associate slavery with American republicanism." He also insists that Walsh defended slavery as a positive good. See Tise, *Proslavery*, 42–74, 98–99; quotations on 49, 42. Tise misreads the thrust of Walsh's argument because he misunderstands the purpose of the debate. Walsh's purpose was not to defend slavery but rather to defend the republican experiment of the United States. Accordingly, he did all he could to dissociate slavery from American republicanism.
53. Walsh, *Appeal*, 407. For the popularity and influence of this work, see *Aurora*, 24 Nov. 1819; *Centinel*, 22 Dec. 1819; *NWR* 18 (5 Aug. 1820): 416; Lochemes, *Robert Walsh*, 89–106.
54. See chap. 8 for a fuller development of Walsh's arguments during the Missouri Crisis.
55. *NWR* 7 (31 Dec. 1814): 286.
56. *NWR* 12 (5 July 1817): 299; see 9 (3 Feb. 1816): 403, for the same kind of article under the same headline. For similar treatments of Britain's failure to stop the slave trade after vanquishing Napoleon, see *NWR* 10 (17 Aug. 1816): 412; *Aurora*, 15 Aug. 1816. For leading Britons' acute embarrassment over the revival of the slave trade within the postwar order they presided over, see Blackburn, *Overthrow of Colonial Slavery*, 413–14.
57. *Aurora*, 19 July 1815. See also *NWR* 10 (20 Apr. 1816): 114; *NWR* 10 (4 May 1816): 166; *NWR* 10 (11 May 1816): 182; *Columbian*, 4 Jan. 1816; *Independent Chronicle*, 29 July 1816, 23 Sept. 1816, 16 July 1817.
58. *NI*, 10 June 1819. See also "WHITE MAN," *NI*, 3 Feb. 1820; *Western American*, 10 June 1815.

59. *Centinel*, 17 Jan. 1810, 14 and 18 July 1810, 10 July 1811, 14 July 1813, 1 Oct. 1814, 21 Aug. 1816.
60. *PADA*, 27 Dec. 1814.
61. *PADA*, 21 July 1818.
62. *Centinel*, 17 July 1816.
63. *PADA*, 22 Oct. 1816.
64. *PADA*, Nov. 1815. See also *PADA*, 8 Feb. 1820, 7 Mar. 1820; *Centinel*, 4 Nov. 1818, 4 Mar. 1820, 19 July 1820; *Newburyport Herald*, 21 Feb. 1817, 4 Mar. 1817, 22 July 1817, 20 Jan. 1818.
65. Kenrick, *Horrors of Slavery*, 5–34; Christie and Dumond, *George Bourne*, 105–206. For other American abolitionists who sought to draw strength from the British example and America's concern for its world image, see Torrey, *Portraiture of Domestic Slavery*, 62–63; *American Convention*, vol. 2. For British abolitionists' similar challenges to their compatriots and Continental powers not to let the Yankees outdo them, see *Courier*, 6 Feb. 1807; *Edinburgh Review* 36 (Oct. 1821): 51; *Parliamentary Debates*, 2d ser., 4:428–29; Davis, *Problem of Slavery in the Age of Revolution*, 310; Fladeland, *Men and Brothers*, ix, 3–79.
66. Ketcham, "Dictates of Conscience," 46–62; quotation on 52.
67. *PADA*, 9 Dec. 1818. This abolitionist lawyer won his case—the judge set the black captives free on habeas corpus; see 10 Dec. 1818.
68. This was also true for British abolitionists. During a later debate, Wilberforce said that it would be lamentable if "any ancient prejudice" between England and America "should be permitted to stand in the way of so desirable a measure" as cooperation against the slave trade; *Parliamentary Debates*, 2d ser., 7:1400. For their part, the nationalists in both countries wished that antislavery advocates would stop giving their political opponents fodder with which to attack them; see *Courier*, 4 and 6 Aug. 1814.
69. Wright, *Refutation of the Sophisms*, vii, 11, 10.
70. Ibid., 23–31.
71. Ibid., 43–44.
72. Ibid., 51.
73. *NWR* 10 (24 Aug. 1816): 427; 14 (18 Apr. 1818): 136; 14 (2 May 1818): 166.
74. *Philadelphia Gazette*, quoted in *Aurora*, 14 Jan. 1819.
75. See also chap. 8 for this tendency in the *Aurora* during the Missouri Crisis.
76. In 1817, for instance, an English lady told a Virginian traveling in England that "to us you are all Yankees, rascals who cheat the whole world"; see Conforti, *Imagining New England*, 162. Howard Temperley has suggested that this form of stereotyping has typified Anglo-American perceptions of one another from the American Revolution down to our day. "In observing one another," he has written, Americans and Britons have overlooked the complexities of the other nation. Instead, preconceived "non-visible concepts" have rendered the observations more illustrative of each nation's drive "to establish their own sense of identity" than of reality. This has served not only to oversimplify both complex and changing societies but also "to exaggerate the differences between the two nations"; see *Britain and America since Independence*, 1–2.
77. *PADA*, 18 July 1820.
78. *Centinel*, 3 Aug. 1816.

79. *North American Review and Miscellaneous Journal* 1 (May 1815): 61–91; quotations on 65. Although this author wrote more along partisan than on strictly sectional lines— leaving the Madison administration, not necessarily the South, out to dry—some readers interpreted this article as symptomatic of New England Federalists' sectionalism; see *NI*, 17 July 1815.

80. This was not always his strategy. Biographer Kenneth Silverman describes his journey from the 1790s to the 1810s well: "Dwight's original 'glorious contrast' had set off England from America. . . . Later it balanced America against France, then America against Connecticut. Now [1815] Dwight lined up the best elements in England and America, Tories and Federalists, against the worst elements, lower-class English radicals and defenders of Madison and Jefferson. . . . He severed Yankees from Americans and tried to demonstrate the continuity of Anglo-Yankee culture"—including its antislavery; see *Timothy Dwight*, 69–71, 111–14, 135–41, 141–49; quotation on 143.

81. Dwight, *Remarks on the Review of Inchiquin's Letters*, 23–24; see also 81. Pointing to passages where Dwight refuses to condemn American slaveholders for receiving slaves by inheritance (Dwight would only condemn cruel treatment of slaves), Larry E. Tise characterizes this book as being proslavery. "Dwight," he submits, "had now come to see that slavery in the United States was quite compatible with American republicanism." Tise reaches this conclusion because Dwight alleged that American slavery was milder than slavery in the West Indies; *Proslavery*, 45. But Tise omits to mention the Yale president's drive to cast the guilt of slavery on the South alone. And to argue that republicanism worked to palliate the cruelties of slavery was far from saying that slavery was "compatible with American republicanism."

82. Dwight, *Travels in New England*, 4:160–61, 185.

83. [Paulding], *United States and England*, 4. See also *NI*, 17 July 1815.

84. *NI*, 30 June 1819.

85. Faux, *Memorable Days in America*, 1:91–95, 96, 115.

86. *Letter to the Edinburgh Reviewers*, 61. The essays were also published in the *Enquirer*, 23 Nov.–7 Dec. 1819. John Wright identified this writer as a prominent Virginian, related by marriage to Monroe; *Refutation of the Sophisms*, vii, 9.

87. *Letter to the Edinburgh Reviewers*, 4–15.

88. Ibid., 7, 17.

89. Ibid., 12–22, 39–40; quotations on 20, 39–40.

90. Ibid., 29–42; quotations on 31–32, 36.

91. Ibid., 22–48; quotations on 37, 30. Similarly, the writings of "Cato" maintained that slavery was a natural institution that throughout history had ensured the poor a subsistence they could gain in no other way. Thus the British had no need to apologize for their part in the African slave trade. Yet he also boasted of how American abolition preceded Britain's. See *NI*, 30 Nov. and 4 Dec. 1819. "An American's" proslavery screed also provoked protest within the same columns that originally published it. "Philanthropos" penned a fervent response to this writer's biblical justifications of slavery and especially to his blanket denunciations of philanthropy. He asserted that the vaunted amelioration of American slaves' condition since the Revolution had been "produced by the very cause which has excited so much of 'An American's'" displeasure —the interference of humanity and philanthropy"; *NI*, 7 Dec. 1819. "A True Virginian" issued a similar rebuke; *NI*, 26 Nov. 1819.

92. For an earlier elaboration of a hesitantly proslavery argument in response to New Englanders and Britons, see Elliott, *Sketch of the Means and Benefits*, 19. The writings of "An American" also included some parallels to an 1807 pamphlet written by a West Indian antagonist of British abolitionists. The West Indian author repeatedly mocked the alleged humanity of the self-styled philanthropist James Stephen. He urged that emancipation schemes would almost inevitably ruin the material prospects of the slaves, for their physical condition was far superior to free laborers. But he also admitted the injustice of slavery from the viewpoint of civil liberty and included the obligatory disclaimer: "I am no defender of slavery"; see *Emancipation in Disguise*; quotation on 207.

93. Welby, *Visit to North America*, 204–5, 228–29, 289–90; *Quarterly Review* 30 (Jan. 1824): 579.

94. See Halevy, *England in 1815*, 459; Anstey, *Atlantic Slave Trade and British Abolition*, 91–153; Blackburn, *Overthrow of Colonial Slavery*, 314; Oldfield, *Popular Politics and British Anti-Slavery*.

95. See *Aurora*, 28 Aug. 1819; *Enquirer*, 2 June 1820; Adams, *Memoirs of John Quincy Adams*, 4:151–52; *AC*, 16th Cong., 1st sess., 697–700; *AC*, 17th Cong., 2d sess., 332, 1147–55.

CHAPTER FIVE

1. The degree to which rumored slave plots were a mere figment of white imaginations has been a matter of controversy among scholars. In the final analysis, however, when it comes to the importance of insurrection anxiety in shaping the politics of slavery, this debate is moot. For whether slave conspiracies were actual or imagined, the vast majority of white Americans acted in politics based on the belief that the danger was real.

2. See chap. 4 herein for slave flight to the British during the War of 1812. For the account of a slave who escaped during the war, see Steward, *Twenty-two Years a Slave*, 49–50, 69–70.

3. Dormon, "Persistent Specter"; Junius Rodriguez, "Rebellion on the River Road: The Ideology and Influence of Louisiana's German Coast Slave Insurrection of 1811," in McKivigan and Harrold, *Antislavery Violence*. This revolt was the largest U.S. slave revolt as measured by the total number of people killed and the number of blacks involved as rebels. Nat Turner's 1831 rebellion in Virginia claimed more white lives but was smaller in scale than the 1811 Louisiana revolt in these other respects.

4. Rodriguez, "Always 'En Garde.'" See also Starobin, *Blacks in Bondage*, 137–38.

5. See Rowland, *Official Letter Books*, 5:34–95; Rothman, "Expansion of Slavery," 97–111; Kennedy, *Mr. Jefferson's Lost Cause*, 115–233.

6. Aptheker, *Documentary History*, 55–57 (quotation); Starobin, *Blacks in Bondage*, 138–40; *NI*, 6 Apr. 1813; *WR* 4 (12 June 1813): 247.

7. *Frederick-Town Herald*, 20 Aug. 1814. See also *Enquirer*, 27 Aug. 1814.

8. See Aptheker, *American Negro Slave Revolts*, 24; Lemmon, *Frustrated Patriots*, 122, 196–98; Rothman, "Expansion of Slavery," 165–66, 231–34.

9. See Pitch, *Burning of Washington*, 128–29, 151.

10. Ibid., 41; Aptheker, *American Negro Slave Revolts*, 25–26.

11. *Enquirer*, 6 Mar. 1816 (quotation); see also 9 Mar. and 22 May 1816. For further details

on Boxley, see Schwarz, *Migrants against Slavery*, chap. 4; Johnston, "Participation of White Men."

12. Governor David R. Williams's 26 Nov. 1816 message to the South Carolina legislature, in *NWR* 11 (1 Feb. 1817): 378–79. The phrase "Boxley's insurrection" is Williams's. South Carolina officials condemned white men fraternizing with unruly slaves in the late 1810s; see Henry, *Police Control of the Slave*, 41, 82. For the complicated interactions between nonslaveholding whites and slaves in one Southern state, see Lockley, *Lines in the Sand*.

13. *NI*, 17 July 1816. See also *Aurora*, 20 July 1816; *NWR* 11 (1 Feb. 1817): 378–79; Henry, *Police Control of the Slave*, 151–52.

14. For conspiracies and riots, see Byrd, "Letter of Richard W. Byrd"; *NI*, 18 Apr. 1817; *Enquirer*, 21 May 1819; *Centinel*, 22 and 25 May 1819. For individual acts of violence against whites, see *Charleston Courier*, 28 Aug. 1812; *NI*, 18 Aug. 1814; *Enquirer*, 27 Aug. 1814; *NWR* 8 (24 June 1815): 292; Lee and Hofstra, "Race, Memory, and the Death of Robert Berkeley." For rising slave crime, see Schwarz, *Twice Condemned*, 200–214, 230–47. For other evidence of Southern officials' jitters in the 1810s, see Meriwether et al., *Papers of John C. Calhoun*, 2:122, 427; 4:490–91, 580.

15. See, e.g., *Enquirer*, 11 Sept. 1812, 2 Apr. 1814, 21 May 1814, 11 and 28 Aug. 1818, 11 Sept. 1818, 16 Nov. 1819; *NWR* 15 (24 Oct. 1818): 139.

16. Quoted in *New-York Evening Post*, 15 Apr. 1814.

17. Quoted in Schwarz, *Twice Condemned*, 200–202.

18. *NWR* 14 (2 May 1818): 176.

19. Herbert Aptheker noted that maroon communities flourished and stubbornly resisted government attempts to root them out in the years following both the American Revolution and the War of 1812; see *American Negro Slave Revolts*, 206–8, 258–62; "Maroons."

20. See Junius Rodriguez, "Rebellion on the River Road: The Ideology and Influence of Louisiana's German Coast Slave Insurrection of 1811," in McKivigan and Harrold, *Antislavery Violence*, 68–70, 73; *Enquirer*, 21 May 1819.

21. Franklin and Schweninger, *Runaway Slaves*, 153–54.

22. *NWR* 11 (1 Feb. 1817): 378–79.

23. *Aurora*, 6 Dec. 1816.

24. *NWR* 13 (3 Jan. 1818): 302; Meriwether et al., *Papers of John C. Calhoun*, 2:122.

25. See Porter, "Negroes and the East Florida Annexation Plot."

26. Rothman, "Expansion of Slavery," 170. See also Covington, "Negro Fort."

27. Quoted in Rothman, "Expansion of Slavery," 171. See also *Georgia Journal*, 26 June 1816; *NWR* 11 (14 Sept. 1816): 37–38. Even after its demise, "the Negro Fort" retained its power as an example to would-be fugitives; Rothman, "Expansion of Slavery," 172–73. And those blacks who escaped the fort's destruction continued "robbing and murdering the frontier inhabitants both of Georgia and Florida indiscriminately"—which was one reason for Andrew Jackson's invasion of Florida in the first Seminole War; see *NWR* 13 (15 Nov. 1817): 190–91.

28. See Ball, *Fifty Years in Chains*, 19–20, 67, 102–4, 392; Young, *Domesticating Slavery*, 158.

29. Phillips, *Freedom's Port*, 29, 57–82; Whitman, *Price of Freedom*, 1, 61–92.

30. Hunt, *Haiti's Influence on Antebellum America*, 37–83; Everett, "Emigres and Militiamen"; Robert L. Paquette, "Revolutionary Saint Domingue in the Making of Territorial

Louisiana," in Gaspar and Geggus, *Turbulent Time*, 219. For general accounts of free people of color in the United States, see Litwack, *North of Slavery*; Berlin, *Slaves without Masters*; Horton and Horton, *In Hope of Liberty*.

31. Cited in Payne, *History of the African Methodist Episcopal Church*, 45. See also George, *Segregated Sabbaths*, esp. chap. 2–3; Litwack, *North of Slavery*, 187–213.

32. No one has shed more light on black life in early national New York City than Shane White. For the points made here, see White, *Somewhat More Independent*, 101–2, chap. 5, 7; White and White, *Stylin'*, chap. 4, (first) quotation on 94; White, *Stories of Freedom*, chap. 1, (second) quotation on 66. See also Gilje, *Road to Mobocracy*, 147–51; Hodges, *Root and Branch*, chap. 7, esp. 187–91; Fearon, *Sketches of America*, 9–10.

33. Phillips, *Freedom's Port*, 83–113; *PADA*, 3 Jan. 1820.

34. Fox, "Negro Vote in Old New York"; Forbes, "Slavery and the Meaning of America," 39–40, 59–65.

35. See, e.g., Gravely, "Dialectic of Double Consciousness"; Nash, *Forging Freedom*, 185–90; Waldstreicher, *In the Midst of Perpetual Fetes*, 323–48; White and White, *Stylin'*, chap. 4.

36. Aptheker, *Documentary History*, 67–69, first quotation on 69; *PADA*, 11 July 1816 (second quotation).

37. For African American patriotism and the War of 1812, see Horton and Horton, *In Hope of Liberty*, 177–202; Forbes, "Slavery and the Meaning of America," 39–40, 59–65.

38. Aptheker, *Documentary History*, 59–66; quotation on 63. The proposal failed.

39. Porter, *Early Negro Writing*, 265–78, 355–63; *Centinel*, 24 June 1818.

40. See Horton and Horton, *In Hope of Liberty*, 177–202, for a good treatment of double consciousness in the early republic.

41. *PADA*, 10 Jan. 1817. See also McGraw, "Richmond Free Blacks."

42. Aptheker, *Documentary History*, 70–72; quotations on 71.

43. Porter, *Early Negro Writing*, 265–68; quotation on 265.

44. James Brewer Stewart has written that black judgments on white-led colonization were part of a variety of efforts by African Americans "on every social level . . . to put themselves forward as equals" in the early nineteenth century; see "Modernizing 'Difference,' " 699–700. For more from the vast secondary literature on this response, see George, *Segregated Sabbaths*, 91, 117, chap. 6; Miller, *Search for a Black Nationality*; Sweet, *Black Images of America*; Winch, *Philadelphia's Black Elite*, chap. 2–3; Bruce, "National Identity."

45. See, e.g., *Georgia Journal*, 16 Sept. 1817.

46. MacLeod, *Slavery, Race, and the American Revolution*, 162–63, 231n56; Berlin, *Slaves without Masters*, esp. chap. 3, 6, 10.

47. Cited in Franklin and Schweninger, *Runaway Slaves*, 301–2.

48. "Arguably," because most historians of the ACS have not adequately emphasized this as a driving principle for ACS supporters. See, e.g., Staudenraus, *African Colonization Movement*; Fox, *American Colonization Society*. Douglas R. Egerton has more recently advanced a revisionist interpretation, presenting Virginian Charles Fenton Mercer as the true founder of the movement and insisting that Mercer impressed his own fear of the free blacks on the ACS; see "Its Origins Are Not a Little Curious" and *Charles Fenton Mercer*, 105–12, 161–75. But Mercer had no need to convince many of his peers to share this fear. Interestingly enough, historians of the Northern response to the ACS have more keenly recognized the importance of free blacks' supposed threat to order;

see esp. Fredrickson, *Black Image in the White Mind*, 5–21; Horton and Horton, *In Hope of Liberty*, 101–24; Melish, *Disowning Slavery*, 192–99.

49. For examples of the variety of reasons that Northerners favored the ACS, see *NWR* 13 (8 Nov. 1817): 164–67; Walsh, *Appeal*, 398–401; *Centinel*, 28 Dec. 1816, 15 May 1819; *PADA*, 28 Dec. 1816, 30 Dec. 1816, 2 Jan. 1817, 19 July 1817, 11 Aug. 1817; *Newburyport Herald*, 12, 15, 22, 26 Oct. 1819, 5 Nov. 1819, 11 Aug. 1820; Price, *Freedom Not Far Distant*, 94–104. For a sampling of anti-ACS Northern voices, see *Aurora*, 18 and 27 Jan. 1817; *PADA*, 12 Aug. 1817.

50. All three surviving Virginia presidents backed the ACS enthusiastically. For Jefferson, see *Enquirer*, 11 Apr. 1817. For Monroe, see Adams, *Memoirs of John Quincy Adams*, 4:292–93. For Madison, see [Rives and Fendall], *Letters and Other Writings of James Madison*, 3:133–38; McCoy, *Last of the Fathers*, 4–6, 165, 252, 276–86, 295–307. For an able discussion of another colonizationist of this stripe, see Papenfuse, *Evils of Necessity*, 2–50, 60–65, 98–118.

51. See *NI*, 24 Dec. 1816; Lee and Hofstra, "Race, Memory, and the Death of Robert Berkeley," esp. 53–59; Taylor, *Arator*, 115–25, 176.

52. See, e.g., *NI*, 16 Jan. 1818; *AC*, 14th Cong., 2d sess., 481–83; Papenfuse, *Evils of Necessity*, 98–118.

53. *NI*, 24 Dec. 1816.

54. *AC*, 14th Cong., 2d sess., 939. The committee consisted of five Northerners and two Southerners, which may account for the "if." See also *AC*, 15th Cong., 1st sess., 237.

55. See *Enquirer*, 16 Jan. 1817; *PADA*, 22 June 1820.

56. *NI*, 24 Oct. 1820. For a similar argument, see *Savannah Republican*, 3 Apr. 1817.

57. *AC*, 12th Cong., 1st sess., 447, 450–51. A writer in the *Virginia Patriot* agreed with Randolph that Southerners must not invade Canada and "leave a worse enemy behind them"; see *PADA*, 22 Jan. 1812. Randolph had plenty of support for his assertions. In 1808, a British traveler bore witness to the alarm Richmond's fire bell produced, "on account of the apprehension that it may be the Signal for, or a Commencement of a rising of the Negroes"; see Iaccarino, "Virginia and the National Contest over Slavery," 133.

58. *AC*, 12th Cong., 2d sess., 701; see also 13th Cong., 3d sess., 331.

59. *Charleston Courier*, 29 March 1813.

60. Despite the seriousness of America's domestic conflict during the War of 1812, relatively few scholars have attended to it, especially in recent years. For some good older treatments, see Adams, *History of the United States*, 896, 1065–68, 1104–7; Samuel Eliot Morison, "Dissent in the War of 1812," in Morison et al., *Dissent in Three American Wars*. For recent examples, see Stagg, *Mr. Madison's War*; Buel, *America on the Brink*. Yet to understand the divisions of the early republic, scholars should know more than they do about this climactic period. See chap. 2 herein for much more on this subject.

61. *AC*, 12th Cong., 2d sess., 645–46.

62. *AC*, 13th Cong., 1st sess., suppl., 527–28.

63. Parish, *Protest against the War*, 16. For a milder version of this vision of slave revolt as a judgment of God on the South for the war, see Perkins, *National Sins, and National Punishment*, 17–18.

64. *Centinel*, 18 July 1812, 24 Feb. 1813, 10 Apr. 1813, 10 and 14 July 1813, 4 Dec. 1813, 31 Dec. 1814.

65. Ibid., 17 Apr. 1813. See also *Courant*, 5 July 1814.

66. *Courant*, 13 and 20 July 1813, 21 Dec. 1813, 7 Feb. 1815.
67. Ibid., 15 June 1813. See also *PADA*, 13 Mar. 1813, 20 Apr. 1813.
68. *Newburyport Herald*, 24 July 1812. See also ibid., 7 Aug. 1812; *PADA*, 30 Jan. 1815.
69. *Courant*, 21 July 1812. "Cato" here anticipated Abraham Lincoln's "house divided" formulation but applied it directly to the South as a region, not to the nation: *the South* could not long endure half slave, half free.
70. Ibid., 28 July 1812.
71. *Centinel*, 4 Apr. 1821; see also 25 Jan. 1817, 22 Nov. 1817, 11 Feb. 1818, 9 May 1818, 21 Mar. 1821, 5 May 1821.
72. *PADA*, 18 Sept. 1818; see also 6 May 1818, 1 June 1818, 27 Feb. 1819.
73. *PADA*, 5 Apr. 1817.
74. New York *Columbian*, quoted in *Aurora*, 2 Dec. 1816. For other uses of Haiti to press a variety of domestic and geopolitical points, see *Centinel*, 25 Jan. 1817, 9 May 1818; *Delaware Gazette*, quoted in *Charleston Courier*, 16 Dec. 1816; *NWR* 6 (25 June 1814): 282; *NWR* 8 (22 Apr. 1815): 136; *NWR* 10 (2 Mar. 1816): 16; *NWR* 10 (20 Apr. 1816): 135; *NWR* 10 (22 June 1816): 282–83; *NWR* 12 (12 Apr. 1817): 109; *NWR* 11 (4 Jan. 1817): 315–17; *Reporter*, 27 Nov. 1816.
75. *Aurora*, 18 May 1818; *Columbian*, 18 May 1818; *NWR* 19 (20 Jan. 1821): 337.
76. *NWR* 14 (13 June 1818): 263–64.
77. See the treatment of slave violence in Boston's *Independent Chronicle*, 2 May 1816, 5 Aug. 1816, 9 Sept. 1816, 4 July 1818, 22 and 26 May 1819; New York's *National Advocate*, 8 Aug. 1816, 17 Nov. 1817, 2 Dec. 1817, 7 Jan. 1818, 24 Mar. 1818, 28 Dec. 1818, 26 Feb. 1819.
78. For Federalist examples, see *Centinel*, 12 Aug. 1818; *Newburyport Herald*, 2 June 1818, 17 Nov. 1820; *ADA*, 14 Nov. 1815. For abolitionists, see Kenrick, *Horrors of Slavery*, 39–41; Christie and Dumond, *George Bourne*, 120–21. Jesse Torrey was more moderate; see *Portraiture of Domestic Slavery*, 18–28.
79. Ellison, *American Captive*, 51. See also Nicholson, *Affecting Narrative*, 7–14.
80. *NWR* 12 (19 July 1817): 323. See also *NWR* 20 (19 May 1821): 192; *Columbian*, 5 Jan. 1817.
81. *NWR* 16 (19 June 1819): 275.
82. *PADA*, 20 Nov. 1815.
83. *American and Commercial Daily Advertiser*, 23 Feb. 1811.
84. *Western Spectator* (Marietta, Ohio), 5 Mar. 1811, quoted in Junius Rodriguez, "Rebellion on the River Road: The Ideology and Influence of Louisiana's German Coast Slave Insurrection of 1811," in McKivigan and Harrold, *Antislavery Violence*, 79. For more on Northern responses to this rebellion and its aftermath, see Thompson, "National Newspaper and Legislative Reactions," 15–21.
85. *Centinel*, 1 Mar. 1820; see also 3 Mar. 1819, 29 May 1819, 18 Dec. 1819, 16 Feb. 1820.
86. *PADA*, 8, 14, 16, 17, 18, 24, 29 Feb. 1820, 7 Mar. 1820; quotations from 17, 18 Feb. 1820.
87. *Centinel*, 26 Nov. 1817.
88. *NWR* 13 (4 Oct. 1817): 82. For a similar argument, see *Columbian*, 24 July 1816.
89. See *Columbian*, 19 June 1818; *Georgia Journal*, 14 Sept., 5 Oct., 12 Oct. 1819; *Charleston Courier*, 11 June 1818; *PADA*, 11 Feb. 1820. Some white Southerners were also aware that the coffles and chains and whips necessary to keep slaves from resisting the interstate slave trade hurt the trade's (and their section's) image in the nation and world. This did not shut the traffic down, of course, but it did help attach a degree of odium to the slave trade, even in the South. See Gudmestad, *Troublesome Commerce*, 153–54.

90. *Savannah Republican*, 14 Aug. 1817.
91. See Finkelman, *Imperfect Union*, esp. 3–4. Finkelman argues that fugitive slave return was usually "the least controversial" of the many cases in which slaves entered free states (e.g., as transients or sojourners with their masters), and that before the 1840s Northern judges as a rule placed maintenance of the Union before their commitment to liberty; 6–13, 27–28 passim. Yet he seems to underestimate the strains such controversies placed on comity between the states, perhaps by focusing less on politicians and editors than on judges who were more sheltered from public opinion. Donald L. Robinson has also written of how the fugitive slave issue "reached deep into the heart of relations within the federal union"; see *Slavery in the Structure of American Politics*, 290.
92. Alilunas, "Fugitive Slave Cases," esp. 170–72.
93. Adams, *Neglected Period of Anti-Slavery*, 235–36.
94. Ethan Allen Brown to Gabriel Slaughter, 14 Feb. 1820, in Smith, *Political History of Slavery*, 1:21. See also Thornbrough, "Indiana and Fugitive Slave Legislation."
95. *AC*, 15th Cong., 1st sess., 825–40; quotation on 826. For a secondary account of this debate, see Morris, *Free Men All*, 33–41.
96. *AC*, 15th Cong., 1st sess., 232.
97. *NWR* 11 (7 Sept. 1816): 28–29.
98. Taylor, *Arator*, 178–80.
99. *NI*, 14 Aug. 1817. See also *Savannah Republican*, 19 Nov. 1816.
100. *NWR* 13 (7 Feb. 1818): 396. The very same issue reported on Kentucky's correspondence with Ohio and Indiana on the same subject; see 386. The governors of Pennsylvania and Delaware essentially ignored Maryland's pleas, recommending only further study by their legislatures, who accordingly buried these proposals in committee. For the official paper trail of this correspondence between Maryland and her neighbors, see entries for 6 Feb. 1817, Feb. 1818, and Jan. 1819, in Maryland Governor's Letterbooks; *Journal of the State of Delaware* (Dover, 1817), 10, 18; *Journal of the State of Delaware* (Dover, 1818), 7; *Journal of the State of Delaware* (Dover, 1819) passim; *Journal of the Senate of the Commonwealth of Pennsylvania* (Harrisburg, 1816), 27:247, index p. 8; *Journal of the Senate of the Commonwealth of Pennsylvania* (Harrisburg, 1817), 28:394–95; and *Journal of the Twenty Eighth House of Representatives of the Commonwealth of Pennsylvania* (Harrisburg, 1817–18), 577–78; all in Jenkins, *Records of the States*.
101. *NWR* 11 (14 Sept. 1816): 46.
102. *AC*, 15th Cong., 1st sess., 828.
103. Ibid., 231–39; quotations on 232, 233–35. Despite (or perhaps because of) the heated rhetoric of these debates, Congress passed no law on fugitive slaves during this session.
104. *NI*, 6 Mar. 1820. See also the cautious tone of the moderately antislavery ACS leader Robert Finley in *Thoughts on the Colonization of Free Blacks*. Historian Early L. Fox argued that the ACS did indeed serve as one arena in which "representative men from New England, the West, and the upper South could stand and discuss dispassionately the negro problem"; *American Colonization Society*, 9–11; quotation on 9. This may have been true *within* the ACS, but was so only to a point in American society in general, especially given some slaveholders' rabid opposition to it. Abolitionists, on the other hand, did not oppose it as a unit in the 1810s; see, for instance, the favorable petitions to Congress from abolition societies in *AC*, 14th Cong., 2d sess., 508; 15th Cong., 1st sess., 517.

105. *Enquirer*, 20 Oct. 1820.

106. *NI*, 9 July 1819.

107. *NI*, 4 Aug., 30 Sept. 1819. For "Limner's" responses, one of which advanced scriptural defenses of slavery, see 3 Sept., 3 Nov. 1819. One Southern colonizationist recognized the dangers of philanthropy in the South even as he sought to advance its cause. He requested readers not to read his essays, "or even converse on the subjects treated of, in the hearing of any sl**ve, no matter how young, or any person who would be so imprudent as to repeat their contents in the hearing of sl**ves. Imprudent conversations in the presence of young ne***es, might be repeated to the older, or would perhaps be remembered by themselves till they became old, and prove the germ of future mischief to the country"; *Georgia Journal*, 25 Aug. 1818.

108. *Georgia Journal*, 18 Jan. 1820.

109. Egerton, *Charles Fenton Mercer*, 161–75; quotation on 162. See also *Enquirer*, 7 Sept. 1816; *NWR* 14 (1 Aug. 1818): 382.

110. "Mitigation of Slavery," in *NWR*, 8 May–21 Aug. 1819.

111. *NI*, 29 May 1819; see also 5 June 1819.

112. Wright, *Refutation of the Sophisms*, 51. He interpreted the Haitian example far differently from how most slaveholders did, for he insisted that the attempts to re-enslave, rather than emancipate, the Africans there had led to racial violence; ibid., 34–40, 51.

113. Evans, *Pedestrious Tour*, 320–24. Evans's account had a nationwide readership, so that the *Baltimore American* referred to him offhand as "the celebrated Pedestrian"; quoted in *Savannah Republican*, 10 Sept. 1818. For other examples of this threatening appeal, see Dupre, *Rational and Benevolent Plan*, 4, 9; Torrey, *Portraiture of Domestic Slavery*, 11–13, 18.

114. See also *Aurora*, 28 July 1818, for another emancipation scheme from an avowed enemy of the slaveholders. On the other hand, at least one Southern editor favored colonization as but one step toward the abolition of slavery; *Georgia Journal*, 1 Jan. 1817.

115. This was true well beyond the specific issue of the ACS. White Southerners argued among themselves on many other matters germane to their fear of African Americans. They showed a divided mind especially when it came to the safety of increasing their labor force by means of the domestic slave trade and the smuggling of slaves from abroad. For a fuller discussion of this point, see Mason, "Rain between the Storms," 224–27.

116. *AC*, 11th Cong., 3d sess., 497–98. The argument was that attaching Louisiana to the Union as a state would oblige the rest of the nation even more to help in putting down a revolt. This debate took place on 4 Jan. 1811, just days before the insurrection broke out in Louisiana.

117. Birkbeck, *Notes on a Journey in America*, 16–17.

118. *New-York Evening Post*, 18 July 1816.

119. *Enquirer*, 30 July 1813. See also *NWR* 7 (4 Feb. 1815): 363–64; *Milledgeville Journal*, cited in *NWR* 8 (15 July 1815): 347; *Charleston Courier*, 20 Feb. 1815. Another related strategy was to hint at the slave threat obliquely, rendering dashes unnecessary; see *WR* 1 (28 Dec. 1811): 299; *Southern Patriot*, 24 Oct. 1814. Another strategy was that of emphasizing British mistreatment of slaves, arguing that the British coerced and/or sold those slaves supposedly fleeing to them for freedom, and so forth. Although this was an

adjunct of American attacks on British hypocrisy (see chap. 4), it was also useful to those who insisted that only with outside interference would their slaves desert them. Those who made these arguments also clearly hoped to keep slaves from their flight to British lines; see *NI*, 9 Oct. 1813; *Enquirer*, 16 Dec. 1813, 11 May 1814; *WR* 4 (8 May 1813): 165; *WR* 4 (15 May 1813): 182; *WR* 4 (3 July 1813): 293; *WR* 4 (31 July 1813): 356; *WR* 5 (2 Oct. 1813): 85; *WR* 5 (27 Nov. 1813): 219; *NWR* 8 (5 Aug. 1815): 403; *NWR* 8, suppl., 190; Bullard, *Black Emancipation*, 58, 62–70; Latour, *Historical Memoir*, 136–37. This point was so useful that it was still not at rest years later; see *Savannah Republican*, 3 Mar. 1818.

120. *Enquirer*, 27 Aug. 1814; *NI*, 24 Aug. 1814. The original newspaper report of the plot, though not under this headline, also downplayed its significance; *Frederick-Town Herald*, 20 Aug. 1814.

121. *Louisiana Gazette*, 17 Jan. 1811, 10–12; *Enquirer*, 19, 22 Feb. 1811. For a similar analysis of this tactic, see Dormon, "Persistent Specter," 400–404.

122. Rowland, *Official Letter Books*, 5:142, 146–47.

123. This even as his letters also bore witness to continued insurrectionary movements among the slaves and anxiety among the whites; ibid., 5:95–124, 6:16–17, 20.

124. Ibid., 5:127–30.

125. *AC*, 12th Cong., 1st sess., 518; see also 457.

126. Ibid., 480.

127. Ibid., 2d sess., 819. Nathaniel Macon joined Calhoun in rebuking Sheffey, hinting significantly that if Sheffey's "observations were intended to warn us, he ought to have considered that others might notice them"; ibid., 755.

128. *NI*, 30 Apr. 1813.

129. *Enquirer*, 3 Aug. 1813.

130. *NI*, 22 May 1819; see also 30 June, 4 Dec. 1819.

131. See *Georgia Journal*, 26 June 1816. See also *WR* 3 (26 Dec. 1812): 259–60.

132. *NI*, 30 Apr. 1813.

133. Elliott, *Sketch of the Means and Benefits*, 19.

134. See *AC*, 15th Cong., 1st sess., 233–35, for this quote and its context in Smith's speech.

135. Rothman, "Expansion of Slavery," 97. He applied this to the Lower Mississippi Valley, but it applies to the entire South.

CHAPTER SIX

1. See Remini, *Course of American Empire*, 191, 231–32, 298–307, 364–65, 384–89, 395–98; Rothman, "Expansion of Slavery."

2. Bingham, *Columbian Orator*, xvii–xviii; Basker, *Amazing Grace*, 354–55.

3. Basker, *Amazing Grace*, 183–86, 289; quotations on 186. At least one audience member at such plays recorded that they strengthened his hatred for slavery; 353.

4. [Colman], *Africans*, esp. 106–9, 161; quotation on 109.

5. Ellison, *American Captive*, 22. See Basker, *Amazing Grace*, xlvii, for antislavery's literary dominance.

6. See Basker, *Amazing Grace*, 268–70.

7. Riley, *Authentic Narrative*, 531–33; Ratcliffe, "Captain James Riley." Riley's life imitated art in this respect, for in writings from twenty years earlier, novelist and playwright

Royall Tyler had one of his characters, an American enslaved by Algerine pirates, pledge that if he could again "taste the freedom of my native country, . . . every moment of my life shall be dedicated to preaching against this detestable commerce" in America. But upon his return to America, a vow to fight slavery was not among his list of intended occupations; see *Algerine Captive*, 1:188–89, 2:227–28; quotation on 1:189. Many American writers between the 1780s and 1810s pointed to the parallels between American and Algerian slavery; see Allison, *Crescent Obscured*, 87–106. (Allison, incidentally, stresses Riley's antislavery contribution—see 222–25—whereas I would stress his relative inaction against slavery.) But an antislavery moral was not the only one that could be drawn from the stories of white Americans in captivity, fictional or factual. One of Riley's shipmates, Archibald Robbins, wrote that after witnessing Africans "take delight in enslaving each other," he had concluded that "it can hardly be expected that an American, who has for months and years been enslaved by them, can feel so much compassion toward a slave *here* as those do, who have always enjoyed the blessings of humanity and liberty." He spoke of his slavery as "the most cruel and oppressive slavery which barbarism . . . could produce"; see *Journal*, v, 91, 251; quotations on 91, v.

8. See, e.g., *American Convention*, vol. 2, passim; Torrey, *Portraiture of Domestic Slavery*, esp. 18–28, 59–62.

9. Rael, "Instruments in the Hands of God," 4. Neither were Quakers an exception to this rule, if the resolutions of an 1809 meeting in North Carolina are any indication; see Schweninger, *Petitions to Southern Legislatures*, 39–40.

10. Vaux, *Memoirs of the Lives of Benjamin Lay and Ralph Sandiford*, 55, 73; quotation on 55.

11. Ashworth, *Commerce and Compromise*, 52–53. The U.S. slave population increased 33 percent between 1800 and 1810 and 29 percent between 1810 and 1820. Many observers noticed this with alarm. See Dillon, *Slavery Attacked*, 121–23.

12. Wright, *Refutation of the Sophisms*, 11–21; quotation on 20. See also Deyle, "Irony of Liberty," esp. 51–53; Deyle, "Domestic Slave Trade in America."

13. See *American Convention*, 2:481–90, 494–98, 577–78, 599–601, 634, 732; *AC*, 12th Cong., 1st sess., 358; *AC*, 14th Cong., 1st sess., 147, 1068; *AC*, 14th Cong., 2d sess., 36, 57, 65, 96, 311–12, 442, 842–43; *AC*, 15th Cong., 1st sess., 61, 92, 829; *WR* 1 (23 Nov. 1811): 224.

14. See esp. Wilson, *Freedom at Risk*, chap. 4.

15. Poulson wrote of "the many projects now in embryo for the abolition of slavery within the United States"; *PADA*, 23 Oct. 1818. Mary Stoughton Locke pointed to the appearance of emancipation schemes between 1783 and 1808 and commented on their novelty; *Anti-Slavery in America*, 188–95. But the real proliferation of emancipation schemes came after 1808, after the abolition of the slave trade proved less effectual than abolitionists had hoped. For further discussion of these schemes in the 1810s, see chap. 5, 8 herein.

16. Christie and Dumond, *George Bourne*. See also McLeod, *Negro Slavery Unjustifiable*, esp. 5–9, 12, 18–20.

17. Kenrick, *Horrors of Slavery*, 38 (quotation), 43–47.

18. For a prime example of high-flying antislavery rhetoric accompanied by programmatic vagueness from this period, see *PADA*, 22 Oct. 1816. This author anticipated later abolitionists in upbraiding his readers for consuming tobacco, cotton, and other slave-grown products. But he called for no organized effort to renounce such consumption;

PADA, 24 Oct. 1816. Furthermore, he was a voice in the wilderness in 1816, as evidenced when Poulson himself printed an article expressing high hopes that Georgia would be able to produce sugar for American consumption! See *PADA*, 25 Dec. 1816.

19. As is common among historians. See, e.g., Adams, *Neglected Period of Anti-Slavery*, 141–43, 152–94; Blackburn, *Overthrow of Colonial Slavery*, 289–90; Wright, *African Americans in the Early Republic*, 182.

20. For the abolitionists' effectiveness in protecting free African Americans and the importance of that achievement, see Torrey, *Portraiture of Domestic Slavery*, 49–58; *American Convention*, 2:679, 746; Steward, *Twenty-two Years a Slave*, x, 67–71; Ball, *Fifty Years in Chains*, 427–30; Wiecek, *Sources of Antislavery Constitutionalism*, 84–106; Wilson, *Freedom at Risk*, chap. 4; and esp. Newman, *Transformation of American Abolitionism*, chap. 1–3.

21. For the growing importance of the slave trade to the Southern economy, see Deyle, "Domestic Slave Trade in America"; Johnson, *Soul by Soul*. For the primacy of, and poignant accounts of the horror of, kidnapping and the slave trade in the early nineteenth century, see Ball, *Fifty Years in Chains*, 28–101, 114–15; Steward, *Twenty-two Years a Slave*, 31–33; Starobin, *Blacks in Bondage*, 59–60, 110, 112–13; Johnson, *Soul by Soul*. For the threat kidnapping posed even to leaders of the free black community, see also George, *Segregated Sabbaths*, 3–4.

22. Evans, *Pedestrious Tour*, 320.

23. Latrobe, *Impressions Respecting New Orleans*, 9–10; quotation on 10.

24. [Paulding], *Letters from the South*, 1:120–31; quotations on 120, 129.

25. *PADA*, 26 July 1820. Robert Pierce Forbes has pointed out that although slavery had previously conjured up vague, exotic (even oriental) images in many Northerners' minds, by the 1810s, the rising slave trade provided them a much more concrete and immediate vision of the horrors of chattel bondage; see "Slavery and the Meaning of America," 21–26.

26. *Centinel*, 17 July 1816; see also 2 Jan. 1819, 8 Sept. 1819.

27. *PADA*, 15 Sept. 1818.

28. This interpretation differs from that of Robert H. Gudmestad, who wrote that before the 1830s most white Americans were apathetic toward the slave trade; *Troublesome Commerce*, chap. 2.

29. See Fogel and Engerman, "Philanthropy at Bargain Prices," esp. 392–93.

30. Whitman, *Price of Freedom*, chap. 3. As such work as Whitman's demonstrates, it is useful to treat Baltimore as closer to the North than to the South in its tone toward slavery by the 1810s; see also Fields, *Slavery and Freedom on the Middle Ground*, esp. chap. 1 and 3; Phillips, *Freedom's Port*, esp. 4, 29. Thus, with few exceptions I will treat Baltimore as more representative of the Mid-Atlantic North.

31. *Aurora*, 14 Jan. 1819.

32. *NWR* 12 (19 July 1817): 323. Note that Niles grouped Maryland among the "middle states."

33. *NWR* 14 (13 June 1818): 280.

34. Whitman, *Price of Freedom*, chap. 3. The law passed in 1817.

35. *NWR* 15, suppl., [Feb. 1819]: 58.

36. Pingeon, "Abominable Business," quotation on 15.

37. *AC*, 15th Cong., 2d sess., 75–76, 78, 254, 336–37; quotation on 336.

38. The parallels with the African trade lent force to the campaign against the domestic

traffic; see Deyle, "Domestic Slave Trade in America," 21–23. For a good example of this parallel, see *PADA*, 9 Jan. 1818.

39. See Nash, *Forging Freedom*, 242–45; Rothman, "Expansion of Slavery," 303–27. For concerns about kidnapping in the 1780s, see Greene, "Prince Hall," 251–54; White, *Somewhat More Independent*, 81, 84.

40. *Centinel*, 30 May 1818; see also 20 July 1816, 26 Oct. 1816, 3 June 1818.

41. *AC*, 14th Cong., 2d sess., 311–12, 442; *AC*, 15th Cong., 1st sess., 61, 92. Shane White has pointed out that the New York Manumission Society was also "at its most effective if the quarantine protecting New York from the South and the West Indies was threatened"; see *Somewhat More Independent*, 85–87; quotation on 85.

42. See Boston's *Independent Chronicle*, 1815 to 1819.

43. See, e.g., New York's *National Advocate*, esp. 28 June 1817, 22 Aug. 1817, 7 June 1819.

44. For a sense of the prominence and persistence of this issue in Pennsylvania and Delaware, see *Aurora*, 1 Nov. 1816, 11 Nov. 1816, 3 July 1818 (quotation), 7 Aug. 1818, 1 June 1819, 2 June 1819; *PADA*, 2 Aug. 1816, 25 June–1 July 1817, 7 July 1817, 24 July 1817, 1–12 June 1818, 13 Aug. 1818, 1 Oct. 1818, 9–10 Dec. 1818, 10 Apr. 1819, 18 May 1819, 31 May 1819, 9 July 1819, 6 Nov. 1819, 1 Dec. 1819, 20 Dec. 1819.

45. *PADA*, 26 May 1818, 3 July 1818.

46. *Federal Republican* (Georgetown, D.C.), cited in *Enquirer*, 31 Jan. 1818.

47. *NWR* 12 (19 July 1817): 323; see also 12 (28 June 1817): 287; 12 (23 Aug. 1817): 415; 13 (31 Jan. 1818): 377; 14 (23 May 1818): 223; 14 (6 June 1818): 256; 14 (4 July 1818): 328; 15 (10 Oct. 1818): 110; 15 (12 Dec. 1818): 267; 16 (24 Apr. 1819): 160; 16 (24 Apr. 1819): 159; 16 (12 June 1819): 272; 16 (10 July 1819): 336.

48. Wilson, *Freedom at Risk*, 10, 69–70.

49. *NI*, 21 Dec. 1818.

50. Wilson, *Freedom at Risk*, chap. 1, 3. This interpretation of Wilson's evidence is at variance with her own. She emphasizes the success kidnappers had in defending themselves and presents federal and state governments' actions against kidnapping as ineffective.

51. Aptheker, *Documentary History*, 73–74.

52. *PADA*, 28 May 1818 (quotation); *Baltimore Patriot*, 15 Nov. 1817. For the progress and passage of a strong antikidnapping law in Maryland, see *Votes and Proceedings . . . Maryland*, 63–65, 78, 80, 85–87, 91, 129.

53. Evans, *Pedestrious Tour*, 105, speaking of the hills of New Hampshire. He wrote similarly of Vermont, as "the peculiar sister of New-Hampshire"; ibid., 108–10.

54. *Centinel*, 31 Oct. 1818; see also 5 Nov. 1814, 28 Dec. 1814.

55. Ibid., 15 Aug. 1818.

56. Ibid., 19 Feb. 1817.

57. *New-York Evening Post*, quoted in *Enquirer*, 8 July 1817. See also *NWR* 12 (19 July 1817): 323.

58. *Aurora*, 3 July 1818.

59. *PADA*, 24 July 1817.

60. Torrey, *Portraiture of Domestic Slavery*, 30–49; quotations on 32, 31.

61. *NWR* 16 (12 June 1819): 269.

62. *PADA*, 7 Jan. 1819.

63. *PADA*, 12 May 1819.

64. *Aurora*, 1 June 1819.

65. Wright, *Refutation of the Sophisms*, 23–27; quotation on 24.

66. *NWR* 12 (19 July 1817): 323.

67. *NWR* 16 (24 Apr. 1819): 159.

68. *WR* 1 (21 Dec. 1811): 283; 1 (8 Feb. 1812): 409–10.

69. *Journal of the Assembly of the State of New-York*, 126–27; see also *Columbian*, 3 Feb. 1817.

70. *National Advocate*, 9 Jan. 1817.

71. It decreed that no one would be held as a slave in New York after 4 July 1827. For more on this law and its significance, see Zilversmit, *First Emancipation*, 211–14.

72. *Journal of the Assembly of the State of New-York*, 558–62.

73. Ibid., 568; *Journal of the Senate of the State of New-York*, 251.

74. For travelers, see Fearon, *Sketches of America*, 56–61, 97, 133, 158, 167–68; Welby, *Visit to North America*, 200, 306; Flint, *Letters from America*, 47, 55; Faux, *Memorable Days in America*, 1:166–67. British travelers, of course, were hardly objective observers of the United States; see chap. 4 herein. For African American testimony, see, e.g., Steward, *Twenty-two Years a Slave*, 77, 81–84. For abolitionist testimony, see, e.g., Wright, *Refutation of the Sophisms*, 21–23. For examples of the mass of modern historians' arguments to this effect, see Berwanger, *Frontier against Slavery*; Nash, *Forging Freedom*, 172–245; Berlin, *Many Thousands Gone*, 358, 364; Winch, *Gentleman of Color*, 162–74 and passim.

75. [Paulding], *Letters from the South*, 1:8; see also 1:110, 117–20. The idea of a separate creation for Africans was slowly gaining currency among some white Americans in the early nineteenth century. See Smith, *Essay on the Causes*, esp. xi–xl; Dain, *Hideous Monster of the Mind*, 72–75.

76. For the petitions, see Winch, *Gentleman of Color*, 168–74. These petitions, however, failed, a fact for which Winch does not adequately account. For the fire company controversy, see *PADA*, 10–16 July 1818.

77. *NWR* 15, suppl., [Feb. 1814]: 58.

78. "To prevent circumvention of their gradual emancipation laws," as Winthrop Jordan put it so well, "many northern states prohibited selling slaves out of state, thereby demonstrating that they valued liberation of Negroes over riddance of them"; *White over Black*, 403–4. Thus Melish, *Disowning Slavery*, is a valuable analysis of white Northerners' drive to distance themselves from slavery and its fruits but exaggerates by suggesting that that drive would be at any cost.

79. Thus in 1817 the leading Federalist organ could find room for a long obituary of the prominent black merchant Paul Cuffee (longer than the one for Jane Austen on the same day, in fact); *Centinel*, 17 Sept. 1817. For other specimens of the Federalist range between sympathy and disdain for people of color, see *PADA*, 4 Mar. 1811, 4 Dec. 1814, 22 Oct. 1816, 15 Feb. 1820, 11 Apr. 1820; *Centinel*, 17 July 1816, 3 June 1818; Dwight, *Charitable Blessed*, 20–23; Dwight, *President Dwight's Decisions*, 49–50, 117–28.

80. Evans, *Pedestrious Tour*, 331–35; see also 281. Another antislavery Yankee, John Kenrick, was one of the early republic's strongest antiracist voices; see *Horrors of Slavery*, 3–34.

81. See *Aurora*, 19 July 1817; *AC*, 11th Cong., 3d sess., 937.

82. [Colman], *Africans*, 89, 98–102.

83. *NWR* 15 (9 Jan. 1819): 384.

84. Newman et al., *Pamphlets of Protest*, 80–83; quotations on 82. See also White, *Somewhat More Independent*, 150–53.

85. Most historians of Northern race relations agree with this, at least implicitly, portraying a hardening of attitudes beginning only in the 1820s or 1830s; see, e.g., Litwack, *North of Slavery*, 64–114; Berwanger, *Frontier against Slavery*, 4–5, 21, 30–59; Fredrickson, *Black Image in the White Mind*, esp. 46–50; White, *Somewhat More Independent*, 72–75, 150–53, 169, 207–9; Phillips, *Freedom's Port*, chap. 4; Whitman, *Price of Freedom*, chap. 6; Harris, *In the Shadow of Slavery*, 5, 72–133; Forbes, "Slavery and the Meaning of America," chap. 2. Some regions of the United States, moreover, remained relatively open spaces where race mattered less than other categories to the "white" inhabitants far into the nineteenth century; see Grivno, " 'Black Frenchmen' and 'White Settlers.' "

86. *AC*, 12th Cong., 1st sess., 171–241 passim, 1155–1431 passim. See also Preyer, "Congressional Fight over the Admission," 52–80.

87. Moore, *Missouri Controversy*, 32.

88. *AC*, 11th Cong., 3d sess., 896, 932–34; 12th Cong., 1st sess., 171–72, 204–7, 1201–9, 1216–18, 1224–26; 12th Cong., 2d sess., 52, 62, 145, 153, 194, 361, 1152; 13th Cong., 3d sess., 177, 1085, 1187–89; 14th Cong., 1st sess., 1300–1301 passim; 14th Cong., 2d sess., passim. In December 1817, the Senate admitted Mississippi unanimously and the House did so without debate; see *AC*, 15th Cong., 1st sess., 20, 409. In early 1819, Alabama sailed through both houses despite the early onset of the Missouri debates; see *AC*, 15th Cong., 2d sess., 75, 79, 114, 121, 252–53, 541, 1240, 1272.

89. See Johnson, "Prelude to the Missouri Compromise."

90. *AC*, 11th Cong., 3d sess., 108–11; 12th Cong., 2d sess., 124–31.

91. "Massachusetts" [Morse], *New States*; [Dwight], *Slave Representation*, 4–6 (quotation).

92. Adams, *History of the United States*, 765–69; quotation on 769.

93. *AC*, 11th Cong., 3d sess., 524–42; quotation on 525.

94. Ibid., 555–70; quotation on 568.

95. Ibid., 38–83, 474–77. See also *Centinel*, 30 Oct. 1811; *WR* 2 (30 May 1812): 201–2; *Courant*, 21 June 1814; Risjord, "Virginia Federalists," 508 (quotation). For Federalists' emphasis on the South over the West during the War of 1812, see chap. 2.

96. *New-York Daily Advertiser*, quoted in *Savannah Republican*, 21 Oct. 1817.

97. *Aurora*, 14 Feb. 1817.

98. Ibid., 26 Aug. 1817 (quotation), 12 Sept. 1817.

99. *AC*, 12th Cong., 1st sess., 426–27. See also Adams, *History of the United States*, 392. For a contrasting interpretation, see Ohline, "Politics and Slavery," 170–86.

100. The United States failed to find a match in the Northern theaters for Jackson in the Southern, helping ensure that "the course of American expansion for the immediate future was directed southward." See Remini, *Course of American Empire*, 191, 231–32, 298–307, 364–65, 384–89, 395–98; quotation on 191.

101. Cunningham, *Circular Letters*, 2:1006.

102. *Columbian*, 26 May 1818 (quotation), 11 Sept. 1817, 8 June 1818, 19 Nov. 1818; *Centinel*, 13 Aug. 1817, 17 Sept. 1817; *Aurora*, 13 Sept. 1817; *Western American*, 31 Aug. 1816.

103. *NWR* 12 (5 July 1817): 304.

104. *Washington City Gazette*, quoted in *Georgia Journal*, 2 Sept. 1817.

105. *AC*, 15th Cong., 2d sess., 1222–23, 1226, 1228, 1235; quotations on 1222 and 1226.

106. *NI*, quoted in *National Advocate*, 22 July 1816.

107. *Address from the Pennsylvania Society for Promoting the Abolition of Slavery*, 4, 6.

108. See *American Convention*, 1:155–209, 340–42; 2:679, 684–85, 698–701, 707, 733–36, 738.

109. Torrey, *Portraiture of Domestic Slavery*, 28–29; quotation on 28.
110. Kenrick, *Horrors of Slavery*, 39n.
111. *North American Review and Miscellaneous Journal* 1 (July 1815): 240.
112. Smith, *Essay on the Causes*, 7–10, 23–92, 169–70; quotation on 169.
113. William M. Wiecek has also argued that the Missouri Crisis, which broke the "federal consensus" by which free and slave states balanced each other, was in part a product of the attempt to move slavery into the Northwest. But he does not develop this theme as I seek to do here; see *Sources of Antislavery Constitutionalism*, 105, 108–10.
114. *AC*, 14th Cong., 2d sess., 254.
115. Finkelman, *Imperfect Union*, chap. 7.
116. Buck, *Illinois in 1818*, 136–40; quotation on 136–37. Pierce, "Luke Decker and Slavery."
117. Onuf, *Statehood and Union*, 113–23; Finkelman, "Evading the Ordinance," 38–49.
118. Barnhart, *Valley of Democracy*, 178–96; Pierce, "Luke Decker and Slavery."
119. Buck, *Illinois in 1818*, 214–19, 233–49.
120. Ibid., 277–82; *NWR* 9 (20 Jan. 1816): 352–53; *NWR* 15 (3 Oct. 1818): 94–96.
121. This interpretation differs from that of Paul Finkelman, who presents the Illinois constitution as a victory for slaveholders; see "Slavery and the Northwest Ordinance," esp. 369. I join other scholars who see it as a victory for the antislavery forces. See Berwanger, *Frontier against Slavery*, 7–29, esp. 18–19; Finnie, "Antislavery Movement in the South," 410–37.
122. *NWR* 13 (4 Oct. 1817): 90.
123. Ibid.
124. Ratcliffe, "Captain James Riley," 80–81; quotations on 81.
125. Ibid., 80. For an earlier use of this tactic, see Ratcliffe, *Party Spirit in a Frontier Republic*, 53–54.
126. *Illinois Intelligencer*, 17 June 1818; see also 12, 19 Aug. 1818.
127. Ibid., 22 July 1818.
128. Ibid., 29 July 1818.
129. Ratcliffe, *Party Spirit in a Frontier Republic*, 107.
130. See MacLeod, *Slavery, Race, and the American Revolution*, 143–45; Cayton, *Frontier Republic*, 57–59; Schwarz, *Migrants against Slavery*; Reda, "Illinois Slavery Reconsidered," esp. 2, 23–27; and esp. Etcheson, *Emerging Midwest*, 67–71, 94–102, 108–39.
131. Berwanger, *Frontier against Slavery*, 20.
132. Hervey Heth to Thomas Posey, 10 Mar. 1814, in "The First American West: The Ohio River Valley, 1750–1820" Collection, <http://memory.loc.gov> (accessed 10 Feb. 2006).
133. Thomas Worthington, 23 Oct. 1817, quoted in Smith, *Political History of Slavery*, 1:21.
134. *Western American*, 9 Dec. 1815, 2 Mar. 1816.
135. Ratcliffe, *Politics of Long Division*, 53. See also *Illinois Intelligencer*, 17 June 1818.
136. Flint, *Letters from America*, 197; see also 215–16.
137. *NWR* 11 (4 Jan. 1817): 313–14; Berwanger, *Frontier against Slavery*, 21 (quotation). See also *NI*, 12 Dec. 1816.
138. Ratcliffe, *Politics of Long Division*, 53.
139. *Aurora*, 13, 16 July 1819. For further details on this settlement of freed people, see Schwarz, *Migrants against Slavery*, 122–48.
140. Reda, "Illinois Slavery Reconsidered," 21.

141. *Illinois Intelligencer*, 29 July 1818; see also 17 June 1818, 1 July 1818; *Western Intelligencer*, 1 Apr. 1818.
142. *Illinois Intelligencer*, 29 July 1818. In the 5 Aug. 1818 issue, "A Friend to Enquiry" responded by refusing to respond to "Prudence"!
143. Nation, "Home in the Hoosier Hills," 464–70.
144. *Newburyport Herald*, 26 Sept. 1817.
145. Ratcliffe, *Politics of Long Division*, 52.
146. *AC*, 15th Cong., 2d sess., 305–11; quotations on 306, 310, 311.
147. *NWR* 16 (12 June 1819): 272; 16 (26 June 1819): 298; 16 (17 July 1819): 347.
148. *Scioto Gazette*, quoted in *PADA*, 26 June 1819.
149. Ibid.
150. Quoted in McCoy, *Last of the Fathers*, 270.
151. As McCoy so aptly demonstrates in ibid., passim.
152. Dickens, *American Notes*, 161.
153. See chap. 3 herein.
154. Adam Rothman has suggested that between 1815 and 1820 "proslavery and antislavery interests combined to define the geographic, political, and moral boundaries of American slavery"; "Expansion of Slavery," 314. It may be better to say that this was the time when both interests *sought* to define those boundaries, but that friction was greatest when the process seemed not to be working. The border had proven all too permeable for many on both sides, which worked in favor of the thickening of the line.
155. Paulding, who so earnestly sought to calm the seas of slavery, struck a confident tone when dismissing the threat of disunion because of westward extension. He did think the subject merited "serious investigation" but calmly asserted that the federal system that incorporated western territories as states militated against any western confederacy like that threatened by Burr ten years earlier. Furthermore, emigration and commerce tied the East and West together. Only encroachment on state rights by the federal government could produce serious divisions on this sectional line; *Letters from the South*, 1:204–26. The subject was still important, but not nearly so alarming as North-South sectionalism. Meanwhile, a Clintonian editor in Albany attacked Monroe's "*sheer jealousy of the state of New-York*," manifested by the president's opposition to "the appropriation of any funds for internal improvements—*in the northern states*"; quoted in *National Advocate*, 16 Dec. 1817. Internal improvements promised to unite the East and the West, and they thus became part of the growing North-South tensions of the Era of Good Feelings.

CHAPTER SEVEN

1. Adams, *History of the United States*, 215–18.
2. *Savannah Republican*, 19 Feb. 1819.
3. Meriwether et al., *Papers of John C. Calhoun*, 1:275–408; 3:xix–xx, 461–72; quotation on 1:361.
4. Dangerfield, *Awakening of American Nationalism*, 15.
5. Quoted in *WR* 3 (19 Dec. 1812): 247.
6. Hickey, *War of 1812*, 244–45. State governments in New England retained their state armies.

7. *WR* 5 (15 Jan. 1814): 330.
8. Rowland, *Official Letter Books*, 5:128.
9. *Georgia Journal*, 26 June 1816.
10. *NWR* 11 (1 Feb. 1817): 378–79.
11. Vipperman, *William Lowndes*, 199–20. Southern dominance of the federal government in the early republic has come to the attention of several other recent historians; see, e.g., Finkelman, *Slavery and the Founders*, esp. x; Richards, *Slave Power*; Rothman, "Expansion of Slavery"; Fehrenbacher, *Slaveholding Republic*. Rothman's account in particular shows how the U.S. government's land and other policies favored the planters in the rush for Southwestern land, which it had itself won by its military exploits against the Indian and European powers; see 54–61, 287–303 passim. All this refutes Jesse T. Carpenter, who emphasized the South's sense of minority status and weakness within the Union over the entire period between 1789 and 1861. But even his own evidence for this point comes from the late eighteenth century and then from the 1830s forward; see *South as a Conscious Minority*, esp. 21–29.
12. Jordan, *White over Black*, 325–31; quotation on 331.
13. For some, that meant state governments; see Hicks, *Observations on the Slavery of the Africans*, 3–12; *NI*, 26 June 1819. But most schemes in this period involved the federal government. Robert P. Forbes has argued that only in the 1810s did the threat of the federal government being used for abolition seem more than hypothetical, for localism was on the decline in this expansive age; see "Slavery and the Evangelical Enlightenment," in McKivigan and Snay, *Religion and the Antebellum Debate*, 77–82, 86. Forbes does not demonstrate these points to the degree well-wishers might desire, but they are suggestive.
14. *NI*, 20 Dec. 1819. For a similar scheme, see *PADA*, 23 Aug. 1817.
15. *NWR* 13 (15 Nov. 1817): 177–81.
16. *NWR* 16 (17 July 1819): 342–44. The scheme is developed in all its complexity in the long series "Mitigation of Slavery," published between 8 May and 21 Aug. 1819.
17. Evans, *Pedestrious Tour*, 320–24.
18. Riley, *Authentic Narrative*, 531–33; quotation on 533.
19. Kenrick, *Horrors of Slavery*, 57–58. The nationalistic judiciary of the Marshall era also proved willing to interfere with state laws respecting slavery; see *NWR* 13 (30 Aug. 1817): 16.
20. *Enquirer*, 4 Jan. 1817, 9 Jan. 1817, 12 June 1818, 30 Mar. 1819; *Georgia Journal*, 1 Jan. 1817.
21. Risjord, *Old Republicans*, 175–87.
22. Nathaniel Macon to Bartlett Yancey, 8 Mar. 1818, in Wilson, *Congressional Career*, 48–49.
23. Macon to Yancey, 15 Apr. 1818, in ibid., 47.
24. Price, "Nathaniel Macon, Planter," 209–10.
25. Cunningham, "Nathaniel Macon and the Southern Protest," 376–84. As a general rule, Macon was not a "typical" figure: "One of his colleagues is reported to have said that if Macon should happen to be drowned, he should look for his body up the stream instead of floating with the current"; see ibid., 377.
26. Cunningham, *Circular Letters*, 2:1001.
27. *AC*, 15th Cong., 2d sess., 336–37. The resolution failed by an undisclosed margin.
28. *Enquirer*, 2 Mar. 1819. These voices, although in the minority, qualify the argument of

some historians that the link between state rights, strict construction, and protecting slavery was weak or invisible before 1819; see Brown, "Missouri Crisis," 58; Bonner, "Americans Apart," 35–40.

29. Thomas P. Abernethy described it well when he wrote that the postwar period was "the high water mark of Southern nationalism, but a closer examination of the situation discloses many crosscurrents"; see *South in the New Nation*, 424–42; quotation on 427. A treatise by Monroe typified the divided Southern Republican mind, arguing that Congress had power to appropriate money for internal improvements but not to actually construct them. As his biographer has noted, this "essay was a baffling production, in which he resorted to a loose interpretation of the power to appropriate money but turned to a strict-construction view when it came to enumerating the purposes for which the money could be spent"; Ammon, *James Monroe*, 390–92; quotation on 390. See also Cooper, *Liberty and Slavery*, 120–34, for a good description of how nationalism vied with Old Republican principles in the minds of most leading Southerners.

30. Skeen, *1816*, chap. 11.

31. *Richmond Compiler*, quoted in *NWR* 15, suppl. (Feb. 1819): 44–45. This account circulated widely; see also *NI*, 29 Oct. 1818; *Savannah Republican*, 10 Nov. 1818. For Las Casas and his proslavery uses beginning in 1787, see Davis, *Problem of Slavery in Western Culture*, 169–73.

32. Adams, *Memoirs of John Quincy Adams*, 4:353–55. At this point in his career Adams was inclined to agree with Hay on most of these points.

33. See Taylor, *Arator*, 176–84; *Enquirer*, 7 Sept. 1816; *Savannah Republican*, 15 July 1817; *NWR* 14 (1 Aug. 1818): 382; *Georgia Journal*, 17 Aug. 1819; Young, *Domesticating Slavery*, 158.

34. See *Letter to the Edinburgh Reviewers*, excerpted in chap. 4 herein.

35. *Savannah Republican*, 19 Nov. 1816.

36. Ibid., 21 Oct. 1817.

37. Wyatt-Brown, "Antimission Movement"; quotation on 510. See also Young, *Domesticating Slavery*, 158. Wyatt-Brown argues that this prejudice was largely limited to non-slaveholders, but Jefferson, perhaps the most cosmopolitan of Southerners, shared this revulsion for New England–centered philanthropy; see Shalhope, "Thomas Jefferson's Republicanism," 539–54.

38. This echoed admissions made earlier in the nineteenth century. "Tell us not of principles" such as liberty and equality, a Virginia legislator said in an 1806 debate over restricting manumissions. "Those principles have been annihilated by the existence of slavery among us"; Jordan, *White over Black*, 576–77. See also Sidbury, *Ploughshares into Swords*, 120–39.

39. These missions were new to the South after the War of 1812; see Tise, *Proslavery*, 293–95.

40. Quoted in *Columbian*, 24 July 1816. See also *Savannah Republican*, 14 Aug. 1817, excerpted in chap. 5 herein.

41. Schweninger, *Petitions to Southern Legislatures*, 47–48, 55–56; quotation on 47.

42. Palmer, *Signs of the Times*; *Charleston Courier*, 31 Mar. 1819, 3 June 1819.

43. *Charleston Courier*, 5 June 1819. On 8 June 1819, however, the editor stated that Faux's letter had prompted an official investigation, which declared his report "greatly exag-

gerated, if not destitute of foundation. . . . In no civilized country, are offences of this character so seldom committed."

44. McColley, *Slavery and Jeffersonian Virginia*, 212–16.

45. Taylor, *Arator*, 185–88; quotation on 185.

46. *NWR* 13 (20 Sept. 1817): 54–58; 17 (18 and 25 Sept. 1819): 45–53. For an analysis of these twin impulses in the antebellum South, see Genovese, *Roll, Jordan, Roll*.

47. [Botsford], *Sambo and Toney*; quotation on 35. For this pamphlet's appeal and context, see Young, *Domesticating Slavery*, 141. For a similar plea for a domesticated slavery, see *NWR* 15 (29 Aug. 1818): 5–6.

48. *NI*, 26 Nov. 1819.

49. *Georgia Journal*, 18 July 1820. Jeffrey Young has aptly observed that although slave-holders worried about the antislavery thrust of the transatlantic intellectual commu-nity in the early nineteenth century, "they exhibited little desire to withdraw from the transatlantic dialogue. . . . They abhorred abolitionism but remained hopeful that their perspective on slavery would sway reasonable minds across the globe"; *Domesticating Slavery*, 140. This passage unduly downplays those who rejected philanthropy, but for other slaveholders it makes a key point.

50. Fredericksburg *Herald*, quoted in *Enquirer*, 8 June 1819. See also *NWR* 12 (19 Apr. 1817): 122; *NWR* 16 (19 June 1819): 287; *NI*, 24–25 June 1819.

51. *NI*, 26 Sept. 1817; *New-Orleans Gazette*, quoted in *Aurora*, 1 Jan. 1817.

52. *Enquirer*, 25 Aug. 1818 (quotation), 31 Jan. 1818; *NI*, 26 Aug. 1817.

53. *Georgia Journal*, 4 Feb. 1817.

54. Quoted in *Aurora*, 7 Aug. 1818.

55. See *NI*, 4 Jan. 1817; *NWR* 11 (8 Feb. 1817): 399–400.

56. *Georgia Journal*, 29 Sept. 1818.

57. *AC*, 14th Cong., 1st sess., 115–17.

58. Randolph's subsequent behavior suggested the degree to which his opposition to the slave trade in the District of Columbia was a public relations campaign. He headed a special committee that gathered evidence of the booming trade but did not report the committee's findings until the last day of the session. When the House ordered his report to merely lie upon the table, Randolph did not call for further action. Neither did he reintroduce the subject into later sessions. He apparently thought it was enough to denounce the trade publicly and thus shore up the image of the paternalist slave-holder; ibid., 1127, 1465. Some of Randolph's biographers have played up his "opposi-tion to slavery." Yet his opposition to the slave trade in Washington, albeit phrased in moralistic tones, by no means suggested opposition to slavery itself. Indeed, at that moment this bundle of contradictions opposed the slave trade largely because of the grasping acquisitiveness it supposedly engrafted onto an otherwise benevolent institu-tion. For the view of Randolph as being antislavery, see Kirk, *John Randolph of Roanoke*, 30 (quotation), 46, 155–89; for evidence to the contrary, see 58–70, 127–28, 157–59, 169, 193, 235–36, 277–78, 283–85, 550.

59. *Georgia Journal*, 4 Dec. 1816.

60. Ibid., 12 Aug. 1817; see also 21 Oct. 1817 and the series by "PHILANTHROPIST" between 18 Aug. 1818 and 10 Nov. 1818. For similar rhetoric from Virginia, see *Enquirer*, 17 July 1818.

61. Ball, *Fifty Years in Chains*, 51–68, 286–87; quotations on 53, 286–87. For more on the status of slave dealers, see Tadman, *Speculators and Slaves*, esp. chap. 7.
62. Gudmestad, *Troublesome Commerce*.
63. *Savannah Republican*, 7 Dec. 1818; *Georgia Journal*, 24 Mar. 1818.
64. *NWR* 15 (12 Dec. 1818): 269.
65. *NWR* 13 (6 Sept. 1817): 32; 13 (27 Dec. 1817): 288–93.
66. *NI*, 9 Dec. 1816; *Georgia Journal*, 28 Apr. 1818, 8 Sept. 1818; *Savannah Republican*, 5 Dec. 1818; *Charleston Courier*, 16 July 1819, 20 July 1819.
67. Meriwether et al., *Papers of John C. Calhoun*, 1:312 (quotation), 364–65.
68. *Enquirer*, 10 Nov. 1818.
69. *American Convention*, 2:605–6. For samples of the outrage, see *Centinel*, 4 Nov. 1818, 25 July 1818; *Aurora*, 31 Aug. 1818, 27 Oct. 1818; *NWR* 14 (1 Aug. 1818): 423; *NWR* 15 (26 Sept. 1818): 80; *AC*, 15th Cong., 2d sess., 77, 87–88, 90, 97, 113, 162, 167, 173, 176, 189, 197.
70. *NWR* 16 (1 May 1819): 165–66.
71. *NI*, 24 Apr. 1819.
72. *Enquirer*, 1 Sept. 1818; see also 16 Mar. 1819.
73. *NI*, 15 Mar. 1819. See also *Georgia Journal*, 13 Apr. 1819.
74. Fowler, *Wandering Philanthropist*, 47–49.
75. See Barrow, *Involuntary . . . Slavery*, esp. iii–vii; quotation on vi. See also Dupre, *Admonitory Picture*, esp. iii–12; Dupre, *Rational and Benevolent Plan*. The Quaker abolitionist Elihu Embree had supporters as well as enemies in Tennessee. In 1815, he founded the Tennessee Manumission Society in Jefferson County, and soon at least six other county societies allied themselves with his small band. The discussion of slavery was settled in Tennessee only in the 1840s at the earliest. See Hoss, *Elihu Embree*, 10–13, 25–27. Much of this room for antislavery was in the upcountry South, but Gordon Esley Finnie has demonstrated that even the Deep South hosted something of an open forum for differing viewpoints. Whites in Mississippi remained open to discussing the merits of slavery as late as the 1820s. In 1816, in fact, the Mississippi Supreme Court ruled that courts should "lean 'in favorem vitae et libertatis,'" because "slavery is condemned by reason and the laws of nature. It exists and can only exist, through municipal regulations"; see "Antislavery Movement in the South," 190–94; quotation on 191. It should be noted, however, that in late 1815, Virginia Presbyterians expelled the most extreme abolitionist of the day, George Bourne. He left for Germantown, Pennsylvania, where the congregation welcomed him unanimously in 1816. The sectional logic of slave and free states was on display in this episode, if still not completely worked out in relation to less radical abolitionists; see Christie and Dumond, *George Bourne*, 47–65.
76. *Georgia Journal*, 1 Sept. 1818.
77. See Morse, *Discourse, Delivered at the African Meeting-House*, 12–13; Jarvis Brewster, *Exposition of the Treatment of Slaves*, 18–20; Kenrick, *Horrors of Slavery*, 56–57n; Wright, *Refutation of the Sophisms*, title page; *Georgia Journal*, 1 Jan. 1817; Allen, "Debate over Slavery," chap. 2.
78. Taylor, *Arator*, 119–25; quotations on 121, 122. See also *Letter to the Edinburgh Reviewers*, 41–48. These writers offer supporting evidence for William Sumner Jenkins's argu-

ment that in the years before the Missouri Crisis the South underwent a "conservative reaction" against the radicalism of the Revolution. The broader manifestation of this reaction was a rejection of all "systems of abstract political theory," the very abstraction that prompted Jefferson's observations on slavery in the *Notes*; see Jenkins, *Pro-Slavery Thought*, 58–65; quotations on 58, 61. See also Hamilton, "Revolutionary Principles and Family Loyalties," 551–53. But it also bears notice that the Virginian George Tucker publicly dissented not from Jefferson's expressions against slavery but from his racist postulations in the *Notes*; see [Tucker], *Letters from Virginia*, 73–103.

79. Birkbeck, *Notes on a Journey in America*, 16–17. See also *Enquirer*, 27 May 1817; *NI*, 14 Aug. 1817.

80. Fearon, *Sketches of America*, 391–419; quotations on 394–95.

81. Flint, *Letters from America*, 140–41.

82. Smith, *In His Image*, 23–73; quotations on 67. See also Young, *Domesticating Slavery*, 153–58.

83. Ketcham, "Dictates of Conscience," 52–54; quotations on 52. For key Founders' accommodation to slavery, see McCoy, *Last of the Fathers*, 221–322; Kaminski, *A Necessary Evil*, 257–67, esp. 260, 263, 265.

84. Welby, *A Visit to North America*, 188.

85. [Tucker], *Letters from Virginia*, 29–35; quotations on 34–35.

86. Quoted in Mathews, *Slavery and Methodism*, 28.

87. *American Convention*, 2:716. For their hopes and solicitude for Southern abolitionism in the 1810s, see 2:424–25, 428, 492–93, 497, 504–5, 550–53, 556–57, 562–63, 574, 582–84, 596.

88. Christie and Dumond, *George Bourne*, 34.

89. Quoted in Finnie, "Antislavery Movement in the South," 143.

90. This argument cuts against two opposing grains in the historiography of proslavery. On the one side are those who minimize the degree to which proslavery theory was developed in the period preceding the Missouri Crisis. Proponents of this view wrongly downplay the degree to which slavery was under attack before Missouri; see, e.g., Jenkins, *Pro-Slavery Thought*, 48–78; Greenberg, "Revolutionary Ideology," 365–84. In the other corner are those who posit a fully developed proslavery ideology well before Missouri burst into view. They either overlook or dismiss the hesitance with which proslavery theorists propounded their views in the 1810s; see, e.g., Tise, *Proslavery*, esp. chap. 3–6; Bailor, "John Taylor of Caroline." Tise notes but discounts the defenders' denials that they were friends of slavery; see *Proslavery*, 30, 37, 46, 233, 246.

91. *NWR* 15, suppl. (Feb. 1819): 44–45.

92. Taylor, *Arator*, 119–25, 176–84; quotations on 182, 180, 124. Given Taylor's disclaimers, Robert McColley erred when he argued that Taylor "fully anticipated the later 'sociology' of George Fitzhugh"; *Slavery and Jeffersonian Virginia*, 4. McColley was right on, however, when he wrote that "Taylor represented a curious point of transition between the high-minded deprecation of slavery of his old law teacher, George Wythe, and the high-minded defense of slavery of his own disciple, George Fitzhugh"; 207.

93. *Georgia Journal*, 10 Aug. 1819–7 Sept. 1819; quotation 24 Aug. 1819. See also *NI*, 14 Sept. 1819, 25 Oct. 1819.

94. *Georgia Journal*, 14 Sept. 1819.

95. *Savannah Republican*, 9 Jan. 1817; see also 19 Nov. 1816.
96. [Pinckney or Smith], "Young Carolinians," 58–111; quotations on 85, 96.
97. Wright, *Refutation of the Sophisms*, 40–43.
98. Barrow, *Involuntary . . . Slavery*, 47.
99. Coker, *Dialogue*. Ira Berlin has written that early national slaveholders "began haltingly to systematize all the crude and perfunctory arguments that had been used to justify African slavery." He points to Coker's imaginary opponent as one who "articulated the full range of slavery's defense" in 1810; see *Many Thousands Gone*, 279. But Coker's Virginian also demonstrated just how halting the whole process still was.

CHAPTER EIGHT

1. Henry Clay to John J. Crittenden, 29 Jan. 1820, quoted in Moore, *Missouri Controversy*, 90. For a good general description of the tense atmosphere in Washington and the all-consuming nature of the debates, see ibid., 90–94; Brown, *Missouri Compromises and Presidential Politics*.
2. Quoted in Cooper, *Liberty and Slavery*, 141.
3. See *NWR* 18 (18 Mar. 1820): 47.
4. *Enquirer*, 22 Jan. 1820.
5. *NI*, 7 Dec. 1819, 25 Dec. 1819, Dec. 1819–Jan. 1820 passim.
6. *NWR* 18 (1 July 1820): 327. For other threats of this kind, see *Aurora*, 21 Dec. 1820, 3 Feb. 1821; *NI*, 16 Sept. 1820.
7. See *Centinel*, 15 Mar. 1820; Moore, *Missouri Controversy*, 269–70. My interpretation of the excitement created by the Missouri Crisis differs from Moore's. He argues that most Americans were generally uninterested in the Missouri debates. This fits well with Moore's thesis that Northern partisans manufactured the Crisis, but not so well with the evidence of widespread popular agitation; see ibid., 65–67, 170–257. For some of the many historians who have nevertheless followed the interpretation of this, the only book-length monograph on Missouri, see Dangerfield, *Awakening of American Nationalism*, chap. 4, esp. 118, 126–27; Foner, *Politics and Ideology*, 22–23, 37–40.
8. *NI*, 22 Mar. 1820.
9. *NWR* 17 (26 Feb. 1820): 441.
10. William Plumer Sr. to William Plumer Jr., 31 Jan. 1820, in Livermore, *Twilight of Federalism*, 89.
11. *AC*, 16th Cong., 1st sess., 389.
12. Ibid., 1291, 1539.
13. *NWR* 17 (19 Feb. 1820): 425–26; see also 17 (26 Feb. 1820): 441; 19 (30 Sept. 1820): 66; 19 (21 Oct. 1820): 113.
14. See *AC*, 15th Cong., 2d sess., 1210; *AC*, 16th Cong., 2d sess., 45–50; *NWR* 17 (20 Nov. 1819): 189; *Centinel*, 10 Nov. 1819; *PADA*, 22–24 Nov. 1819, 30 Nov. 1819, 14 Dec. 1819, 17 Dec. 1819, 22 Jan. 1820, 29 Jan. 1820, 19 Feb. 1820, 21 Feb. 1820, 4 Mar. 1820, 24 Mar. 1820, 21 Apr. 1820, 27 Apr. 1820, 30 June 1820, 27 July 1820, 1 Aug. 1820, 16 Aug. 1820; [Walsh], *Free Remarks*, 21–24; Hillhouse, *Pocahontas*, 10, 12–13.
15. *PADA*, 21 Feb. 1820; also reprinted in Embree, *Emancipator*, 16.
16. *AC*, 16th Cong., 1st sess., 1205–18; quotations on 1207, 1214.

17. *PADA*, 10 July 1820; see also 24 July 1820.
18. *New York Daily Advertiser*, in *PADA*, 4 Nov. 1820 (first quotation), 2 Sept. 1820 (second quotation); see also 20 Nov. 1820, 22 Nov. 1820, 25 Nov. 1820, 5 Dec. 1820.
19. *New York Commercial Advertiser*, in *PADA*, 4 May 1820.
20. Rufus King, as both a Federalist and a New Yorker, naturally carried both traditions and sets of concerns into the Missouri debates; see King, *Life and Correspondence*, 6:278–80, 282. So did Zachariah Poulson, a Philadelphia Federalist and staunch restrictionist.
21. *NWR* 17 (5 Feb. 1820): 399.
22. *NWR* 17 (29 Jan. 1820): 381. Compare the Massachusetts governor's avoidance of the Missouri issue; 368–71.
23. *NWR* 17 (1 Jan. 1820): 296–97.
24. See King, *Life and Correspondence*, 259–61, 273–74; *Centinel*, 20 Jan. 1821, 21 Feb. 1821; Morison, *Life and Letters of Harrison Gray Otis*, 2:223–33; Moore, *Missouri Controversy*, 81–82, 277–81; Sheidley, *Sectional Nationalism*, 17–21; Forbes, "Slavery and the Meaning of America," 202–50. For the origins and possible meanings of the term "doughfaces," see *PADA*, 26 June 1820, 19 Dec. 1820; Richards, *Slave Power*, 85–88.
25. *Newburyport Herald*, 21 Apr. 1820, 16 May 1820. This sheet typified the overall pattern for New England. Between late 1819 and early 1821, it was nearly silent on the subject. If any one story took pride of place it was the constitutional convention in Massachusetts, which obviously struck closer to home. The editor's interest spiked at various points, but in March 1820 he complained mildly about how much time Congress had consumed with the single question of slavery in Missouri; 7 Mar. 1820. This editor's reticence on Missouri may have been part of his general retreat from "party spirit"; see 6 July 1821, 10 July 1821, 19 July 1822, 13 Dec. 1822.
26. Parish, *Sermons, Practical and Doctrinal*, xv–24.
27. Rufus King to J. A. King and C. King, 20 Feb. 1820, in King, *Life and Correspondence*, 279. See also *NWR* 18 (8 July 1820): 338.
28. Ratcliffe, "Captain James Riley," 81; the bracketed insertion is Ratcliffe's.
29. *AC*, 16th Cong., 1st sess., 1174–1201; quotation on 1184.
30. Ibid., 1354.
31. Ibid., 1111. This exchange foretold the repeal of the Missouri Compromise in the Kansas-Nebraska Act.
32. In the *Louisiana Public Advertiser*, quoted in *Enquirer*, 6 Apr. 1821.
33. *AC*, 16th Cong., 2d sess., 83–85.
34. See ibid., 97–98, 114.
35. Moore, *Missouri Controversy*, 85; Pease, *Illinois Election Returns*, 1–6. Cook's margin was 58 percent to 41 percent in 1819, and 65 percent to 35 percent in 1820. In 1819, 3,775 voted statewide, whereas in 1820 the turnout was 6,944. It appears the Missouri Controversy galvanized voters in Illinois, contrary to Moore's argument that Illinois was essentially a slave state in 1819; see Moore, *Missouri Controversy*, 53–55, 281–87. See also Harris, *History of Negro Servitude in Illinois*, 6–29.
36. *Detroit Gazette*, 9 Mar. 1821 (quotation). For indifference in Michigan to slavery in Missouri, see 24 Mar. 1820, 9 June 1820, 7 July 1820, 10 Nov. 1820, 8 Dec. 1820. For the use of slavery in Missouri in the rivalry for settlers, see 12 Nov. 1819, 25 Feb. 1820.
37. Richmond *Compiler*, quoted in *NI*, 16 Sept. 1816. For Southern settlers in Missouri after

the Louisiana Purchase, see Shoemaker, *Missouri's Struggle for Statehood*, chap. 4, esp. 114–16.

38. *AC*, 15th Cong., 2d sess., 1203. See also Moore, *Missouri Controversy*, 62.

39. [Walsh], *Free Remarks*, 44, 76–77; quotations on 76. For similar arguments, see King, *Life and Correspondence*, 692, 694, 702.

40. *Centinel*, 24 Nov. 1819.

41. *Enquirer*, 7 Mar. 1820.

42. *AC*, 16th Cong., 1st sess., 125.

43. See *NWR* 9 (10 Feb. 1816): 405; *NWR* 12 (10 May 1817): 175; *NWR* 14 (6 June 1818): 246; *Aurora*, 23 Apr. 1817, 8 May 1817; Lewis, *American Union and the Problem of Neighborhood*, chap. 3–4; Rothman, "Expansion of Slavery," 282–86; Dangerfield, *Awakening of American Nationalism*, 37.

44. *NWR* 14 (23 May 1818): 218, 223; *NWR* 14 (11 July 1818): 334; *Columbian*, 20 June 1818; *Centinel*, 21 and 28 Feb. 1818; *National Advocate*, 18 Sept. 1818; *Enquirer*, 27 Mar. 1818.

45. *NWR* 16 (13 Mar. 1819): 45; see also 16 (27 Feb. 1819): 3–4; 16 (6 Mar. 1819): 28–33.

46. See Dangerfield, *Era of Good Feelings*, 136–37, 199; Adams, *Memoirs of John Quincy Adams*, 4:102, 107–17; Risjord, *Old Republicans*, 188–91.

47. Adams, *Memoirs of John Quincy Adams*, 4:480; see also 5:19. In March 1820, Adams himself, who had long sought Florida, became reluctant to annex Florida or Texas without restricting slavery in the treaties; see 5:54, 68.

48. *PADA*, 17 Mar. 1820; see also *Aurora*, 3 Apr. 1820; *Centinel*, 3 Mar. 1821.

49. *PADA*, 21 Apr. 1820; see also 27 Apr. 1820.

50. *AC*, 16th Cong., 1st sess., 965–66.

51. *NWR* 17 (11 Dec. 1819): 241–42.

52. *AC*, 16th Cong., 1st sess., 336.

53. Fehrenbacher, *Slaveholding Republic*, 119. See also Lewis, *American Union and the Problem of Neighborhood*, 127, 132–33, 147–48, 172; *NWR* 18 (11 Mar. 1820): 25–26.

54. *Brookville Enquirer*, 23 July 1819. See also *Ohio Repository*, 12 Apr. 1821.

55. Dangerfield, *Awakening of American Nationalism*, 71.

56. As early as October 1819, a traveler assumed that the Congress would put the Missouri question "at rest" by drawing a "line of demarcation"; Flint, *Letters from America*, 192.

57. Eaton, *Growth of Southern Civilization*, xiii.

58. Quoted in Moore, *Missouri Controversy*, 254.

59. Taylor, *Construction Construed*, 291–99; quotation on 291.

60. *AC*, 16th Cong., 1st sess., 1320.

61. Adams, *Memoirs of John Quincy Adams*, 4:531; see also 5:67–68.

62. Taylor, *Construction Construed*, 295.

63. Calhoun to Virgil Maxcy, 12 Aug. 1820, in Meriwether et al., *Papers of John C. Calhoun*, 5:327.

64. See *AC*, 16th Cong., 1st sess., 999, 1014–15, 1536–37; *Kentucky Reporter*, 29 Mar. 1820; Moore, *Missouri Controversy*, 258–59.

65. King to John Adams, 12 July 1818, in King, *Life and Correspondence*, 153.

66. See *WR* 2 (21 Mar. 1812): 54–55; Dangerfield, *Era of Good Feelings*, 105; Hammack, *Kentucky and the Second American Revolution*, 111–12; Remini, *Course of American Empire*, 298–304; Owsley, *Struggle for the Gulf Borderlands*, 192–95; Stagg, *Mr. Madison's War*,

211–12; Hickey, *War of 1812*, 137; Kastor, *Nation's Crucible*, 136–49, 165–67, 178–80, 183–200, 203, 226.

67. *AC*, 13th Cong., 3d sess., 1162, 1166; *WR* 3 (9 Jan. 1813): 300; *NWR* 6 (28 May 1814): 207; *NWR* 7 (19 Nov. 1814): 169; *NWR* 8, suppl., [Aug. 1815]: 161; Waldstreicher, *In the Midst of Perpetual Fetes*, 289.

68. *AC*, 14th Cong., 1st sess., 108–9 (quotation); *NWR* 12 (8 Mar. 1817): 19.

69. See *Columbian*, 29 Oct. 1819, 19 July 1820; *NWR* 12 (26 July 1817): 340.

70. Rufus King to J. A. King and C. King, 20 Feb. 1820, in King, *Life and Correspondence*, 6:279. See also ibid., 330, 698–700; *PADA*, 17 Jan. 1820, 26 Jan. 1820, 22 Mar. 1820, 17 Apr. 1820.

71. Hillhouse, *Pocahontas*, 3–13; quotations on 3, 13.

72. *Aurora*, 29 Nov. 1819. In a biblical incident, "Mene" meant "God hath numbered thy kingdom, and finished it," whereas "Tekel" meant "thou art weighed in the balances, and art found wanting"; see Daniel 5, esp. verses 25–27.

73. *Aurora*, 23 Dec. 1820; see also 4 Dec. 1819, 4 Jan. 1820, 21 Feb. 1820, 12 Apr. 1820, 17 Apr. 1820, 19 Apr. 1820, 28–31 Oct. 1820, 27 Nov. 1820, 30 Dec. 1820.

74. *NWR* 17 (27 Nov. 1819): 200.

75. *NWR* 17 (22 Jan. 1820): 342.

76. *AC*, 16th Cong., 1st sess., 124, 966, 1437–39.

77. *Columbian*, 16 Nov. 1820; see also 21 Nov. 1820, 12 Dec. 1820, 22 Dec. 1820.

78. Quoted in Moore, *Missouri Controversy*, 240.

79. Adams, *Memoirs of John Quincy Adams*, 4:492–93.

80. Ibid., 5:4, 11–12.

81. *Centinel*, 4 Dec. 1819.

82. *Independent Chronicle*, 29 Sept. 1819, 2 Oct. 1819, 20 Nov. 1819, 27 Nov. 1819, 1–15 Dec. 1819, 1 Feb. 1820, 4 Feb. 1820.

83. Quoted in Moore, *Missouri Controversy*, 310.

84. *Aurora*, 16 May 1820.

85. Ibid., 2, 9 Mar. 1820.

86. *PADA*, 26 July 1820. See also *PADA*, 26 Jan. 1820; *NWR* 17 (2 Oct. 1819): 71.

87. *AC*, 16th Cong., 1st sess., 150.

88. *NWR* 18 (17 June 1820): 293–95.

89. See, e.g., Welby, *Visit to North America*, 309–12; *Quarterly Review* 30 (Oct. 1823): 40; *Blackwood's Edinburgh Magazine* 16 (Dec. 1824): 641. I am indebted to Professor Nicholas Mason for this reference from *Blackwood's*.

90. *Illinois Intelligencer*, 23 Dec. 1818.

91. *AC*, 15th Cong., 2d sess., 1210–13; quotations on 1210–11. See also *AC*, 16th Cong., 1st sess., 1374.

92. *AC*, 16th Cong., 1st sess., 1108; see also 1042, 1467.

93. *NWR* 18 (8 July 1820): 339.

94. *Centinel*, 19 July 1820.

95. *Columbian*, 19 Nov. 1820. See also *Columbian*, 11 Feb. 1820, 29 Nov. 1820; *NI*, 9 Nov. 1819; *Centinel*, 25 Dec. 1819; *Aurora*, 23 Nov. 1819, 3 Dec. 1819, 6 Mar. 1820, 15 Dec. 1820, 25 Jan. 1821; *PADA*, 22 Nov. 1819, 29 Dec. 1819, 25 Mar. 1820, 30 Mar. 1820, 27 Apr. 1820, 12 May 1820, 14 July 1820, 18 July 1820, 26 July 1820, 16 Aug. 1820; *North American Review and Miscellaneous Journal* 10 (Jan. 1820): 137–45.

96. [Walsh], *Free Remarks*, 80–81; see also 81–93. Such comments turned white Southerners against Walsh; *Enquirer*, 1 Aug. 1820; 4 Aug. 1820.

97. [Walsh], *Free Remarks*, 32–33, 100.

98. See Meriwether et al., *Papers of John C. Calhoun*, 5:672–73; Remini, *Course of American Empire*, 391; Wilson, *Congressional Career*, 53, 60.

99. Moore accepted this characterization of himself in *Missouri Controversy*. But a picture of politicians manipulating popular sentiments presupposes sentiments available for manipulation.

100. *NWR* 19 (3 Feb. 1821): 371.

101. *AC*, 16th Cong., 1st sess., 1090. For some few other examples of the Federalist plot argument, see *AC*, 16th Cong., 2d sess., 1102–13; *NI*, 24 Mar. 1820; *National Advocate*, 25 Jan. 1820, 24 Aug. 1820; *Independent Chronicle*, 26 Feb. 1820; *Savannah Republican*, 23 Jan. 1820; Dillon, *Benjamin Lundy*, 37. Jefferson was a leading practitioner of this device, although even the nuanced reading of Stuart Leibiger does not characterize it as such. Elsewhere in a valuable article, he argues that "the hand-wringing apparent in Jefferson's shrillest letters" over the danger the Missouri Crisis posed to the Union "may have been calculated for effect"—scaring Yankees into jettisoning restriction—"and possibly should not be taken at full face value." This was in keeping with "his political habit of sometimes using hysterical language to influence public opinion." This is a valuable reading, although I would not box it in by "may haves." But Leibiger proceeds to take at full face value Jefferson's statements that Federalists got the Missouri agitation up to secure national power. Why take the fears for the Union—which had much more basis in fact—as a bugaboo and the Federalist plot angle as descriptive? See "Thomas Jefferson and the Missouri Crisis"; quotations on 121, 122.

102. *New Hampshire Patriot*, quoted in *Enquirer*, 21 Nov. 1820. See also *AC*, 16th Cong., 1st sess., 1372–73; *Enquirer*, 10 Feb. 1821.

103. *NWR* 18 (5 Aug. 1820): 403–12; *NI*, 13 Jan. 1820 (quotation).

104. *Aurora*, 19 Dec. 1820. See also *Columbian*, 12 Dec. 1820.

105. *Western Herald*, reprinted in *Brookville Enquirer*, 13 Apr. 1820. See also *PADA*, 25 Feb. 1820.

106. *AC*, 16th Cong., 1st sess., 331.

107. Lewis, *American Union and the Problem of Neighborhood*, 135.

108. *AC*, 16th Cong., 1st sess., 219–20; *Southern Patriot*, quoted in *Columbian*, 29 Feb. 1820; [Rives and Fendall], *Letters and Other Writings of James Madison*, 3:142, 157.

109. *NI*, 7 Feb. 1821.

110. *Boston Daily Advertiser*, in *PADA*, 15 Apr. 1820. See also King, *Life and Correspondence*, 388.

111. For exceptions, see *AC*, 16th Cong., 1st sess., 995–96, 1231–32; *Enquirer*, 8 Jan. 1820, 13 Jan. 1820.

112. *Savannah Republican*, 6 Nov. 1820.

113. *Independent Chronicle*, 22 Mar. 1820. See also *Independent Chronicle*, 12 Apr. 1820; *AC*, 16th Cong., 1st sess., 942–47, 966–90; *NWR* 17 (26 Feb. 1820): 442; *NI*, 14 Sept. 1820; *Kentucky Reporter*, 15 Mar. 1820.

114. See *Charleston Courier*, 13 Dec. 1820; *AC*, 16th Cong., 1st sess., 1021.

115. See, e.g., *Brookville Enquirer*, 5 Dec. 1820; *PADA*, 29 Apr. 1820.

116. *Independent Chronicle*, 5 Feb. 1820. See also *AC*, 16th Cong., 1st sess., 187–95; *Enquirer*, 14 Dec. 1819.

117. *Kentucky Reporter*, 4 Jan. 1820. See also *Kentucky Reporter*, 12 May 1819; *AC*, 16th Cong., 1st sess., 129, 315, 394–401, 999–1004, 1072–73; Cunningham, *Circular Letters*, 3:1093.

118. *NWR* 16, suppl. (Aug. 1819): 177–79. See also Cunningham, *Circular Letters*, 3:1109–15, 1122; *PADA*, 14 Nov. 1820.

119. *Boston Patriot*, quoted in *NI*, 15 Jan. 1820.

120. *AC*, 16th Cong., 1st sess., 967. This speech as a whole is a handy anthology of the doughface creed, as well as a revival of arguments Holmes used against Federalists during the war; see 966–90.

121. *AC*, 15th Cong., 2d sess., 1227–35. This was actually uttered in the debate over restricting slavery in Arkansas, but McLane repeated this line of argument in the Missouri debates; see *AC*, 16th Cong., 1st sess., 1138–68. For other examples of antirestrictionists posing as opponents of slavery and defenders of the Union, see *NI*, 24 Dec. 1819, 14 Sept. 1820; *Independent Chronicle*, 15 Dec. 1819, 12 Jan. 1820, 26 Jan. 1820; *National Advocate*, 19 Feb. 1820, 23 Feb. 1820; *Columbian*, 20 Jan. 1820; *Centinel*, 25 Mar. 1820; *Brookville Enquirer*, 21 Nov. 1820; Cunningham, *Circular Letters*, 3:1101–4, 1109–15.

122. *PADA*, 11 Feb. 1820. See also *Independent Chronicle*, 8 Dec. 1819.

123. King, *Life and Correspondence*, 702; see also 286, 357.

124. *Brookville Enquirer*, 13 Apr. 1820; see also 23 May 1820, 21 Nov. 1820.

125. *Portland Gazette*, quoted in Richards, *Slave Power*, 88.

126. *PADA*, 30 Mar. 1820 (quotation). For just some of the many examples of attacks on doughfaces, see ibid., 8 Feb. 1820, 12 Feb. 1820, 14 Feb. 1820, 27 Feb. 1820, 6–7 Mar. 1820, 11 Mar. 1820, 21–22 Mar. 1820, 28 Mar. 1820, 10–11 Apr. 1820, 1 May 1820, 20 May 1820, 18 July 1820; Hillhouse, *Pocahontas*, 6–7, 10–12.

127. Of the eighteen doughfaces in the House in the 16th Congress, only five were reelected. For their travails, see *AC*, 16th Cong., 1st sess., 1113; *NWR* 19 (17 Feb. 1821): 415–16; Moore, *Missouri Controversy*, 170–217; Forbes, "Slavery and the Meaning of America," 250–56, 285–90.

128. See *Independent Chronicle*, 13 May 1820; *National Advocate*, 10 Feb. 1820; *PADA*, 14 Nov. 1820.

129. *AC*, 16th Cong., 1st sess., 345–59.

130. See Meriwether et al., *Papers of John C. Calhoun*, 5:413–14, 6:413–15; Capers, "Reconsideration," esp. 40–42. Robert E. Bonner has presented evidence of a continuing commitment, particularly in the Deep South, to a strong central government, despite the Missouri Crisis; see "Americans Apart," 35–40. For examples of the literature painting an overwhelming switch to state rights during and after Missouri, see Risjord, *Old Republicans*, 175–87, 213–23; Ammon, *James Monroe*, 463–64; Durden, *Self-Inflicted Wound*, 1–19; Vipperman, *William Lowndes*, 181–83, 193–97; Forbes, "Slavery and the Meaning of America," 359–82.

131. *Petersburg [Va.] Intelligencer*, quoted in *Aurora*, 16 Dec. 1820.

132. *Georgia Journal*, 19 Sept. 1820.

133. *PADA*, 14–18, 21, 23–24, 29 Feb. 1820. See Davis, *Challenging the Boundaries*, chap. 2, for a good discussion of prominent Americans who advocated loose interpretation of the Constitution and of the Bible in 1819, which "represented two prongs of a common modernizing culture" that alarmed slaveholders then and thereafter; quotation on 57.

134. Roane to James Barbour, 29 Dec. 1819, in "Missouri Compromise: Letters to James Barbour," 7.

135. *NWR* 17 (8 Jan. 1820): 311–14; 17 (22 Jan. 1820): 343.

136. See "Missouri Compromise: Letters to James Barbour," 6–7, 11–14, 16–17; Fehrenbacher, "Missouri Controversy," 19–20.

137. Shalhope, *John Taylor of Caroline*, 193–217. The book was *Construction Construed*. As William Cooper has put it, Missouri and surrounding events "turned a [state rights] minority into a majority"; *Liberty and Slavery*, 134.

138. *AC*, 16th Cong., 1st sess., 1265. It bears notice that some Northerners pushed state rights theory to its logical conclusions in support of restriction. One denied that holding slaves was "a right derived from the Constitution of the United States," for some states had outlawed it. If it was a national right, any American citizen could hold slaves "in any State of the Union." If slavery were a municipal concern only, Southerners could claim no constitutional right to carry their slaves to Missouri or elsewhere; see 146–48.

139. *Enquirer*, 10 Feb. 1820, quoted in Fehrenbacher, "Missouri Controversy," 19.

140. Quoted in Fehrenbacher, "Missouri Controversy," 10.

141. Charles Yancey to James Barbour, 16 Feb. 1820, in "Missouri Compromise: Letters to James Barbour," 14.

142. Linn Banks to James Barbour, 20 Feb. 1820, in ibid., 21.

143. *AC*, 16th Cong., 1st sess., 1070–84; quotations on 1076–77.

144. Ibid., 1567; see also 925–26. Northerners turned strict construction against the South in Missouri's second round. Niles, for instance, argued that Missouri's ban on free blacks violated "the *express letter* of the constitution"; *NWR* 19 (4 Nov. 1820): 146.

145. Adams, *Memoirs of John Quincy Adams*, 292; see also 308–9.

146. *AC*, 15th Cong., 2d sess., 1179–83; *AC*, 16th Cong., 1st sess., 957, 1035–42; Zeitz, "Missouri Compromise Reconsidered," 453–62.

147. See *NWR* 18 (8 July 1820): 337–38. Philadelphia's restrictionists met in the statehouse where the Declaration was signed—"appropriately," wrote one observer; see *Aurora*, 23 Nov. 1819.

148. Adams, *Memoirs of John Quincy Adams*, 5:6; see also 4:492–93.

149. *PADA*, 8 Nov. 1820.

150. Embree, *Emancipator*, 68. See also [Walsh], *Free Remarks*, 3–33.

151. *AC*, 16th Cong., 1st sess., 1004; emphasis added.

152. Ibid., 1071.

153. Ibid., 225.

154. Ibid., 301–3, 309, 618, 1383–85. They specifically excluded white women.

155. Hardin of Kentucky dismissed the force of constituents' expressed wishes, insisting that "our instructions come from higher authority"—the Constitution; see ibid., 1075. A Tennessee congressman rejoiced that his constituents had held no town meetings, for "the people there seem disposed first to hear what Congress has to say upon the subject." A representative from Massachusetts lectured him that it was "in vain . . . that gentlemen would confine the discussion of such a question as this to the hall of legislation. . . . Public opinion . . . is the real sovereignty of the people"; see ibid., 1457–58, 1466–67.

156. Moore, *Missouri Controversy*, 254–56; quotation on 256.

157. See *AC*, 16th Cong., 1st sess., 150, 155–56, 957, 1011–12, 1135, 1399–1402, 1427–28; *Centinel*, 1 Dec. 1819; *PADA*, 25 Feb. 1820, 30 Nov. 1820. For use of other Virginia

patriots' antislavery, see *PADA*, 14 Dec. 1819 (George Mason); 30 Dec. 1819 (Washington, Patrick Henry, and Jefferson); 29 Apr. 1820 (Henry). John Randolph's 1811 antiwar speech joined Jefferson's *Notes* in the catalog of harmful past candor when Theodore Dwight used it in responding to those who objected when Dwight raised the specter of slave rebellion; *New York Evening Post*, quoted in *Brookville Enquirer*, 23 Mar. 1820.

158. *Georgia Journal*, 1 Aug. 1820.

159. *AC*, 16th Cong., 1st sess., 228–29, 268–69, 332 (quotation).

160. Ibid., 133, 1010–12, 1032–33, 1086–89. One antirestrictionist even published his screed under the name "Wilberforce," insisting that his position was in the tradition of this reformer, who was "one of the benefactors of mankind"; see *Enquirer*, 6 Jan. 1820.

161. *Georgia Journal*, 18 July 1820, 15 Aug. 1820, 17 Oct. 1820 (quotation).

162. *Enquirer*, 2 June 1820, 1 Dec. 1820; Egerton, *Charles Fenton Mercer*, 165–68, 176–96.

163. *NI*, 25 Aug. 1819. See also *NI*, 29 July 1820; *AC*, 16th Cong., 1st sess., 1384.

164. Thomas B. Robertson to Calhoun, 24 Apr. 1820, in Meriwether et al., *Papers of John C. Calhoun*, 5:74; see also Schweninger, *Petitions to Southern Legislatures*, 62–63.

165. *Enquirer*, 14 Dec. 1819.

166. *AC*, 16th Cong., 2d sess., 543–53; quotation on 549.

167. Shalhope, "Thomas Jefferson's Republicanism," 552.

168. *AC*, 15th Cong., 2d sess., 1205; see also 16th Cong., 1st sess., 1023–24. Black residents of the District did witness the Missouri debates; see Moore, *Missouri Controversy*, 91.

169. *AC*, 16th Cong., 1st sess., 1018–20.

170. Ibid., 329–31; quotation on 330.

171. Taylor, *Construction Construed*, 299–303, 314; quotations on 301.

172. *AC*, 16th Cong., 1st sess., 1371.

173. Ibid., 1370–71. See also ibid., 329–31; *Charleston Courier*, 14 Aug. 1820.

174. Ironically enough, this exposed them to charges of inconsistency, for as they took up new positions that worked better for the Missouri debates, their opponents dug up their old positions and held up the contrast; see *PADA*, 15 Jan. 1820, 4 Mar. 1820.

175. Embree, *Emancipator*, x, 95–96. Moore also recognized the continuing variety of Southern thought; see Moore, *Missouri Controversy*, 346–49.

176. *Natchez Republican*, 11 Jan. 1820, quoted in *PADA*, 17 Feb. 1820. See also *PADA*, 18 Feb. 1820.

177. The *Charleston Courier* exemplified this phenomenon. It was like a ship without a compass in the turbulent seas of Missouri until February 1820, when its editor began reprinting the teachings of the *Richmond Enquirer* as gospel truth. The Charleston printer even quoted St. Peter, declaring that since "it is important that we should be able to give 'a reason for the faith that is in us,' whenever this important discussion may occur, we readily insert the article"; *Charleston Courier*, 15 July 1820; see also 23 Feb. 1820, 28 Feb. 1820, 14 Feb. 1821.

178. *AC*, 16th Cong., 1st sess., 1391. See also *Savannah Republican*, 11 July 1820, 6 Nov. 1820; *NWR* 19 (16 Dec. 1820): 241; *Enquirer*, 17 Apr. 1821. For some good secondary treatments of diffusionism, see McCoy, *Last of the Fathers*, 265–80; Papenfuse, *Evils of Necessity*, 65–67. Antirestrictionists in Missouri advocated diffusion when speaking to a national audience but not when debating among themselves; see Shoemaker, *Missouri's Struggle for Statehood*, 81–134.

179. *Centinel*, 8 Dec. 1819. See also *AC*, 16th Cong., 1st sess., 953; Otis, *Speech of Mr. Otis*, 20–22; *North American Review and Miscellaneous Journal* 10 (Jan. 1820): 160; *PADA*, 20 Dec. 1819. These rejections of diffusionism call into question Steven Deyle's assertion that Virginians thereby convinced most other Americans that the slave trade could be acceptable; see "Irony of Liberty," 46–48.

180. *AC*, 16th Cong., 1st sess., 1133.

181. Ibid., 1108; see also 286.

182. *NWR* 16 (14 Aug. 1819): 403.

183. *Columbian*, 24 Aug. 1820.

184. *PADA*, 29 Jan. 1820; see also 2 Mar. 1819, 5 Aug. 1820.

185. Adams, *Memoirs of John Quincy Adams*, 5:10. See also *AC*, 15th Cong., 2d sess., 1170–79; *AC*, 16th Cong., 1st sess., 207, 1246–47; [Walsh], *Free Remarks*, 75; *NWR* 17 (2 Oct. 1819): 71, 17 (8 Jan. 1820): 307; *Centinel*, 24 Nov. 1819; *Brookville Enquirer*, 6 Aug. 1819, 21 Nov. 1820; Embree, *Emancipator*, 2–8, 17–19, 112; Zeitz, "Missouri Compromise Reconsidered," 460–61. For secondary discussions, see Davis, *Problem of Slavery in the Age of Revolution*, 342; Fehrenbacher, "Missouri Controversy," 23; Fehrenbacher, *Dred Scott Case*, 111; Forbes, "Slavery and the Meaning of America," 267–70.

186. *AC*, 16th Cong., 1st sess., 333–35.

187. *Kentucky Reporter*, 12 Jan. 1820. See also *AC*, 16th Cong., 1st sess., 159–63; *AC*, 16th Cong., 2d sess., 1204–6; *Georgia Journal*, 9 Jan. 1820; *Enquirer*, 18 Jan. 1820, 8 Feb. 1820, 10 Feb. 1820; Hamilton, "Revolutionary Principles and Family Loyalties," esp. 554.

188. *AC*, 16th Cong., 1st sess., 1244.

189. John Randolph to Dr. John Brockenbrough, 24 Feb. 1820, quoted in Risjord, *Old Republicans*, 215–16. See also Forbes, "Slavery and the Meaning of America," 275–79.

190. *Enquirer*, 1 Jan. 1820; see also 8 Jan. 1820. "An American" was Monroe's son-in-law, George Hay, and Monroe helped him gather material for these essays. Although Hay may have exceeded Monroe's views on slavery, they were both unalterably opposed to restriction; see Ammon, *James Monroe*, 451, 654n5.

191. *AC*, 16th Cong., 2d sess., 259–75; quotations on 267. Smith did implicitly condemn the Atlantic slave trade, however, by seeking to saddle the North and Britain with its guilt. For a good discussion of the importance and accuracy of this part of his speech, see McMillin, *Final Victims*, chap. 4.

192. *AC*, 16th Cong., 2d sess., 226–28, 232, 1135–38, 1324–25. Macon had traveled some distance since 1797, when he declared slavery to be a "curse"; see Price, "Nathaniel Macon, Planter," 202. Such evidence refutes Larry E. Tise's assertion that "the Missouri controversy of 1819–1820 did not elicit a single proslavery response" from the South, which perceived no danger from the North until ten years later; see Tise, *Proslavery*, 57–74; quotation on 57. His evidence that positive good hardly swept the South uniformly in the 1820s is good, but otherwise this argument is unfathomable—unless Tise defines proslavery too narrowly for the Missouri debates, just as he defines it too broadly elsewhere in his book.

193. *AC*, 16th Cong., 1st sess., 279; see also 341–42, 1379. Jeffrey Robert Young has convincingly argued that a paternalistic, unambiguously positive view of chattel bondage had already emerged within the Lower South, but Missouri moved it into national politics; see *Domesticating Slavery*, 162–67, 191–92.

194. *PADA*, 2 Feb. 1820.

195. See Embree, *Emancipator*, 20; *Columbian*, 6 Jan. 1820; *Brookville Enquirer*, 30 Mar. 1820; *Centinel*, 14 Apr. 1821; Adams, *Memoirs of John Quincy Adams*, 4:524–25, 528–29.

196. *AC*, 16th Cong., 1st sess., 338, 344.

197. Ibid., 1425–26.

198. As quoted by William Smith in ibid., 380–81. "So far as I know," David Brion Davis has written, "up to that time no statesman or political leader in the world had publicly made such a radical declaration of slavery's illegality"; Davis, *Challenging the Boundaries*, 42. No wonder this Federalist backed away from this speech.

199. King, *Substance of Two Speeches*, 3. See also King, *Life and Correspondence*, 233–34, 235–37, 276–78, 324–26.

200. See also *AC*, 15th Cong., 2d sess., 1192–93; 16th Cong., 1st sess., 1395–1401. As George Dangerfield put it, there "were antislavery men in" the 16th Congress but "no abolitionists," which blunted the North's competitive edge; see *Era of Good Feelings*, 226–28; quotations on 226.

201. *AC*, 16th Cong., 1st sess., 999; see also 1088–89.

202. Ibid., 402–14.

203. *National Advocate*, 18 Nov. 1819.

204. *Columbian*, 16 Dec. 1820. Two weeks earlier, this paper's editor had vigorously contested a doughface's charge that New York itself was still a slave state; see 1 Dec. 1820. The court's ruling was widely reported; see, e.g., *PADA*, 19 Dec. 1820; *Ohio Repository*, 11 Jan. 1821.

205. *Reports of the Proceedings and Debates of the Convention of 1821*, 167.

206. *PADA*, 13 Dec. 1820.

207. *PADA*, 2 Mar. 1820; see also 25 Jan. 1820.

208. For the tortuous progress of this bill, see the index references for it in the *Journal of the Senate of the Commonwealth of Pennsylvania*, vols. 28–30 (Harrisburg, 1817–1820), and *Journal of the . . . House of Representatives of the Commonwealth of Pennsylvania*, vols. 28–30 (Harrisburg, 1817–1820); all in Jenkins, *Records of the States*. See also Turner, *Negro in Pennsylvania*, 115–18.

209. *Pennsylvania Gazette*, quoted in *Aurora*, 26 June 1820; see also 11 July 1820. New York's factions also accused one another of being either advocates of or actual participants in slavery; see *National Advocate*, 22 Apr. 1820, 6 Sept. 1820, 7 Oct. 1820, 27 Dec. 1820.

210. *AC*, 16th Cong., 2d sess., 986–89; quotation on 988. See also ibid., 45–50, 109; Adams, *Memoirs of John Quincy Adams*, 5:210.

211. *AC*, 16th Cong., 1st sess., 217.

212. Ibid., 2d sess., 625–26.

213. Ibid., 556. See also ibid., 51–77, 543–53; *Charleston Courier*, 29 Dec. 1820.

214. *AC*, 16th Cong., 2d sess., 596–99, 630–33, 637 (quotation). See also *Centinel*, 29 Nov. 1820.

215. *Reports of the Proceedings and Debates of the Convention of 1821*, 180–81; for similar arguments, see 191, 198–99.

216. *National Advocate*, 21 Apr. 1819; see also 23 Apr. 1819, 21 Apr. 1820.

217. *Columbian*, 20 Apr. 1820. Clinton won reelection in both 1819 and 1820. Racial egalitarians also spoke up in the Northwest; see *PADA*, 4 Jan. 1820.

218. *Reports of the Proceedings and Debates of the Convention of 1821*, 184 (quotations), 186–89.

219. *NWR* 19 (9–16 Sept. 1820): 26–36; *NWR* 19 (17 Feb. 1821): 415; *NWR* 20 (30 June 1821): 278; Adams, *New England in the Republic*, 59.

220. *NWR* 17 (27 Nov. 1819): 201–2.

221. *AC*, 16th Cong., 1st sess., 390. John Ashworth rightly described the Missouri debates as important because they "clarified many issues which had hitherto remained obscure" and foreshadowed later debates; see *Commerce and Compromise*, 56–58, 61–68; quotation on 56.

CHAPTER NINE

1. See, e.g., *PADA*, 11, 14, 23 Mar. 1820.

2. Meriwether et al., *Papers of John C. Calhoun*, 6:329.

3. *PADA*, 16 Oct. 1820; see also 20–21 Oct. 1820.

4. Brown, *Missouri Compromises and Presidential Politics*, 47–50, 55, 58–59, 65, 117–21, 133; quotation on 65. See also Ratcliffe, *Politics of Long Division*, 54–63, 80–97, 138–59.

5. For good discussions of this, see Ashworth, *Commerce and Compromise*, 333–36; Miller, *Arguing about Slavery*, chap. 10, 12; and esp. Grimsted, *American Mobbing*.

6. Brown, "Missouri Crisis"; quotations on 69–70.

7. Adams, *Memoirs of John Quincy Adams*, 11:72–73n.

8. Miller, *Arguing about Slavery*, 438–39.

9. Ibid., 441. See also Adams, *Memoirs of John Quincy Adams*, 11:84.

10. *Newburyport Herald*, 20, 27 Feb., 2–23 Mar., 6–9 Apr., 28 May 1824; Garrison, *Letters*, 1:39–42; Sheidley, *Sectional Nationalism*, 72–85, 148–68.

11. Haynes, "An Ally in the Centre of the American Line," 7–14; Hinks, *To Awaken My Afflicted Brethren*, 237–38, quotation on 237.

12. Ashworth, *Commerce and Compromise*, 341–42; quotations on 341. See also Earle, "Marcus Morton," 68–69; Banner, *To the Hartford Convention*, 109n.

13. Quoted in Ratcliffe, *Politics of Long Division*, 278; see also 277–310.

14. For a good portrait of an antislavery Northerner struggling with his Whig loyalties, see Stewart, *Joshua R. Giddings*, chap. 3–8. For a general treatment, see Foner, *Free Soil*, chap. 5–6.

15. Foner, *Free Soil*, 101, 308–9; quotation on 101.

16. Richards, *Gentlemen of Property and Standing*, 160–65; quotations on 164.

17. The literature on this is enormous; for good examples, which this paragraph has followed, see Nye, *Fettered Freedom*, esp. 32–176, 217–51; Stewart, *Holy Warriors*, 75–120; Freehling, *Road to Disunion*; Grimsted, *American Mobbing*.

18. Sheidley, *Sectional Nationalism*, 70–71.

19. Quincy, *Address . . . Power of the Slave States*, 2–20, 29; quotations on 2, 5, 12.

20. Adams, *Memoirs of John Quincy Adams*, 11:29. See also ibid., 11:65, 86, 381; Quincy, *Address . . . Power of the Slave States*, 5–6, 13–32; Richards, *Slave Power*.

21. Adams, *Memoirs of John Quincy Adams*, 11:65.

22. Ibid., 11:103, 336 (first quotation), 381, 408 (second quotation).

23. Richards, *Life and Times*, 10–15, 31–32.

24. Adams, *Memoirs of John Quincy Adams*, 11:116 (quotation), 159, 382–84.

25. For the history of these resolves, see ibid., 11:455, 457–58, 462, 464, 472–73 (quota-

tion), 481–82, 498–99, 511–13, 527; *Congressional Globe*, 28th Cong., 1st sess., 62–66, 179–80, 244.

26. *Congressional Globe*, 28th Cong., 1st sess., 62.
27. Quoted in Stewart, *Joshua R. Giddings*, 91.
28. *Congressional Globe*, 28th Cong., 1st sess., 64–66.
29. Ibid., 62–64; quotation on 62.
30. Ibid., 244.
31. Ames, *Proposed Amendments*, 46–49; quotations on 47, 48n1.
32. Ames, *State Documents on Federal Relations*, 239–40.
33. For other antebellum defenders of slave representation, see [Holland], *Refutation of the Calumnies*, 8–10, 36–40; *Proslavery Argument: As Maintained by the Most Distinguished Writers*, 112–13, 168–69.
34. Wallenstein, "Slavery, Race, and Representation," 1–9; quotation on 8.
35. The 1827 Georgia legislature recognized the Federalists' place in the history of anti-slavery and sectional politics; see Ames, *State Documents on Federal Relations*, 212. So have certain modern historians, who have pointed to echoes between the Federalists and the antebellum Republicans; see, e.g., Nagel, *One Nation Indivisible*, 235–46; Banner, *To the Hartford Convention*, 108–9. For examples of those who have downplayed Federalist antislavery and its impact on sectional politics, see Foner, *Politics and Ideology*, 22–23, 37–40; Buel, *America on the Brink*, 243.
36. Starobin, *Blacks in Bondage*, 150–53 (quotations); Walter L. Arnstein, "Queen Victoria and the United States," in Leventhal and Quinault, *Anglo-American Attitudes*, 95–96.
37. Quoted in Arnstein, "Queen Victoria and the United States," 97.
38. McPherson, *Crossroads of Freedom*, 143–45.
39. For New England and the North, see Dickens, *American Notes*, 75–159, 289, 306. For slavery as the cause of North-South distinction, see 180. The chapter on slavery is chap. 17.
40. Ibid., 128, 151, 181, 270 (quotation).
41. Dickens, *Martin Chuzzlewit*, chap. 16–17, 21–23, 33–34, esp. 194, 242 (quotation), 244, 260, 312, 330–31, 476, 481, 600, 755.
42. Ibid., 338 (quotations), 341, 491, 500. See also Dickens, *American Notes*, 309. His professions of friendship begin with the very dedication of the latter book; see ibid., 45.
43. Dickens, *American Notes*, 329.
44. Stewart, "Boston, Abolition, and the Atlantic World," 101–25, esp. 115–17.
45. For the Turner rumors, see Oates, *Fires of Jubilee*, 82–83. For Southern Anglophobia, see Greenberg, *Masters and Statesmen*, 111–23; Davis, *Challenging the Boundaries*, 78–91.
46. Richards, *Gentlemen of Property and Standing*, 62–71; quotation on 66.
47. [Paulding], *Sketch of Old England*, 1:227–33; see also 2:233, 244.
48. Paulding, *Slavery in the United States*, 109–39.
49. Adams, *Memoirs of John Quincy Adams*, 6:37.
50. See ibid., 3:96–98, 3:556–59, 4:353–55, 5:181–84, 5:189–93, 5:214–19, 5:225–26; Soulsby, *Right of Search*, 13–27; Perkins, *Castlereagh and Adams*, 275–77; *AC*, 15th Cong., 1st sess., 73–75.
51. *Reports of the Proceedings and Debates of the Convention of 1821*, 374–76.
52. Ratcliffe, "Captain James Riley," 90–91.
53. Hinks, *David Walker's Appeal*, 43; see also L, 51, 53, 58, 121–22.

54. Whittier, *Complete Poetical Works*, 266–68, 298, 303, 309; Cain, *William Lloyd Garrison and the Fight against Slavery*, 80, 82, 112–15, 117–18; Lowance, *House Divided*, 102, 215.

55. See Foner, *Free Soil*, 72.

56. Eaton, *Growth of Southern Civilization*, 1–3, 323–24; quotation on 323. See also Scarborough, *Masters of the Big House*, for planters' cosmopolitanism and Anglophilia.

57. Dickens, *American Notes*, 315–18; quotations on 318, 315.

58. See Forbes, "Slavery and the Meaning of America," 342, 599–602; *Proslavery Argument: As Maintained by the Most Distinguished Writers*, 129–40, 145–46. Rugemer, "Southern Response to British Abolitionism," overemphasizes the novelty of what were often not new arguments but does make a suggestive case for the way British abolitionism shaped the proslavery response.

59. Fitzhugh, *Cannibals All!*, 158.

60. Hamer, "Great Britain"; quotations on 9, 7, 11, 26.

61. Fox, "Negro Vote in Old New York"; Gellman and Quigley, *Jim Crow New York*. See also Dangerfield, *Awakening of American Nationalism*, 114–15, 130–32; Harris, *In the Shadow of Slavery*, chap. 5.

62. See esp. Rael, *Black Identity and Black Protest*, 44, 72–81, 118–208; Rael, "Instruments in the Hands of God"; Harris, *In the Shadow of Slavery*, chap. 5; White, *Stories of Freedom*, esp. 5–6, 66.

63. For the influence of earlier black writings, see Newman et al., *Pamphlets of Protest*, 1–2, 8, 66; Hinks, *To Awaken My Afflicted Brethren*, 14–62, chap. 3, 6. For free blacks' influence on white abolitionists, see Newman, *Transformation of American Abolitionism*, esp. chap. 4–5.

64. See, e.g., Schweninger, *Petitions to Southern Legislatures*, 76–83; Berlin et al., *Slaves No More*, 203, 206–7. See also Ira Berlin's striking characterization of Northern free black communities as maroon communities, in *Generations of Captivity*, 230–44.

65. Gilje, *Road to Mobocracy*, 151–70; White and White, *Stylin'*, chap. 4; Hodges, *Root and Branch*, 197–98, 205–13.

66. Hodges, *Root and Branch*, 216. See also Richards, *Gentlemen of Property and Standing*, chap. 2; Melish, *Disowning Slavery*.

67. Ratcliffe, *Politics of Long Division*, 53 (Ratcliffe's words).

68. Winch, *Gentleman of Color*, 182; Blight, *Frederick Douglass' Civil War*, 168–69, 187–88.

69. Starobin, *Blacks in Bondage*, 169.

70. Fehrenbacher, *Slaveholding Republic*, 265–66.

71. Egerton, *He Shall Go Out Free*, 44, 98–100, 109–25, 130–31; quotation on 131. See also Pearson, *Designs against Charleston*, 77–103, 119–22.

72. Egerton, *He Shall Go Out Free*, 224–25; Oates, *Fires of Jubilee*, 133–34.

73. *New York Daily Advertiser*, 31 July 1822, in Pearson, *Designs against Charleston*, 340. See also Egerton, *He Shall Go Out Free*, 224–25; *Newburyport Herald*, 12 July 1822, 6, 9, 13 Aug. 1822, 28 Oct. 1823. For a Southern response to these responses to Vesey, see [Holland], *Refutation of the Calumnies*, 10–14, 75–82.

74. Dillon, *Slavery Attacked*, 162–66; quotation on 165.

75. Whittier, *Complete Poetical Works*, 288.

76. Thoreau, *Civil Disobedience*, 40–48.

77. Furman, *Exposition of the Views of the Baptists*; Freehling, *Drift towards Dissolution*; Egerton, *He Shall Go Out Free*, 203–21; Pearson, *Designs against Charleston*, 147–62.

78. Miller, *Arguing about Slavery*, 36–39, 60–62, 117, 221–22, 251; quotations on 37, 39.

79. Hammond, *Selections from the Letters and Speeches*, 31–32, 35–37; [Drayton], *South Vindicated*, 295–309; *Proslavery Argument: As Maintained by the Most Distinguished Writers*, 74–82, 112, 127, 201–7, 220–21, 223–24, 457–60, 462–82. Antislavery men were especially fond of John Randolph's 1811 antiwar speech; see Miller, *Arguing about Slavery*, 136; Quincy, *Address . . . Power of the Slave States*, 26.

80. *Proslavery Argument: As Maintained by the Most Distinguished Writers*, 133.

81. Quoted in Aptheker, *American Negro Slave Revolts*, 105.

82. Some of the most useful treatments among the vast literature on this include Morris, *Free Men All*; Finkelman, *Imperfect Union*; Oakes, "Political Significance of Slave Resistance"; Grimsted, *American Mobbing*.

83. Fehrenbacher, *Dred Scott Case*, 114–17.

84. Miller, *Arguing about Slavery*, 210–12, 278, chap. 24.

85. Ames, *State Documents on Federal Relations*, 225.

86. Scarborough, *Masters of the Big House*, 417; Dunning, "Manifest Destiny," esp. 113–15.

87. See Crocker, "Missouri Compromise"; and esp. May, *Southern Dream*. Compare their descriptions of the South as a bloc with William W. Freehling's emphasis on the diversity of Southern voices even on expansionism; *Reintegration of American History*, chap. 8.

88. Quoted in Miller, *Arguing about Slavery*, 468.

89. This is another point on which the literature is huge; Grimsted offers a good discussion in *American Mobbing*.

90. Epperson, "Lee's Slave-Makers," esp. 48.

91. Jacobs, *Incidents in the Life of a Slave Girl*, 176.

92. Ratcliffe, "Captain James Riley," 88; see also 93.

93. Bagby, "Randolph Slave Saga," esp. chap. 8–9.

94. Etcheson, *Emerging Midwest*, 100–101.

95. Schwalm, "Overrun with Free Negroes." See also Berlin et al., *Slaves No More*, 127–28, in which the authors describe both "Negrophobic hysteria" in 1862 and a more welcoming attitude in fall 1863.

96. Ames, *State Documents on Federal Relations*, 203–4; quotation on 204. See also Ratcliffe, "Captain James Riley," 88–90.

97. Davis, "Emergence of Immediatism," esp. 226–27; quotation on 226.

98. Cain, *William Lloyd Garrison and the Fight against Slavery*, 93.

99. Ibid., 84–89, 114, 142.

100. See Mason, "Attacking the 'Covenant with Death.' "

101. Dillon, *Elijah P. Lovejoy*, 2–4. Lovejoy's brother Owen, another of many Lovejoy abolitionists, named a son Elijah Parish; Garrison, *Letters*, 5:341.

102. Abzug, *Passionate Liberator*, 7, 16–27. For Theodore Dwight's abolitionism and influence, see Locke, *Anti-Slavery in America*, 126; Stout and Minkema, "Edwardsean Tradition," 14, 16–17; Hinks, "It Is at the Extremest Risque."

103. Mason, "Attacking the 'Covenant with Death.' "

104. Fox, "Negro Vote in Old New York," 257, 260 (first quotation), 270 (second quotation).

105. Quoted in Cain, *William Lloyd Garrison and the Fight against Slavery*, 114. For more samples of this "covenant" rhetoric, see 165–66, 174. Garrison encountered this rhetoric in the back files of the *Newburyport Herald*; see *Newburyport Herald*, 18 Feb.

1814; emphasis added. Allen was quoting the *Courant*, 15 Feb. 1814, cited and discussed in chap. 2 herein. Thus Fehrenbacher erred when he stated that "it was Garrison . . ., of course, who coined the phrase, 'a covenant with death, and an agreement with hell.'" Fehrenbacher, *Slaveholding Republic*, 39. Based on the fact that I could not find this phrase applied to the Constitution by Northern Antifederalists, it appears that that distinction belongs to the Federalists.

106. See Lowance, *House Divided*, 223, 230–31, 340, 345–46, 438–49.

107. Cain, *William Lloyd Garrison and the Fight against Slavery*, 143.

108. Stewart, *Holy Warriors*, 132. For more suggestive evidence of Federalism's good reputation among antislavery proponents, see Lowance, *House Divided*, 194.

109. The literature on this is also vast. For a good synthetic discussion, see Stewart, *Holy Warriors*, 75–120. For Garrison's ambivalence about politics, see Stewart, *William Lloyd Garrison*, 146–51, 159–74.

110. Nye, *Fettered Freedom*, 32–176, 217–51; quotations on 54, 114.

111. Whittier, *Complete Poetical Works*, 271–72; see also 273–76, 282, 286–88, 291–94, 304, 308, 314–16, 322–23, 326.

112. See Cain, *William Lloyd Garrison and the Fight against Slavery*, 18–19, 36, 80–83, 153–55. See also Mason, "Attacking the 'Covenant of Death,'" for these points more generally.

113. Christie and Dumond, *George Bourne*, esp. 27, 66–98. For Garrison's use of these terms, see Cain, *William Lloyd Garrison and the Fight against Slavery*, 88–89, 92.

114. Rowan, *Tribute to the Memory of Alexander McLeod*, 9–10.

115. Whittier, *Complete Poetical Works*, xi, 276, 280, 282, 329.

116. Stewart, *William Lloyd Garrison*, 23–39; see also 45–51. Evangelical and Quaker influences also brought Sarah and Angelina Grimke to antislavery; see Perry, *Lift Up Thy Voice*, 38–40, 52–54, 61, 77.

117. Hinks, *David Walker's Appeal*, 47ff, 123.

118. Cain, *William Lloyd Garrison and the Fight against Slavery*, 79. See also Deyle, "Domestic Slave Trade in America." Walter Johnson has downplayed the slave trade's role in antebellum abolitionism. But his discussion rests on a seemingly arbitrary designation of Weld's *American Slavery As It Is*—which emphasizes physical brutality over the slave trade—as "the central document of early abolitionism." Besides the issue of centrality, its 1839 publication date was not even "early" in antebellum abolitionism—indeed, this was eight years after Garrison put an auction block on his paper's masthead, which Johnson himself later mentions! See Johnson, *Soul by Soul*, 217–19; quotation on 217.

119. Cain, *William Lloyd Garrison and the Fight against Slavery*, 146–47.

120. Quincy, *Address . . . Power of the Slave States*, 24–25; Garrison, *Letters*, 1:112; Cain, *William Lloyd Garrison and the Fight against Slavery*, 158–59; Lowance, *House Divided*, 372, 472; Hinks, *David Walker's Appeal*, 77–79; Miller, *Arguing about Slavery*, 111, 441–43.

121. Oates, *Fires of Jubilee*, 130.

122. *Proslavery Argument: As Maintained by the Most Distinguished Writers*, 5–14, quotations on 6, 8; see also 109–10, 250–60, 455–61. See also [Drayton], *South Vindicated*, 83–84.

123. Carey, *Some Thoughts*, 6–31; quotation on 12.

124. Levine, *Half Slave and Half Free*, 138.

125. *Proslavery Argument: As Maintained by the Most Distinguished Writers*, 1–5, 15–27, 28–61, 88; quotations on 88, 15.

126. Takaki, *Pro-Slavery Crusade*, quotations on 4. See also Thornton, *Politics and Power*, 375–76; Faust, *Creation of Confederate Nationalism*, 74–75.

127. For a sampling of this attention to proslavery extremists, see Jenkins, *Pro-Slavery Thought*; Genovese, *The World the Slaveholders Made*; Faust, *Ideology of Slavery*; Tise, *Proslavery*.

128. Perhaps no one among the writers on the "many Souths" has made these points better than the Freehlings. See Allison Goodyear Freehling, *Drift towards Dissolution*, for Virginia; and for the South as a whole, William W. Freehling, *Road to Disunion* and *South vs. the South*.

129. Takaki, *Pro-Slavery Crusade*, esp. 1–8, 231–43; quotation on 6.

130. See Tallant, *Evil Necessity*; Freehling, *Drift towards Dissolution*; Freehling, *Road to Disunion*; Link, *Roots of Secession*, esp. 11–27; Iaccarino, "Virginia and the National Contest over Slavery," chap. 5; Bagby, "Randolph Slave Saga," 1–103; Ammon, *James Monroe*, 565.

131. Ames, *State Documents on Federal Relations*, 206.

132. Masur, *1831*, 40–41.

133. Freehling, *Prelude to Civil War*.

134. [Holland], *Refutation of the Calumnies*, 7–8, 14–22, 40–86; quotations on 49, 7.

135. [Dalcho], *Practical Considerations*, 6–21; quotation on 6.

136. Furman, *Exposition of the Views of the Baptists*, 7–15, esp. 11–13.

137. Rugemer, "Southern Response to British Abolitionism," 237–38.

138. [Drayton], *South Vindicated*, 19–79, 81, 88–122; quotations on 31, 100, 38.

139. Carey, *Some Thoughts*, esp. 6–31. Carey, *Slavery in Maryland*, 7–51; quotation on 33.

140. Winch, *Gentleman of Color*, 239–41, 244; quotation on 239.

141. Lowance, *House Divided*, 409 (quotation), 483; see also Cain, *William Lloyd Garrison and the Fight against Slavery*, 14, 104, 110–11, 161. Steven Hahn has argued that many late antebellum slaveholders "believed that the winds of history might now be blowing in their direction even if it required rebelling against . . . the national government and risking civil war." Only the slaves "sensed the prospects of emancipation" in this increasingly conservative world; *Nation under Our Feet*, 62–64; quotations on 64. But this makes little sense: why take such a risk if history was on your side anyway? Slaveholders hardly read the signs—especially the rise of the Republican Party—as consolingly conservative, at least by the late 1850s.

142. John Patrick Daly has written convincingly that few evangelicals, who led the proslavery ranks, left the mainstream of Western thought by defending slavery in the abstract; see *When Slavery Was Called Freedom*, esp. chap. 2.

Interestingly enough, at least some modern neo-Confederates, fringe as they are, do the 1810s-style back-step, apparently for similar reasons. In *The South Was Right!* (2d ed., Gretna, La.: Pelican Publishing, 1994), James Ronald Kennedy and Walter Donald Kennedy paint a glowing picture of Southern slavery. They argue that it was a system "in which many blacks were free from want and violence," unlike today's inner cities. Moreover, "today more families are broken in one year in the black community than were ever separated by white masters during the slavery era." "Now," they backtrack, "if the foregoing sounds as if we are advocating the return of the system of African servitude, let us restate emphatically that this is not what we are suggesting. . . . If indeed the black people were better off in some respects under the system of slavery, that does not justify or warrant its return." Just as illogical as backtrackers two centuries earlier, these men obviously realize that slavery is in even more disrepute now than then. See <http://www.okaloosanaacp.com/confederate—heritage—month.htm>, pp. 89–90.

143. Dickens, *American Notes*, 269–71, 321.

144. Hammond, *Speech*, 18.

145. *Proslavery Argument: As Maintained by the Most Distinguished Writers*, 100 (quotation), 103–11.

146. Kirk, *John Randolph of Roanoke*, 16, 24, 85–121, 421–22, 428, 469 (quotation).

147. Nathaniel Macon to Bartlett Yancey, 26 Dec. 1824, 8 Dec. 1825, in Wilson, *Congressional Career*, 72 (quotations), 76–78.

148. The states were Georgia, South Carolina, Mississippi, Louisiana, Alabama, and Missouri; see Ames, *State Documents on Federal Relations*, 203–9, quotations on 208–9.

149. Freehling, *Prelude to Civil War*, chap. 4; Ames, *State Documents on Federal Relations*, 133–51.

150. Points made well by Sydnor, *Development of Southern Sectionalism*, 177–202, 222. For more on Calhoun's and others' slow conversion, see Capers, "Reconsideration"; Dangerfield, *Awakening of American Nationalism*, 205–6, 218.

151. In practice, as Fehrenbacher has recently pointed out so well, it was often different. Whether using the federal government to track down fugitive slaves or calling for a federal slave code for the territories, Southern politicians rarely hesitated to apply central power to *upholding* slavery, especially as the sectional crisis advanced in the 1850s. See Fehrenbacher, *Slaveholding Republic*.

Bibliography

MANUSCRIPT SOURCES

Richard W. Byrd, "Letter of Richard W. Byrd to Governor John Tyler Giving Details of Peter's Insurrection Plans for Rebellion, May 30, 1810." Broadsides, Rare Books and Special Collections, Library of Congress, Washington, D.C.

Sir Alexander Cochrane Papers, Manuscript Division, Library of Congress, Washington, D.C.

Sir George Cockburn Papers, Manuscript Division, Library of Congress, Washington, D.C.

John Randolph–Josiah Quincy Letters, John Randolph Collection, Manuscript Division, Library of Congress, Washington, D.C.

Senate Documents 4820, Massachusetts Archives, Boston

NEWSPAPERS AND CONTEMPORARY JOURNALS

American and Commercial Daily Advertiser (Baltimore)

Aurora (Philadelphia)

Balance (Hudson, N.Y.)

Baltimore Patriot and Mercantile Advertiser

Blackwood's Edinburgh Magazine

Brookville [Ind.] Enquirer

Charleston Courier

Columbian (New York)

Columbian Centinel (Boston)

Connecticut Courant (Hartford)

Courier (London)

Detroit Gazette

Edinburgh Review

Elihu Embree, *Emancipator* (Jonesborough, Tenn., 1820. Reprint, Nashville: B. H. Murphy, 1932)

Enquirer (Richmond) / *Richmond Enquirer*

Frederick-Town [Md.] Herald

Georgia Journal (Milledgeville)

Illinois Intelligencer (Kaskaskia)

Independent Chronicle (Boston)

Independent Chronicle and Boston Patriot

Investigator (Charleston)

Kentucky Reporter (Lexington)

Louisiana Gazette (New Orleans)

Morning Chronicle (London)

National Advocate (New York)

National Intelligencer (Washington, D.C.)

Newburyport [Mass.] Herald

New-York Evening Post

Niles' Weekly Register (Baltimore)

North American Review and Miscellaneous Journal (Boston)

Ohio Repository (Canton, Ohio)

Phenix (Providence, R.I.)

Poulson's American Daily Advertiser (Philadelphia)

Quarterly Review (London)

Reporter (Lexington, Ky.)

Republican and Savannah Evening Ledger

Savannah Republican

Southern Patriot and Commercial Advertiser
(Charleston, S.C.)
The Weekly Register (Baltimore)

Western American (Williamsburgh, Ohio)
Western Intelligencer (Kaskaskia, Ill.)

LEGISLATIVE RECORDS

Annals of the Congress of the United States. 9th Cong., 1st sess.–17th Cong., 2d sess. Washington, D.C.: Gales and Seaton, 1852–55.
Congressional Globe. Washington, D.C.: Blair and Rives, 1834–73.
Journal of the Assembly of the State of New-York: At Their Fortieth Session. Albany: J. Buel, 1816.
Journal of the Senate of the State of New-York: At Their Fortieth Session. Albany: J. Buel, 1816.
The Parliamentary Debates. 1st ser., vol. 22–2d ser., vol. 16. London: T. C. Hansard, 1812–27. Reprint, Kraus Reprint Co., 1970.
Reports of the Proceedings and Debates of the Convention of 1821, Assembled for the Purpose of Amending the Constitution of the State of New-York. Albany: E. and E. Hosford, 1821. Reprint, New York: Da Capo Press, 1970.
Votes and Proceedings of the House of Delegates of the State of Maryland, December Session, 1817. Annapolis: Jonas Green, 1818.

PAMPHLETS AND CONTROVERSIAL LITERATURE

An Address from the Pennsylvania Society for Promoting the Abolition of Slavery, for the Relief of Free Negroes Unlawfully Held in Bondage and for Improving the Condition of the African Race; on the Origin, Purposes, and Utility of Their Institution. Philadelphia: Hall and Atkinson, 1819.
The American Convention for Promoting the Abolition of Slavery and Improving the Condition of the African Race: Minutes, Constitution, Addresses, Memorials, Resolutions, Reports, Committees and Anti-Slavery Tracts. 3 vols. New York: Bergman Publishers, 1969.
Barrow, David. *Involuntary, Unmerited, Perpetual, Absolute, Hereditary Slavery, Examined; On the Principles of Nature, Reason, Justice, Policy and Scripture.* Lexington, Ky.: D. and C. Bradford, 1808.
"Benevolus, Hector." *The Hartford Convention in an Uproar! And the Wise Men of the East Confounded! Together with a Short History of the Peter Washingtonians, Being the First Book of the Chronicles of the Children of Disobedience; Otherwise Falsely Called "Washington Benevolents."* Windsor, Vt.: Josiah Stone, 1815.
[Botsford, Edmund]. *Sambo and Toney: A Dialogue between two Africans in South Carolina.* Baltimore: John Kingston, 1811.
Branagan, Thomas. *Serious Remonstrances, Addressed to the Citizens of the Northern States, and Their Representatives, . . . on the Recent Revival of the Slave Trade in the American Republic.* Philadelphia: Thomas T. Stiles, 1805.
Brewster, Jarvis. *An Exposition of the Treatment of Slaves in the Southern States, Particularly in the States of Maryland, Virginia, North Carolina, South Carolina and Georgia.* New Brunswick, N.J.: D. and J. FitzRandolph, 1815.
Carey, John L. *Some Thoughts Concerning Domestic Slavery.* 1838. 2d ed. Baltimore: D. Brunner, 1839.
——. *Slavery in Maryland Briefly Considered.* Baltimore: John Murphy, 1845.
[Carey, Matthew]. *A Calm Address to the People of the Eastern States on the Subject of the Repre-*

sentation of Slaves; the Representation in the Senate; and the Hostility to Commerce Ascribed to the Southern States. By the Author of the Olive Branch. Boston: Rowe and Hooper, 1814.

——. *The Olive Branch; or, Faults on Both Sides, Federal and Democratic. A Serious Appeal on the Necessity of Mutual Forgiveness and Harmony.* 10th ed. Philadelphia: M. Carey and Son, 1818. Reprint, Freeport, N.Y.: Books for Libraries Press, 1969.

Coker, Daniel. *Dialogue between a Virginian and an African Minister.* Baltimore: Benjamin Edes, 1810.

[Dalcho, Frederick]. *Practical Considerations Founded on the Scriptures, Relative to the Slave Population of South Carolina.* Charleston: A. E. Miller, 1823.

[Drayton, William]. *The South Vindicated from the Treason and Fanaticism of the Northern Abolitionists.* Philadelphia: H. Manly, 1836. Reprint, New York: Negro Universities Press, 1969.

Dupre, Lewis. *An Admonitory Picture, and a Solemn Warning Principally Addressed to Professing Christians in the Southern States of North America. Being an Introduction and Pressing Invitation to the Establishment of a System of Progressive Emancipation.* Charleston, 1810.

——. *A Rational and Benevolent Plan for Averting Some of the Calamitous Consequences of Slavery, Being a Practicable, Seasonable, and Profitable Institution for the Progressive Emancipation of Virginia and Carolina Slaves.* 1810.

[Dwight, Sereno Edwards]. *Slave Representation, by Boreas. Awake! O Spirit of the North.* New Haven, 1812.

Dwight, Timothy. *Remarks on the Review of Inchiquin's Letters.* Boston: Samuel Armstrong, 1815. Reprint, New York: Garrett Press, 1970.

Elliott, Benjamin. *A Sketch of the Means and Benefits of Prosecuting This War against Britain.* Charleston: John L. Wilson, 1814.

Emancipation in Disguise; or, The True Crisis of the Colonies. London: J. Ridgway and J. M. Richardson, 1807.

Finley, Robert. *Thoughts on the Colonization of Free Blacks.* Washington, D.C., 1816.

Fitzhugh, George. *Cannibals All! or, Slaves without Masters.* 1857. Edited by C. Vann Woodward. Cambridge, Mass.: Belknap Press of Harvard University Press, 1960.

"A Friend to Freedom." *Southern Oppression: An Address to the People of the Eastern States, Developing the Causes of Their Oppression.* New York: John Forbes, 1813.

Furman, Richard. *Exposition of the Views of the Baptists, Relative to the Coloured Population of the United States, in a Communication to the Governor of South-Carolina.* Charleston: A. E. Miller, 1823.

Hicks, Elias. *Observations on the Slavery of the Africans. Recommended to the Serious Perusal, and Impartial Consideration of the Citizens of the United States of America, and Others Concerned.* New York: Samuel Wood, 1811.

Hillhouse, James. *Pocahontas: A Proclamation.* New Haven: J. Clyme, 1820.

Hinks, Peter, ed. *David Walker's Appeal to the Coloured Citizens of the World.* University Park: Pennsylvania State University Press, 2000.

[Holland, Edwin Clifford]. *A Refutation of the Calumnies Circulated against the Southern and Western States, Respecting the Institution and Existence of Slavery among Them.* Charleston: A. E. Miller, 1822. Reprint, New York: Negro Universities Press, 1969.

Kenrick, John. *Horrors of Slavery, in Two Parts . . . Demonstrating That Slavery Is Impolitic, Antirepublican, Unchristian, and Highly Criminal; and Proposing Measures for Its Complete Abolition through the United States.* Cambridge, Mass.: Hilliard and Metcalf, 1817.

[307]

King, Rufus. *Substance of Two Speeches, Delivered in the Senate of the United States, on the Subject of the Missouri Bill.* New York: Kirk and Mercein, 1819.

Letter to the Edinburgh Reviewers: By "An American." Washington, D.C., 1819. First published in *National Intelligencer,* 18–25 Nov. 1819.

"Massachusetts" [Sidney Edwards Morse]. *The New States; or, A Comparison of the Wealth, Strength, and Population of the Northern and Southern States; As Also of Their Respective Powers in Congress, with a View to Expose the Injustice of Erecting New States at the South.* Boston: Belcher, 1813.

[McKean, William?]. *An Answer to Certain Parts of a Work Published by Mathew Carey, Entitled "The Olive Branch" . . . by a Federalist.* New York, 1816.

Otis, Harrison Gray. *Speech of Mr. Otis, on the Restriction of Slavery in Missouri: Delivered in the Senate of the United States, January 25, 1820.* Washington, D.C., 1820.

[Paulding, James Kirke]. *The United States and England: Being a Reply to the Criticism on Inchiquin's Letters Contained in the Quarterly Review for January, 1814.* New York: A. H. Inskeep / Philadelphia: Bradford and Inskeep, 1815.

———. *Slavery in the United States.* 1836. Reprint, New York: Negro Universities Press, 1968.

The Proslavery Argument: As Maintained by the Most Distinguished Writers of the Southern States, Containing the Several Essays, on the Subject, of Chancellor Harper, Governor Hammond, Dr. Simms, and Professor Dew. 1852. Reprint, New York: Negro Universities Press, 1968.

Smith, Samuel Stanhope. *An Essay on the Causes of the Variety of Complexion and Figure in the Human Species.* 1810. Reprint, edited by Winthrop D. Jordan. Cambridge, Mass.: Belknap Press of Harvard University Press, 1965.

[Stephen, James]. *The Dangers of the Country.* Philadelphia: Samuel J. Bradford, 1807.

Taylor, John. *Arator: Being a Series of Agricultural Essays, Practical and Political: In Sixty-four Numbers.* 2d ed. Georgetown, D.C., 1814. Reprint, edited by M. E. Bradford. Indianapolis: Liberty Fund, 1977.

———. *Construction Construed and Constitutions Vindicated.* Richmond: Shepherd and Pollard, 1820. Reprint, New York: Da Capo Press, 1970.

Thoreau, Henry David. *Civil Disobedience and Other Essays.* New York: Dover Publications, 1993.

Torrey, Jesse, Jr. *A Portraiture of Domestic Slavery in the United States with Reflections on the Practicability of Restoring the Moral Rights of the Slave, without Impairing the Legal Privileges of the Possessor, etc.* Philadelphia: John Bioren, 1817.

Walsh, Robert. *An Appeal from the Judgments of Great Britain Respecting the United States of America. Containing an Historical Outline of Their Merits and Wrongs as Colonies; and Strictures upon the Calumnies of British Writers.* Mitchell, Ames, and White, 1819. Reprint, New York: Negro Universities Press, 1969.

[———]. *Free Remarks on the Spirit of the Federal Constitution, the Practice of the Federal Government, and the Obligations of the Union, Respecting the Exclusion of Slavery from the Territories and New States. By a Philadelphian.* Philadelphia: A. Finley, 1819.

Wesley, John. *Thoughts upon Slavery.* London, 1774. Reprint, Philadelphia: Joseph Crukshank, 1774.

Wright, John. *A Refutation of the Sophisms, Gross Misrepresentations, and Erroneous Quotations Contained in "An American's" Letter to the Edinburgh Reviewers; or, Slavery Inimical to the Character of the Great Father of All, Unsupported by Divine Revelation, a Violation of Natural Justice, and Hostile to the Fundamental Principles of American Independence.* Washington, D.C., 1820.

SERMONS AND ORATIONS

Bangs, Edward Dillingham. *An Oration, Pronounced at Sutton, Massachusetts, July 5th, 1813, in Commemoration of American Independence.* Boston: J. Belcher, 1813.

Carter, Nathaniel H. *An Oration, Delivered before the Republicans of Portland, on the Thirty-ninth Anniversary of American Independence.* Portland, Maine: F. Douglas, 1815.

Cumings, Henry. *A Sermon, Preached at Billerica, April 9th, 1801; Being the Day of the Annual Fast.* Amherst, N.H.: Samuel Preston, 1801.

Dwight, Timothy. *The Duty of Americans, at the Present Crisis, Illustrated in a Discourse, Preached on the Fourth of July, 1798.* New Haven: Thomas and Samuel Green, 1798.

——. *The Charitable Blessed. A Sermon Preached in the First Church in New Haven, Aug. 8, 1810.* [New Haven]: Sidney's Press, 1810.

——. *A Discourse, in Two Parts, Delivered July 23, 1812, on the Public Fast, in the Chapel of Yale College.* New Haven: Howe and Deforest, 1812.

Emmons, Nathanael. *A Discourse, Delivered on the Annual Fast in Massachusetts, April 9, 1801.* Salem, Mass.: Joshua Cushing, 1802.

——. *Discourse, Delivered November 25, 1813; on the Day of the Annual Thanksgiving.* Dedham, Mass.: Gazette Office, 1813.

——. *A Discourse, Delivered on the National Thanksgiving, April 13, 1815.* Dedham, Mass.: Gazette Office, 1815.

Evarts, Jeremiah. *An Oration, Delivered in Charlestown, (Mass.) on the Fourth of July, 1812.* Charlestown, Mass., 1812.

Gray, Thomas. *A Sermon Delivered in Boston before the African Society on the 14th day of July, 1818; the Anniversary of the Abolition of the Slave Trade.* Boston: Parmenter and Norton, 1818.

Hammond, James H. *Speech of the Hon. James H. Hammond, Delivered at Barnwell C.H., October 29th, 1858.* Charleston: Walker, Evans, 1858.

Kidder, David. *An Oration, Pronounced at Bloomfield, (Me.) July 4th, 1814.* Hallowell, Maine: N. Cheever, 1814.

Mallary, Rollin Carolus. *An Oration, Addressed to Republicans, Delivered at Poultney, Vermont, July 4, 1814.* Rutland, Vt.: Fay and Davison, 1814.

McLeod, Alexander. *Negro Slavery Unjustifiable: A Discourse.* New York: T. and J. Swords, 1802.

——. *Scriptural View of the Character, Causes, and Ends of the Present War.* New York: Paul and Thomas, 1815.

Miltimore, William. *A Discourse, Delivered at Falmouth, March 1, 1815, on the Ratification of Peace, between America and Great-Britain.* Portland, Maine: F. Douglas, 1815.

Moore, Humphrey. *An Oration Delivered at Bedford, New-Hampshire, February 22, 1815, at the Request of the Washington Benevolent Society.* Concord, N.H.: George Hough, 1815.

Morse, Jedidiah. *A Sermon, Exhibiting the Present Dangers, and Consequent Duties of the Citizens of the United States of America. Delivered at Charlestown, April 25, 1799. The Day of the National Fast.* Charlestown, Mass.: Samuel Etheridge, 1799.

——. *A Discourse, Delivered at the African Meeting-House, in Boston, July 14, 1808, in Grateful Celebration of the Abolition of the African Slave Trade, by the Governments of the United States, Great Britain and Denmark.* 2d ed. Boston: Lincoln and Edmands, 1808.

Osgood, David. *The Wonderful Works of GOD Are to Be Remembered. A Sermon, Delivered on the Day of Annual Thanksgiving, November 20, 1794. 3d ed. Boston: Samuel Hall, 1795.

[———]. *The Devil Let Loose; or, The Wo Occasioned to the Inhabitants of the Earth by His Wrathful Appearance among Them, Illustrated in a Discourse Delivered on the Day of the National Fast, April 25, 1799.* Boston: Samuel Hall, 1799.

———. *A Discourse, Delivered before the Lieutenant-Governor, the Council, and the Two Houses Composing the Legislature of the Commonwealth of Massachusetts, May 31, 1809.* Boston: Russell and Cutler, 1809.

———. *A Solemn Protest against the Late Declaration of War. In a Discourse, Delivered on the Next Lord's Day after the Tidings of It Were Received.* Cambridge, Mass.: Hilliard and Metcalf, 1812.

Palmer, Benjamin Morgan. *The Signs of the Times Discerned and Improved, in Two Sermons, Delivered in the Independent or Congregational Church, Charleston, S.C.* Charleston: J. Hoff, 1816.

Parish, Elijah. *An Oration Delivered at Byfield, July 4, 1799.* Newburyport, Mass.: Angier March, 1799.

———. *Ruin or Separation from Anti-Christ. A Sermon Preached at Byfield, April 7, 1808, on the Annual Fast in the Commonwealth of Massachusetts.* Newburyport, Mass.: R. W. and W. S. Allen, 1808.

———. *A Sermon, Preached at Boston, before His Excellency Christopher Gore, Governor, . . . the Council and Legislature, upon the Annual Election, May 30, 1810.* Boston, 1810.

———. *A Sermon, Preached at Byfield, on the Annual Fast, April 11, 1811.* Newburyport, Mass.: E. W. Allen, 1811.

———. *A Protest against the War. A Discourse Delivered at Byfield, Fast Day, July 23, 1812.* Newburyport, Mass.: E. W. Allen, 1812.

———. *A Discourse, Delivered at Byfield, on the Annual Fast, April 8, 1813.* Newburyport, Mass.: E. W. Allen, 1813.

———. *A Discourse, Delivered at Byfield, on the Public Fast, April 7, 1814.* Newburyport, Mass.: William B. Allen, 1814.

———. *Sermons, Practical and Doctrinal, by the Late Elijah Parish, D.D., with a Biographical Sketch of the Author.* Boston: Crocker and Brewster, 1826.

Payson, Seth. *An Abridgement of Two Discourses, Preached at Rindge, N.H., at the Annual Fast, April 13, 1815.* New-Ipswich, N.H.: Simeon Ide, 1815.

Perkins, Nathan. *The National Sins, and National Punishment in the Recently Declared War; Considered in a Sermon Delivered, July 23, 1812.* Hartford: Hudson and Goodwin, 1812.

[Plumer, William]. *Address to the Clergy of New-England, on Their Opposition to the Rulers of the United States. By a Layman.* Concord, N.H.: L. and W. R. Hill, 1814.

Popkin, John Snelling. *A Sermon, Preached in Newbury, First Parish, on the Day of Annual Thanksgiving in the Commonwealth of Massachusetts, November 25, 1813.* Newburyport, Mass.: William B. Allen, 1814.

Prince, John. *A Discourse, Delivered at Salem, on the Day of the National Fast, May 9, 1798; Appointed by President Adams, on Account of the Difficulties Subsisting between the United States and France.* Salem, Mass.: Thomas C. Cushing, 1798.

Quincy, Josiah. *An Oration Delivered before the Washington Benevolent Society of Massachusetts, on the Thirtieth Day of April, 1813, Being the Anniversary of the First Inauguration of President Washington.* Boston: William S. and Henry Spear, 1813.

——. *Address Illustrative of the Nature and Power of the Slave States and the Duties of Free States.* Boston: Ticknor and Fields, 1856.

Sprague, Peleg. *An Oration Pronounced at Worcester, July 4, 1815. The Thirty-ninth Anniversary of American Independence.* Worcester, Mass.: Henry Rogers, 1815.

Strong, Nathan. *A Sermon, Preached at the Annual Thanksgiving, November 16, 1797.* Hartford: Hudson and Goodwin, 1797.

——. *Political Instruction from the Prophecies of God's Word. A Sermon, Preached on the State Thanksgiving, November 29, 1798.* Reprint, New York: G. Forman, 1799.

——. *A Fast Sermon, Delivered in the North Presbyterian Meeting House, in Hartford, July 23, 1812.* Hartford: Peter B. Gleason, 1812.

Van Ness, Cornelius Peter. *An Oration Delivered at Williston, July 4th, 1812, to a General and Very Numerous Meeting of the Republicans of Chittenden County.* Burlington, Vt.: Samuel Mills, 1812.

Van Pelt, Peter I. *The Goodness of God, to Be Praised by Men, &c. A Discourse, Delivered on the Fourth of July, in the North Brick Church.* New York: Pelsue and Gould, 1812.

[Webster, Noah]. *The Revolution in France, Considered in Respect to Its Progress and Effects. By an American.* New York: George Bunce, 1794.

TRAVEL, BIOGRAPHICAL, AND MILITARY ACCOUNTS

Ashe, Thomas. *Travels in America, Performed in 1806, for the Purpose of Exploring the Rivers Allegheny, Monongahela, Ohio, and Mississippi, and Ascertaining the Produce and Condition of Their Banks and Vicinity.* London: Cramer and Spear, 1808.

Ball, Charles. *Slavery in the United States; A Narrative of the Life and Adventures of Charles Ball, a Black Man.* Lewistown, Pa.: John W. Shugert, 1836. Reprint, Detroit: Negro History Press, 1970.

——. *Fifty Years in Chains; or, The Life of an American Slave.* New York: H. Dayton, 1859. Reprint, Detroit: Negro History Press, 1971.

Birkbeck, Morris. *Letters from Illinois.* London: Taylor and Hessey, 1818.

——. *Notes on a Journey in America, from the Coast of Virginia to the Territory of Illinois.* 3d ed. London: Severn, 1818.

Bradbury, John. *Travels in the Interior of America, in the Years 1809, 1810, and 1811.* 2d ed. London, 1818. Reprint, Cleveland: Arthur H. Clark, 1904.

Cobbett, William. *A Year's Residence in the United States of America.* London: Sherwood, Neely, and Jones, 1818. Reprint, New York: Augustus M. Kelley, 1969.

Cuming, Fortescue. *Sketches of a Tour to the Western Country . . . Commenced at Philadelphia in the Winter of 1807, and Concluded in 1809.* Pittsburgh: Cramer, Spear, and Bichbaum, 1810. Reprint, Cleveland: Arthur H. Clark, 1904.

Dickens, Charles. *American Notes for General Circulation.* 1842. Baltimore: Penguin Books, 1972.

Dwight, Timothy. *Travels in New England and New York.* New Haven: S. Converse, 1821–22. Reprint, edited by Barbara Miller Solomon. Cambridge, Mass.: Belknap Press of Harvard University Press, 1969.

Evans, Estwick. *A Pedestrious Tour of Four Thousand Miles through the Western States and Territories during the Winter and Spring of 1818.* Concord, N.H.: Joseph C. Spear, 1819. Reprint, Cleveland: Arthur H. Clark, 1904.

Faux, William. *Memorable Days in America; Being a Journal of a Tour to the United States.* 2 vols. London: W. Simpkin and R. Marshall, 1823. Reprint, Cleveland: Arthur H. Clark, 1905.

Fearon, Henry Bradshaw. *Sketches of America: A Narrative of a Journey Five Thousand Miles through the Eastern and Western States of America.* 2d ed. London: Longman, Hurst, Rees, Orme, and Browne, 1818.

Flint, James. *Letters from America, Containing Observations on the Climate and Agriculture of the Western States, the Manners of the People, the Prospects of Emigrants, &c., &c..* Edinburgh: W and C Tait, 1822. Reprint, Cleveland: Arthur H. Clark, 1904.

Flint, Timothy. *Recollections of the Last Ten Years, Passed in Occasional Residences and Journeyings in the Valley of the Mississippi . . . in a Series of Letters to the Rev. James Flint, of Salem, Massachusetts.* Edited by C. Hartley Grattan. Boston: Cummings, Hilliard, 1826. Reprint, New York: Alfred A. Knopf, 1932.

Fowler, George. *The Wandering Philanthropist; or, Letters from a Chinese, Written during his Residence in the United States. Discovered and Edited by George Fowler of Virginia.* Philadelphia, 1810.

Gleig, G. R. *The Campaigns of the British Army at Washington and New Orleans.* London, 1821. Reprint, Totowa, N.J.: Rowman and Littlefield, 1972.

Jacobs, Harriet A. *Incidents in the Life of a Slave Girl, Written by Herself.* 1861. Reprint, edited by Jean Fagan Yellin. Cambridge, Mass.: Harvard University Press, 1987.

Lambert, John. *Travels through Lower Canada, and the United States of North America, in the Years 1806, 1807, and 1808.* London: Richard Phillips, 1810.

Latour, Arsene La Carriere. *Historical Memoir of the War in West Florida and Louisiana in 1814–1815.* Philadelphia, 1816. Expanded edition, edited by Gene A. Smith, Gainesville: University Presses of Florida, 1999.

Latrobe, Benjamin Henry Boneval. *Impressions Respecting New Orleans. Diary and Sketches, 1818–1820.* Edited by Samuel Wilson, Jr. New York: Columbia University Press, 1951.

Melish, John. *Travels in the United States of America in the Years 1806 and 1807, and 1809, 1810 and 1811.* Philadelphia, 1812, and London, 1818. Reprint, New York: Johnson Reprint, 1970.

Morse, Jedidiah. *The American Geography; or, A View of the Present Situation of the United States of America.* Elizabethtown, N.J.: Shepard Kollock, 1789. Reprint, Arno Press and New York Times, 1970.

Nicholson, Thomas. *An Affecting Narrative of the Captivity and Sufferings of Thomas Nicholson, (A Native of New Jersey), Who Has Been Six Years a Prisoner among the Algerines.* Boston: H. Trumbull, 1816.

Nuttall, Thomas. *Journal of Travels into the Arkansas Territory, during the Year 1819.* Philadelphia, 1821.

[Paulding, James Kirke]. *Letters from the South, Written during an Excursion in the Summer of 1816.* 2 vols. New York: James Eastburn, 1817.

[——]. *A Sketch of Old England, by a New-England Man.* 2 vols. New York: Charles Wiley, 1822.

Riley, James. *An Authentic Narrative of the Loss of the American Brig Commerce, Wrecked on the Western Coast of Africa, in the Month of August, 1815.* New York: T. and W. Mercein, 1817.

Robbins, Archibald. *A Journal, Comprising an Account of the Loss of the Brig Commerce . . . ; Also, of the Slavery and Sufferings of the Author and the Rest of the Crew, upon the Desert of*

Zahara, in the Years 1815, 1816, 1817 . . . 1818. Reprint, Hartford: Silas Andrus and Son, 1848.

Rowan, Stephen N. *Tribute to the Memory of Alexander McLeod, D.D.* New York: Peter Hill, 1833.

Steward, Austin. *Twenty-two Years a Slave and Forty Years a Freeman.* 1857. Reprint, edited by Jane H. and William H. Pease. Reading, Mass.: Addison-Wesley, 1969.

Strickland, William. *Journal of a Tour in the United States of America, 1794–1795.* Edited by J. E. Strickland. New York: New-York Historical Society, 1971.

[Tucker, George]. *Letters from Virginia, Translated from the French.* Baltimore: Fielding Lucas, Jr., 1816.

Welby, Adlard. *A Visit to North America and the English Settlements in Illinois.* London: J. Drury, 1821. Reprint, Cleveland: Arthur H. Clark, 1905.

Wright, Frances. *Views of Society and Manners in America.* London, 1821. Edited by Paul R. Baker. Cambridge, Mass.: Belknap Press of Harvard University Press, 1963.

PLAYS AND LITERATURE

Bingham, Caleb. *The Columbian Orator: Containing a Variety of Original and Selected Pieces Together with Rules, Which Are Calculated to Improve Youth and Others, in the Ornamental and Useful Art of Eloquence.* 1797. Reprint, edited by David Blight. New York: New York University Press, 1998.

[Colman, George]. *The Africans; or, War, Love, and Duty: a Play, in Three Acts: As Performed at the Philadelphia Theatre.* Philadelphia: M. Carey, 1811.

Dickens, Charles. *Martin Chuzzlewit.* 1843–44. Ware, England: Wordsworth Editions, 1994.

Ellison, James. *The American Captive; or, Siege of Tripoli.* Boston: Joshua Belcher, 1812.

Murdock, John. *The Triumphs of Love; or, Happy Reconciliation: A Comedy.* Philadelphia: R. Folwell, 1795.

———. *The Politicians; or, A State of Things: A Dramatic Piece. Written by an American, and a Citizen of Philadelphia.* Philadelphia, 1798.

[Pinckney, Maria, or Sarah Pogson Smith]. "Young Carolinians, or, Americans in Algiers." In *Essays, Religious, Moral, Dramatic and Poetical.* Charleston: Archibald E. Miller, 1818.

Tyler, Royall. *The Algerine Captive; or, The Life and Adventures of Doctor Updike Underhill, Six Years a Prisoner among the Algerines.* 2 vols. 1797. Reprint, Gainesville, Fla.: Scholars' Facsimiles and Reprints, 1967.

EDITED PRIMARY SOURCE COLLECTIONS

Adams, Charles Francis, ed. *Memoirs of John Quincy Adams, Comprising Portions of His Diary from 1795 to 1848.* Philadelphia, 1874–77. 12 vols. Reprint, Freeport, N.Y.: Books for Libraries Press, 1969.

Adams, Henry, ed. *Documents Relating to New-England Federalism, 1800–1815.* Boston, 1877. Reprint, New York: Burt Franklin, 1969.

Ames, Fisher. *The Works of Fisher Ames.* Edited by Seth Ames and W. B. Allen. Boston: Little, Brown, 1854. Reprint, Indianapolis: Liberty Fund, 1983.

Ames, Herman V. *The Proposed Amendments to the Constitution of the United States during the First Century of Its History*. Washington, D.C.: Government Printing Office, 1897. Reprint, New York: Burt Franklin, 1970.

——, ed. *State Documents on Federal Relations: The States and the United States*. Philadelphia: University of Pennsylvania, 1906. Reprint, New York: Da Capo Press, 1970.

Aptheker, Herbert, ed. *A Documentary History of the Negro People in the United States*. Vol. 1 of *From Colonial Times through the Civil War*. New York: Citadel Press, 1951.

Baepler, Paul, ed. *White Slaves, African Masters: An Anthology of American Barbary Captivity Narratives*. Chicago: University of Chicago Press, 1999.

Basker, James G., ed. *Amazing Grace: An Anthology of Poems about Slavery, 1660–1810*. New Haven: Yale University Press, 2002.

Battle, Kemp P., ed. *Letters of Nathaniel Macon, John Steele and William Barry Grove. James Sprunt Historical Monographs* 3. Chapel Hill: University of North Carolina, 1902.

Brown, Everett Somerville, ed. *The Missouri Compromises and Presidential Politics, 1820–1825: From the Letters of William Plumer, Junior, Representative from New Hampshire*. St. Louis: Missouri Historical Society, 1926. Reprint, New York: Da Capo Press, 1970.

Bruns, Roger, ed. *Am I Not a Man and a Brother: The Antislavery Crusade of Revolutionary America, 1688–1788*. New York: Chelsea House, 1977.

Cain, William E., ed. *William Lloyd Garrison and the Fight against Slavery: Selections from* The Liberator. Boston: Bedford Books of St. Martin's Press, 1995.

Cunningham, Noble E., Jr., ed. *Circular Letters of Congressmen to Their Constituents, 1789–1829*. 3 vols. Chapel Hill: University of North Carolina Press for the Institute of Early American History and Culture, 1978.

Duane, William. "Letters." In Massachusetts Historical Society, *Proceedings*, edited by Worthington C. Ford, 2d ser., 20 (1906–7): 257–394.

Dwight, Timothy, Jr., ed. *President Dwight's Decisions of Questions Discussed by the Senior Class in Yale College in 1813 and 1814*. New York: Joshua Leavitt, 1833.

Faust, Drew Gilpin, ed. *The Ideology of Slavery: Proslavery Thought in the Antebellum South, 1830–1860*. Baton Rouge: Louisiana State University Press, 1981.

Garrison, William Lloyd. *Letters of William Lloyd Garrison*. Edited by Louis Ruchames and Walter Merrill. 6 vols. Cambridge, Mass.: Belknap Press of Harvard University Press, 1971–1981.

Gellman, David N., and David Quigley, eds. *Jim Crow New York: A Documentary History of Race and Citizenship, 1777–1877*. New York: New York University Press, 2003.

Hammond, James Henry. *Selections from the Letters and Speeches of the Hon. James H. Hammond, of South Carolina*. New York: J. F. Trow, 1866.

Hunt, Gaillard, ed. *The Writings of James Madison*. New York: G. P. Putnam's, 1900–1910.

Jenkins, William Sumner, ed. *Records of the States of the United States of America*. Microfilm collection. Washington, D.C., 1949.

Kaminski, John P., ed. *A Necessary Evil? Slavery and the Debate over the Constitution*. Madison, Wis.: Madison House, 1995.

King, Charles R., ed. *The Life and Correspondence of Rufus King*. Vol. 6. New York: G. P. Putnam's, 1900.

Lowance, Mason I., Jr., ed. *A House Divided: The Antebellum Slavery Debates in America, 1776–1865*. Princeton, N.J.: Princeton University Press, 2003.

Meaders, Daniel, ed. *Advertisements for Runaway Slaves in Virginia, 1801–1820*. New York: Garland, 1997.

Meriwether, Robert L., Clyde N. Wilson, W. Edwin Hemphill, and Shirley B. Cook, eds. *The Papers of John C. Calhoun*. 28 vols. Columbia: University of South Carolina Press, 1959–2003.

"Missouri Compromise: Letters to James Barbour, Senator of Virginia in the Congress of the United States." *William and Mary Quarterly*, 1st ser., 10 (July 1901): 5–24.

Newman, Richard, Patrick Rael, and Philip Lapsansky, eds. *Pamphlets of Protest: An Anthology of Early African-American Protest Literature, 1790–1860*. New York: Routledge, 2001.

Pearson, Edward A., ed. *Designs against Charleston: The Trial Record of the Denmark Vesey Conspiracy of 1822*. Chapel Hill: University of North Carolina Press, 1999.

Pease, Theodore C., ed. *Illinois Election Returns, 1818–1848*. Springfield: Illinois State Historical Library, 1923.

Porter, Dorothy, ed. *Early Negro Writing, 1760–1837*. Boston: Beacon Press, 1971.

Price, Clement Alexander, comp. and ed. *Freedom Not Far Distant: A Documentary History of Afro-Americans in New Jersey*. Newark: New Jersey Historical Society, 1980.

[Rives, William C., and Philip R. Fendall, eds.]. *Letters and Other Writings of James Madison*. 4 vols. Philadelphia, 1865.

Rowland, Dunbar, ed. *Official Letter Books of W. C. C. Claiborne, 1801–1816*. 6 vols. Jackson, Miss., 1917.

Sandoz, Ellis, ed. *Political Sermons of the American Founding Era: 1730–1805*. Indianapolis: Liberty Press, 1991.

Schmidt, Fredrika Teute, and Barbara Ripel Wilhelm. "Early Proslavery Petitions in Virginia." *William and Mary Quarterly*, 3d ser., 30 (Jan. 1973): 133–46.

Schweninger, Loren, ed. *Petitions to Southern Legislatures, 1778–1864*. Vol. 1 of *The Southern Debate over Slavery*. Urbana: University of Illinois Press, 2001.

Starobin, Robert S., ed. *Blacks in Bondage: Letters of American Slaves*. 1974. New York: Markus Wiener Publishing, 1988.

Whittier, John Greenleaf. *The Complete Poetical Works of John Greenleaf Whittier: Cambridge Edition*. Boston: Houghton, Mifflin, 1894.

Wiltse, Charles M., ed. *1798–1824*. Vol. 1 of *The Papers of Daniel Webster: Correspondence*. Hanover, N.H.: University Press of New England, 1974.

BOOKS AND ARTICLES

Abernethy, Thomas Perkins. *The Burr Conspiracy*. New York: Oxford University Press, 1954.

———. *The South in the New Nation, 1789–1819*. Baton Rouge: Louisiana State University Press, 1961.

Abzug, Robert H. *Passionate Liberator: Theodore Dwight Weld and the Dilemma of Reform*. New York: Oxford University Press, 1980.

Adams, Alice Dana. *The Neglected Period of Anti-Slavery in America, 1808–1831*. Radcliffe College, 1908. Reprint, Williamstown, Mass.: Corner House Publishers, 1973.

Adams, Henry. *History of the United States during the Administrations of James Madison*. New York, 1889–1891. Reprint, New York: Library of America, 1986.

Adams, James Truslow. *New England in the Republic, 1776–1850*. Boston: Little, Brown, 1926.

Alden, John. *The First South*. Baton Rouge: Louisiana State University Press, 1961.

Alilunas, Leo. "Fugitive Slave Cases in Ohio prior to 1850." *Ohio Archaeological and Historical Quarterly* 49 (1940): 160–84.

Allegro, James J. " 'Increasing and Strengthening the Country': Law, Politics, and the Antislavery Movement in Early-Eighteenth-Century Massachusetts Bay." *New England Quarterly* 75 (Mar. 2002): 5–23.

Allison, Robert J. *The Crescent Obscured: The United States and the Muslim World, 1776–1815*. New York: Oxford University Press, 1995.

Altoff, Gerard T. *Amongst My Best Men: African-Americans and the War of 1812*. Put-in-Bay, Ohio: Perry Group, 1996.

Ammon, Harry. *James Monroe: The Quest for National Identity*. New York: McGraw-Hill, 1971.

Anstey, Roger. *The Atlantic Slave Trade and British Abolition, 1760–1810*. Atlantic Highlands, N.J.: Humanities Press, 1975.

Aptheker, Herbert. "Maroons within the Present Limits of the United States." *Journal of Negro History* 24 (1939): 167–84.

———. *American Negro Slave Revolts*. New York: Columbia University Press, 1943.

Ashworth, John. *Commerce and Compromise, 1820–1850*. Vol. 1 in *Slavery, Capitalism, and Politics in the Antebellum Republic*. Cambridge: Cambridge University Press, 1995.

Ayers, Edward L., Patricia Nelson Limerick, Stephen Nissenbaum, and Peter S. Onuf. *All over the Map: Rethinking American Regions*. Baltimore: Johns Hopkins University Press, 1996.

Bailor, Keith M. "John Taylor of Caroline: Continuity, Change and Discontinuity in Virginia's Sentiments toward Slavery, 1790–1820." *Virginia Magazine of History and Biography* 75 (July 1967): 290–304.

Bailyn, Bernard. *The Ideological Origins of the American Revolution*. Enlarged ed. Cambridge, Mass.: Belknap Press of Harvard University Press, 1992.

Bancroft, Frederic. *Slave Trading in the Old South*. 1931. Reprint, Columbia: University of South Carolina Press, 1996.

Banner, James M., Jr. *To the Hartford Convention: The Federalists and the Origins of Party Politics in Massachusetts, 1789–1815*. New York: Alfred A. Knopf, 1970.

Barnhart, John D. *Valley of Democracy: The Frontier versus the Plantation in the Ohio Valley, 1775–1818*. Bloomington: Indiana University Press, 1953.

Beeman, Richard, Stephen Botein, and Edward C. Carter II, eds. *Beyond Confederation: Origins of the Constitution and American National Identity*. Chapel Hill: University of North Carolina Press for the Institute of Early American History and Culture, 1987.

Ben-Atar, Doron, and Barbara B. Oberg, eds. *Federalists Reconsidered*. Charlottesville: University Press of Virginia, 1998.

Berlin, Ira. *Slaves without Masters: The Free Negro in the Antebellum South*. New York: Pantheon, 1974.

———. *Many Thousands Gone: The First Two Centuries of Slavery in North America*. Cambridge, Mass.: Belknap Press of Harvard University Press, 1998.

———. *Generations of Captivity: A History of African-American Slaves*. Cambridge, Mass.: Belknap Press of Harvard University Press, 2003.

Berlin, Ira, and Ronald Hoffman, eds. *Slavery and Freedom in the Age of the American Revolution*. Charlottesville: University Press of Virginia, 1983.

Berlin, Ira, and Philip D. Morgan, eds. *Cultivation and Culture: Labor and the Shaping of Slave Life in the Americas*. Charlottesville: University Press of Virginia, 1993.

Berlin, Ira, Barbara J. Fields, Steven F. Miller, Joseph P. Reidy, and Leslie S. Rowland. *Slaves No More: Three Essays on Emancipation and the Civil War*. Cambridge: Cambridge University Press, 1992.

Berwanger, Eugene H. *The Frontier against Slavery: Western Anti-Negro Prejudice and the Slavery Extension Controversy*. Urbana: University of Illinois Press, 1967.

Blackburn, Robin. *The Overthrow of Colonial Slavery, 1776–1848*. London: Verso Press, 1988.

Blight, David W. *Frederick Douglass' Civil War: Keeping Faith in Jubilee*. Baton Rouge: Louisiana State University Press, 1989.

Broussard, James H. *The Southern Federalists, 1800–1816*. Baton Rouge: Louisiana State University Press, 1978.

Brown, Everett S. *The Constitutional History of the Louisiana Purchase, 1803–1812*. Berkeley: University of California Press, 1920.

Brown, Richard H. "The Missouri Crisis, Slavery, and the Politics of Jacksonianism." *South Atlantic Quarterly* 65 (Winter 1966): 55–72.

Bruce, Dickson D., Jr. "National Identity and African-American Colonization, 1773–1817." *Historian* 58 (Autumn 1995): 15–28.

Buck, Solon Justus. *Illinois in 1818*. Chicago: A. C. McClurg, 1918.

Buel, Richard, Jr. *America on the Brink: How the Political Struggles over the War of 1812 Almost Destroyed the Young Republic*. New York: Palgrave McMillan, 2005.

Bullard, Mary R. *Black Emancipation at Cumberland Island in 1815*. De Leon Springs, Fla.: E. O. Painter, 1983.

Capers, Gerald M. "A Reconsideration of John C. Calhoun's Transition from Nationalism to Nullification." *Journal of Southern History* 14 (Feb. 1948): 34–48.

Carpenter, Jesse T. *The South as a Conscious Minority, 1789–1861: A Study in Political Thought*. New York: New York University Press, 1930.

Cassell, Frank A. "Slaves of the Chesapeake Bay Area and the War of 1812." *Journal of Negro History* 57 (Apr. 1972): 144–55.

Cayton, Andrew R. L. *The Frontier Republic: Ideology and Politics in the Ohio Country, 1780–1825*. Kent, Ohio: Kent State University Press, 1986.

———. " 'Separate Interests' and the Nation-State: The Washington Administration and the Origins of Regionalism in the Trans-Appalachian West." *Journal of American History* 79 (June 1992): 39–67.

———. *Frontier Indiana*. Bloomington: Indiana University Press, 1996.

Christie, John W., and Dwight L. Dumond. *George Bourne and "The Book and Slavery Irreconcilable."* Wilmington and Philadelphia: Historical Society of Delaware and Presbyterian Historical Society, 1969.

Condit, Celeste Michelle, and Lucaites, John Louis. *Crafting Equality: America's Anglo-African Word*. Chicago: University of Chicago Press, 1993.

Colley, Linda. *Britons: Forging the Nation, 1707–1837*. New Haven: Yale University Press, 1992.

Conforti, Joseph A. *Imagining New England: Explorations of Regional Identity from the Pilgrims to the Mid-Twentieth Century*. Chapel Hill: University of North Carolina Press, 2001.

Cooper, William J., Jr. *Liberty and Slavery: Southern Politics to 1860*. New York: McGraw Hill, 1983.

Covington, James W. "The Negro Fort." *Gulf Coast Historical Review* 5 (1990): 78–91.

Crocker, Matthew H. "The Missouri Compromise, the Monroe Doctrine, and the Southern Strategy." *Journal of the West* 43 (Summer 2004): 45–52.

Cunningham, Noble E., Jr. "Nathaniel Macon and the Southern Protest against National Consolidation." *North Carolina Historical Review* 32 (July 1955): 376–84.

Curtin, Philip D. *The Rise and Fall of the Plantation Complex: Essays in Atlantic History*. Cambridge: Cambridge University Press, 1990.

Dain, Bruce. *A Hideous Monster of the Mind: American Race Theory in the Early Republic*. Cambridge, Mass.: Harvard University Press, 2002.

Daly, John Patrick. *When Slavery Was Called Freedom: Evangelicalism, Proslavery, and the Causes of the Civil War*. Lexington: University Press of Kentucky, 2002.

Dangerfield, George. *The Era of Good Feelings*. New York: Harcourt, Brace, 1952.

———. *The Awakening of American Nationalism, 1815–1828*. New York: Harper and Row, 1965.

Davis, David Brion. "The Emergence of Immediatism in British and American Antislavery Thought." *Mississippi Valley Historical Review* 49 (Sept. 1962): 209–30.

———. *The Problem of Slavery in Western Culture*. Ithaca, N.Y.: Cornell University Press, 1966.

———. *The Problem of Slavery in the Age of Revolution, 1770–1823*. Ithaca, N.Y.: Cornell University Press, 1974.

———. "Looking at Slavery from Broader Perspectives." *American Historical Review* 105 (Apr. 2000): 452–66.

———. *Challenging the Boundaries of Slavery*. Cambridge, Mass.: Harvard University Press, 2003.

Deyle, Steven. "The Irony of Liberty: Origins of the Domestic Slave Trade." *Journal of the Early Republic* 12 (Spring 1992): 37–62.

Dillon, Merton L. *Elijah P. Lovejoy: Abolitionist Editor*. Urbana: University of Illinois Press, 1961.

———. *Benjamin Lundy and the Struggle for Negro Freedom*. Urbana: University of Illinois Press, 1966.

———. *Slavery Attacked: Southern Slaves and Their Allies, 1619–1865*. Baton Rouge: Louisiana State University Press, 1990.

Dormon, James H. "The Persistent Specter: Slave Rebellion in Territorial Louisiana." *Louisiana History* 28 (Fall 1977): 389–404.

Dunning, Mike. "Manifest Destiny and the Trans-Mississippi South: Natural Laws and the Extension of Slavery into Mexico." *Journal of Popular Culture* 35 (Mar. 2001): 111–27.

Durden, Robert F. *The Self-Inflicted Wound: Southern Politics in the Nineteenth Century*. Lexington: University Press of Kentucky, 1985.

Dwight, Theodore. *History of the Hartford Convention, with a Review of the Policy of the United States Government Which Led to the War of 1812*. New York and Boston, 1833. Reprint, New York: Da Capo Press, 1970.

Earle, Jonathan. "Marcus Morton and the Dilemma of Jacksonian Antislavery in Massachusetts, 1817–1849." *Massachusetts Historical Review* 4 (2002): 61–87.

Eaton, Clement. *The Growth of Southern Civilization, 1790–1860.* New York: Harper and Row, 1961.

Egerton, Douglas R. " 'Its Origins Are Not a Little Curious': A New Look at the American Colonization Society." *Journal of the Early Republic* 5 (Winter 1985): 463–80.

———. *Charles Fenton Mercer and the Trial of National Conservatism.* Jackson: University Press of Mississippi, 1989.

———. *Gabriel's Rebellion: The Virginia Slave Conspiracies of 1800 and 1802.* Chapel Hill: University of North Carolina Press, 1993.

———. *He Shall Go Out Free: The Lives of Denmark Vesey.* Madison, Wis.: Madison House, 1999.

Epperson, James F. "Lee's Slave-Makers." *Civil War Times Illustrated* (Aug. 2002): 44–51.

Essig, James D. *The Bonds of Wickedness: American Evangelicals against Slavery, 1770–1808.* Philadelphia: Temple University Press, 1982.

Etcheson, Nicole. *The Emerging Midwest: Upland Southerners and the Political Culture of the Old Northwest, 1787–1861.* Bloomington: Indiana University Press, 1996.

Everett, Donald E. "Emigres and Militiamen: Free Persons of Color in New Orleans, 1803–1815." *Journal of Negro History* 38 (1953): 377–402.

Faust, Drew Gilpin. *Creation of Confederate Nationalism: Ideology and Identity in the Civil War South.* Baton Rouge: Louisiana State University Press, 1988.

Fehrenbacher, Don E. *The Dred Scott Case: Its Significance in American Law and Politics.* New York: Oxford University Press, 1978.

———. "The Missouri Controversy and the Sources of Southern Sectionalism." In *The South and Three Sectional Crises.* Baton Rouge: Louisiana State University Press, 1980.

———. *The Slaveholding Republic: An Account of the United States Government's Relations to Slavery.* Edited by Ward M. McAfee. New York: Oxford University Press, 2001.

Fields, Barbara Jeanne. *Slavery and Freedom on the Middle Ground: Maryland during the Nineteenth Century.* New Haven: Yale University Press, 1985.

Finkelman, Paul. *An Imperfect Union: Slavery, Federalism, and Comity.* Chapel Hill: University of North Carolina Press, 1981.

———. "Slavery and the Northwest Ordinance: A Study in Ambiguity." *Journal of the Early Republic* 6 (Winter 1986): 343–70.

———. "Evading the Ordinance: The Persistence of Bondage in Indiana and Illinois." *Journal of the Early Republic* 9 (Spring 1989): 21–51.

———. *Slavery and the Founders: Race and Liberty in the Age of Jefferson.* Armonk, N.Y.: M. E. Sharpe, 1996.

Fischer, David Hackett. *The Revolution of American Conservatism: The Federalist Party in the Era of Jeffersonian Democracy.* New York: Harper and Row, 1965.

Fladeland, Betty. *Men and Brothers: Anglo-American Antislavery Cooperation.* Urbana: University of Illinois Press, 1972.

Fogel, Robert William, and Stanley L. Engerman. "Philanthropy at Bargain Prices: Notes on the Economics of Gradual Emancipation." *Journal of Legal Studies* 3 (June 1974): 377–401.

Foner, Eric. *Free Soil, Free Labor, Free Men: The Ideology of the Republican Party before the Civil War.* New York: Oxford University Press, 1970.

———. *Politics and Ideology in the Age of the Civil War.* New York: Oxford University Press, 1980.

Fox, Dixon Ryan. "The Negro Vote in Old New York." *Political Science Quarterly* 32 (June 1917): 252–75.

Fox, Early L. *The American Colonization Society, 1817–1840*. Baltimore: Johns Hopkins University Press, 1919.

Fox-Genovese, Elizabeth, and Eugene D. Genovese. *Fruits of Merchant Capital: Slavery and Bourgeois Property in the Rise and Expansion of Capitalism*. New York: Oxford University Press, 1983.

Franklin, John Hope, and Loren Schweninger. *Runaway Slaves: Rebels on the Plantation*. New York: Oxford University Press, 1999.

Fredrickson, George M. *The Black Image in the White Mind: The Debate on Afro-American Character and Destiny, 1817–1914*. New York: Harper and Row, 1971.

Freehling, Alison Goodyear. *Drift towards Dissolution: The Virginia Slavery Debate of 1831–1832*. Baton Rouge: Louisiana State University Press, 1982.

Freehling, William W. *Prelude to Civil War: The Nullification Controversy in South Carolina, 1816–1836*. New York: Oxford University Press, 1965.

———. *The Road to Disunion: Secessionists at Bay, 1776–1854*. New York: Oxford University Press, 1990.

———. *The Reintegration of American History: Slavery and the Civil War*. New York: Oxford University Press, 1994.

———. *The South vs. the South: How Anti-Confederate Southerners Shaped the Course of the Civil War*. New York: Oxford University Press, 2001.

Frey, Sylvia R. *Water from the Rock: Black Resistance in a Revolutionary Age*. Princeton, N.J.: Princeton University Press, 1991.

Gannon, Kevin M. "Escaping 'Mr. Jefferson's Plan of Destruction': New England Federalists and the Idea of a Northern Confederacy, 1803–1804." *Journal of the Early Republic* 21 (Fall 2001): 413–43.

Gaspar, David Barry, and David Patrick Geggus, eds. *A Turbulent Time: The French Revolution and the Greater Caribbean*. Bloomington: Indiana University Press, 1997.

Geggus, David P., ed. *The Impact of the Haitian Revolution in the Atlantic World*. Columbia: University of South Carolina Press, 2001.

Genovese, Eugene D. *The World the Slaveholders Made: Two Essays in Interpretation*. New York: Pantheon, 1969.

———. *Roll, Jordan, Roll: The World the Slaves Made*. New York: Pantheon, 1974.

George, Carol V. R. *Segregated Sabbaths: Richard Allen and the Emergence of Independent Black Churches, 1790–1840*. New York: Oxford University Press, 1973.

George, Christopher T. "Mirage of Freedom: African Americans in the War of 1812." *Maryland Historical Magazine* 91 (Winter 1996): 427–50.

Gilje, Paul A. *The Road to Mobocracy: Popular Disorder in New York City, 1763–1834*. Chapel Hill: University of North Carolina Press for the Institute of Early American History and Culture, 1987.

Gravely, William B. "The Dialectic of Double Consciousness in Black American Freedom Celebrations, 1808–1863." *Journal of Negro History* 67 (1982): 302–17.

Greenberg, Kenneth S. "Revolutionary Ideology and the Proslavery Argument: The Abolition of Slavery in Antebellum South Carolina." *Journal of Southern History* 42 (Aug. 1976): 365–84.

———. *Masters and Statesmen: The Political Culture of American Slavery*. Baltimore: Johns Hopkins University Press, 1985.

Greene, John C. "The American Debate on the Negro's Place in Nature, 1780–1815." *Journal of the History of Ideas* 15 (June 1954): 384–96.

Greene, Lorenzo J. *The Negro in Colonial New England, 1620–1776*. New York: Columbia University Press, 1942.

———. "Prince Hall: Massachusetts Leader in Crisis." *Freedomways* 1 (Fall 1961): 238–58.

Gribbin, William. *The Churches Militant: The War of 1812 and American Religion*. New Haven: Yale University Press, 1973.

Grimsted, David. *American Mobbing, 1828–1861: Toward Civil War*. New York: Oxford University Press, 1998.

Grivno, Max L. " 'Black Frenchmen' and 'White Settlers': Race, Slavery, and the Creation of African-American Identities along the Northwest Frontier, 1790–1840." *Slavery and Abolition* 21 (Dec. 2000): 75–93.

Gudmestad, Robert H. *A Troublesome Commerce: The Transformation of the Interstate Slave Trade*. Baton Rouge: Louisiana State University Press, 2003.

Hahn, Steven. *A Nation under Our Feet: Black Political Struggles in the Rural South from Slavery to the Great Migration*. Cambridge, Mass.: Belknap Press of Harvard University Press, 2003.

Halevy, Elie. *England in 1815*. 1913. Translated from the French by E. I Watkin and D. A. Barker. New York: Barnes and Noble, 1961.

Hamer, Philip M. "Great Britain, the United States, and the Negro Seamen Acts, 1822–1848." *Journal of Southern History* 1 (Feb. 1935): 3–28.

Hamilton, Phillip. "Revolutionary Principles and Family Loyalties: Slavery's Transformation in the St. George Tucker Household of Early National Virginia." *William and Mary Quarterly*, 3d ser., 55 (Oct. 1998): 531–56.

Hammack, James Wallace, Jr. *Kentucky and the Second American Revolution: The War of 1812*. Lexington: University Press of Kentucky, 1976.

Hanyan, Craig R. "DeWitt Clinton and Partisanship: The Development of Clintonianism from 1811 to 1820." *New-York Historical Society Quarterly* 56 (Apr. 1972): 109–31.

Harris, Leslie M. *In the Shadow of Slavery: African Americans in New York City, 1626–1863*. Chicago: University of Chicago Press, 2002.

Harris, Norman Dwight. *History of Negro Servitude in Illinois and of the Slavery Agitation in That State, 1719–1864*. Chicago: A. C. McClurg, 1904.

Henry, H. M. *The Police Control of the Slave in South Carolina*. Emory, Va., 1914.

Hickey, Donald R. "New England's Defense Problem and the Genesis of the Hartford Convention." *New England Quarterly* 50 (Dec. 1977): 587–604.

———. *The War of 1812: A Forgotten Conflict*. Urbana: University of Illinois Press, 1989.

Hinks, Peter P. *To Awaken My Afflicted Brethren: David Walker and the Problem of Antebellum Slave Resistance*. University Park: Pennsylvania State University Press, 1997.

Hodges, Graham Russell. *Root and Branch: African Americans in New York and East Jersey, 1613–1863*. Chapel Hill: University of North Carolina Press, 1999.

Horton, James Oliver, and Lois E. Horton. *In Hope of Liberty: Culture, Community, and Protest among Northern Free Blacks, 1700–1860*. New York: Oxford University Press, 1997.

Hoss, E. E. *Elihu Embree, Abolitionist*. Nashville, Tenn.: University Press Company, 1897.

Hunt, Alfred N. *Haiti's Influence on Antebellum America: Slumbering Volcano in the Caribbean.* Baton Rouge: Louisiana State University Press, 1988.

Jenkins, William Sumner. *Pro-Slavery Thought in the Old South.* Chapel Hill: University of North Carolina Press, 1935.

Johnson, Walter. *Soul by Soul: Life inside the Antebellum Slave Market.* Cambridge, Mass.: Harvard University Press, 1999.

Johnson, William R. "Prelude to the Missouri Compromise: A New York Congressman's Effort to Exclude Slavery from Arkansas Territory." *New-York Historical Society Quarterly* 48 (Jan. 1964): 31–50.

Johnston, James Hugo. "The Participation of White Men in Virginia Negro Insurrections." *Journal of Negro History* 16 (Apr. 1931): 158–67.

Jordan, Winthrop D. *White over Black: American Attitudes toward the Negro, 1550–1812.* Baltimore: Penguin Books, 1968.

Kastor, Peter J. *The Nation's Crucible: The Louisiana Purchase and the Creation of America.* New Haven: Yale University Press, 2004.

Kennedy, Roger G. *Mr. Jefferson's Lost Cause: Land, Farmers, Slavery, and the Louisiana Purchase.* New York: Oxford University Press, 2003.

Kerber, Linda K. *Federalists in Dissent: Imagery and Ideology in Jeffersonian America.* Ithaca, N.Y.: Cornell University Press, 1970.

Ketcham, Ralph L. "The Dictates of Conscience: Edward Coles and Slavery." *Virginia Quarterly Review* 36 (Winter 1960): 46–62.

Kirk, Russell. *John Randolph of Roanoke: A Study in American Politics.* 4th ed. Chicago, 1951. Reprint, Indianapolis: Liberty Fund, 1997.

Konig, David Thomas, ed. *Devising Liberty: Preserving and Creating Freedom in the New American Republic.* Stanford, Calif.: Stanford University Press, 1995.

Lachance, Paul F. "The Politics of Fear: French Louisianans and the Slave Trade, 1786–1809." *Plantation Society* 1 (June 1979): 162–97.

Lee, Deborah A., and Warren R. Hofstra. "Race, Memory, and the Death of Robert Berkeley: 'A Murder . . . of . . . Horrible and Savage Barbarity.' " *Journal of Southern History* 65 (Feb. 1999): 41–76.

Legal and Moral Aspects of Slavery: Selected Essays. New York: Negro Universities Press, 1969.

Leibiger, Stuart. "Thomas Jefferson and the Missouri Crisis: An Alternative Interpretation." *Journal of the Early Republic* 17 (Spring 1997): 121–30.

Lemmon, Sarah M. *Frustrated Patriots: North Carolina and the War of 1812.* Chapel Hill: University of North Carolina Press, 1973.

Leventhal, Fred M., and Roland Quinault, eds. *Anglo-American Attitudes: From Revolution to Partnership.* Aldershot, England: Ashgate, 2000.

Levine, Bruce. *Half Slave and Half Free: The Roots of Civil War.* New York: Hill and Wang, 1992.

Lewis, James E., Jr. *The American Union and the Problem of Neighborhood: The United States and the Collapse of the Spanish Empire, 1783–1829.* Chapel Hill: University of North Carolina Press, 1998.

Lindsay, Arnett G. "Diplomatic Relations between the United States and Great Britain Bearing on the Return of Negro Slaves, 1783–1828." *Journal of Negro History* 5 (Oct. 1920): 391–419.

Link, William A. *Roots of Secession: Slavery and Politics in Antebellum Virginia*. Chapel Hill: University of North Carolina Press, 2003.

Littlefield, Daniel C. "John Jay, the Revolutionary Generation, and Slavery." *New York History* 81 (Jan. 2000): 91–132.

Litwack, Leon F. *North of Slavery: The Negro in the Free States, 1790–1860*. Chicago: University of Chicago Press, 1961.

Livermore, Shaw, Jr. *The Twilight of Federalism: The Disintegration of the Federalist Party, 1815–1830*. Princeton, N.J.: Princeton University Press, 1962.

Lochemes, Sister M. Frederick. *Robert Walsh: His Story*. Washington, D.C.: Catholic University of America Press, 1941.

Locke, Mary Stoughton. *Anti-Slavery in America from the Introduction of African Slaves to the Prohibition of the Slave Trade*. Boston, 1901. Reprint, Gloucester, Mass.: Pete Smith, 1965; Johnson Reprint Corp., 1968.

Lockley, Timothy James. *Lines in the Sand: Race and Class in Lowcountry Georgia*. Athens: University of Georgia Press, 2001.

MacLeod, Duncan J. *Slavery, Race, and the American Revolution*. London: Cambridge University Press, 1974.

Malone, Dumas, and Allen Johnson, eds. *Dictionary of American Biography*. New York: Charles Scribner's, 1927–36.

Mason, Matthew E. "Slavery Overshadowed: Congress Debates Prohibiting the Atlantic Slave Trade to the United States, 1806–1807." *Journal of the Early Republic* 20 (Spring 2000): 59–81.

———. "The Battle of the Slaveholding Liberators: Great Britain, the United States, and Slavery in the Early Nineteenth Century." *William and Mary Quarterly*, 3d ser., 59 (July 2002): 665–96.

———. "'Nothing Is Better Calculated to Excite Divisions': Federalist Agitation against Slave Representation during the War of 1812." *New England Quarterly* 75 (Dec. 2002): 531–61.

Masur, Louis P. *1831: Year of Eclipse*. New York: Hill and Wang, 2001.

Mathews, Donald G. *Slavery and Methodism: A Chapter in American Morality, 1780–1845*. Princeton, N.J.: Princeton University Press, 1965.

———. *Religion and the Old South*. Chicago: University of Chicago Press, 1977.

May, Robert E. *The Southern Dream of a Caribbean Empire, 1854–1861*. Rev. ed., Gainesville: University Press of Florida, 2002.

McCaughey, Robert A. *Josiah Quincy, 1772–1854: The Last Federalist*. Cambridge, Mass.: Harvard University Press, 1974.

McColley, Robert. *Slavery and Jeffersonian Virginia*. 2d ed. Urbana: University of Illinois Press, 1973.

McCoy, Drew R. *Last of the Fathers: James Madison and the Republican Legacy*. Cambridge: Cambridge University Press, 1989.

McDonald, Forrest. *States' Rights and the Union: Imperium in Imperio, 1776–1876*. Lawrence: University Press of Kansas, 2000.

McGraw, Marie Tyler. "Richmond Free Blacks and African Colonization, 1816–1832." *Journal of American Studies* 21 (Aug. 1987): 207–24.

McKivigan, John R., and Stanley Harrold, eds. *Antislavery Violence: Sectional, Racial, and Cultural Conflict in Antebellum America*. Knoxville: University of Tennessee Press, 1999.

McKivigan, John R., and Mitchell Snay, eds. *Religion and the Antebellum Debate over Slavery*. Athens: University of Georgia Press, 1998.

McManus, Edgar J. *Black Bondage in the North*. Syracuse, N.Y.: Syracuse University Press, 1973.

McMillin, James A. *The Final Victims: Foreign Slave Trade to North America, 1783–1810*. Columbia: University of South Carolina Press, 2004.

McPherson, James M. *Crossroads of Freedom: Antietam*. New York: Oxford University Press, 2002.

Melish, Joanne Pope. *Disowning Slavery: Gradual Emancipation and "Race" in New England, 1780–1860*. Ithaca, N.Y.: Cornell University Press, 1998.

Miller, Floyd J. *The Search for a Black Nationality: Black Emigration and Colonization, 1787–1863*. Urbana: University of Illinois Press, 1975.

Miller, William Lee. *Arguing about Slavery: The Great Battle in the United States Congress*. New York: Alfred A. Knopf, 1996.

Minkema, Kenneth P. "Jonathan Edwards' Defense of Slavery." *Massachusetts Historical Review* 4 (2002): 23–60.

Moore, Glover. *The Missouri Controversy*. Lexington: University of Kentucky Press, 1953.

Morgan, Kenneth. "Slavery and the Debate over Ratification of the United States Constitution." *Slavery and Abolition* 22 (Dec. 2001): 40–65.

Morison, Samuel Eliot. *The Life and Letters of Harrison Gray Otis, Federalist, 1765–1848*. 2 vols. Boston: Houghton Mifflin, 1913.

Morison, Samuel Eliot, Frederick Merk, and Frank Freidel. *Dissent in Three American Wars*. Cambridge, Mass.: Harvard University Press, 1970.

Morris, Thomas D. *Free Men All: The Personal Liberty Laws of the North, 1780–1861*. Baltimore: Johns Hopkins University Press, 1974.

Morton, Louis. *Robert Carter of Nomini Hall: A Virginia Tobacco Planter of the Eighteenth Century*. 1941. Reprint, Charlottesville: University of Virginia Press, 1964.

Mullin, Gerald W. *Flight and Rebellion: Slave Resistance in Eighteenth-Century Virginia*. New York: Oxford University Press, 1972.

Nagel, Paul C. *One Nation Indivisible: The Union in American Thought, 1776–1861*. New York: Oxford University Press, 1964.

Nash, Gary B. *Forging Freedom: The Formation of Philadelphia's Black Community, 1720–1840*. Cambridge, Mass.: Harvard University Press, 1988.

Nash, Gary B., and Jean R. Soderlund. *Freedom by Degrees: Emancipation in Pennsylvania and Its Aftermath*. New York: Oxford University Press, 1991.

Newman, Richard S. *The Transformation of American Abolitionism: Fighting Slavery in the Early Republic*. Chapel Hill: University of North Carolina Press, 2002.

Nye, Russel B. *Fettered Freedom: Civil Liberties and the Slavery Controversy*. East Lansing: Michigan State College Press, 1949.

Oakes, James. "The Political Significance of Slave Resistance." *History Workshop Journal* 22 (1986): 89–107.

Oates, Stephen B. *The Fires of Jubilee: Nat Turner's Fierce Rebellion*. New York: Harper and Row, 1975.

Oldfield, J. R. *Popular Politics and British Anti-Slavery: The Mobilisation of Public Opinion against the Slave Trade, 1787–1807*. London: Frank Cass, 1998.

Onuf, Peter S. *Statehood and Union: A History of the Northwest Ordinance.* Bloomington: Indiana University Press, 1987.

——. "The Expanding Union." In *Devising Liberty: Preserving and Creating Freedom in the New American Republic,* edited by David Thomas Konig. Stanford, Calif.: Stanford University Press, 1995.

Owsley, Frank Lawrence, Jr. *Struggle for the Gulf Borderlands: The Creek War and the Battle of New Orleans, 1812–1815.* Gainesville: University Presses of Florida, 1981.

Papenfuse, Eric Robert. *The Evils of Necessity: Robert Goodloe Harper and the Moral Dilemma of Slavery.* Philadelphia: American Philosophical Society, 1997.

Pasley, Jeffrey L. *"The Tyranny of the Printers": Newspaper Politics in the Early American Republic.* Charlottesville: University Press of Virginia, 2001.

Pasley, Jeffrey L., Andrew W. Robertson, and David Waldstreicher, eds. *Beyond the Founders: New Approaches to the Political History of the Early American Republic.* Chapel Hill: University of North Carolina Press, 2004.

Payne, Daniel A. *History of the African Methodist Episcopal Church.* 1891. Reprint, edited by C. S. Smith. New York: Arno Press, 1969.

Pease, Jane, and William Pease. *Bound with Them in Chains: A Biographical History of the Antislavery Movement.* Westport, Conn.: Greenwood Press, 1972.

Perkins, Bradford. *Castlereagh and Adams: England and the United States, 1812–1823.* Berkeley: University of California Press, 1964.

Perry, Mark. *Lift Up Thy Voice: The Grimke Family's Journey from Slaveholders to Civil Rights Leaders.* New York: Viking Penguin, 2001.

Peskin, Lawrence A. "How the Republicans Learned to Love Manufacturing: The First Parties and the 'New Economy.'" *Journal of the Early Republic* 22 (Summer 2002): 235–62.

Peterson, Mark A. "The Selling of Joseph: Bostonians, Antislavery, and the Protestant International, 1689–1733." *Massachusetts Historical Review* 4 (2002): 1–22.

Peterson, Merrill D. *Thomas Jefferson and the New Nation: A Biography.* New York: Oxford University Press, 1970.

Phillips, Christopher. *Freedom's Port: The African American Community of Baltimore, 1790–1860.* Urbana: University of Illinois Press, 1997.

Phillips, Kim T. "William Duane, Philadelphia's Democratic Republicans, and the Origins of Modern Politics." *Pennsylvania Magazine of History and Biography* 101 (July 1977): 365–87.

Pierce, Merrily. "Luke Decker and Slavery: His Cases with Bob and Anthony, 1817–1822." *Indiana Magazine of History* 85 (Mar. 1989): 31–49.

Pingeon, Frances D. "An Abominable Business: The New Jersey Slave Trade, 1818." *New Jersey History* 109 (Fall/Winter 1991): 15–35.

Pitch, Anthony S. *The Burning of Washington: The British Invasion of 1814.* Annapolis, Md.: Naval Institute Press, 1998.

Porter, Kenneth Wiggins. "Negroes and the East Florida Annexation Plot, 1811–1813." *Journal of Negro History* 30 (Jan. 1945): 9–29.

Price, William S., Jr. "Nathaniel Macon, Planter." *North Carolina Historical Review* 78 (Apr. 2001): 187–214.

Pybus, Cassandra. "Jefferson's Faulty Math: The Question of Slave Defections in the American Revolution." *William and Mary Quarterly,* 3d ser., 62 (Apr. 2005): 243–64.

Rael, Patrick. *Black Identity and Black Protest in the Antebellum North*. Chapel Hill: University of North Carolina Press, 2003.

Ratcliffe, Donald J. "Captain James Riley and Antislavery Sentiment in Ohio, 1819–1824." *Ohio History* 81 (Spring 1972): 76–94.

———. *Party Spirit in a Frontier Republic: Democratic Politics in Ohio, 1793–1821*. Columbus: Ohio State University Press, 1998.

———. *The Politics of Long Division: The Birth of the Second Party System in Ohio, 1818–1828*. Columbus: Ohio State University Press, 2000.

Ratner, Lorman. *James Kirke Paulding: The Last Republican*. Westport, Conn.: Greenwood Press, 1992.

Remini, Robert V. *The Course of American Empire, 1767–1821*. Vol. 1 in *Andrew Jackson*. New York: Harper and Row, 1977.

Richards, Leonard L. *Gentlemen of Property and Standing: Anti-Abolition Mobs in Jacksonian America*. New York: Oxford University Press, 1970.

———. *The Life and Times of Congressman John Quincy Adams*. New York: Oxford University Press, 1986.

———. *The Slave Power: The Free North and Southern Domination, 1780–1860*. Baton Rouge: Louisiana State University Press, 2000.

Risjord, Norman K. *The Old Republicans: Southern Conservatism in the Age of Jefferson*. New York: Columbia University Press, 1965.

———. "The Virginia Federalists." *Journal of Southern History* 33 (Nov. 1967): 486–517.

Robinson, Donald L. *Slavery in the Structure of American Politics, 1765–1820*. New York: Harcourt Brace Jovanovich, 1971.

Rodriguez, Junius. "Always 'En Garde': The Effects of Slave Insurrection upon the Louisiana Mentality." *Louisiana History* 33 (Fall 1992): 399–416.

Rogers, George C., Jr. *Evolution of a Federalist: William Loughton Smith of Charleston (1758–1812)*. Columbia: University of South Carolina Press, 1962.

Rose, Willie Lee. "The Domestication of Domestic Slavery." In *Slavery and Freedom*, edited by William W. Freehling. New York: Oxford University Press, 1982.

Rugemer, Edward B. "The Southern Response to British Abolitionism: The Maturation of Proslavery Apologetics." *Journal of Southern History* 70 (May 2004): 221–48.

Sassi, Jonathan D. *A Republic of Righteousness: The Public Christianity of the Post-Revolutionary New England Clergy*. Oxford: Oxford University Press, 2001.

Scarborough, William Kauffman. *Masters of the Big House: Elite Slaveholders of the Mid-Nineteenth-Century South*. Baton Rouge: Louisiana State University Press, 2003.

Schrader, Arthur. "Singing SHEAR History: A Commentary and Music Sampler." *Journal of the Early Republic* 21 (Winter 2001): 674–77.

Schwalm, Leslie A. " 'Overrun with Free Negroes': Emancipation and Wartime Migration in the Upper Midwest." *Civil War History* 50 (June 2004): 145–74.

Schwarz, Philip J. *Twice Condemned: Slaves and the Criminal Laws of Virginia, 1705–1865*. Baton Rouge: Louisiana State University Press, 1988.

———. *Migrants against Slavery: Virginians and the Nation*. Charlottesville: University Press of Virginia, 2001.

Shalhope, Robert E. "Thomas Jefferson's Republicanism and Antebellum Southern Thought." *Journal of Southern History* 42 (Fall 1976): 529–56.

——. *John Taylor of Caroline: Pastoral Republican*. Columbia: South Carolina University Press, 1980.

Sharp, James Rogers. *American Politics in the Early Republic: The New Nation in Crisis*. New Haven: Yale University Press, 1993.

Sheidley, Harlow W. *Sectional Nationalism: Massachusetts Conservative Leaders and the Transformation of America, 1815–1836*. Boston: Northeastern University Press, 1998.

Shoemaker, Floyd Calvin. *Missouri's Struggle for Statehood, 1804–1821*. Jefferson City, Mo.: Hugh Stephens Printing Co., 1916. Reprint, New York: Russell and Russell, 1969.

Shugerman, Jed Handelsman. "The Louisiana Purchase and South Carolina's Reopening of the Slave Trade in 1803." *Journal of the Early Republic* 22 (Summer 2002): 263–90.

Sidbury, James. *Ploughshares into Swords: Race, Rebellion, and Identity in Gabriel's Virginia, 1730–1810*. Cambridge: Cambridge University Press, 1997.

——. "Saint Domingue in Virginia: Ideology, Local Meanings, and Resistance to Slavery, 1790 to 1800." *Journal of Southern History* 63 (Aug. 1997): 531–52.

Silverman, Kenneth. *Timothy Dwight*. New York: Twayne Publishers, 1969.

Simeone, James. *Democracy and Slavery in Frontier Illinois: The Bottomland Republic*. DeKalb: Northern Illinois University Press, 2000.

Simpson, Albert F. "The Political Significance of Slave Representation, 1787–1821." *Journal of Southern History* 7 (Aug. 1941): 315–42.

Skeen, C. Edward. *1816: America Rising*. Lexington: University Press of Kentucky, 2003.

Smelser, Marshall. *The Democratic Republic, 1801–1815*. New York: Harper and Row, 1968.

Smith, H. Shelton. *In His Image, But . . . : Racism in Southern Religion, 1780–1910*. Durham, N.C.: Duke University Press, 1972.

Smith, William Henry. *A Political History of Slavery*. 2 vols. New York: G. P. Putnam's, 1903.

Soulsby, Hugh G. *The Right of Search and the Slave Trade in Anglo-American Relations, 1814–1862*. Baltimore: Johns Hopkins University Press, 1933.

Stagg, J. C. A. *Mr. Madison's War: Politics, Diplomacy, and Warfare in the Early American Republic, 1783–1830*. Princeton, N.J.: Princeton University Press, 1983.

Stampp, Kenneth M. "The Concept of a Perpetual Union." In *The Imperiled Union: Essays on the Background of the Civil War*. New York: Oxford University Press, 1980.

Starobin, Robert S., ed. *Blacks in Bondage: Letters of American Slaves*. 1974. Reprint, New York: Markus Wiener, 1988.

Staudenraus, P. J. *The African Colonization Movement, 1816–1865*. New York: Columbia University Press, 1961.

Stewart, James Brewer. *Joshua R. Giddings and the Tactics of Radical Politics*. Cleveland: Press of Case Western Reserve University, 1970.

——. *Holy Warriors: The Abolitionists and American Slavery*. 1976. Rev. ed., New York: Hill and Wang, 1996.

——. *William Lloyd Garrison and the Challenge of Emancipation*. Arlington Heights, Ill.: Harlan Davidson, 1992.

——. "Boston, Abolition, and the Atlantic World, 1820–1861." In *Courage and Conscience: Black and White Abolitionists in Boston*, edited by Donald Jacobs. Bloomington: Indiana University Press, 1993.

——. "The Emergence of Racial Modernity and the Rise of the White North, 1790–1840." *Journal of the Early Republic* 18 (Summer 1998): 181–236.

——. "Modernizing 'Difference': The Political Meanings of Color in the Free States, 1776–1840." *Journal of the Early Republic* 19 (Winter 1999): 691–712.

Sweet, Leonard I. *Black Images of America, 1784–1870.* New York: W. W. Norton, 1976.

Sydnor, Charles S. *The Development of Southern Sectionalism, 1819–1848.* Baton Rouge: Louisiana State University Press, 1948.

Tadman, Michael. *Speculators and Slaves: Masters, Traders, and Slaves in the Old South.* Madison: University of Wisconsin Press, 1989.

Takaki, Ronald T. *A Pro-Slavery Crusade: The Agitation to Reopen the African Slave Trade.* New York: Free Press, 1971.

Tallant, Harold D. *Evil Necessity: Slavery and Political Culture in Antebellum Kentucky.* Lexington: University Press of Kentucky, 2003.

Temperley, Howard. *Britain and America since Independence.* New York: Palgrave, 2002.

Thompson, Thomas Marshall. "National Newspaper and Legislative Reactions to Louisiana's Deslondes Slave Revolt of 1811." *Louisiana History* 33 (Winter 1992): 5–29.

Thornbrough, Emma Lou. "Indiana and Fugitive Slave Legislation." *Indiana Magazine of History* 50 (Sept. 1954): 201–28.

Thornton, J. Mills III. *Politics and Power in a Slave Society: Alabama, 1800–1860.* Baton Rouge: Louisiana State University Press, 1978.

Tise, Larry E. *Proslavery: A History of the Defense of Slavery in America, 1701–1840.* Athens: University of Georgia Press, 1987.

Turner, Edward Raymond. *The Negro in Pennsylvania: Slavery-Servitude-Freedom, 1639–1861.* Washington, D.C.: American Historical Association, 1911. Reprint, New York: Arno Press / New York Times, 1969.

Vaux, Roberts. *Memoirs of the Lives of Benjamin Lay and Ralph Sandiford; Two of the Earliest Public Advocates for the Emancipation of the Enslaved Africans.* Philadelphia: Simon W. Conrad, 1815.

Vipperman, Carl J. *William Lowndes and the Transition of Southern Politics, 1782–1822.* Chapel Hill: University of North Carolina Press, 1989.

Waldstreicher, David. *In the Midst of Perpetual Fetes: The Making of American Nationalism, 1776–1820.* Chapel Hill: University of North Carolina Press for the Omohundro Institute for Early American History and Culture, 1997.

White, Shane. *Somewhat More Independent: The End of Slavery in New York City, 1770–1810.* Athens: University of Georgia Press, 1991.

——. *Stories of Freedom in Black New York.* Cambridge, Mass.: Harvard University Press, 2002.

White, Shane, and Graham White. *Stylin': African American Expressive Culture from Its Beginnings to the Zoot Suit.* Ithaca, N.Y.: Cornell University Press, 1998.

Whitman, T. Stephen. *The Price of Freedom: Slavery and Manumission in Baltimore and Early National Maryland.* Lexington: University Press of Kentucky, 1997.

Wiecek, William M. *The Sources of Antislavery Constitutionalism in America, 1760–1848.* Ithaca, N.Y.: Cornell University Press, 1977.

Wills, Gary. *"Negro President": Jefferson and the Slave Power.* Boston: Houghton Mifflin, 2003.

Wilson, Carol. *Freedom at Risk: The Kidnapping of Free Blacks in America, 1780–1865.* Lexington: University Press of Kentucky, 1994.

Wilson, Edwin Mood. *The Congressional Career of Nathaniel Macon.* No. 2 of *James Sprunt Historical Monographs.* Chapel Hill: University of North Carolina, 1900.

Winch, Julie. *Philadelphia's Black Elite: Activism, Accommodation and the Struggle for Autonomy, 1787–1848*. Philadelphia: Temple University Press, 1988.

——. *A Gentleman of Color: The Life of James Forten*. New York: Oxford University Press, 2002.

Wood, Peter H. *Black Majority: Negroes in Colonial South Carolina from 1670 through the Stono Rebellion*. New York: W. W. Norton, 1974.

Wright, Donald R. *African Americans in the Early Republic, 1789–1831*. Arlington Heights, Ill.: Harlan Davidson, 1993.

Wyatt-Brown, Bertram. "The Antimission Movement in the Jacksonian South: A Study in Regional Folk Culture." *Journal of Southern History* 36 (Nov. 1970): 501–29.

Young, Jeffrey Robert. *Domesticating Slavery: The Master Class in Georgia and South Carolina, 1670–1837*. Chapel Hill: University of North Carolina Press, 1999.

Zeitz, Joshua Michael. "The Missouri Compromise Reconsidered: Antislavery Rhetoric and the Emergence of the Free Labor Synthesis." *Journal of the Early Republic* 20 (Fall 2000): 447–85.

Zilversmit, Arthur. *The First Emancipation: The Abolition of Slavery in the North*. Chicago: University of Chicago Press, 1967.

DISSERTATIONS, THESES, AND CONFERENCE PAPERS

Allen, Jeffrey Brooke. "The Debate over Slavery and Race in Ante-Bellum Kentucky: 1792–1850." Ph.D. diss., Northwestern University, 1973.

Bagby, Ross Frederick. "The Randolph Slave Saga: Communities in Collision." Ph.D. Diss., Ohio State University, 1998.

Bonner, Robert E. "Americans Apart: Nationality in the Slaveholding South." Ph.D. diss., Yale University, 1997.

Deyle, Steven. "The Domestic Slave Trade in America: The Lifeblood of the Southern Slave System." Paper presented at a conference at the Gilder Lehrman Center for the Study of Slavery, Resistance, and Abolition at Yale University, 22–24 Oct. 1999.

Dupre, Daniel S. "The Panic of 1819 and the Political Economy of Sectionalism." Paper presented at the conference "The Past and Future of Early American Economic History: Needs and Opportunities, the Program in Early American Economy and Society," Philadelphia, 20–21 Apr. 2001.

Finnie, Gordon Esley. "The Antislavery Movement in the South, 1787–1836: Its Rise and Decline and Its Contribution to Abolition in the West." Ph.D. diss., Duke University, 1962.

Forbes, Robert Pierce. "Slavery and the Meaning of America, 1819–1837." Ph.D. diss., Yale University, 1994.

Haynes, Sam W. " 'An Ally in the Centre of the American Line': Anglophobia and the Nullification Crisis." Paper presented to SHEAR / BrANCH Conference, Cambridge University, England, Oct. 2003.

Hinks, Peter P. " 'It Is at the Extremest Risque If We Still Hold Fast the Accursed Thing': Connecticut's Abolition Bill of 1794, the New Divinity, and Antislavery in the Late Eighteenth Century Atlantic World." Paper delivered at the conference "Yale, New Haven, and American Slavery," Yale University, 27 Sept. 2002.

Iaccarino, Anthony Alfred. "Virginia and the National Contest over Slavery in the Early Republic, 1780–1833." Ph.D. diss., University of California–Los Angeles, 1999.

Lampi, Philip J. "The Embargo Reaction and the Federalist Revival, 1808–1816." Paper presented at the SHEAR/BRANCH Conference, Cambridge University, England, 5 Oct. 2003.

Mason, Matthew E. "Labor Supply in the Age of Toussaint: The Decision to Outlaw the Atlantic Slave Trade to the United States." Presented at the meeting of the Southeastern American Society for Eighteenth-Century Studies, Savannah, Ga., 4 Mar. 2000.

——. "The Rain between the Storms: The Politics and Ideology of Slavery in the United States, 1808–1821." Ph.D. diss., University of Maryland, 2002.

——. "Attacking the 'Covenant with Death' Across the Generations: The Link between New England's Federalists and Abolitionists." Presented at "New England Slavery and the Slave Trade" conference of the Colonial Society of Massachusetts, Boston, 22 Apr. 2004.

Nation, Richard Franklin. "Home in the Hoosier Hills: Agriculture, Politics, and Religion in Southern Indiana, 1810–1870." Ph.D. diss., University of Michigan, 1995.

Ohline, Howard Albert. "Politics and Slavery: The Issue of Slavery in National Politics, 1787–1815." Ph.D. diss., University of Missouri, 1969.

Preyer, Norris W. "The Congressional Fight over the Admission of Kentucky, Tennessee, Louisiana, and Alabama into the Union." Master's thesis, University of Virginia, 1950.

Rael, Patrick. " 'Instruments in the Hands of God': Black Activism and Black Agency in the Age of Emancipation." Paper delivered at "New England Slavery and the Slave Trade" conference, Boston, 23 Apr. 2004.

Reda, John. "Illinois Slavery Reconsidered: The Significance of the Northwest Ordinance." Paper delivered at Society for Historians of the Early Republic conference, Columbus, Ohio, Oct. 2003.

Rothman, Adam. "Expansion of Slavery in the Deep South, 1790–1820." Ph.D. diss., Columbia University, 2000.

Scott, Julius S. "The Common Wind: Currents of Afro-American Communication in the Era of the Haitian Revolution." Ph.D. diss., Duke University, 1986.

Stout, Harry S., and Kenneth P. Minkema. "The Edwardsean Tradition and Antebellum Antislavery." Paper delivered at "Yale, New Haven, and American Slavery" conference, Yale University, 27 Sept. 2002.

Wallenstein, Peter. "Slavery, Race, and Representation: From the Hartford Convention to the Fourteenth Amendment." Paper presented to SHEAR/BRANCH Conference, Cambridge University, England, 5 Oct. 2003.

Index

Whittier, John Greenleaf, 225, 231–32
Wilberforce, William, 91, 98, 101, 165, 265
  (n. 68); as pseudonym, 190, 294 (n. 160)
Williams, David R., 69
Wilson, James, 24
Wisconsin, 228
Wolcott, Oliver, 191

Worthington, Thomas, 152
Wright, Frances, 94
Wright, John, 93, 100–101, 103, 125, 175–76,
  273 (n. 112)

Yancey, Bartlett, 162–63, 236